TAIPEI In A Day

台 北 一 日 遊

Includes: **Taiwan From A To Z**

<u>Taipei In A Day</u> is the most comprehensive,
up-to-date guide to thoroughly enjoy Taiwan.
http://www.TaipeiInADay.com

By Scott B. Freiberger

Friends may come and go but family is forever.

Taipei In A Day is dedicated to my mother, father, and brothers Glen, Jay, and Todd. I love you.

Many thanks to Ariel Tsao and family, Chin-Man Chang, Gavin Phipps, James Tsao, Jason Huang, Scott Greenwald, and to hundreds of gracious unknown pedestrians.

Scott Freiberger uses his B.A. in Psychology/Chinese from Queens College, C.U.N.Y., Masters in Pacific International Affairs from UC San Diego and fluency in seven languages to provide expert consulting advice. He has contributed dozens of articles to regional tour guides and is a contributing reporter for the China Post newspaper. When not at a desk, the author rises early to explore remote mountain areas, practice tai chi, tour museums, and sip tea at traditional teahouses. After the sun has set, Scott strolls through night markets snacking on local delicacies and later dances in Asia's finest clubs.

Taipei In A Day Includes: Taiwan From A To Z, First Edition

ISBN 978-1-4357-0332-2

After arriving on Taiwan in 1997, I was astonished to find that available tour guides failed to mention the best places to visit and most interesting things to see. Although the capital has changed drastically, the quality of resources available for international guests has not. When my brother Jay visited, he was so taken by what he had experienced that he suggested I expand my Taipei tour guide, originally completed in 2002, and write a Taiwan traveler's guide so others could enjoy Taiwan as he had.

"From Hell Valley to Snake Alley, **Taipei In A Day** is the most comprehensive, up-to-date tour guide to thoroughly enjoy Taipei and its vicinities. Inside you'll find the most diverse Taipei Dining Guide on the market, discover relics with Taipei Historic Sites, and know where to stay and play by using the complete Taipei Hotel Guide, Taipei Museum Guide, Taipei Parks Guide and Taipei Pub Guide. There is a special Taipei Guide to Mountain Climbing for active globe trekkers, and overseas adventurers will appreciate the descriptive Taipei Night Market Guide. Use the in-depth Taipei Temple Guide to explore Taiwanese religious beliefs and culture. For a soothing spot of tea, find serenity at Tea Station. Names and addresses are also listed in Chinese, along with local phone numbers, so major attractions and interesting out-of-the-way locales are readily found. Helpful communication tips, important vocabulary and useful phrases are at your fingertips. The encompassing "Taiwan From A To Z" section introduces local cues, customs and important cultural information so readers can be Taiwan travelers rather than tourists. After reading **Taipei In A Day** you should be prepared for your visit, whether it spans a month, week, or weekend." Gavin Phipps, Staff Reporter, International Community Radio Taipei (ICRT).

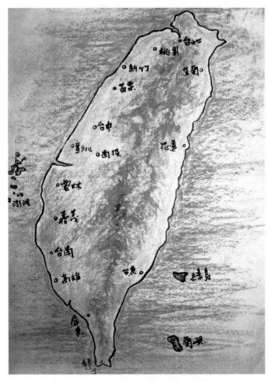

Discover the resplendent Republic of China.

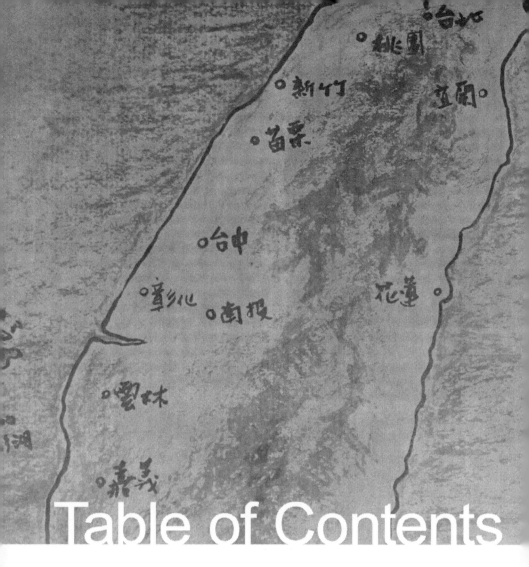

Table of Contents

MAPS (地圖)

Taiwan From A to Z

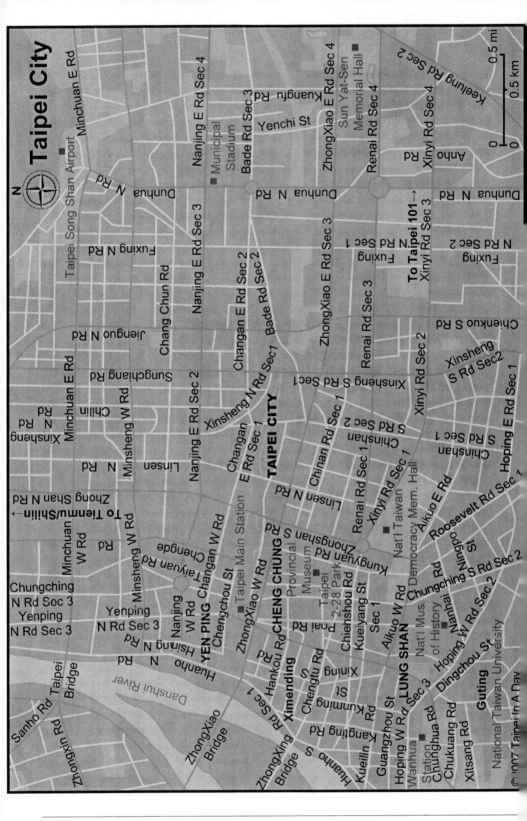

Taipei City

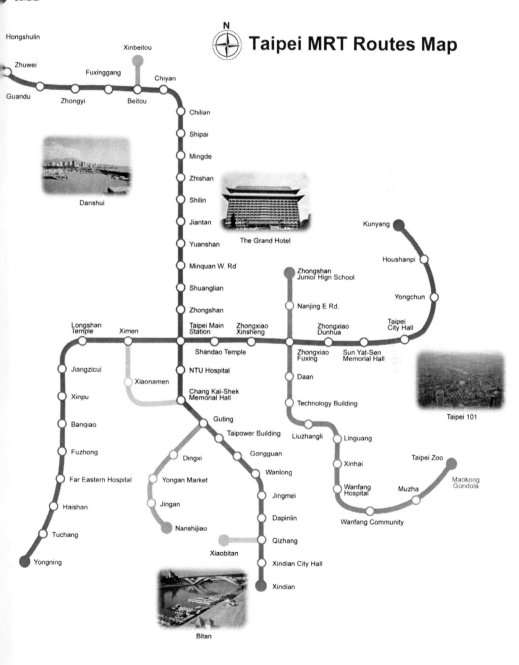

Danshui

Hongshulin

Xinbeitou

Taipei MRT Routes Map

Zhuwei

Fuxinggang

Chiyan

Guandu

Zhongyi

Beitou

Chilian

Shipai

Mingde

Zhishan

Shilin

Jiantan

The Grand Hotel

Kunyang

Yuanshan

Minquan W. Rd

Houshanpi

Zhongshan
Junior High School

Shuanglian

Yongchun

Zhongshan

Nanjing E Rd.

Longshan
Temple

Ximen

Taipei Main
Station

Zhongxiao
Xinsheng

Zhongxiao
Dunhua

Taipei
City Hall

Jiangzicui

Shandao Temple

Zhongxiao
Fuxing

Sun Yat-Sen
Memorial Hall

Xiaonamen

NTU Hospital

Daan

Xinpu

Chang Kai-Shek
Memorial Hall

Technology Building

Taipei 101

Banqiao

Guting

Taipower Building

Liuzhangli

Linguang

Fuzhong

Dingxi

Gongguan

Xinhai

Taipei Zoo

Far Eastern Hospital

Yongan Market

Wanlong

Wanfang
Hospital

Muzha

Maokong
Gondola

Haishan

Jingan

Jingmei

Wanfang Community

Tuchang

Nanshijiao

Dapinlin

Yongning

Xiaobitan

Qizhang

Xindian City Hall

Xindian

Bitan

Introduction

Official name: Republic of China

Population: 23 million

Total area: 36,179 square kilometers

Population density: 626 people per square kilometer

Average life expectancy: 73.40 (men) 79.31 (women)

Population to age 14: 19.83 percent

Population between the ages of 13-64: 70.93 percent

Population over the age of 65: 9.24 percent

Major religions: Buddhism (佛教) and Taoism (道家)

Capital: Taipei (台北)

Capital population: 2.7 million

Capital population density: 9,666 people per square kilometer

Airports: 40

Golf courses: 80

Electricity: 110V/60 cycles

Major aboriginal tribes: 12

National parks: 6

Number of islands: 86

Mountain ranges: 5

Shue Mountain (雪山) highest peak: 3,886 meters

Central Mountain Range (中央山脈) highest peak: 3,703 meters

Jade Mountain (玉山) highest peak: 3,952-meters, the highest in Northeast Asia

Alishan (阿里山) highest peak: 2,663 meters, Alishan's Data Mountain range (大塔山)

East Coast Mountains (東部海岸山脈) highest peak: 1,682 meters,

Hsingang Mountain (新港山)

National flower: plum blossom

As my brothers and I were growing up in Queens, New York, we often heard our father caution, "Good is not cheap, and cheap is not good," meaning the cost of an item usually determines its quality. In Taipei, however, you can find a plethora of outstanding native foods, comfortable clothing, modern electronic equipment and high-quality computer components for very reasonable prices. Night markets brim with vibrant vendors that sell exceptional edible enigmas and trendy consumer goods well after the sun has set. Young people share laughter, class notes and wireless Internet connections in contemporary coffee shops and big boss bookstores while discussing politics, art, economics, global events, and the most important topic of all, the opposite sex. Literally teeming with life at all hours, Taipei puts my hometown, the city that never sleeps, to shame.

In addition to its curious confluence of ancient Chinese tradition meets 21st century cyber city, what visitors tend to find most alluring about Taipei is the city's close proximity to the gorgeous green mountains that surround it. You can spend the entire morning relaxing in the mountains with a picturesque view of Taipei, hop on the clean, modern Mass Rapid Transit (MRT) system (捷運 jie yun), and in less than an hour, visit magnificent cultural attractions in the city all afternoon and evening. Or, explore the city during the day and relax in the mountains at night, sipping Chinese tea while snacking on delicious local delicacies at a traditional teahouse. Then, soak the night away in one of New Beitou's fine natural hot springs before turning in.

Business travelers may find city hotels convenient due to proximity to the Taipei World Trade Center and other international business centers. If you're visiting Taiwan for leisure, however, you may want to reside in Taipei's Beitou (北投 Bay Toe) district during your stay. Beitou is situated comfortably between Taipei and Danshui (淡水), an exciting waterfront town and the last stop on the MRT heading north, away from Taipei. (More on Danshui later.) From Beitou, Taipei and Danshui are both approximately twenty-five minutes in either direction by MRT.

The Author Recommends:

. EVA Air for international travel to and from Taiwan (excellent food and service).
. Using an Easy Card and public transportation.
. Reading Do's and Don'ts under "XY & Z (Useful Information) (很有用的信息)."
. Bringing a good camera, sneakers or walking shoes, sunglasses, hat, suntan lotion, and a portable umbrella (although one can be purchased easily).
. Visiting New Beitou, Danshui, Taipei 101, Shilin Night Market and Yangmingshan National Park.
. Exploring Taipei's historic, almost ethereal temples; you'll find a wide selection under "Taipei Temple Guide (台北寺廟指南)."
. Teatime at The Grand Hotel (圓山大飯店), listed under "Taipei Hotel Guide (台北飯店指南)."
. Tienmu and "Dinghao" (Zhongxiao East Road, Section 4) for unique boutique shopping and people watching.
. Bathing at Spring City Resort's replenishing outdoor hot springs, listed under "Hot Springs (溫泉)" and "Taipei Hotel Guide (台北飯店指南)" under "Hotels, Beitou (飯店, 北投)."

Arrivals and Departures

Once you arrive at Taiwan Taoyuan International Airport, approximately an hour southwest of Taipei, four major bus companies transport passengers from the airport to Taipei: Toward You Air Bus (大有巴士), Evergreen (長榮), Fe Go Express (飛狗) and Taiwan Bus Corp. (桃園汽車). Show the salespeople the name of your hotel in Chinese as some buses may stop closer to your destination than others (for your convenience, hotel names and addresses are listed in both English and Chinese under

"Taipei Hotel Guide (台北飯店指南)."

The International Airport Tourist Service Center (中正國際機場旅客服務中心) (03) 383-4631, open from 7 am to 11:30 pm at the lobby entrance of Terminal 1, offers maps and other helpful information about Taiwan travel. A twenty-four hour monorail and a free shuttle bus that runs from 5:20 am to 1:10 am transports passengers between terminals one and two. For additional information the Visitor Information Center, open from 8 am to 7 pm, is located in Taipei on Dunhua North Road, #240 (台北市敦化北路240號) (02) 2717-3737. Many area hotels offer similar information.

From the airport, taxi fares cost around NT $1,000 (US $30.00), although you may be able to shave a few bucks (NT $100) if you ask. Many drivers offer this set fare in advance of departure rather than turn on the meter. Traffic tends to be heavier during weekends and holidays so on your return plan to depart two to three hours in advance of checking in.

For domestic air travel, four airlines operate out of Taipei Songshan Airport (台北松山機場), Dunhua North Road, #340-9 (台北國際航空站 台北市敦化北路340之9號). The airport is at the intersection of Minchuen East Road, Section 4, Guangfu North Road and Dunhua North Road. Airlines operate from 6:00 am to 8:30 pm.
Service desk: (02) 8770-3460.

Far Eastern Transport Corp. (FAT)
遠東航空 (02) 2712-1555
http://www.fat.com.tw.

Mandarin Airlines (MDA)
華信航空公司 (02) 2717-1230
http://www.mandarin-airlines.com.

TransAsia Airways (TNA)
復興航空公司 (02) 2972-4599
http://www.tna.com.tw.

UNI AIR (UIA)
立榮航空 (02) 2518-5166
http://www.uniair.com.tw.

Cab It

From 6 am to 11 pm a Taipei taxi costs NT $70 (US $2.10) for the first 1.25 kilometers and NT $5 (US $.15) every two hundred and fifty meters thereafter. From 11 pm until 6 am the fare starts the same but the meter will run faster. Some companies charge NT $10 for "trunk service" or for telephone booking. For taxi rides that originate and end in Danshui, which include the neighboring towns of Hongshulin and Zhuwei, you will now need to add NT $30 to the fare, presumably to prevent cab drivers from playing musical prices. Fares for public transportation are set to increase due to skyrocketing gas prices. For updates please check http://www.OnTaiwan.com.

In Taipei, Smile Taxi (賓樂 *Binluh*) claims to have English-speaking drivers: (02) 2746-9988, 8787-0088. New Life (新生活 *Hsin Shenghuo*) also claims to have a handful of drivers that can speak English: (02) 2753-2000. In Taipei, the number for the English Taxi Drivers Association (ETA), which provides English-speaking taxi drivers, is (02) 2799-7997, their toll-free number is 0800-055-850, dial "2."

As a note of caution, many taxi drivers aren't fluent in English, so each time you take a taxi, make sure the driver knows where you want to go before the meter starts running.

Currency Exchange

The name of the local currency is the New Taiwan Dollar (NT$ or NTD). To keep things simple, US $3.00 = NT $100.00 is used in **Taipei In A Day**. During the past several years the exchange rate has fluctuated between NT $29 to NT $34, check http://www.OnTaiwan.com to see what the exchange rate will be during your stay. You may find a better deal if you change your currency at a local bank on Taiwan (passport required) rather than overseas or at the airport. However, some local banks will not accept bills prior to the year 2003 and tellers are fastidious about marks and tears on bills. Bring new, unmarked bills and you shouldn't encounter major problems. Also, while some tour guides advocate using Traverlers Checks, most merchants prefer cash or credit.

Easy Card, Easy Go

If you've ever driven in a large metropolis, imagine dividing the width of the streets in half. Now try to imagine, during rush hour, adding twice as many cars. Add impatient drivers to the mix and that's pretty much what driving in Taipei is like. Parking is a veritable nightmare as spaces are few and far between. Public transportation is modern, inexpensive, and reliable, and for unfamiliar visitors, a much better option than renting a car. You'll find a sobering, albeit humorous, take on the capital's terrifying traffic in "Traffic Tips (Or, "Invasion of the Mopeds!") (交通安全)" found under "XY & Z (Useful Information) (很有用的信息)."

For those that love adventure, renting a moped to explore Beitou (北投), Yangmingshan (陽明山) and Tienmu (天母) may provide an opportunity to visit out of the way areas and leave an entirely different impression. Some local repair shops rent mopeds for approximately NT $1,000 (US $30.00) a day. Bear in mind, however, that riding a moped through the streets of Taipei can be dangerous, especially if you are unfamiliar with the terrain and hasty nature of local drivers. **_Renting a moped is not advisable for new visitors to the island_**.

Before taking the MRT, it's wise to purchase a stored-value Easy Card (悠遊卡) from one of the machines inside the MRT station to avoid long lines during peak hours. A stored-value card in Taipei is similar to the Transit Metro Card used in New York City, it may be used at MRT stations, on buses and in some parking lots. NT $1000 (US $30.00) is the maximum stored-value amount, and you may return the card at any MRT station to receive a refund for the unused stored card value and NT $200 deposit (NT $100 if you had purchased a card for NT $500 or NT $300). Single trip tickets or one-way coins range from NT $20 (US $.60) to NT $65 (US $1.95) depending on distance traveled. You can also purchase a one-day pass for NT $200, and groups of ten receive a 20% discount on tickets.

Automatic Fare Collection (AFC) gates similar to the ones used in Hong Kong are also in use, press the Easy Card against the front ticket sensor zone, the card's remaining monetary amount appears on a screen and the gates open. Children 115 cm and under enter free when accompanied by an adult.

Some MRT stations provide maps of Taipei and the MRT system. For your convenience, maps are included in **Taipei In A Day** so you should be better acquainted with Taiwan and some of its enchanting scenic spots before you arrive.

Address Mess?

Addresses on Taiwan may appear confusing, as buildings sometimes appear on a lane (巷 shang) or an alley (弄 nom). Unlike in the West, where alleys may be small and dangerous, alleys and lanes on Taiwan are often well-lit and not difficult to find off major intersections. Main roads may also be divided into sections (段 duan). Be aware that street signs may be spelled differently throughout the city. For instance, Zhongxiao East Road (忠孝東路) and Zhongxiao West Road (忠孝西路), a main thoroughfare that runs east to west across Taipei past Taipei Main Station (台北火車站), is spelled "Chung Hsiao" in certain areas, and "Chunghsiao," "Chong Hsiao" or "Chong Shiao" in others. In Danshui, Zhongzheng Road is spelled "Jong Jeng Road" or "Jhong

Jheng Road," Yingzhuan Road, the night market, may be spelled "Ying Juan Road" and Zhongshan Road is spelled "Jeng Shan Road." Tienmu (天母) may also be spelled "Tienmou" or "Tian Mu." Wenchuen Road (溫泉路) in Beitou (北投) is spelled "Wenquan Road" in certain areas, and Guangming Road (光明路), a main Beitou road is spelled with a "K" (Kuang Ming Road) in certain areas of New Beitou (新北投 Xinbeitou). On Taiwan, there is an ongoing debate as to how Chinese characters should be phonetically translated into English. In certain instances translations render street signs more easily discernable, yet at other times the "improved" versions serve only to confuse tourists and expatriates. Should Guang be spelled with a "G" or with a "K?" The debate continues.

Taiwan High-Speed Rail (THSR)

The face of Taipei continues to change, with **Taiwan High-Speed Rail (THSR)** (台灣高鐵 Taiwan Gaotie) connecting Taipei in the north and Kaohsiung (Zuoying) in the south. THSR is a modern high-speed railway system comparable to the TGV trains in France, the Amtrak American Flyer that connects New York, Boston and Washington, D.C., and the Shinkansen "bullet train" that connects Tokyo and Osaka in Japan.

THSR, which makes traversing the island from north to south possible in around two hours, currently stops at Taipei, Banciao, Taoyuan, Hsinchu, Taichung, Chiayi, Tainan and Zuoying (Kaohsiung). Stations in Nankang, Miaoli, Changhua and Yunlin are slated to open in 2010. Call (02) 4066-5678 for general inquiries or (02) 6626-8000 for phone booking.

If you have the time and inclination, the eastern side of the island, which includes Pingtung (屏東), Hualien (花蓮) and Taitung (台東), is known for its natural beauty and preservation of aboriginal culture. Down south, Kaohsiung (高雄) has a climate and temperature all its own—hot! If you choose to visit, the weather down south is hotter and dryer than its northern counterpart, so dress accordingly. From Kaohsiung, you may opt to take a bus to explore other areas of the island, such as Kenting National Park (墾丁國家公園) in Pingtung, which graces the southern tip of the island.

Important Numbers

Emergency Fire or Medical Emergency: 119
Information (Chinese): 104
Information (English): 106
English-speaking police: (02) 2555-4275 (Taipei), 2881-3853 (Tienmu)
Taipei Police Hotline: 110
Taiwan Country Code: 886
Taipei City Code: 02.

Taipei Railway Station Information Desk: (02) 2381-6595
For 24-hour MRT service dial (02) 2181-2345
For Taipei bus route information call the Department of Transportation toll-free at 0800-223-650.

The Taiwan country code is 886 and Taipei area code is 02. From the United States, to dial the Chinatrust Executive Suites, Beitou one would dial 011 886 2 2893-0911. When dialing a local number in Taipei it is not necessary to dial the area code, 02, first. To dial abroad while on Taiwan dial 002 and then the country code (44 for the U.K., 1 for the U.S., and so on), the city code and then the number.

Moving At The Speed Of Taipei

If you're looking to unwind, southern Taiwan offers a slower life pace. Taiwan's outlying islands or the capital's surrounding mountains may also provide the serenity you seek; please see "Islands In The Strait (台灣本島)" or "Taipei Guide To Mountain Climbing (台北登山指南)." The frenetic pace of the capital leaves many expatriates feeling as if they're on a 24-hour caffeine buzz without having touched a single cup of java (although you'll find plenty of local options to get that caffeine kick!). Since Taiwanese tend to go by trends (see "Get With The Fad, Dad!" under "XY & Z (Useful Information) (很有用的信息)," please call in advance to ensure that the establishment you wish to frequent is still thriving.

Name Cards

It's imperative that your name card be in both English and Chinese. Some put both English and Chinese writing on one side of the card, while others prefer to use English on one side, Chinese on the other. It shows respect for the local culture if you've had your name, title and any promotional literature translated into Chinese, and goes a long way as far as establishing "face" and making contacts. "Face" is described in greater detail under "XY & Z (Useful Information) (很有用的信息)."

Pay Phones

Two types of public pay phones prevail on Taiwan, coin-operated phones and stored-value card phones. For coin-operated phones insert at least NT $1 to make a local call, you can deposit NT $1, NT $5, or NT $10 at a time. Local calls cost NT $1/minute. Stored-value IC calling cards are available in NT $200 and NT $300 denominations. IC calling cards, which have a golden square strip on one side corner, can only be inserted top first into the sky blue or cloudy gray IC card public phones. You may find another type of stored-value public pay phone in which the cards are inserted horizontally, side first. Again, it's not necessary to dial the local area code when making a local call, so if you're in Taipei there's no need to dial "02" before the number. IC calling cards are available at most convenience stores.

Ping Me

On occasion you may find a hotel boasting of a large room size in "pings." Real estate property on Taiwan is measured in pings, or the size of a tatami mat. This measurement system, used by the Japanese on Taiwan from 1895 to 1945, is still in place today. For reference, 1 ping = 3.3 square meters. Aside from metric units, common units used are the catty or jin (斤) (1.1 lb or 0.4989 kilograms) and li (里) (0.5 kilometers or 0.31 miles).

Doing Business

Schedule an appointment in advance and don't show up during lunch, which typically runs from noon until around 1:30 pm, otherwise you're likely to find a dark office full of napping employees. Why? While Westerners have power lunches, Easterners enjoy power naps. Make sure your card is in both English and Chinese to make a better impression, and of course, choose your Chinese name carefully to avoid looking foolish. For other helpful tips please see "XY & Z (Useful Information) (很有用的信息)."

Forget Something?

If you forget personal effects, 24-hour convenience stores appear on seemingly every other block. Hong Kong-based **Watson's**® (屈臣士® Chuchengshi) is also easily recognized around town by its trademark blue sign and red logo and carries most daily necessities, such as pain relievers, tampons, vitamin pills, towels, and under garments. If you don't come across a Watson's try **Cosmed**® (康是美® Kangshimei), there are over seventy Cosmed stores in Taipei alone. If you sojourn to other parts of the island these stores may be harder to come by. Several of these drugstore chain locations are listed under "Toiletries (盥洗用具)."

Dress In Layers

For weather information see "Weather (天氣)" under "XY & Z (Useful Information) (很有用的信息)." The best times to visit are during cool autumn and temperate spring months, but the Taiwanese won't hold it against you if you visit during the winter (the frequent rainclouds might) or summer (typhoon season). If you plan on hiking see "Taipei Guide to Mountain Climbing (台北登山指南)" and bear in mind that it's cooler at higher altitudes. Bring a hat, sunglasses and a good bottle of sun tan lotion, preferably one that offers a high level of Pf protection, as sunscreen tends to be expensive on Taiwan. Small portable umbrellas go for around NT $120 (US $3.60) at most convenience stores and come in handy. Also, remember to bring a good pair of sneakers or walking shoes, as there is a lot to do and see in this exciting city.

National Palace Museum
(故宮博物院)

Take the MRT to Shilin Station (士林站) and exit Zhongzheng Road (Exit 1). In front of the station take either the 304, 255, Small 18 (小18), Small 19 (小19), or Red 30 (紅30) to the **National Palace Museum** (故宮博物院 Gugong Bowuyuan), Zhishan Road, Section 2, #221, Shilin (台北市士林區至善路2段221號) (02) 2881-2021. About seven minutes into the bus ride you'll spot "Chinese Culture and Movie Center." Chinese Culture and Movie Center once housed a small insect and dinosaur exhibit, a poor excuse for a haunted house, as well as early black and white Chinese movies with hard-to-discern subtitles. Though closed for the past few years, politicians are still debating the area's fate. Fast food eateries and cartoon-like statues continue to lure tourists. Unless you're under ten you're better off remaining on the bus.

Outside the National Palace Museum, a stupendous sanguine sign with caramel characters reads, "For All People Under Heaven," inviting all to enjoy the splendors inside. A statue of Dr. Sun Yat-sen towers above tourists as they give their cameras a workout, enamored with the museum's architectural beauty and with the area's magnificent mountain terrain. There are over 600,000 ancient artifacts on display, which run the gamut from musical instruments and art to wine vessels and pottery. The treasures at this museum were carefully removed from Mainland China by truck, railway, and boat before the Civil War. Admission to the National Palace Museum is NT $150 (US $4.50) per adult. If you don't mind splurging NT $150 (US $4.50) on a cup of coffee or tea, an upscale café on the top floor boasts a scenic view.

Adjacent to the museum is **Zhishan Garden** (至善公園). On your left, peacocks and other exotic birds peer curiously through cages. Who's watching whom? Glass windows provide an excellent opportunity to interact with and film these fine feathered friends. You'll also find placid, pulchritudinous ponds teeming with captivatingly colorful carp, grudging gray pheasants, a traditional tearoom overlooking the park and singular statues of ancient Chinese along the pathways. Purchase fish food at machines for only NT $10 and create a carp mosh-pit! Amuse yourself by watching these colossal chromatic carp slam dance into one another, opening and closing their monstrous mouths while seemingly stage-diving over one another for fresh fish pellets. Admission to the park is only NT $10 (US $ .30) and is a relaxing way to spend time.

Ximending
(西門町)

Buses run from in front of the National Palace Museum to Shilin Station. At Taipei Main Station transfer to the blue line heading in the direction of Xinpu and get off at the first stop, Ximen Station (西門站). You've now arrived at **Ximending** (西門町), "West Gate District," an area that boasts the youthful energy, creativity and spirt of Greenwich Village in New York City or Tokyo's Shibuya shopping district. This large urban sprawl that runs west of Zhonghua Road (中華路) to just north of Guiyang Street (貴陽街) is especially popular with young people as East meets West in fun foods and fashion fads. Ximending boasts curious cultural attractions such as **The Red Playhouse** (紅樓劇場), a traditional market-turned-playhouse and movie theater on Chengdu Road, #10, Ximending (台北市萬華區成都路10號) (02) 2311-9380. Not far from Ximen Station, street performers break out rare routines, particularly during weekends, and Asian pop artists hold live concerts (over prerecorded music) to promote new recordings. Explore a historic heavenly hot spot, **Tienho Temple** (天后宮 *Tienho Gong*), Chengdu Road, #51, Ximending (台北市成都路51號) (02) 2331-0421. The temple is within walking distance from the heart of the shopping area. Guang Shu, a former Ch'ing dynasty emperor, donated the sign that hangs at the entrance of the temple.

Skylark at rockin' restaurants, cool cafés and steakhouses (TGI Friday's® does quite well on Wuchang Street, Section 2, #72 (台北市武昌街2段72號2樓) (02) 2388-0679), and be sure to nosh on nectareous native foods during your stay. Ximending is rife with vendors! On Hanchung Street, vendors dish out everything from roasted chicken butt (雞屁股 *ji pigoo*), chicken claws (雞腳 *ji jiao*), pig blood mixed with rice (豬血糕 *zhu xue gao*), to fresh fruits, barbeque corn, and cotton candy. Personal favorites include candied cherry tomatoes and strawberries (糖葫蘆 *tanghulu*), which usually go for NT $30 (US $ .90) per stick of four, and sweet gluttonous rice with peanut or sesame seed shavings (麻糬 *mwaji*). Mwaji, or "mochi" as the snack is called by Japanese, typically costs NT $10 (US $ .30) each or NT $100 (US $ 3.00) for a box of ten. For tips on tasty Taiwanese tidbits, please see the section entitled, "Native Foods (台灣食物)."

Multinational Corporations (MNCs) often test market products or services on Taiwan before rolling them out across Asia or the rest of the world. McDonald's® (麥當勞® *My Dang Lao*) McCafé® coffeehouse chain entices, and the enormous McDonald's that once stood directly across from Ximen Station has been replaced by the company's ambitious McTreat® restaurant, a new chain catering to a more upscale, health-conscious crowd. Burger lovers will be disappointed to find that McTreat offers sandwiches, pastries and finger foods rather than burgers. Sorry folks, there's no seating at this McTreat, you'll have to get that tiramisu to go.

National Taiwan Democracy Memorial Hall
(國立臺灣民主紀念館)

Two stops from Ximending is **National Taiwan Democracy Memorial Hall** (國立臺灣民主紀念館 *Guoli Taiwan Minzhu Jinian Guan*). Formerly known as "Chiang Kai-Shek Memorial Hall," the area encompasses 250,000 square meters and officially opened on April 5, 1980, exactly five years after the first Republic of China (ROC) president's passing. There is an ongoing debate on Taiwan regarding the historical significance of Chiang Kai-shek, the first president of the republic. For more information please see "Politics and Government" under "XY & Z (Useful Information) (很有用的信息)."

The octagon-shaped roof of the Memorial Hall resembles a traditional Chinese alter. You'll need to climb over a hundred steps to reach the enormous paternal-looking Chiang monument that weighs 21.5 metric tons and towers nearly 10 meters tall. From 9 am to 5 pm, armed guards stand on either side of the monument, and every hour, on the hour, visitors bear witness to the changing of the guard. You'll know it's the ceremonial changing of the guard from the sudden stream of camera flashes.

At the base of the monument, on either side, are entrances to the Memorial Hall Museum. There is no admission fee to enter the Memorial Hall or the museum. Inside the main hall a display room exhibits clothing worn by the late leader, the central lobby sports his two black Cadillacs, and a lecture hall shows movies about the late leader's life. There's also an art gallery, memorial room, and memorial library which houses the late president's works, as well as over thirty thousand books and a hundred and fifty volumes of journals.

On the Great Lawn, admire the traditional Chinese architecture of the National Theater and National Concert Hall. The National Theater boasts lively ballet, recital and phenomenal Peking Opera performances. Pick up a free Monthly Program Guide at Eslite (誠品書局), Kingstone (金石堂), or Caves Books (敦煌書局), where event tickets may be purchased. Locations are listed under "Bookstores (書局)."

Tienmu
(天母)

From National Taiwan Democracy Memorial Hall take the MRT to Taipei Main Station, transfer to the green (Beitou) or red (Danshui) lines and exit at Shipai (石牌站). If you cross Shipai Road (石牌路), the main road directly in front of the station, you'll be heading towards Beitou. To the right of the MRT, Donghua Street, Section 2 (東華街2段) divides Shipai Road (石牌路) into sections one and two. Cross Donghua Street and head in the direction of Shipai Road, Section 2 (石牌路2段). After crossing Yumin 4th Road (裕民四路) you'll see bus stops. Take the 285, 645 or Red 12 (紅12) buses that stop at Miramar Cinemas, Zhongcheng Road, Section 2, #202 4F (intersection of Tienmu East and Tienmu West Roads) (台北市天母美麗華 忠誠路2段202號4樓) (02) 2876-3300 or the Red 19 (紅19) that stops at Tienmu Village Square on Zhongshan North Road, Section 7 (中山北路7段). Welcome to **Tienmu** (天母)!

Tienmu Square (天母廣場), the intersection where Tienmu East Road and Tienmu West Road meet Zhongshan North Road, Section 7, is a good starting point. There is no direct MRT line to Tienmu. If you opt not to wait for the bus, hail a taxi adjacent to the station and head to the intersection of Tienmu East Road and Zhongshan North Road, Section 7 (天母東路和中山北路7段路口). From here you can either walk up Zhongshan North Road, Section 7 or explore the shops and boutiques around Tienmu West Road. A taxi fare from Shipai Station to Tienmu costs around NT $130 (US $3.90).

There are several myths as to how the town

got its name and each is unique. According to one legend, when foreigners asked how to get to Tienmu over a century ago locals would respond, "tia boh," or "I don't understand" in Taiwanese (閩南語 *milanyu*). The town of Tia Boh later became Tienmu, a more dulcet-sounding name in Mandarin. The two Chinese characters for "Tienmu" mean "sky mother." Another tale relates to Matsu, the goddess of heaven. One name for Matsu is Tien Shang Shen Mu (天上聖母). During the 1920s, when Taiwan was still under Japanese rule, the town name was shortened from Tien Shang Shen Mu to Tienmu in her honor.

If you've visited Long Island, New York, you'll have a general idea of what the town is like. Tienmu is a quaint, bustling town much like the Long Island towns of Great Neck or Roslyn, but with a Taiwan flavor all its own. If you're arriving from California, Tienmu may remind you of Westwood in Los Angeles. Tienmu boasts a wide selection of Western restaurants such as Kentucky Fried Chicken®, McDonald's, Pizza Hut®, Round Table Pizza®, Swenson's®, or Sizzler®. Indulge at cafés (a la Starbucks®) or chill at a huge Häagen-Dazs® on Tienyu Street, behind Tienmu West Road, directly across from a Wellcome supermarket. Aside from McDonald's, which are easily located in most neighborhoods, glance through "Taipei Dining Guide (台北餐廳指南)" for some savory suggestions. Many Western restaurants, considered local teen hangouts and nothing spectacular back home, are monumental here, marketed as upscale Western dining establishments. Take a gander at the two-story Pizza Hut on Zhongxiao East Road, Section 3, opposite Dr. Sun Yat-sen Memorial Hall (Zhongxiao East Road, Section 4 and Guofu South Road intersection) or the one on Zhongshan North Road, Section 7.

Ice cream, anyone? You'll be amazed at Taipei's enormous Häagen-Dazs ice cream parlors. On Dunhua South Road, Section 1, #173 (台北市敦化南路1段173號) (02) 2776-

9553, Häagen-Dazs towers four stories and appears as spectacular as some of the artifacts at the National Palace Museum. On Tienyu Street, Lane 38, Alley 18, #1 (台北市天玉街38巷18弄1號) (02) 2874 5223, Häagen-Dazs is also singularly impressive. With white holiday lights, spacious seating and an outdoor garden, this ice cream parlor appears more like an emperor's palace than a place to sample your favorite flavors. (Häagen-Dazs recently opened in Ximending by Ximen Station, as well.) Needless to say, you'll find fine local and international cuisine in Tienmu.

On the same street as Häagen-Dazs (across town) is **Liuligongfang Tienmu International Gallery** (琉璃工房天母國際藝廊), Tienyu Street, #7 (台北市士林區天玉街7號) (02) 2873-0258. This handicrafts museum established in 1987 is making a splash in establishing a new culture of image creation. With galleries across the globe, the Tienmu gallery boasts impressive glass works that include Buddhist figures, Chinese horoscopes, legends and auspicious animals. In addition to a work area and audio-visual room, guests frequent the upscale café for fine coffee, tea, pastries and ambiance.

Taipei American School and Taipei Japanese School face each other at the tail end of Zhongshan North Road, Section 6, where expat children enjoy their formative years. Stroll along Tienmu East Road or walk up Zhongshan North Road, Section 7 to frequent Tienmu's current clothing boutiques, where styles run from classy to trendy to punk. In Tienmu you'll find fantastic foods and a variety of clothing, from local Taiwanese styles to international super brands: The Body Shop®, Adidas®, Puma®, Nike®, and a Major League Baseball® sportswear store are frequented here. In addition to professional basketball, which is somewhat of an obsession to Taiwan's youth, baseball has become a popular local pastime. For more information please see "Baseball (棒球)." Tienmu

Baseball Stadium, which is across the street from Dayeh Takashimaya department store where games are sometimes broadcast live, is "Taipei Physical Education College" during the off-season.

Spring City Resort (春天酒店)

After dinner take either the Red 19 (紅19), 216, 218, 223, or the 508 bus to Shipai Station and return to Beitou, it's fairly easy to get around and residents will point you in the right direction. At Beitou Station take bus 218 to Xinbeitou (New Beitou) Station. There is no fare to use the bus from Beitou to New Beitou after 9 pm because the New Beitou MRT line doesn't operate until 6 am the following morning. At Xinbeitou Station take the free hotel shuttle bus or a taxi a few hundred yards up the mountain to **Spring City Resort** (春天酒店 *Chuntien Jiudian*), Youya Road, #18 (台北市北投區幽雅路18號) (02) 2897-5555. The address, phone number and hotel description are also listed under "Taipei Hotel Guide (台北飯店指南)."

Many contend that the hot springs at Spring City Resort are not only the best in Taipei, but also the best on Taiwan. The first shuttle bus runs at 6:55 am from New Beitou Park, directly across from Xinbeitou Station, and the last one departs from the park at 11:10 pm. Call the hotel to arrange for a pick-up. If you opt for a taxi, the resort is about a five-minute ride from Xinbeitou Station and the fare costs around NT $130 (US $3.90). Make sure the driver knows where you want to go before the meter starts running.

Live in luxury (NT $7,000/night and up) or visit the Melody Sky Lounge on the first floor for choice cocktails and a romantic Taipei view just outside. See if Melody Sky Lounge is running any special promotions as the strawberry margaritas and tropical fruit drinks typically tantilize tastebuds. After relaxing at the Melody Sky Lounge, visit Spring City Resort's spectacular outdoor hot springs. Wooden reclining chairs and natural whirlpools ease tension. There are both cold and hot springs for those who may wish to cool off after a hot dip. The outdoor springs are open from 9 am to 10 pm and at NT $800 (US $24.00) it's time and money well spent. The indoor hot springs cost NT $600 (US $18.00) per person per hour, the springs are new and comfortable but the room itself is small. Amenities include a shower cap, comb, razor, towels, bathing lotion, shampoo and mineral water. The hotel sometimes runs promotions for an inclusive dinner/spring experience. Wear a bathing suit to enjoy Spring City Resort's outdoor springs but only your birthday suit to soak in your own private indoor hot spring bath.

Hall Yard Resort
(花月溫泉館)

If you're visiting during the winter or if the weather's too wet for an outdoor dip try **Hall Yard Resort** (花月溫泉館 *Huayue Wenchuenguan*), Xinmin Road, Lane 1, #2.4 (台北市北投區新民路1巷2.4號) (02) 2893-9870. Also in New Beitou, bathe in one of the resort's fine indoor hot springs. Like the indoor springs of Spring City Resort (and most indoor springs, for that matter), there are no whirlpool jets. Some rooms have a hot spring while others boast both hot and cold spring faucets, so if you'd like a room with both temperatures available make a request beforehand. Like Spring City Resort, amenities are available free of charge, such as a shower cap, comb, razor, towels, bathing lotion, moisturizer, shampoo and mineral water. Unlike Spring City Resort, however, rooms are spacious and have a couch/rest area to relax between bathing sessions and have a separate shower area. Hall Yard charges NT $1000/ hour and a half, during weekends and national holidays the price increases to NT $1,200. Currently undergoing renovation, please call first.

Spring City Resort and Hall Yard Resort

are relatively new, clean, and modern. Addresses and phone numbers for these and other select hot springs are listed under "Hot Springs (溫泉)." Relax and unwind, you've experienced your first day in Taipei.

Beitou Traditional Market
(北投傳統市場)

Wake up early to experience a traditional Taiwan market. If you're staying in Beitou, walk from Beitou Station to Xinshi Street (新市街), the bustling outdoor **Beitou Traditional Market** (北投傳統市場) is two blocks behind Beitou Station. The mid-way point of the traditional market is near the busy Beitou intersection of Chingchiang Street (清江街) and Zhongzheng Street (中正街). The area becomes a night market after sunset. Another travel book incorrectly refers to night markets as "wet markets," the only time these markets are wet is when it rains! Don't make the same mistake my brother Jay made and search for a "wet market," you'll only be making yourself all wet in the process.

Vendors begin flooding traditional markets around 6 am, if you've never visited the outdoor markets of South America you should be in for a fun time. At Taiwan's traditional markets you can buy just about anything, from plastic and porcelain wares, flowers, fresh fish, tropical fruits and vegetables, and sometimes even live chickens. Even if you opt not to purchase anything, the market in and of itself is an interesting introduction to Taiwanese foods and conventional culture.

Bewitching jade bracelets, found in most day/night markets, are usually used for religious purposes. Followers of the Buddhist faith hold a bracelet in one hand while silently chanting, "Omi tofo, omi tofo," running a thumb over each bead. After the thumb has run over every bead, the individual feels more at ease and hopes that his prayers will be answered. On Taiwan, you may witness individuals using these beaded bracelets at airports, in restaurants, or while using public transportation. Prayer beads hang from the front mirrors of many

taxis and are sold in most temples. It's understandable that many use silent prayer to escape the stresses of everyday life. For more information please see "Religion on Taiwan" under "XY & Z (Useful Information) (很有用的信息)."

If prices are not listed at day/night markets, vendors may hit you with what I refer to as the "foreign face tax." This "tax" on appearance may be far more blatant in other countries. If a price is written on a cardboard poster above the items, you have a better idea of what the fair market value for the goods are and can negotiate a more reasonable price. At day/night markets, beaded jade prayer bracelets typically sell for between NT $100 to NT $200, if a vendor asks for more than chances are the price isn't reasonable. More on bargaining/negotiation on Taiwan can be found under "XY & Z (Useful Information)(很有用的信息)," in the section entitled, "Communication Corner: Important Cultural Do's & Don'ts."

Renting a moped is not advisable for new visitors to the island.

This next section describes in detail a moped ride through **Beitou** (北投) over the mountain to **Lungfeng and Sulfur Valley** (硫磺谷) and on to **Tienmu** (天母) for breakfast. This section has been included to introduce readers to attractions that are popular with local residents and expatriates who reside on Taiwan. If you opt to take a taxi you may want to pay a few extra NT$ so your ride waits for you. From Tienmu, readers sojourn to **Yangmingshan Houshan** (陽明山後山) for a picturesque view of Taipei just behind **Chinese Culture University** (中國文化大學). Visitors can then choose to experience Chianshan Park (陽明山前山公園) with its flurry of food and toy vendors. Just down the road is **Yangmingshan National Park** (陽明山國家公園), famous for its manicured flower clock that tells the accurate local time, hiking trails and scenic beauty. Then head up to **Juzihu Lookout Point** (竹子湖觀景平台) in the mountains where nearby vendors sell fresh fruits and flowers. Afterwards dwell deep in the depths of **Hell Valley** (地熱谷) to experience the eerie beauty of a natural sulfuric pond. Readers can then take the MRT to **Danshui** (淡水) to enjoy a historic town with a carnival atmosphere and soothing sunset. This may take more than one day via MRT, bus and on foot, but as a note of caution, some of the hike could be steep. *Renting a moped is not advisable for new visitors to the island*.

Taipei traffic is chaotic, accidents and altercations appear with frightening frequency on late-night news programs. If you're absolutely set on cruising over the mountains (the spirit of James Dean lives on—in Taipei), speak with a local friend or long-term expatriate about taking you to where you would like to go. If someone you trust is willing to ride in Yangmingshan, New Beitou or Tienmu, it is suggested that he or she use a medium-sized or larger bike with a 100 cc or 125 cc engine as a smaller engine may not be equipped to make it up steeper areas. International drivers must have an international permit and a license from their home country to drive on Taiwan for thirty days, after which one must apply for a local license. If you've never ridden a moped, it's similar to riding a bicycle except that on a moped you use your right hand to add gas to accelerate. Much like a bicycle, brakes are also found in front of the handlebars.

Two important notes on motorbike safety: First, while riding on a moped, always wear your helmet. Even if you're tempted to feel the cool mountain breeze, don't take your helmet off, it's against the law and it's simply not safe. You never know when a reckless or irritable driver may attempt to pass you on a winding road. Local police, who may appear somewhat cold or aloof, rarely hassle visitors, they recognize that

international guests are probably not familiar with local customs and tend to overlook minor offenses. If you obey traffic laws and wear your helmet, it's doubtful you'll have trouble. You will be stopped, however, for riding a moped without a helmet.

Betelnut Beauties
(檳榔西施)

Second, try not to allow yourself to become distracted by "spicy girls" (辣美 *la mei*) that ride mopeds in spandex or mini-skirts, or by betelnut beauties (檳榔西施 *binglang shishih*). There were four absolutely stunning women in Chinese history and Shi Shih (西施) was one of them; charming Chinese women, therefore, are sometimes called this name. Betelnut beauties are typically young ladies who wear practically nothing to sell betelnuts (檳榔 *binglang*) and other addictive substances, such as cigarettes and alcohol, in glass window booths decorated in neon lights alongside main roads. These small, innocent-looking green nuts, jokingly referred to locally as "Taiwanese chewing gum," release the addictive arecoline stimulant, leaving your throat feeling hot and a blood-red stain on your teeth. After chewing one you may appear as if you've just bitten into a live squirrel. To try and introduce as many quintessentially local (道地 *dao di*) items as possible, every friend and relative of the author that has visited Taiwan has tried one.

So far the consensus seems to be that betelnut tastes like a raw, bitter vegetable such as celery. Is betelnut widely consumed? Consider this: Next to rice, betelnut is Taiwan's second-largest cash crop. The legalities of chewing betelnuts are continually debated as the short roots of betelnut trees cause erosion and may be responsible for deadly mudslides. In addition, citizen groups complain about negative stereotypes and health effects (a recent law bans the sale of betelnuts to minors). Since chewing betelnut is one aspect of traditional Taiwanese culture and the industry reportedly generates upwards of US $2 billion a year, don't expect these small green nuts or the accompanying debates to disappear anytime soon.

Betelnut beauties typically work in more traditional areas of the island along major roadways so drivers can briefly stop and get their daily dose of arecoline, nicotine and oogling. Not far from Beitou, betelnut beauties work on Minchuan Road (台北縣淡水鎮民權路) and Zhongzheng Road, Sections 1 and 2 (台北縣淡水鎮中正路1段、2段) that lead to Danshui.

If you're not attracted to fetching women, betelnut beauties shouldn't be a problem; however, as a note of caution, keep your eyes on the road. Spicy betelnut women are notorious for causing rubber necking (or necking with rubbers, with the harsh-looking guys that run the stands) and traffic accidents.

You may want to visit an automobile club before your departure to purchase an international driver's license. Chances are you won't need it, but if an officer asks to see your license, it's a good idea to have one with you.

Betelnut beauties provide daily doses of arecoline, nicotine, and oogling——and traffic accidents?

Gasoline on the island has been relatively inexpensive, and only recently has the price of Octane 98 risen to NT $30 (US $.90) a liter. This is because China Petroleum Corporation, which runs the distribution of gasoline on the island, is a government-subsidized monopoly. (Power generation and telecommunications industries have recently been deregulated; legal monopolies on Taiwan included Chung Hwa Telecom, Taiwan Salt Works, Taiwan Sugar Corporation, Taiwan Power Co., or Taipower, and Taiwan Wine and Tobacco.) Fill up with at least Octane 98 to help prevent any unforeseen difficulties, the last thing you need is to be stranded because you filled up with a low-grade of gas. Most moped tanks can be filled on ten to twelve liters and you could probably ride around for an entire week on one full tank of gas, although for newcomers it's not advisable.

Some expatriates claim that navigating over the mountains from Beitou to Tienmu and Yangmingshan National Park is relatively easy. How so? Only a few main roads wind around the mountain. Residents are also generally friendly and offer assistance.

Let's Get It Started

Beitou Station is across the street and one block south of Chinatrust Executive Suites, Beitou on Beitou Road, Section 2. A long row of yellow taxis line the front of Beitou Station. Ride the moped to the back of the MRT station, to Guangming Road (光明路). Guangming Road runs through Beitou from Beitou Station to Xinbeitou Station.

Heading away from Beitou Station ride up Guangming Road (光明路). Pass the Family Mart convenience store on your left, local shops, a Super Lotto store to the right, and Beitou Elementary School on the left. If there isn't a line halfway down the block, you may want to stop in and purchase a lotto ticket. Before Taiwan initiated the national lotto draw, local residents would collect their receipts and try and match the serial numbers on top of their receipts with a winning number drawn every three months. With the recent craze over the national lotto, however, many residents are throwing their receipts away rather than wait to see if they've hit the jackpot. Instant gratification wins again.

After you pass Beitou Elementary School on the left, Guangming Road winds towards the right. You should find yourself at a busy four-way intersection. To your left is Beitou Police Station and the Beitou branch of Taipei Fubon Bank, which bears the company's trademark green, blue and white sign. (Fubon Corporation recently acquired Taipei Bank.) Directly across the street, on the corner, is a 7-Eleven® convenience store. A sign directly in front of you indicates Zhongyang North Road, Section 1 (中央北路1段) is to the left and Zhongyang South Road, Section 1 (中央南路1段) is to the right. Don't turn onto either road. Go straight, bearing right around the circle, heading up the main road towards New Beitou (新北投 Xinbeitou).

If you make a sharp right onto Huanggang Road (礦港路) immediately after the 7-Eleven on the corner you'll be going towards Beitou Traditional Market. Continue going straight on Guangming Road (光明路), you should pass an I-Mei (義美 E May), Guangming Road, #132 (台北市北投區光明路132號) (02) 2891-3690. I-Mei bakery sells the best soft ice cream on the island for NT $20 (US $.60) a cone. Just up the road from I-Mei you'll see another 7-Eleven on your right and Beitou Fire Station on your left. On your right you'll pass Milkhouses (米哥烘焙坊), Guangming Road, #158 (台北市北投區光明路 158 號) (02) 2898-2258. Milkhouses bakery chain wins customers for its choice cakes, piquant pastries and delicious pudding desserts.

Once you pass Beitou Post Office on your left you've entered New Beitou. The white and green sign above the post office bears the Beitou zip code, 112. You'll pass a two-story Blockbuster® Video (百事達® Baishida) on the right, and Watson's drug store (屈臣士 Chuchengshi) on the left. Next to Watson's is Yoshinoya® (吉野家® Jiyejia), a Japanese fast food restaurant (orange sign, white logo), try a beef or chicken bowl. Adjacent to Yoshinoya is KFC®, which bears the same red and white logo found around the world, except in Asia a giant statue of Colonel Sanders greets customers outside. KFC replaced a Kipo Chicken Rice®, a spicy chicken chain from Singapore. Oddly enough, the sign for that fast food restaurant bore a picture of a kindly grandmother. In the West, not many grandmothers would serve food that spicy to their grandkids.

You've now arrived at a main intersection of New Beitou. McDonald's and a 24-hour Wellcome supermarket are to the right. Is the store spelled with two "l"s intentionally or was that originally a typo? Some expats like to joke, "The well come to Wellcome, the sick stay home" or "You are welcome to spend your money at Wellcome." Wellcome, based out of Hong Kong, is the largest supermarket chain on Taiwan and one of the largest in Asia. These supermarkets are easily recognizable by their large red signs bearing the white and yellow Wellcome logo.

Across from McDonald's and Wellcome is New Beitou Park (新北投公園). Continuing straight, Xinbeitou Station should be on your left, directly across from New Beitou Park. To the left of the entrance to New Beitou Park and directly across from McDonald's once stood a Burger King®. Alas, burger giants from the West are facing off ferociously in the East. In its place is now a large electronics chain with a red and white logo, "Chuenguo Dianzi" (全國電子). To the left, adjacent to Xinbeitou Station, is Dayeh Road (大業路), which runs from New Beitou to a main thoroughfare leading to Taipei.

Continue going straight past Chuenguo Dianzi (全國電子) and bear to the right, you should see a bus stop on your right and be on Chuenyuen Road (泉源路), a narrow road that winds up the mountain. By bus the Small 9 (小\9), Small 22 (小\22) and Small 25 (小\25) head up the mountain from this stop. Don't turn right onto Xinming Road (新民路) or you'll end up in a residential area behind Hsin Ming Junior High School. Bear to the *left* at the fork, Chuenyuen Road twists to the left past a 7-Eleven before bending sharply to the right past an OK convenience store. By now you should notice that, due to a dearth of space and frenetic Taipei lifestyles, fast food restaurants and convenience stores have become exceedingly popular. Beware of mopeds and cars that may be pulling out of driveways and alleyways.

After five minutes you should find yourself at a crossroad and spot a brown wooden sign for Yangmingshan National Park (陽明山國家公園). To the right of this sign is a small white sign with red Chinese characters for Spring City Resort (春天酒店). A sign for Taiwan Folk Arts Museum should be to your right. Here you'll find terrific mountain terrain and the enchanting scent of...sulfur? Yes, sulfur! If the air begins to smell like eggs it's not you (well, hopefully it's not you), nor is it your gasoline (it shouldn't be if you had filled up with a higher grade, such as Octane 98).

Make a right and continue on Chuenyuen Road, heading in the direction of Spring City Resort and Taiwan Folk Arts Museum. You should pass a retirement home and a black and yellow-striped shoulder on the right before reaching another fork. You should see signs for Spring City Resort, Taiwan Folk Arts Museum and Shann Garden, a teahouse adjacent to the museum. Directly in front of you, slightly to the left, should be a large sign for Yangmingshan National Park.

Stop and admire the towering red-faced statue of **Guan Gong** (關公), the God of War, by the temple at the fork in the road. Local residents stop here and pray to Guan

Gong for safety, health and prosperity. If time permits, walk up the small road directly to the left of the statue to see a unique statue, approximately five meters high, of Buddha.

Make a left at the statue of Guan Gong and head in the direction of the sign pointing toward Yangmingshan National Park. Chuenyuen Road twists and turns, ride slowly and be sure to stop along the way, perhaps at the wooden pagoda and benches near Xingyi Road (行義路) to view Sulfur Valley.

Lungfeng and Sulfur Valley (硫磺谷)

Lungfeng and Sulfur Valley (硫磺谷 *Liuhuanggu*) boast amazing fumaroles, natural hot springs (too hot for bathing) and sulfur pits. Sulfur Valley is between Beitou's Chuenyuen Road (泉源路) and Xingyi Road (行義路). Lungfeng Valley is just beyond the intersection of Chuenyuen Road and Xingyi Road, on the opposite side of the large four-way intersection. These hot springs are not for bathing, as the green and yellow volcanic topography of Sulfur Valley emit spirals of hot steam year-round.

For a closer look at Sulfur Valley, make a *left* at the Chuenyuen Road crossroad and continue to go straight until you see the sign for Sulfur Valley on the right. The entrance

If the air begins to smell like eggs it's not you. Well, hopefully it's not you...

Yangming Mountain, once mined for its sulfur deposits, is home to some fantastic splendors of nature.

sign reads, "Liuhuangku Geothermal Scenic Area." To get to Lungfeng and Sulfur Valley by bus, take the 230, which runs from Beitou over Yangmingshan (陽明山) to Shilin (士林). You can find this bus at Beitou Station or at the main bus stop across from Taipei Fubon Bank in Beitou. Make sure the driver knows where you want to go. Two small blue buses, the Small 22 (小22) and Small 25 (小25), now pick up passengers directly in front of Beitou Station. You can depart either of these buses at the Chuenyuen Road/ Xingyi Road intersection, the highest part of

Chuenyuen Road, and walk for about fifteen minutes to reach Sulfur Valley. Buses do not stop here frequently.

Once you reach Xingyi Road, you should come to another four-way fork in the road. From here you could either go straight for twenty minutes to reach Chinese Culture University, make a left to head to Yangmingshan National Park, or make a right to go to Tienmu. Stop and take a glimpse at the local market on the right side of the road. At the intersection of Xingyi Road and Chuenyuen Road (行義路和泉源路口), vendors sell fresh fruits, flowers and vegetables to morning commuters. The area becomes particularly busy during weekends and Chinese holidays.

Make a right onto Xingyi Road and head towards Tienmu, the road winds past Sa Mao Valley Hot Springs Area (紗帽山溫泉區). For a more traditional hot spring bath, try **Tang Wu** (湯屋溫泉 *Tangwu Wenchuen)*, Xingyi Road, #296-2 (台北市北投區行義路296號之2) (02) 2875-5808. Tang Wu charges NT $100 per person per hour for a private bath (個人池 *geren chih*). Two notes: bring your own towel, and staff is not bilingual. For more information please see the section entitled, "Hot Springs (溫泉)."

Near the bottom of Xingyi Road you should pass a 7-Eleven, a motorbike shop and a temple on your right by the small circle fork. Don't go straight onto Shipai Road, make a *left* at the circle onto Tienmu North Road (天母北路) and head straight. Cross the small bridge where fresh stream water flows below, pass car repair shops, restaurants, residential buildings and, on your left, Mos Burger® (摩斯漢堡® *Moxi Hanbao*), the Japanese equivalent of McDonald's.

Cross Tienmu West Road and continue straight, Tienmu North Road winds to the left. Make a right onto Zhongshan North Road, Section 6 and enjoy a delicious Western-style breakfast at **Jake's Country Kitchen** (鄉香美墨餐廳), Zhongshan North

Road, Section 6, #705 (台北市中山北路6段705號) (02) 2871-5289. Founded in 1979 by Jake Lo, expats and locals alike are fond of Jake's down-home country cooking. This Tienmu staple boasts hearty homemade Western and Mexican foods and free coffee refills.

From Jake's Country Kitchen head up Zhongshan North Road, Section 6 (中山北路6段) towards Zhongshan North Road, Section 7. Pass Taipei American School on your right and Taipei Japanese School on your left. You should arrive at an intersection with a large underground parking lot directly in front of you. To the left is Tienmu West Road (天母西路), to the right is Tienmu East Road (天母東路) and straight ahead, across the intersection, is Zhongshan North Road, Section 7 (中山北路7段).

Turn right onto Tienmu East Road (天母東路). You'll notice an interesting contrast between ancient and modern here as **Sanyu Temple** (三玉宮), a historic Buddhist temple on Tienmu East Road, #6 (台北市士林區天母東路6號) (02) 2871-3000, is adjacent to a three-story KFC. People come here (to the temple, not KFC) to pray to Matsu (媽祖), the goddess of heaven, the seven statues of celestial beings (七尊大神像 *chee shen da zhen zhu*), the god of farming (神農大帝 *Shen Nong Da Di*, also referred to as 五穀先帝 *Wu Guh Xian Di*), as well as other gods. The temple was built over two centuries ago when thousands, mostly farmers, immigrated from China's Fujian and Chuenchou provinces. The temple was moved to its current location and opened in January, 1979.

Stop at Watson's or at Family Mart to pick up bottled water and light snacks and continue on Tienmu East Road. At the intersection of Tienmu East Road and Zhongcheng Road (忠誠路) you should see a McCafé on your left, and on your right, Shin Kong Mitsukoshi department store. After crossing Zhongcheng Road pass The

Pig, Green Bar, and Tequila Sunrise on your right. Some expats find the The Pig, an old British-style pub, a welcome respite for throwing darts or dancing. Check out "Taipei Pub Guide (台北PUB指南)" for a list of happening hot spots.

Continue straight, pass Sanyu Elementary School (三玉國小) and Taipei Municipal Tienmu Junior High (天母國中) on the right. After passing Tienmu Junior High, Tienmu East Road winds sharply to the right and become Dongshan Road (東山路). At the first traffic light, which you should see about a hundred meters after turning the corner, turn *left* onto Dongshan Road, Lane 25 (東山路25巷) and follow the signs for Chinese Culture University. From Tienmu, you'll be heading up the back of Yangmingshan. This is a steep, winding road, so be thankful you're riding a 100 or 125 cc moped and have filled up with a high grade of gasoline (Octane 98 or higher). You should soon pass traditional teahouses built alongside the mountain. In addition to Tienmu and Yangming Mountain, a handful of expatriates have also settled in the hilly and secluded Wellington Heights area of Beitou.

Yangmingshan Houshan (陽明山後山)

Continue going up Dongshan Road, Lane 25 (東山路25巷), after the road turns into Kaishuen Road (台北市陽明山凱旋路) you should arrive at the back of **Chinese Culture University** (中國文化大學). Kaishuen Road winds up and to the right, behind the campus basketball courts. The back of Chinese Culture University is known as **Yangmingshan Houshan** (陽明山後山), enjoy the picturesque view of Tienmu below, Shipai and Beitou to the right and Taipei off in the distance. During the evening, food vendors line the road selling everything from roasted corn (烤玉米 *kao yu mi*) and stinky tofu (臭豆腐 *chou dofu*) to barbeque squid (烤魷魚 *kao you yu*). Yangmingshan Houshan is usually lined with couples after sunset. From the road below, just outside

The Top (屋頂上) (formerly "Dongshan Teahouse & Hotspring"), it appears as if everyone is staring at a large movie screen. The Top, Kaishuen Road, Lane 61, Alley 4, #33 (台北市陽明山凱旋路61巷4弄33 號) (02) 2862-2255 is a hot pot spot for Taiwanese, Cantonese and Southeast Asian cuisine, fish, shrimp and tofu, sumptuous soups, choice coffee and Chinese teas. Open from 5 pm to 3 am weekdays, 12 pm to 3 am weekends, some young people spend the entire night enjoying the food, drinks and view.

Chianshan Park
(陽明山前山公園)

After you exit Chinese Culture University you should be on Gejr Road (格致路), turn left, you should soon see a sign for Yangmingshan National Park. As the road winds make a left onto Shamao Road (紗帽路). After crossing Shamao Road, make a right and then another quick right onto Jianguo Street (建國街). You've arrived at **Chianshan Park** (陽明山前山公園 Chianshan Gongyuan), which boasts a pristine lake, hiking trails and a public natural hot spring. Here you'll find local merchants selling everything from cooked bamboo (竹子 zhu zi) to purple herbal pancakes (山藥 shan yao), which many Taiwanese consider to be a form of medicine. More daring adventurers can consider bathing in the natural pubic hot spring, free of charge. This is a traditional Japanese-style spring, where typically older men or women bathe together in rooms separated by sex. Wearing a bathing suit here isn't permitted, so those embarrassed to disrobe in front of strangers may prefer to frequent a private hot spring bathhouse instead.

Yangmingshan National Park
(陽明山國家公園)

On Gejr Road (格致路) make a left, heading in the direction you were going before you turned left onto Shamao Road (紗帽 路). You should pass Taipei Teachers In-Service Education Center (台北市教師研習中心) on the *left*, bear to the left at the military base to arrive at a fork in the road. The road to the right leads to Gold Mountain (金山 Jinshan). Take the road to the *left* and ride for five minutes to arrive at **Yangmingshan National Park** (陽明山國家公園 Yangmingshan Guojia Gongyuan), Zhuzihu Road, #1-20 (台北市陽明山竹子湖路1-20號) (02) 2861-3601.

Once called "Grass Mountain" (草山 Caoshan), the name was changed to Yangming Mountain (陽明山 Yangmingshan) in 1950 in honor of Ming dynasty Chinese laureate Wang Yang Ming (王陽明) (1472-1529), a favored author of the late Chiang Kai-shek. Discover metallic Chinese scrolls displaying some of Wang Yang Ming's works, fetching flowers, towering trees, magnificent mountain ranges, a fantastic fountain, hiking trails, and a manicured flower clock that tells the accurate local time. The area becomes particularly popular in spring when bright pink plum blossoms, the national flower, and cherry blossoms, are in bloom. You'll also find traditional red pagodas and immense, life-like monuments dedicated to significant figures in Chinese history, such as Sun Yat-sen and Wang Yang Ming. Yangmingshan National Park is a national cultural attraction and a visit is well worth your time.

Head back to the fork in the road by 7-Eleven and Starbucks. Are Taiwanese people that enthusiastic about the trademark burnt-tasting Western coffee? It seems that they are. There are over a hundred Starbucks cafés on Taiwan, with the trademark green and brown signs popping up at nearly every major tourist attraction.

Zhuzihu Lookout Point
(竹子湖觀景平台)

Follow the roundabout road to **Zhuzihu** (竹子湖), "Bamboo Lake," and stop at scenic **Zhuzihu Lookout Point** (竹子湖觀景平台) on the left for an outstanding view of Chinese Culture University and Taipei. For more information please see "Taipei Guide To Mountain Climbing (台北登山指南)." The winding road becomes steep in a few areas, so be sure you're on a moped that is equipped to handle the journey. Near the lookout point are fruit and vegetable merchants, and flower vendors selling exotic flowers that include the white calla lily (海芋 *hai yu*). Further along the road, five minutes by bus, twenty-five by foot, visitors unwind and sip teas just beyond fields where leaves are cultivated. Ride carefully along the steep, winding mountain road. By bus take the Small 9 (小9) from Beitou Station. The Small 9 also stops across the street from Starbucks, about a twenty-minute walk from the main entrance area of Yangmingshan National Park.

Hell Valley
(地熱谷)

After you return to the fork in the road, follow the signs that lead to Beitou. From New Beitou Park across from Xinbeitou Station turn *right* onto Zhongshan Road (中山路), just behind the electronics chain store Chuenguo Dianzi (全國電子). Pass Ketagalan Culture Center on the left and Beitou Hot Springs Museum on the right on Zhongshan Road (北投區中山路), bear slightly to the right at the fork in the road and pay a visit to **Hell Valley** (地熱谷 *Di Ruh Gu*). Entrance is free, and after a visit here you can tell friends back home you've been to hell and back—literally!

Hell Valley is a sulfuric pond that appears much like a large witch's cauldron. Residents once boiled eggs in the water, but after complaints from local hospitals that

children were burning their hands the town erected a wooden fence around the edge of the path, just beyond the water's edge. Thankfully, visitors can still experience the eerie beauty of the park. A Buddhist alter in the woods just inside the park, a flowing stream and natural waterfall create the impression that Taipei's own Hell Valley may not be so hellish after all. Hell Valley, open Tuesday to Sunday, 9 am to 5 pm, closed Mondays, is about a ten-minute walk to the end of Zhongshan Road from Xinbeitou Station (地熱谷 台北市北投區中山路底) (02) 2888-2117.

Hell Valley is part of Yangmingshan, an inactive volcano that isn't about to erupt anytime soon. In times past, aboriginal people feared that evil spirits and witches lurked about due to the viridian volcanic topography and constant stream of sulfuric steam. Now that New Beitou and its hot spring resorts have been renovated, revamped and rebuilt, residents have little to fear other than a sharp increase in tourism. To the left of Hell Valley are advertisements for local spas. At the fork is a ramen eatery, stop if you have time to unwind (fantastic food, slow service). Otherwise, several fine cafés and restaurants line Guangming Road near Wellcome, adjacent to New Beitou Park.

Beitou Hot Springs Museum
(北投溫泉博物館)

After lunch, walk through **Beitou Hot Springs Museum** (北投溫泉博物館), Zhongshan Road, #2, Beitou (台北市北投區中山路2號) (02) 2896-9918. Admission is free and all are welcome. As is the custom before you enter Chinese homes, guests are expected to put shoes into a cubby and change into a pair of slippers available at the entrance. You may be surprised to learn that Beitou had once been a popular respite for Japanese soldiers during their fifty-year (1895-1945) occupation. In the early 1900's, the crown prince and future emperor of

Discover Beitou's fascinating hot springs history at **Beitou Hot Springs Museum**.

Singular wooden statues greet guests outside **Ketalagan Culture Center** in Beitou.

Japan, Hirohito, paid the hot springs a visit. Beitou Hot Springs Museum was once known as "Beitou Hot Springs Bathhouse," and in the basement you'll find the original hot spring pool used by Japanese soldiers. During this era, the combination of restless soldiers and natural hot springs turned Beitou into a rowdy red-light district (風化區 fenghuachu). Today, however, Beitou is a thriving family-oriented community, and prostitutes are no longer in the area. Learn more about the seedier sights on Taiwan (basically, what to avoid) in the "XY & Z (Useful Information) (很有用的信息)" section entitled, "Barber Shops."

Adjacent to the museum is **Millennium Hot Springs** (千禧湯 Chianxitang), public springs with four large natural spring pools. Admission is only NT $20 (US $.60) weekdays, NT $40 (US $1.30) weekends. Not recommended to those averse to crowds.

Ketagalan Culture Center
(凱達格蘭文化中心)

Near Xinbeitou Station is a new museum dedicated to the preservation of aboriginal language and culture on Taiwan, **Ketagalan Culture Center** (凱達格蘭文化中心), Zhongshan Road, #3-1 (台北市北投區中山路3-1號) (02) 2898-6500. The center offers performances, language and culture classes on floors four through seven, and an impressive collection of native art works on the first three floors. Admission is free and all are welcome.

Buses travel from Beitou over the mountains every twenty to thirty minutes but it may not be easy to get around the mountains by walking and taxis are not easy to come by. Be sure to visit Yangmingshan National Park and Hell Valley, and if time permits, Sulfur Valley, Ketagalan Culture Center and Beitou Hot Springs Museum.

Guandu Temple
(關渡宮)

Built in 1661, **Guandu Temple** boasts a sacred tunnel, elaborate architecture and a sprawling mountainside park that overlooks Bali to one side and the Guandu Plains and Taipei to the other.

After unwinding in New Beitou, take the MRT to Danshui (淡水), a wondrous waterfront town just north of the city. On the MRT heading to Danshui you should see Guanyin Mountain (觀音山 *Guanyinshan*) on Bali towering 616 meters above sea level, surrounded by eighteen smaller peaks. The mountain is named after Guanyin, the Bodhisattva goddess of mercy and is a northern Taiwan landmark. The number for the Guanyinshan Visitor Center is (02) 2292-8888.

Explore what is said to be the oldest temple on Taiwan, **Guandu Temple** (關渡宮 *Guandu Gong*), Zhixing Road, #360, Taipei (台北市北投區知行路360號). To reach Guandu Temple by foot, depart Guandu Station Exit 1, make a right and walk towards Dadu Road (大度路). You can either walk down the one-way street, Dadu Road, Section 3, Lane 296 (大度路3段296弄), or make a right at the narrow, two-way Zi Hsien Road (自線路), immediately past the one-way street. Zi Hsien Road leads to Dadu Road. You should see a fire station under the overpass when you arrive at the intersection of Zi Hsien Road, Dadu Road, and, as you pass the fire station, Zhixing Road (知行路). There are no traffic lights here so be careful as mopeds and cars seem to race through the streets in an attempt to be the first to reach the traffic light up around the bend. Cross Dadu Road (walk under the large overpass) and head down Zhixing Road (知行路) until you arrive at the temple. By foot the temple is a little over nine hundred meters from Guandu Station and takes about fifteen minutes to reach. By bus the Red 35 (紅35) runs to Guandu Temple from Exit 1 of Guandu Station.

Each year the temple comes alive during religious holidays such as Chinese New Year and the Lantern Festival. During this time children are delighted by electronic puppet theatre performances akin to a religious "It's A Small World" Disney® -inspired exhibit.

Since the city government recently completed about a hundred kilometers of hiking and biking trails, cycling is quickly becoming a popular leisure activity. You'll notice several bike rental shops in Guandu on the way to the temple that charge reasonable rates (some stores charge only NT $100 for a full-day rental). Taipei City has also established the Guandu Bicycle Service Center at Guandu Wharf specifically for this purpose, bikes can be rented for NT $40/hr, NT $60/2 hours, NT $90/3 hours, NT $120/4 hours or NT $150 for the day. Guandu Bikeway starts across from Guandu Temple and winds around the protected marsh area of Guandu Nature Park.

Danshui
(淡水)

Once known as Huwei (滬尾), this titillating town came to be called "Danshui" (淡水 *Dan Shway*) because the Taiwanese pronunciation of Huwei sounds like Kobe, Japan. You may see signs with "Tamsui," "Tamshui" or "Tamshuei" from its Taiwanese (閩南語 *milanyu*) phonetic translation, Danshui is pronounced "Tam Swee," hence the odd English translation.

From sprawling parks, historic relics and savory local selections, **Danshui** has become a must-see town.

As the MRT pulls into Danshui Station the sun glitters high above Guanyin Mountain to your left and modern eats are on your right. It's hard to imagine that the four-story McDonald's across from the MRT was constructed only a decade ago. Danshui turns into a carnival of sorts on weekends, artists arrive with pencils, markers and paint brushes in hand to portray tourists willing to pose for thirty minutes and part with around NT $500 (US $15). You may also see blind or elderly musicians performing near the

MRT station and Danshui River.

At **Riverbank Park** (河濱公園 *Hobing Gongyuan*) behind the MRT station you should spot cylindrical wind socks with vermeil and champagne-colored ribbons, funky animals and divine-looking dragons soaring high above Danshui River. Inside the park is a rink where young people show off their latest moves on roller blades. Horseback riding is another fun option for both young and old.

Taiwanese have a keen interest in lifestyle trends popular abroad, and modern cafés and coffee shops now line the road by Danshui River. Saunter down Zhengzheng Road, **Danshui Historic Street** (淡水老街 *Danshui Laojie*), an entrance is on Gongming Street adjacent to the park, to find famous local foods, trinkets, toys, clothing, and eating establishments. An old movie theater (淡江戲院), Gongming Street, #48 (台北縣淡水鎮公明街48號) (02) 2621-2144 shows films (NT $150/100) a few months after their release (sound quality is questionable). Aside from antique theater projectors, however, you're more likely to come across Condomania® on Gongming Street than classical Chinese artifacts.

What are those tiny black things, you ask? No, they're not gun pellets, although they may appear that way, they're "iron eggs" (鐵蛋 *tie dan*), chicken eggs that are cooked until they become small, black, hard and chewy. Danshui is also famous for its tantalizing native tofu with green bean noodles smothered in tangy sauce (阿給 *a-gei*) as well as for fresh fish meatballs, and there is a quaint **Fishball Museum** (魚丸博物館) on Zhongzheng Road, #117 (台北縣淡水鎮中正路117號) (02) 2629-3312. Although signs are in Chinese you may enjoy some of the exhibits. Mind your head while walking up to the second floor. A venerable Danshui fishball establishment is *Kekou Yuwan* (可口魚丸), Zhongzheng Road, #232 (台北縣淡水鎮中正路232號) (02) 2623-3579. For delectable dumplings try Danshui mainstay Wenzhou Wonton (百葉溫州餛飩), Zhengzheng Road, #177 (台北縣淡水鎮中正路177號) (02) 2621-7286.

Danshui River (淡水河), which provides a pristine panorama, is behind Danshui Historic Street. From Danshui Historic Street make a left to walk alongside the river. Here you'll find local food and souvenir shops, and ice cream vendors that will give you a vanilla, chocolate or mixed ice cream cone that towers fifty centimeters into the air for only NT $20 (US $.60).

Rev. George Leslie Mackay (馬偕 *Ma Jie*), an adventurous Canadian missionary who arrived on Taiwan in 1872, had a profound influence on this waterfront town. Mackay Monument (馬偕雕像 *majie diao shang*) was erected in his honor in the center of town on Zhongzheng Road. To learn more about Mackay's accomplishments please see the section entitled, "Danshui (淡水)."

Taipei's answer to San Francisco, **Fisherman's Wharf** (漁人碼頭 *Yuren Matou*), also makes for a pleasant excursion. Red 26 (紅26) and 836 buses run to Fisherman's Wharf run every twenty minutes from the MRT station bus terminal. After a fifteen-minute bus ride you'll find a park brimming with kite-flyers, local artists and musicians, a sea wall, pier, various food and trinket shops and Lover's Bridge, (情人橋 *Chingrenchiao*), which may inspire you to get down on bended knee and propose on Taiwan. If you purchase a kite let it soar! The white lighthouse at the end of the pier had once been a scenic picture spot but is now off-limits to tourists.

The fifteen-minute speed boat ride from Danshui Historic Street to the wharf or from the wharf back to Danshui Historic Street is NT $50 one-way and provides more excitement than many Hollywood action flicks. Local boat companies also attempt to lure tourists with fifty-minute scenic tours of Danshui River (NT $250-300).

Danshui Night Market (淡水夜市) is on Yingzhuan Road (英專路), directly across from Danshui Station, taste local culinary creations such as barbeque corn, squid and milk tea with chewy tapioca candy pearls (珍珠奶茶 *jenzhu naicha*). The original **OCoco's** opened in the Danshui night market in 1997 on Chingshui Street, #14-1 (淡水鎮清水街14-1號) (02) 8631-0491, stop by to find out why young people crave this native Taiwanese drink around the world.

Fort San Domingo (紅毛城 *Hungmaocheng*), Zhongzheng Road, Lane 28, #1 (台北縣淡水鎮文化里中正路28巷1號) (02) 2623-1001 is a first-class relic on Taiwan. The fort (NT $60) was built by the Spanish and later run by the Dutch. Red 26 (紅26) and 836 buses stop in front of the fort. If you're impatient and opt not to wait, taxis are always an option. Passengers must add NT $30 to any fare that originates and ends in Danshui, so if the meter reads NT $100 you'll need to pay the driver NT $130.

Consider eating at a café or restaurant opposite the fort. You won't need a passport to eat at **The Consulate** (領事館 *Lingshiguan*), Zhongzheng Road, #257 (台北縣淡水鎮中正路257號) (02) 2622-8529. Open 10:30 am to midnight, The Consulate boasts Eastern and Western dishes (NT $250 and up), as well as fine coffees, teas and juice drinks.

From Fort San Domingo, cross Zhongzheng Road and make a right, pass the decrepit Danshui police substation (aging white buildings surrounded by a tall wall with barbed wire) to arrive at wooden promenade alongside the Danshui River. The road winds until it reaches **Tsway Yuan** (翠園), also called "Yakiniku," a fun cook-it-yourself barbeque with unlimited servings on Zhongzheng Road, Section 1, #3 (台北縣淡水鎮中正路1段3號) (02) 2805-6293. Lunch is NT $299 and dinner is NT $359, add a 10% service charge. Menus are in Chinese so you may want to bring a local friend.

Built in 1782, Danshui's **Fu Yo Temple** (福佑宮) is one of the oldest Matsu temples on Taiwan.

On Danshui Historic Street is **Fu Yo Temple** (福佑宮 *Fu Yo Gong*), Zhongzheng Road, #200 (台北縣淡水鎮中正路200號) (02) 2625-2084. Open 5 am to 9 pm. Like most of Taipei, this area is well-lit and safe, even evenings. At night, find the alley on Zhongzheng Road that leads to **Red Castle** (紅樓 *Hong Lo*), Sanmin Street, Lane 2, #6 (台北縣淡水鎮三民街2巷6號) (02) 8631-1168. It's hard to imagine that construction started on Red Castle in 1895, when invading Western nations (English, French and Dutch) used Taiwan as a military base and trading port. Times have certainly changed as Red Castle now boasts a classy café on the top floor. You'll have to climb over a hundred steps up a narrow winding alley to reach the restaurant but the frothy cappuccinos, smooth lattes and exotic fruit drinks are worth the trek. The pasta and chicken dishes are also delectable. Some Canadian expats have suggested, however, that the waffles would make good hockey pucks. You'll also find that Taiwanese restaurants aren't accustomed to providing hot maple syrup with pancakes and waffles. If you request syrup and are not at a Western-style restaurant, you may receive a small cup of cold honey.

At Red Castle, ask for an outside balcony seat for a panoramic view. Try a cappuccino, fruit smoothie or the rich vanilla popcorn. As the sun slowly sets you may hear people shooting off fireworks, Taiwanese people believe that loud noises and scintillating colors scare off evil spirits, but you can simply relax and appreciate the ambiance.

To better understand the history of this wondrous waterfront town and the island itself please read the section entitled, "Ilhas Formosa! A Brief History of Taiwan."

Bali (八里)

Take the ferry from Danshui to **Bali Wharf** (八里碼頭). In addition to snack stands and trinket vendors, **Left Bank Park** (八里左岸公園) makes a visit to this once-barren destination a pleasant experience. The relaxing ten-minute boat ride is worth the price (NT $25/ $50 roundtrip). The ferry also runs to Bali from Fisherman's Wharf (NT $50/ $100 roundtrip).

If time permits, take bus Red 13 (紅13) to **Shihsanhang Museum of Archaeology** (十三行博物館), Bowuguan Road, #200 (台北縣八里鄉博物館路200號) (02) 2619-1313, a Bali cultural attraction that boasts sui generis archeological findings. Brave souls traverse a transparent glass walkway on the top floor to view exhibits four floors below.

For information on climbing Bali's Guanyinshan please see "Taipei Guide to Mountain climbing (台北登山指南)."

At night ease your mind and bathe again in a natural hot spring. Too bad you can't bring these heavenly hot springs home. Enjoy them while you can.

Jiufen
(九份)

Are you excited to visit **Jiufen** (九份), a quaint mountain village just beyond Keelung (基隆 *ji lung*), the largest trading port in northern Taiwan? In case you're curious, "nine" in Chinese is "jiu," and "fen" is a measure word meaning "item." It is said that at one point only nine families inhabited this small mountain village. When one of the villagers sojourned down the mountain to purchase something in town, he had to purchase nine items for each of the nine families.

Once known as "Little Hong Kong" due to a gold rush that sparked a flurry of excitement and thousands of settlers to the area in the late 1800's, Jiufen was like a ghost town until Hou Hsiao-hsien (侯孝賢) directed "City of Sadness" (悲情城市 *Beiqing Chengshi*) here in 1989. The hit movie once again sparked interest in this placid mountain town. Jiufen's winding mountain pathways, serene coffee and teashops, souvenir stands and art galleries provide a welcome respite.

Begin the day with a breakfast suited for royalty at **Royal Host** (樂雅樂 *Leyale*). In Beitou the restaurant is on Beitou Road, Section 2, #9 (台北市北投區北投路2段9號) (02) 2897-6248, adjacent to Chinatrust Executive Suites. Those staying at the Chinatrust Executive Suites, Beitou enjoy a complimentary breakfast. Otherwise enjoy an All-American or Japanese-style breakfast at reasonable prices. Pick up a drink and snack at a convenience store for the train ride, there are several near Beitou Station. Take the MRT to Taipei Main Station and ride the escalator upstairs to the main lobby. You should see a food court on the second floor, a wall-size table listing train departure and arrival times, ticket vending machines and vendors selling tickets.

There are three types of trains, express trains (自強號 *zi chiang hao*), which rarely stop except at main stations, semi-express trains (莒光號 *chu guang hao*) and (復興號 *fu hsing hao*), which stop at main stations as well as some of the larger local stations, and local trains (普通號 *pu tong hao*) and (電聯車 *dian lian che*), which stop at most stations. To save time, it would make sense to purchase a ticket for an express train.

Purchase a ticket to **Ruei (Ray) Fang** (瑞芳). A one-way express fare from Taipei to Rueifang should be NT $80.00 (US $2.60). The train does not run directly to mountainous Jiufen and Rueifang is a quaint nearby Taipei County town. Be sure to request a ticket with a seat (我希望這班列車還有位子 *Wo xiwong jeban liehche haiyo weizi.*) Afterwards take the escalator downstairs and follow the signs that lead to Taiwan Railway Authority (TRA) Station (台北火車站). If these signs are not easily discernable, ask an employee seated at the exits where the boarding entrance is. For the next hour, relax and take in the sights of Taipei City, Taipei County and Keelung.

Make sure you exit the train at **Rueifang** (瑞芳), you should see a four-way intersection across from the train station. At the telephone pole on the corner, across from the OK convenience store, is where the bus to Jiufen stops every twenty minutes, the fare is NT $19 (US $.57). Be warned that many taxi drivers try to negotiate a fare as opposed to turning on their meters and charge NT $300 and up for the brief ride. Enjoy the fifteen-minute bus ride, if possible sit on the left (driver side) for the best views of Keelung Harbor. Once you depart, a lookout point with a magnificent view of the town, mountains, and Keelung is about twenty meters up to your right. From here you should see the alley entrance to the main village shopping area. Sample native foods, peruse art galleries, souvenir shops, or relax at a local eatery or coffee shop.

Drinks and snacks at local coffeehouses and teashops tend to be pricey (NT $190 and up) since business is seasonal. For more information please see the section below, "Jiufen (九份)."

After a fun-filled afternoon, take the bus back to Rueifang train station. From here you can either take the train one stop to arrive at Keelung City or take the train directly from Rueifang back to Taipei. Should you decide to walk around Keelung, most vendors don't appear at **Miaoko** (基隆廟口), a Keelung night market and tourist attraction, until after 5 pm. For more Keelung attractions please see "Keelung (基隆)."

Shilin Night Market (士林夜市)

From Taipei Main Station take the MRT to Jiantan Station (劍潭站) and experience one of the largest night markets on Taiwan, **Shilin Night Market** (士林夜市 *Shilin Yeshi*). Shop for just about anything imaginable, from foods and clothes to live animals. Brace yourself, those adorable puppies can fetch over NT $12,000 (US $360.00), a truly astounding amount to spend at a night market. Price depends on how adorable or rare the animal is and how well the customer negotiates. To be safe, purchase dear items at department stores, items sold here may be imitation goods (仿冒品 *fangmaopin*).

For years this outdoor extravaganza boasted an outdoor eating area, but Taipei City Government established a separate indoor food court for easier regulatory management. Shilin Night Market is distinctly chaotic, illegal vendors hock their wares, slowing the flow of pedestrian traffic to a virtual halt, especially during weekends and holidays. Police occasionally show up and issue tickets as illegal vendors pack up and scatter to the sides; after a few minutes the chaos returns to normal. Adventuresome globe trekkers should visit Shilin Night Market now in its original, frenzied form.

To learn more about religion on Taiwan, please see the "XY & Z (Useful Information) (很有用的信息)" section entitled, appropriately enough, "Religion On Taiwan."

Longshan Temple
(龍山寺)

Take the MRT to Taipei Main Station and transfer to the blue line heading in the direction of Xinpu. The first stop is Ximen Station. Exit at the second station, **Longshan Temple** (龍山寺), Guangzhou Street, #211 (廣州街211號) (02) 2302-5162. Food and trinket vendors congregate just outside the temple, but once inside the gates, you'll be amazed to find a temple yard that appears celestial, almost as if you've left the city and entered into a separate, more ethereal world. At Longshan Temple discover a flowing waterfall, man-made but calming azure ponds, an immense golden urn for burning incense and magnificent traditional Chinese architecture.

The history of **Longshan Temple** is as colorful as its decor. Built in 1738, a devastating earthquake in 1815 all but destroyed the temple. It was rebuilt but leveled by a tremendous storm several decades later, in 1867. The temple was again rebuilt, but in 1919 a scourge of white ants ate most of the wooden structure and foundation. The temple was reconstructed but destroyed yet again in a 1945 Allied Forces bombing raid to purge Taiwan of the Japanese. Although most of the temple was destroyed in the air raid, a statue of Guanyin, the goddess of mercy, withstood the attack, and local residents hid under her for protection. Believing that the goddess was watching over them, local residents rebuit the temple, a symbol of the importance of religion on Taiwan and perseverance of the Taiwanese.

If you decide to bring a camera or camcorder, try to be respectful of local worshippers. While cameras are permitted, consider how you would feel if tourists photographed your most intimate spiritual moments.

Xingtian Temple
(行天宮)

Next, take a taxi to **Xingtian Temple** (行天宮 *Xingtiengong*), Minchuan East Road, Section 2 # 109 (台北市民權東路2段109號) (02) 2503-1831. From Longshan Temple, the fare to Xingtian Temple should cost under NT $200 (US $6.00). The Buddha inside is the God of War, "Guan Shen Di Zhuen" (關公 *Guan Gong*). All five entrances to the temple are only opened on important religious holidays, and the underground walkway is where fortune-tellers predict your future (算命 *suan ming*), but for a price. Fortune-tellers consider a person's name, date and time of birth, facial characteristics, and lines on palms. While you may laugh at the prospect of paying money to a complete stranger to tell you whether your next three to five years will be auspicious, consider this: fortune-tellers do quite well on Taiwan, generally earning anywhere from NT $800 (US $24.00) to NT $3000 (US $90.00) per brief prediction session.

While terrific temples dot Taipei, the aforementioned are two of the most famous and are usually flooded with worshipers eager to pay homage to the gods, especially during holidays. Peruse "Taipei Temple Guide (台北寺廟指南)" for more ethereal exploring.

Topview Taipei
(新光摩天展望台)

Return to Taipei Main Station (台北火車站), depending on traffic a taxi shouldn't cost more than NT $180. Cross the street to arrive at **Shin Kong Life Building**, Zhongxiao West Road, Section 1, # 66 (台北市新光三越, 站前店), a Taipei landmark opposite Taipei Main Station. The roads around Taipei Main Station are one-way and difficult for drivers to navigate, if you don't mind spending an extra eight to ten minutes in the taxi then go directly to Shin Kong Mitsukoshi department store.

Topview Taipei, Shin Kong Observatory (新光摩天展望台), Zhongxiao West Road, Section 1, # 66 (台北市忠孝西路1段66號) (02) 2388-6130 is atop Shin Kong Life Tower. Take one of the fastest elevators in Taipei (it climbs 540 meters per minute!) to the 46th floor and visit the Observatory for fantastic 360-degree city views. The Observatory (NT $150/$120) is open 11 am to 10 pm daily.

that run to Taipei 101. In addition to local and international companies that have rented office space in the skyscraper, trendy shops and large food courts line the bottom floors for those that are hungry for luxury goods as well as lunch (five floors are underground in this 106-floor building). Admission to the observatory is NT $350/$320, NT$300 for groups of 20 or more, children under 70 cm admitted free. Located in the bustling Xinyi business district of Taipei at Shifu Road #45, Taipei 101 is singularly impressive (台北市信義區市府路45號) (02) 8101-7777.

For lunch stay in Taipei or return to Danshui where patrons marvel at the soothing blue waterway. It all depends on what whets your appetite. If you crave international cuisine, visit Fuxing North Road (台北市復興北路). By MRT, return

Grab a bite at the underground mall or dine in style at the highest restaurant in the world.

Taipei 101
(台北 101)

Or, take the world's fastest elevator to the 89th floor observatory of Taipei Financial Center 101 (台北國際金融中心), **Taipei 101** (台北 101), a Taipei landmark that towers 508 meters above the city! Taipei 101 is one of the tallest skyscrapers not only on Taiwan but also in the world. The building elevator travels upwards at 1,010 meters (60.6 kilometers) per minute, and the world's largest wind damper, weighing 660 metric tons, is also on the 89th floor. By MRT, transfer at Taipei Main Station for the Kunyang line and exit at Taipei City Hall, then catch one of the free buses

to Taipei Main Station and go down one flight to the blue line that runs from Xinpu to Kunyang. Take the MRT heading in the direction of Kunyang and transfer at Zhongxiao Fuxing Station for the brown Muzha line. The Muzha line runs from Zhongshan Middle School to Taipei Zoo, exit at Zhongshan Middle School Station. Once you exit the station you should be on Fuxing North Road. Or, take a taxi to the corner of Minchuan East Road and Fuxing North Road (台北市民權東路和復興北路口). Either way you should arrive at Zhongshan Middle School Station (捷運中山國中). From Fuxing North Road, head south towards Minsheng East Road. You're about to encounter a number of good dining options, which include **The Stinking Rose** (裝蒜 *Zhuanshuang*), Fuxing North Road, #342 (台北市復興北路342號) (02) 2516-8880, 2506-2727, a fun garlic restaurant established in San Francisco. There are currently Stinking Rose restaurants in Los Angeles, San Francisco and Taipei. Don't expect to meet any vampires here! On the same road you'll find Western, African and Indian restaurants as well as charming cafés. If you don't discover an excitable eatery try the pasta dishes at **My Other Place**, Fuxing North Road, #303 (台北市復興北路303號) (02) 2718-7826. My Other Place is where Fuxing North Road meets Minsheng East Road, within walking distance to Sherwood Hotel. My Other Place becomes a hoppin' local pub on the weekends. For more dining options turn left and head down Minsheng East Road.

For ice skating action scrambled or sunny side up visit "Taipei Giant Egg," **Taipei Arena** (台北巨蛋), Nanjing East Road, Section 4, #2 (台北市南京東路4段2號) (02) 8023-9339 Ice skating (冰上樂園): (02) 2570-1136. Taipei Arena boasts eateries, a shopping arcade and a stadium that comfortably seats fifteen thousand. Opposite Asia World Department Store (環亞百貨). By MRT depart Nanjing East Road Station and take either bus Brown 9 or Brown 10.

At night hit the Taipei pub scene, there are plenty of hot spots to choose from depending on your mood or musical taste, check out "Taipei Pub Guide (台北PUB指南)." For jumpin' live jazz, **Brown Sugar**, Jinshan South Road, Section 2, #218 (台北市金山南路2段218號) (02) 2322-4677, is a sweet spot to chill. Get there early before afficianados start swinging. For fresh disco and mainstream pop try **Mint** in the lower level of Taipei 101. Mint boasts an enormous new bar, flashing L.E.D. displays, glassy thermoplastic furniture typically used by artists and a futuristic illuminated dance floor. The hefty cover charge includes one menu drink. Shifu Road, #45, B1 (台北市信義區市府路45號B1樓) (02) 8101-8662.

For a Taipei meets Sex & The City experience visit **Room 18** at Warner Brothers Village, Songshou Road, #22, B1 (Neo19 building) (台北市松壽路 22 號 B1) (02) 2345-2778. This posh discoteque in the Xinyi business district attracts a younger crowd that knows how to have fun. **Fresh**, Jinshan South Road, #7, 2nd Floor (台北市金山南路7號2F) (02) 2358-7706, is a fun Western-style gay and gay-friendly pub with three floors, stop by for good conversation and drinks, or dance to techno and trance on the second floor. Rap and R&B lovers, see you at **Pub TU**, Fuxing South Road, Section 1, #249, B1, (台北市復興南路249號B1) (02) 2704-7920.

For great alternative music, rock out at local clubbing favorite since 1982, **Roxy Vibe**, Jinshan South Road, Section 1, #155, B2 (台北市金山南路1段155號) B2 (02) 2341-0642. Many expatriates frequent **45 Pub**, Heping East Road, Section 1, #45, 2F (和平東路1段45號2F) (02) 2321-2140 for a few drinks before stumbling around the corner and a few blocks down to Vibe. If you're in the mood to unwind, consider a visit to a natural hot spring. The night is young and so are you, and even if you're not young chronologically you can still feel that way in Taipei.

SHOPPING
(購物)

There are a number of ways you could spend the day, and activities vary depending on your tastes and the weather. Here is a suggested itinerary:

After breakfast, take the MRT heading in the direction of Xindian and depart at **Gongguan** (公館). This area makes for some particularly hopping shopping as it is directly across from "Taida," National Taiwan University (國立台灣大學). Known as "Empire University" during the Japanese colonization period, National Taiwan University is the highest-ranked private university on Taiwan. Walk around and enjoy the lively, carnival-like atmosphere.

Take the MRT to Taipei Main Station and transfer to the blue line heading towards Kunyang, exit at Zhongxiao Fuxing Station. Find Exit 4, the exit for "Sogo Department Store" (Pacific Sogo), enter directly from the station or take the escalator up to the front of Sogo on **Zhongxiao East Road, Section 4** (忠孝東路4段). This is "Dinghao," where urbanites buy new digs at snazzy boutiques and distinctive department stores, such as Sogo and ATT, which has nothing to do with AT&T, a large U.S.-based telecommunications service provider. Jive with jamocha junkies at a cool coffeehouse or dine at trendy cafés and upscale eateries (T.G.I. Friday's is adjacent to Sogo). Dinghao is a shopper's paradise and many urbanites shop until they drop (from the weight of their packages, of course). Cutting-edge cafés, regal restaurants and unique boutiques are adjacent to or within walking distance of one another.

For a fantastic ferris wheel experience hop on the MRT and head to **Miramar Entertainment Park** (美麗華百樂園 *Meilihua*) (台北市大直敬業三路20號) (02) 2175-3456, an upscale department store that boasts a movie complex, fine dining and of course, hopping shopping. A free bus runs to Miramar from Jiantan Station.

Miramar (美麗華) boasts upscale shopping, dining, a current cinema complex and one of Asia's largest ferris wheels that soars eighteen stories above the city. One rotation lasts seventeen thrilling minutes.

National Dr. Sun Yat-sen Memorial Hall (國父紀念館)

From Zhongxiao Fuxing Station, take the MRT two stops west heading in the direction of Kunyang to arrive at **National Dr. Sun Yat-sen Memorial Hall** (國父紀念館 *Guofu Jinianguan*), Renai Road, Section 4, #505 (台北市110信義區仁愛路4段505號) (02) 2758-8008. The Memorial Hall hosts a myriad of concerts (sometimes even loud rock shows!) and other high-caliber dance and theatrical performances. Call the theater, pick up a guide at a local bookstore or stop by to see if touring acts can quench your thirst for live entertainment. Inside the picturesque park at National Dr. Sun Yat-sen Memorial Hall, kites fly high and roller blades rundle while charming couples hold hands and traverse around the tranquil lake. At the park you'll notice no shortage of food, beverage and trinket vendors.

Snake Alley
(華西街夜市)

Are you in the mood for some grilled snake meat? How about fresh turtle soup? You can experience these goodies and more at **Huaxi Street Night Market** (華西街夜市), known to expatriates as **Snake Alley**. Hop on the MRT heading in the direction of Xinpu, you won't need to change trains to reach Snake Alley, it's around the corner from Longshan Temple. You may have visited the temple and seen the area in the morning, but the indoor night market comes alive in the late afternoon to early evening, when local residents dine on delicacies that may have been crawling or slithering moments earlier. Shop owners put on demonstrations to lure customers by taking a stupendous slithering snake out of a cage to show how a rabbit or other animal reacts. It's all for show (unless you order it, of course). Be mindful of your wallet and other valuables while visiting Snake Alley. It's not advisable to walk around alone, especially at night, as prostitutes and seedy-looking characters sometimes hang around.

National Taiwan Normal University
(國立臺灣師範大學) (師大 *Shida*)

If Snake Alley didn't spoil your appetite (or if you're not already full), take the MRT back to Taipei Main Station, transfer to the green line heading south towards Xindian and exit at Taipower Building Station. You're not far from National Taiwan Normal University (國立臺灣師範大學), also known as "Teacher's College" (師大 *Shida*), Heping East Road, Section 1, #162 (台北市和平東路1段162號). The Mandarin Training Center is quite reputable. Walk from Taipower Building Station to Shida Road (師大路) until you

arrive at the night market. Young people often crowd the night market and local shops to dine on delectable dumplings and other (now that you've visited Snake Alley, perhaps less shocking) edible items.

Warner Brothers Village
(華納威秀)

Take the blue MRT line heading towards Kunyang, exit at Taipei City Hall to reach **Warner Brothers Village** (華納威秀 *Wana Huishou*), Sungshou Road, #18 (台北市松壽路18號) (02) 8502-2208 (dial "9" for English service). Pub hop, speed shop or watch the latest Hollywood hits at the massive (seventeen cinemas!) 24-hour movie complex. From Taipei City Hall Station it's a twelve-minute walk to Warner Brothers Village, hop a cab if you're pressed for time. New York, New York (紐約紐約 展覽購物中心), Sungshou Road, #12 (台北市松壽路12號) (02-8780-8111) is a digable department store less than a stone's throw from Warner Brothers Village. The Chinese restaurant on the top (seventh) floor is particularly good and prices are reasonable. You may also enjoy the food and drinks at Chili's® Grill & Bar, Sungshou Road, #22, 2nd Floor (台北市松壽路22號 2F) (02) 2345-8838, a fun place to grab a burger, soup, salad or fajita. Chili's is next to Warner Brothers Village. Some people seem to float on air as they shop, and their feet never touch the ground—literally. Xinyi Circle Sky Corridor, nearly three thousand meters of roomy red ramps, runs from Taipei World Trade Center to Taipei 101, New York, New York to the nearby Hyatt and New York, New York to Warner Brothers Village. It also connects to Shin Kong Mitsukoshi New Life Square, which breathes new life into any Taipei shopping adventure.

A visit to **Yongkang Street** (永康街) should also not disappoint. Located at the intersection of Yongkang Street and Xinyi Road, Section 2 (台北市信義路2段和永康街口), this seemingly serene neighborhood comes alive at night as people seek out the area's fine local eateries and cafés. Yongkang Street is only a few blocks from National Taiwan Normal University (師大 Shida) and is within walking distance from Taipower Building Station. For delectable dumplings, the exceedingly popular Dintaifung (頂泰豐) is at the intersection of Xinyi Road, Section 2 and Yongkang Street (信義路2段194號，永康街口) (02) 2721-1890. The wait can be substantial during peak dining hours.

Experience a hot pot, literally "fire pot" (火鍋 huo guo), meal during your stay. Hot pot restaurants provide bowls on hot plates, and at some restaurants, you pay according to the number of items you add to the bowl. At most restaurants, however, there are set prices for set meals. The food served is typically not spicy (as the "hot" in "hot pot" may lead you to believe), you would need to order a spicy dish or request chili peppers be added to your bowl. These kinds of restaurants won't be difficult to come by as Taiwanese enjoy hot pot meals, particularly during cold wet winters. Several heavenly hot pot restaurants are listed under "Taipei Dining Guide (台北餐廳指南)."

Food cooked in front of you teppanyaki-style on a grand grill (鐵板燒 tie ban shiao) is also a lot of fun. At "tie ban shiao" restaurants there are often set meals with set prices ranging from NT $120 (US $3.60) to NT $350 ($10.50) depending on the location and what you order. If you do not wish to devour spicy flavoring be sure to tell the chef you do not want spicy (不辣 bu la), otherwise you may see a handful of small red hot chili peppers tossed into your food as it is being prepared. These small red vegetables may look innocent, but they sure are pungent!

Make sure you sample local fruits and vegetables during your stay. Taiwanese children often moan when parents bring home durian (榴槤 liulian), a green, oval-shaped fruit with spikes that resembles an evil pineapple imported from Thailand.

The smell is so pungent that many upscale Thailand hotels forbid guests from bringing the local fruit back to their rooms. Perhaps children have reason to moan, as many expatriates check the soles of their shoes, mistaking the pong of fresh cut durian for another substance. Don't be scared off, though, the fruit is actually light, creamy, delicious--and expensive, so make sure you don't waste it (pun intended). Just make sure to wash your hands afterwards so the neighbors don't think you had an accident.

Weekend Jade & Flower Markets (建國假日花市 與 建國假日玉市)

The empty parking lots under Jianguo Expressway become the touristy but popular **Weekend Jade & Flower Markets** (建國假日花市 與 建國假日玉市). As the name implies, these markets are only open Saturday and Sunday 9 am to 6 pm. Weekend Jade & Flower Markets are under Jianguo South Road (建國南路) between Xinyi Road (信義路) and Renai Road (仁愛路), at the east end of Daan Forest Park. This may be a haggler's paradise, but prices not listed on many items means you may be in for a game of musical prices. The markets are a twelve-minute walk from Daan Station.

However you decide to spend your final day in Taipei, make it an enjoyable ending to a convivial vacation. Take lots of pictures and enjoy the memories. There's no place quite like Taipei.

Zhishan Garden (至善公園) is adjacent to the National Palace Museum (故宮博物院).
A stroll through the park costs only NT $10 and makes for a memorable experience.

Lin Antai Historic Home

Taipei Confucius Temple

Dadaocheng Wharf

Horseback ride in Danshui's **Riverbank Park**.

Fishing boats docked in **Danshui River**.

Tiande Temple (天德宮) is raised after floods in Taipei's **Sanjiaodu Riverside Area** (三腳渡碼頭).

Tour this traditional temple in **Jiufen** (九份).

Jazzy sculptures jam at **Taipei Fine Arts Museum**.

Dadaocheng Wharf, Taipei

Clean, modern, and air-conditioned, the Mass Rapid Transit (MRT) (捷運 *jie yun*) railway system transports passengers around Taipei within walking distance from national attractions.

Feeling romantic? Visit Lover's Bridge at Danshui's Fisherman's Wharf (漁人碼頭).

Taipei Martyrs' Shine (忠烈祠)

Splendors beckon at the National Palace Museum.

The Grand Hotel is a popular respite for dignitaries.

Xiahai City God Temple, Dihua Street, Taipei.

Mackay Monument (馬偕雕像) in Danshui honors the late Rev. George Leslie Mackay, an adventurous Canadian missionary.

The solemn changing of the guard at Taipei Martyrs' Shine (忠烈祠).

Longnaitang (瀧乃湯) in Beitou is one of Taiwan's oldest operating hot springs.

At Taiwan's traditional markets you can buy just about anything, from plastic and porcelain wares, flowers, fresh fish, tropical fruits and vegetables, and sometimes even live chickens.

Entrance to **Hell Valley** (地熱谷) in Beitou is free,
after a visit you've been to hell and back!

For java, tea or a **Jiufen** (九份) trinket spree, sojourn
high above the rolling hills of **Keelung** (基隆).

Many Taiwan families use mopeds and helmets rather than deal with the "car hassle."

Glean insight into history at **Taipei Story House**.

Grand appearance aside, **Danshui Martyrs' Shrine** (淡水忠烈祠) manifests a modern park manicure.

Moving at the speed of Taipei.

Shilin, Taipei

Yangming Mountain (陽明山 *Yangmingshan*) boasts lush green terrain and outstanding scenery. Chinese Culture University's vista offers weary students pensive moments.

Meilun Science Park, Taipei

A

ABORIGINAL CULTURE
(原著民文化)

When Chiang Kai-shek arrived from China, Taiwanese language, art and culture were outlawed, and in the decades that followed, students were beaten at school for speaking Taiwanese (閩南語 *milanyu*). Aborigines were also treated harshly by the new Chinese administration. Now, however, aboriginal clothing and works of art have found their way into the mainstream of Taiwanese society. Perhaps this reawakening was sparked by the success of pop diva Zhang Hui-mei (張惠妹), "Ah-mei" to her legion of fans, an aboriginal woman from Taitung (台東), southeastern Taiwan. Ah-mei burst onto the Taiwanese music scene in the early 1990's and has sold millions of records. Whatever the reason, aboriginal art and clothing is colorful and full of life, much like the aboriginal Taiwanese who create them.

There are currently twelve major tribes of indiginous peoples on Taiwan: Amis (阿美族), Atayal (泰雅族), Bunun (布農族), Kavalan (噶瑪蘭族), Paiwan (排灣族), Pinuyumayan (卑南族), Rukai (魯凱族), Saisiyat (賽夏族), Thao (邵族), Truku (太魯閣族), Tsou (鄒族), and Yami (雅美族). The Amis tribe, numbering just under two hundred thousand, is the largest of Taiwan's native peoples. For centuries, the Amis cultivated Taiwan's eastern and coastal plains areas. Today, a large Amis population thrives in the eastern city of Taitung (台東). Slightly under ninety thousand Atayal live in the north of Taiwan's central mountain region and around forty-six thousand Bunun live on Taiwan's Central Mountain Range (中央山脈 *Zhongyang Sanmai*). Six hundred Kavalan, also known as plains-roaming Pingpu (平埔), cultivate the land on the eastern plains

of Hualien and Taitung. Along eastern Taitung County are nearly ten-thousand Pinuyumayan, and among Taiwan's indigenous peoples they are known for their expert combat skills (so don't pick a fight!).

The Rukai number around eleven thousand, and the seventy-nine thousand Paiwan are famous for their outstanding glass beads and woodcarving arts. A little over five thousand Saisiyat cultivate valuable crops on Taiwan such as mushrooms, bamboo and rare flowers while the dwindling Thao (around five hundred now) live around Sun Moon Lake (日月潭 *Reyetan*). The Thao have an interesting farming technique, they place soil and grass on bamboo shafts and grow crops on the river.

Roughly seven thousand Truku live in Hualien and Nantou, they wear a traditional white outfit and speak their own aboriginal dialect. Truku women can be distinguished by their circular facial tattoos. Around six thousand Tsou live in the Jade Mountain area, and approximately three thousand Yami live on Orchid Island (蘭嶼 *Lanyu*). The Yami are known for their hand-carved fishing boats and fishing expertise.

To experience a touristy taste of aboriginal culture, **Wulai** (烏來) is an aboriginal village in Taipei County about fifty minutes outside the city by car and a little over an hour by bus. The town boasts a hot springs village and Wulai Falls (烏來瀑布 *Wulai Pubu*), the largest waterfall on Taiwan at around eighty meters. A tourist train (烏來觀光台車) (NT $50) runs 1.6 kilometers from the village to the falls area. Tourists are also fond of riding the cable car that runs from Wulai Falls to Dreamland (雲仙樂園 *Yunxian Leyuan*), an amusement park that boasts pricey (NT $500) yet lively aboriginal culture shows. By MRT exit Xindian Station, the bus heading towards Wulai is the only one in front of the station without a number and has the Chinese characters "Wulai"

(烏來) on the front. The MRT fare from Taipei Main Station to Xindian is NT $30, have some change handy, you'll need to add NT $25 once you swipe your Easy Card while boarding the bus. The ride from Xindian Station to Wulai takes about twenty-five minutes.

Daytrip in **Wulai** for vivid vistas and a touristy but terrific taste of aboriginal culture.

Taiwan Folk Arts Museum (台灣民俗北投文物館) and **Ketagalan Culture Center** (凱達格蘭文化中心) in Beitou, **Taiwan Provincial Museum** (台灣博物館), walking distance from Taipei Main Station, and **Shunyi Museum of Formosan Aborigines** (順益台灣原著民博物館 *Shunyi Taiwan Yuenzhumin Bowuguan*), near the National Palace Museum, are museums in Taipei which boast aboriginal artifacts, clothing and artwork. **Tamkang University Maritime Museum** (淡江大學 海事博物館) also displays an exact replica of a hand-carved Yami fishing boat, as well as pictures and information about this sea-faring tribe, on the first floor. Addresses and phone numbers are found under "Taipei Museum Guide (台北博物館指南)."

Every Thursday and Saturday evening, after 9:30 pm, patrons can hear live aboriginal singing at **Aboriginal Stones** (漂流木原住民餐廳 *Piaoliumu*). The restaurant boasts a wide selection of Taiwanese aboriginal food and is open until 1 am Monday through Thursday and until 3 am Friday through Sunday. You'll find this happening aboriginal hot spot on Roosevelt Road, Section 3, Lane 316, Alley 9, #4 (台北市羅斯福路3段316巷9弄4號) (02) 2365-7413.

Another fine choice for aboriginal food, libations and live music in the Shilin area is **Vuvu Rock** (原住民主題餐廳), Zhishan Road, Section 2, #3 (台北市士林區至善路2段3號, 中影文化城附近). Vuvu Rock, known for its dried tofu, appetizing pork and papaya stew and delectable desserts, is near Shunyi Museum of Formosan Aborigines. Meals range from NT $250 (US $7.50) to NT $300 (US $9.00). Their vintage red wine also has a reputation for excellence.

If you have the time and inclination, aboriginal tribes once thrived in the southern and eastern Taiwan counties of Pingtung (屏東), Hualien (花蓮) and Taitung (台東). Aboriginal clothing, foods and art are more prevalent in these areas.

ATM MACHINES (提款機)

Most Taipei hotel concierges can point you to a nearby Automatic Transfer Machine (ATM). International banking facilities display Cirrus, Interlink, Plus, Star, and/or other international settlement systems, and currency is withdrawn in the local New Taiwan Dollar (NT$) currency. Depending on your bank you may be hit with a small international transaction fee for using a local ATM. Along Minsheng East Road, Section 3, from Fuxing North Road to Dunhua South Road, are posh restaurants and plenty of banks. You shouldn't have difficulty finding an ATM to withdraw funds in this area. Although Taipei Main Station has ATM machines, be warned that suspicious characters sometimes hang around at night. ATM machines are also found in most twenty-four hour convenience stores.

B ALI (八里)

Take the ferry from Danshui across the river to **Bali** (八里), a wharf and Left Bank Park (八里左岸公園) have recently been constructed, making a visit to this once-barren destination pleasant. The relaxing ten-minute boat ride is worth the NT $18 price, NT $36 roundtrip. If you have a few hours to spare, take the Red 13 (紅13) bus to **Shihsanhang Museum of Archaeology** (十三行博物館), Bowuguan Road, #200 (台北縣八里鄉博物館路200號) (02) 2619-1313. Daring individuals walk across the top floor glass walkway to view exhibits four floors below. The Red 13 (紅13) bus also runs to the museum from Guandu Station. For information on climbing Bali's Guanyinshan please see "Taipei Guide to Mountain climbing (台北登山指南)."

B ANKS (銀行)

Banks are open from 9 am to 3:30 pm, and international banks are prevelant throughout Taipei. Here are several in convenient locations:

Bank SinoPac (永豐銀行) 24-hour customer service: (02) 2505-9999
Shilin: Chengde Road, Section 4, #300, 302 (台北市士林區承德路4 段300, 302 號)
(02) 2881-1867
Tienmu: Zhongcheng Road, Section 2, #249 (台北市士林區忠誠路2段249號
(02) 2872-1177
Ximen: Chengdu Road, #75, 77 Ximending (台北市萬華區成都路75, 77 號)
(02) 2381-8255
Xinyi: Xinyi Road, Section 4, #252, 256 2F-1

(台北市大安區信義路4 段252 號, 256 號2 樓之1) (02) 2705-8322
Zhongxiao: Zhongxiao East Road, Section 4, #48 (台北市大安區忠孝東路4 段48 號1, 2 樓) (02) 2771-7011.

Bank of Taiwan (台灣銀行)
is also conveniently located around town:
Beitou: Zhongyang South Road, Section 1, #152 (台北市北投區中央南路1段152號)
(02) 2895-1200
Minsheng: Chengdu Road, Section 2, #239 (台北市大同區承德路2段239號)
(02) 2553-0121
Shilin: Zhongshan North Road, Section 6, #197 (台北市中山北路6段197號)
(02) 2836-7080
Tienmu: Zhongshan North Road, Section 7, #18 (台北市中山北路7段18號)
(02) 2875-5222
Zhongshan North Road, Section 1, #150 (台北市中山北路1段150號) (02) 2542-3434
Zhongxiao East Road, Section 4, #560 (台北市忠孝東路4段560號) (02) 2707-3111.

Mega International Commercial Bank (兆豐國際商業銀行) (International Commercial Bank of China, ICBC) offers international banking services:
Shilin: Zhongshan North Road, Section 6, #126 (台北市中山北路6段126號)
(02) 2838-5225
Taipei Songshan Airport, Dunhua North Road, 340-9 (台北國際航空站 台北市敦化北路340之9號) (02) 2715-2385
Tienmu: Zhongshan North Road, Section 7, #193 (台北市中山北路7段193號)
(02) 2871-4125
Zhongxiao: Zhongxiao East Road, Section 4, #233 (台北市中山北路4段233號)
(02) 2771-1877.

In addition to banking services, **American Express Bank** (美國運通銀行) offers Moneygram® wire services:
Dunhua North Road, #214, 2nd Floor (敦化北路214號2樓) (02) 2715-1581

Of course, there's always **Citibank** (花旗銀行 *Huachi Yinhang*), the bank that never sleeps (except when it's not normal banking hours):

Minsheng East Road, Section 3, #117-1 (台北市民生東路3段117-1號) (02) 2725-5931. For Citibank banking services in Taipei dial: 0800-012-345.

Baseball (棒球)

In addition to professional basketball, which is something of an obsession to Taiwan's youth, baseball has become a popular local pastime. Taiwanese pitcher Wang Chien-ming (王建民) has become a starter for the New York Yankees® and local favorite Chen Chin-feng (陳金鋒), a former pinch-hitting star for the Los Angeles Dodgers®, recently returned home to play for the Chinese Professional Baseball League (CPBL) Bears. Six teams duke it out to become league champion during the 300-game CPBL season, which runs from March until October. There are the Sinon Bulls (興農牛), Macoto Cobras (誠泰 *Cobras*), Uni-President Lions (統一獅), Chinatrust Whales (中信鯨), Brother Elephants (兄弟象) and La New Bears (La New 熊). Unlike in the West, where home teams are associated with cities, teams on Taiwan are associated with brands. So far the Elephants have been the most triumphant team in the league's history and as such seem to have garnered the most loyal fans. Player nicknames are particularly intriguing to Westerners, such as Uni-President Lions' right-hander Lin "Big Pancake" Yue-ping, slugger Lin "Wild Hog" Hong-yuan, and Taiwan's answer to The Yankees' Babe "The Bambino" Ruth, Cobras' hitting star Hsu "The Bamboo" Chu-chien.

Baseball enthusiasts may want to check out Taiwan's largest baseball stadium built in Kaohsiung in 1999, home to the island's only **Baseball Museum** (棒球博物館), Dabi Road, #113, Niausung Shiang, Kaohsiung County (高雄縣鳥松鄉鳥松村大埤路113號) (07) 733-8602. The stadium and museum, reachable by city buses 70, 79, and 102,

are outside the city, so a visit may not be convenient if you are not a die-hard fan of the Chinese Professional Baseball League (CPBL). http://www.cpbl.com.tw.

Explore the **Northcoast Scenic Area** for white sandy beaches and Taiwanese-style fun in the sun.

Beaches (海邊)

From Danshui, traveling north towards Keelung on Highway 2, or North Second Highway (北二高速公路 *Bei Er Gao*), is **White Sand Bay** (白沙灣 *Baishawan*). There may be a small fee to enter the beach during summer when snack stands summon and cautious lifeguards are on duty. The beach is typically crowded summer weekends and holidays, and local businesses tend to be seasonal. For more information contact North Coast & Guanyinshan Scenic Area Administration (北海岸及觀音山國家風景區管理處), Siayuankeng, Demao Village, #33-6, Shimen (台北縣石門鄉德茂村下員坑33-6號) (02) 2636-4503. On the left you should spot Sanjhih's bizarre, abandoned UFO-style apartment complexes before seeing **Qianshuiwan** (淺水灣), a less-crowded beach.

Green Bay, commonly referred to by its Chinese name, *Feitsuiwan* (翡翠灣), is perhaps the nicest beach on Taiwan because, although smaller than most beaches, it's not typically crowded. There is a high fee (NT $550) to enter the beach during summer, and some may find the price of exclusivity to be too high. The beach is located near **Howard Beach Resort Pacific Green Bay** (太平洋翡翠灣福華渡假飯店 *Taipingyang Feitsuiwan Fuhua Fandian*), Feicui Road, #1-1, Wanli (台北縣萬里鄉翡翠路1-1號) (02) 2492-6565. Howard Beach is an upscale resort that boasts one of the largest outdoor pools in Taipei, a fitness center, bar, and fine Chinese or Western dining. For the high seasonal rates, however, rooms could use refurbishing. During summer DJs sometimes spin phat tunes by the pool.

During weekends, standard rooms go for NT $5000 (US $150.00) and up, weekday rates drop to NT $3,600 (US $108.00). By car head north on North Second Highway (北二高速公路 *Beiergao*) in the direction of Keelung and continue in the direction of Wanli (萬里), the resort is on the right. Buses run to the resort from the Chung Lun Bus Station behind Taipei Train Station, or from Zhongxiao East Road, Section 5, at the bus stop between Taipei City Hall and Yongchun Station, across from the Sunrise Department Store (中興百貨 *Zhongxing Baihuo*), Zhongxiao East Road, Section 5, #297 (台北市忠孝東路5段297號). Take the bus bound for Jinshan (Gold Mountain) and make sure the driver knows where you want to depart.

Buses heading to Keelung from Danshui Station also stop at these beaches, they start running around 7 am and depart approximately every forty minutes thereafter. The sign in front of the buses say "Keelung → Jinshan → Danshuei" and signs on the back say "Taipei → Chiufen → Chinkuashih." From Danshui the fare is NT $48 for the forty-five minute ride to Baishawan (白沙灣), NT $115 for the hour ride to Feitswaywan (翡翠灣).

The toll-free number for Keelung Bus Company (基隆汽車客運) is 0800-588-010. A handful of other northeastern beaches are listed under "Taipei County (台北縣)."

B EITOU (北投)

Fearful of witches? The Pingpu (平埔) aboriginal tribe that once thrived here were, and they named the area "Beitou," or "witch" in their aboriginal dialect. Why? Aboriginals once feared that, due to Beitou's natural sulfuric topography, witches lurked in the area. Today, however, residents have little to fear other than a steep increase in tourism.

At the base of Yangmingshan (陽明山) and close to **Yangmingshan National Park** (陽明山國家公園), Beitou is a suburb of Taipei teeming with well-maintained parks, new or remodled hotels, regal restaurants, magnetic museums, natural hot springs, and cultural life. Surrounding Beitou is Datun Mountain (大屯山 *Datunshan*), the main mountain range of Yangmingshan. From Beitou Station you can see Shin Kong Mitsukoshi Life Tower, a Taiwan landmark directly across from Taipei Main Station, and Taipei 101. The highest peak of Datun Mountain reaches 1,081 meters, or 3,545 feet.

Beitou is home to rare crystallized stones such as hokutolite (also known as anglesobarite). "Hokuto" means "Beitou" in Japanese, this rare stone was discovered in Beitou by Okamoto Youhachiro in 1876, you'll find this and other rare stones on display at Beitou Hot Springs Museum. In Beitou visit **Hell Valley** (地熱谷 *Di Ruh Gu*), a sulfuric pond, and relax in the town's relatively new natural hot springs.

BEITOU INCINERATOR
(北投垃圾焚化廠)

One doesn't typically think of an incinerator as an ideal location to relax, swim, or bring the kids, but Taipei City Government has turned a recycling plant into a popular tourist attraction. Perhaps the city could spruce up their marketing a bit and call the incinerator Taipei Garbage Fun Park? At Beitou Refuse Incineration Plant (BTRIP) you'll find an outdoor heated swimming pool, a sports park, children's playground, car wash, and rainbow-colored smokestack that stands 150 meters above the ground. This colorful tower is visible on the Danshui MRT line. The restaurant (set to close this year) and observatory rotate 360 degrees, offering panoramic views of Shipai, Beitou, Yangmingshan, Guanyinshan, and, off in the distance, Taipei. Observatory tickets cost NT $40, NT $20 for students.

Once known for having what I term a *plastic bag culture*, convenience stores would give out platic bags to customers for a purchase as insignificant as a pack of gum. In only a few years, Taipei has come a long way in ensuring that its population remains healthy. At convenience stores, supermarkets and hypermarts, residents must now purchase plastic bags if they have not brought their own. In addition, the city requires residents to dispose of trash and recycled goods in separate bags available at 24-hour convenience stores and hypermarts. This helps reduce trash and ensures that plastic bags are kept to a minimum; according to the city government, the new policy has reduced Taipei's waste by 38% and increased household recycling 3.4 times the previous rate. In addition, fast food establishments now provide trash receptacles that enable customers to separate waste from recyclables. Even some Western countries have not yet taken such prudent measures.

At a cost of approximately NT $7.44 billion and opened in 1998, Beitou Incinerator disposes of 1800 metric tons of general and industrial waste every twenty-four hours. The plant generates electricity from recoverd heat that can be used by the city, and as a result BTRIP has been awarded ISO14001 certification, a very high international standard of environmental efficiency. Indeed, Taipei seems on track to meet its goal of becoming a "Zero-Landfill, 100% Recyclable" city by 2010. BTRIP is open from 9 am to midnight every day of the week. Tours may be arranged by calling Division 3 of the plant at (02) 2836-0500 Ext. 103 or by calling (02) 2832-7474. In spite of its name, BTRIP is not close to the heart of Beitou, it's approximately four kilometers from Danshui River. By MRT, BTRIP is 1.55 kilometers from Qilian Station (其哩岸站), buses 217, 218, 266 and 302 stop at Jili Street, about a kilometer hike. The quickest way to reach the plant would be to take the MRT to Qilian Station and take a taxi, the fare costs around NT $150 (US $4.50). Zhoumei Street, #271, Beitou, Taipei (台北市政府環境保護局北投垃圾焚化廠) (台北市北投區洲美街271號) (02) 2836-0500.

BOAT RIDES (搭船)

Danshui River, Xindian (Hsindian) River and Keelung River form a natural blue border around parts of Taipei County. Since boating is being promoted by the government and is becoming a popular leisure activity, routes along these rivers are now known as the "Blue Highway" (藍色公路). For a relaxing twenty-minute boat ride across Danshui River, take the ferry and visit Bali (八里) (Taiwan's Bali, not the one in Indonesia). Aside from sampling native foods and purchasing souvenirs, which you can do plenty of in Danshui, the relaxing ten-minute boat ride from Danshui to Bali is well worth the NT $25 ticket price (NT $50 roundtrip). Shuen Feng Ferry Company (順風航業股份有限公司) (02) 8630-1845 runs a ticket booth by Danshui River, ferries run from 6:15 am to 8 pm. For a one-way ticket (NT $50) you can also ride from Danshui Historic Street (淡水老街) to Fisherman's Wharf (漁人碼頭) or back, or from Fisherman's Wharf to Bali for the same price. These ferries run from 9 am to 8 pm and until 10 pm on weekends.

Ferries also run from either Bali or Danshui to Guandu Wharf (關渡碼頭) from Danshui Historic Street (NT $80) and take ten minutes. Guandu Wharf is adjacent to Guandu Riverside Park and is a five-minute walk from Guandu Temple. From Guandu you can also visit Bali (NT $40), Fisherman's Wharf (NT $120) or Danshui Historic Street, Bali and Fisherman's Wharf (NT $200). Ferries run Monday through Friday from

12:30 pm to 7:30 pm, 10:30 am to 8 pm during weekends and holidays. Contact Taipei Cruise Co., Ltd. (台北航運) (02) 2805-9022, toll-free at 0800-002-277.

By foot, the ferry departure point is ten minutes from Danshui Station. During weekends expect a ten to fifteen-minute wait for boarding. For landlubbers wishing to stretch their sea legs, a few private charter companies depart from Fisherman's Wharf to neighboring Sanjhih (三芝). A roundtrip ticket (NT $250 to NT $300) includes complimentary coffee, tea and karaoke, so you may want to bring earplugs for off-key crooners. The ride lasts approximately fifty minutes.

Depending on the weather, you can also board a boat at Guandu Wharf from Hao Le Hao, Ltd. (好樂好股份有限公司) (02) 2553-1368 and venture to Taipei's Dadaocheng Wharf (大稻埕碼頭) (NT $150 one-way). From Neihu's Dajia Wharf (大佳碼頭) tour the Keelung River in the Dajia-Neihu Technology Area aboard Sea Sky Ltd.'s eighty-passenger Taipei Star (NT $120 day, NT $150 night) or have a lick of a good time aboard the sixteen-passenger motor boat Lollipop (NT $150 day, NT $180 night) (02) 2618-6348. From Yuanshan Station buses 33, 49, 72, 222, 286 and Brown 13 run to Dajia Elementary School (台北市大稻國民小學), Dajia Wharf is within walking distance. Nearby scenic areas include Dajia Riverside Park (大佳河濱公園) and Xinsheng Park (新

生公園), listed under "Taipei Parks Guide (台北公園指南)."

BOOKSTORES (書局)

Some of Taipei's boss bookstores boast comfortable cafés for those who choose to relax with a pastry and cup of coffee or tea. While many smaller stores carry only Chinese titles, the following stores carry a wide selection of imported English-language material. For a full listing of bookstores around the island visit http://www.OnTaiwan.com.

Caves Books (敦煌書局 *Dunhuang Shuju*)
Tienmu: Tienyu Street, Lane 38, #5 (台北市天母天玉街38巷5號)(near Häagen-Dazs) (02) 2874-2199
Zhongshan: Zhongshan North Road, Section 2, #103 (台北市中山北路2段103號) (02) 2537-1666.

Eslite (誠品書局 *Chungpin Shuju*)
Songgao Road, #11 (台北市信義區松高路11號) (Xinyi business district, the largest bookstore on Taiwan boasts an art gallery and theater) (02) 8789-3388
Tienmu: Zhongcheng Road, Section 2, #188 (台北市士林區忠誠路2段188號) (02) 2873-0966
Dunhua South Road, Section 1, #245 (24-hour megastore) (台北市敦化南路1段245號2F) (新光大樓) (02) 2775-5977
Zhongxiao West Road, Section 1, #50 (2nd/4th floors) (台北市忠孝西路1段50號2F/ 4F) (02) 2370-3100.

Kingstone Books (金石文化廣場, 金石堂 *Jinshitang*)
Minsheng East Road, Section 5, #119 (台北市民生東路5段119號) (02) 2768-2757
Zhongxiao East Road, Section 1, #78 (台北市忠孝西路1段78號) (02) 2371-0306
Zhongxiao East Road, Section 4, #230 (台北市忠孝東路4段230號) (02) 2781-0987.

BOWLING (保齡球)

Yuanshan Sports Center (圓山育樂中心) near the Grand Hotel in Shilin, Taipei boasts a restaurant, bowling alley and ping-pong tables to bring out the competitive Forrest Gump in you. Monday through Friday from 8 am to 12 pm, a game costs NT $50 each, NT $60 from 12 to 6 pm, NT $60 before 12pm, NT $80 after on weekends. Shoes cost a reasonable NT$ 30 to rent. Although "no smoking" signs dot the alley, smoking is permitted inside. Open 8 am to 10:30 pm. By MRT it's a five-minute walk from Exit 2 of Jiantan Station. Zhongshan North Road, Section 5, #6 (台北市中山北路5段6號) (02) 2881-2277.

Another fun option for the young and young-at-heart in Taipei is **City Jungle** (士林都會叢林) near Shilin Night Market. On the first lower level you'll find a mechanical bull thrashing guests around and bumper cars. One level down guests play at E7Play, a new bowling alley replete with a bar, fluorescent lights, video screens and hip-hop hits, an ambiance strikingly similar to Strike®, a hip New York bowling spot, or the international Lucky Strike® Lanes chain. The company's pirate mascot looks like he could be a cousin of Captain Jack from Disney's "Pirates of the Caribbean." An alley goes for NT $360/hour during peak hours and shoe rental costs NT $20. Open 12 pm to 6 am weekdays, 11 am to 6 am weekends. By MRT it's a five-minute walk from Exit 1 of Jiantan Station. Keeho Road, #15, B1-B2, Shilin (台北市士林區基河路15號B1-B2樓, 近劍潭捷運站) (02) 6610-1177.

International visitors with larger feet should be warned that many alleys don't carry shoe sizes larger than ten or eleven. For a detailed list of bowling alleys around the island visit http://www.OnTaiwan.com.

CHANGHUA 彰化

(Area Code: 04)
Population: 1,316,762

Located along the West Coast of southcentral Taiwan, Changhua, once called "Ban Hsian," was the political and economic center of central Taiwan before the Japanese developed Taichung. A Changhua famous food is the "cow tongue cookie" (牛舌餅 *niushibing*) because these fresh, sweet, soft dough cookies are shaped like cow tongues.

Major Attractions

Changhua is home to **Lukang Historical District** (彰化縣鹿港), one of Taiwan's most famous historic districts. A testament to Lu Kang's importance in Taiwan's development is **Lukang Folk Arts Museum** (鹿港民俗文物館), Zhongshan Road, #152 (彰化縣鹿港鎮泰興里中山路152號) (04) 777-2019. Dramatic dragon boat races are held in Lukang every Dragon Boat Festival that attract thousands, and Changhua's three main temples are lit up as bright as New York's Times Square during the Lantern Festival. In the Lukang district you'll find historic temples such as Changhua's **Longshan Temple** (彰化縣鹿港鎮龍山寺), Jinmen Gang, #81 (彰化縣鹿港鎮龍山里金門巷81號) (04) 777-2472. The temple was constructed in 1653 and is open daily from 5 am to 9:30 pm.

Here you'll also discover **Tianho Temple** (彰化縣天后宮), a classic Chinese temple constructed in 1647 and dedicated to Guanyin, the Goddess of Mercy. The temple is open from 6 am to 10 pm and is located on Zhongshan Road, #430 (彰化縣鹿港鎮中山路430號) (04) 777-9899. Inside the temple you'll find **Matzu Folklore Culture Museum of Tianhou Temple** (鹿港天后宮媽祖文物館) (04) 777-9899 ext. 27. Lukang Historical District can be walked in just under two hours.

Changhua also boasts a traditional **Confucius Temple** (孔廟), built in 1726. It's on Kongmen Road, #6 (彰化市永福里孔門路6號).

In the center of town is **National Changhua University of Education** (國立彰化師範大學), a premier Taiwan university dedicated to higher learning. The two campuses are in the downtown area. For more information visit http://www.ncue.edu.tw.

Stone art lovers may appreciate **Erhshui Loshi Stone Art Museum** (二水螺溪石藝館), Shenghua Village, #72 (彰化縣二水鄉聖化村溪邊巷72號) (04) 879-4333. **Tungtso Ink Slab Art Museum** (董坐石硯藝術館) is also here on Yuanji Road, Section 4, #286 (彰化縣二水鄉員集路4段286號) (04) 879-6135.

The Culture Club is the first Western-style restaurant and pub that becomes a deluxe discoteque during weekends, make friends with karma chameleons on San-Min Road #9-1, Changhua City (彰化縣彰化市三民路9-1號) (04) 722-9190.

To spend the night, **The Grand View Hotel** (昇財麗禧酒店) boasts fine Eastern and Western dining, a spa, and daily rates that start at NT $1,399 for two. Zhongshan Road, Section 2, #395, Yunlin Township, Changhua County (彰化縣員林鎮中山路2段395號) (04) 833-3999 http://www.grand-view.com.tw.

From Taipei: Tong Lien Bus Company (統聯客運) (02) 2555-0085 runs to Lukang from its terminal near Taipei Train Station on Chengde Road (台北市承德站), it takes approximately three hours and twenty minutes to reach Changhua and four hours to reach Lukang.

A creative betelnut vendor lures customers with scantily-clad pigs rather than alluring adolescents.

From Taichung: Changhua Bus Company has a terminal in Taichung behind the train station at Fuxing Road, Section 4, #179 (復興路4段179號) (04) 225-6430. It takes approximately two hours to reach the Lukang bus stop (鹿港站), Minchuan Road, #190 (彰化縣鹿港民權路190號) (04) 777-2611.

After arriving in Changhua, the Changhua Bus Company (彰化客運) is located directly across the street from Changhua Train Station on Zhongzheng Road, #561 (中正路561號) (04) 722-4603. From here it takes about 40 minutes to reach Lukang.

CHIAYI (嘉義)

(Area Code: 05)
Population: 557,903

With its natural rivers, enormous traditional temples and placid small town feel, the southern town of Chiayi may make a pleasant escape from the hustle and bustle of northern city life. Chiayi boasts full flower fields, nearly three-dozen non-smoking restaurants, and a city government that is working assiduously to turn Chiayi City into the next great national tourist destination. Therefore, the city's goal of becoming a 100% "wireless city" may be attained in the coming years. If you visit try the native square cracker cookie (方塊酥 *fangkuai shu*).

One popular Chiayi tourist destination is **Chiayi Farm** (嘉義農場), just off of Taiwan Highway 3 (嘉義縣大埔鄉西興村四鄰3號, 台三線349公里處) (05) 252-2285. Here you can pick your own fruit and walnuts (pay by weight), order local drinks and delicacies, and examine local flora, fauna and insects. Guests typically see between twelve and fifteen different butterfly species during their visit. The farm is adjacent to the placid Zengwun Reservoir (曾文溪). Adult admission to the family fun farm costs NT $280. For guests that choose to stay overnight, Chiayi Farm boasts Chiayi Farm Ecological Resort where rooms start at NT $3000 per night; family-size tents may also be rented for a fee. Buses run from Chiayi Train Station to Chiayi Farm three times a day, at 8 am, 1:30 pm and again at 5:00 pm for those who may have been partying a little too hard the previous evening. Heading from Tainan by car turn onto Taiwan Highway 3. From Chiayi City take Taiwan Highway 18 and turn onto Taiwan Highway 3. http://www.chiayifarm.com.tw.

Alishan National Scenic Area (阿里山國家風景區), undoubedtly one of Taiwan's most popular tourist destinations, is only a few hours outside the city. From Taipei take the train to Chiayi, Alishan is about 2 to 2.5 hours by bus from Chiayi Train Station. More information about visiting Alishan is available at http://www.OnTaiwan.com.

From Taipei you can fly to **Chiayi Shuishang Airport** (嘉義水上航空站), from Chiayi there are nearly a dozen flights every day to Taipei, two to Penghu, and two to Kinmen. A taxi to the airport (15 minutes from downtown) will set you back about NT $300. Uni Air (立榮航空 *Li Rong Hang Kong*) (05) 286-2363 operates most of the flights into and out of Chiayi Shuishang Airport, call for departure and arrival information.

Aside from catching a bus, **Taiwan High-Speed Rail (THSR)** (台灣高鐵 *Taiwan Gaotie*) stops in Chiayi, the ride from Taipei takes around an hour and a half and a one-way economy (standard) ticket costs NT $1080. Kaotie West Road, #168, Taibao City, Chiayi County (嘉義縣太保市高鐵西路168號) (02) 4066-5678.

Chiayi Hotels

Chiayi Chinatrust Hotel (嘉義中信大飯店 *Chiayi Zhongxin Dafandian*) Rooms start at NT $2880/night and include a Western or Chinese-style buffet breakfast. Call in advance for a complimentary car to pick you up from Chiayi Train Station, otherwise it's a 15 to 20-minute walk to reach Wenhua Road, #257 (嘉義市文化路257號) (05) 229-2233.

Chiayi Golden Dragon Hotel (金龍大飯店 *Jinlong Dafandian*) Established over thirty years ago, this no frills hotel offers rooms for NT $1000 or NT $1,200 per night. Rates are seasonal so call in advance for the current room rate. By foot it's ten minutes from Chiayi Train Station and there are ample restaurants closeby. Minsheng North Road, #130 (民生北路130號) (05) 222-2049.

Alishan Golden Dragon Hotel (吳鳳賓館 *Wufeng Bingguan*) This four-floor hotel

is somewhat like a Taiwanese version of Motel 6, a cozy but simple American chain. Here you'll find friendly service, a traditional Chinese restaurant and twenty-six clean rooms with refrigerators to store local delicacies. Rooms start at NT $2800/night for two, NT $2000 for singles, smaller rooms have no windows. Zhongzheng Village, #48 (阿里山鄉中正村48號) (05) 267-9730.

To learn more about Alishan visit
http://www.OnTaiwan.com.

CHINESE HOLIDAYS
(台灣的假日)

Chinese Lunar New Year
(中國新年 Zhongguo Xinnian)
First new moon of the lunar year, falls in late January or early February on the Western calendar

Taipei becomes a veritable ghost town during the largest festival in Chinese culture as people return home during the fifteen-day Lunar New Year holiday. Chinese people clean the house (打掃 da sao), try not to break anything, and try not to cry, show anger or scold children to avoid bad luck. Never give a clock (signifies that time, like life, will run out) or gifts in sets of four, as the Chinese character for "four" sounds similar to that of death. Children receive red envelopes filled with money (紅包 hong bao) from family and close friends, and employees receive a bonus from the boss, typically a red envelope filled with one to two month's salary. Say "Happy New Year!" (新年快樂 Xinnian Kwaile!) and expect loud firecrackers to chase away evil spirits and usher in a year of health, happiness and luck.

Lantern Festival
(元宵節 Yuenxiaojie)
Fifteenth day of the first month of the Lunar Year

The Lantern Festival signifies the culmination of Chinese Lunar New Year. According to one legend, ancient Chinese used lanterns to see spirits by the light of the full moon. According to another, Ming Tai Chu, the first Ming dynasty emperor, found a local village decorated with red lanterns during the last day of the Lunar New Year. When a townsperson made fun of his wife, he asked his servants to write the Chinese character for luck (福 fu) on his door so he could later kill him. Upon hearing of her husband's plot, the kindly Queen Ma instructed palace servants to write the character on all homes, and the king was subsequently unable to find him. After this incident, Chinese people began hanging lucky Chinese characters such as luck (福 fu) and spring (春 chun), for rebirth and renewal, on their doors during the Lunar New Year to usher in good fortune. You may also see these characters hung upside down (luck will be forthcoming). Many Chinese partake in folk dancing while the city becomes aglow with bright red lanterns. Try some delicious red or white sweet glutinous rice balls (元宵 yuenxiao) or (湯圓 tang yuan) that symbolize family unity.

Dragon Boat Festival
(端午節 Dwan Wu Jie)
Fifth day of the fifth lunar month

There is a famous folklore behind the history of the Dragon Boat Festival. During the ancient Chinese Warring States period (475 BC to 221 BC), a loyal poet and bureaucrat named Chu Yuan (屈原) served the king until begrudging bureaucrats led the king to dismiss him. Dismayed, Chu Yuan tied a rock to his chest and threw himself in Hunan Province's Milo River. Local residents took rice dumplings and set out in boats in a frantic attempt to find him, throwing the dumplings into the river in an attempt to thwart fish from eating Chu Yuan's body. This is why Chinese people eat scrumptious rice dumplings (粽子 zhong zi) and hold dragon boat races today.

Double Ten Day
(雙十節 Shuangshijie)
October 10

The Republic of China on Taiwan celebrates Double Ten Day on October 10 to commemorate the Wuchang Uprising in China's Szechuan Province. Although the holiday was officially founded on January 1, 1912, this potent event led to the downfall of the Chinese Manchu Ch'ing dynasty. Much like Independence Day in the United States, this event is typically commemorated with exciting performances and colorful fireworks on Taiwan.

Labor Day
(勞動節 Laogongjie)
May 1

Labor Day falls on May 1st. Not all salaried employees on Taiwan are permitted to take the day off, but banks and some businesses do close. Most factory workers are excused from work and ports are closed for the day.

Mid-Autumn Festival
(中秋節 *Zhongchiujie*)
Fifteenth day of the eighth lunar month
The Mid-Autumn Festival takes place under a full moon when the moon is said to be roundest and brightest. Like Chinese Lunar New Year, this is another important Chinese holiday for family reunion and togetherness. Delicious round moon cakes (月餅 *yue bing)* are typically given as gifts.

2-28 Peace and Remembrance Day
(二二八和平紀念日 *Er Er Ba Hoping Jinianre)*
In 1947, over thirty thousand Taiwanese were killed in what is now referred to as the *Er Er Ba*, or 2-28, incident. Lee Teng-hui, Taiwan's first democratically elected president, issued a formal apology for the 2-28 incident and introduced legislation that compensated victims' families. February 28 was declared a national holiday of remembrance in 1997. To learn more please see the section below entitled, "2-28 Incident (二二八 *Er Er Ba).*"

Teacher's Day
(教師節 *Laoshijie)*
Falls on September 28, which commemorates the birth of Confucius (孔子 *Kong Zi)*. Confucius is considered one of the most influential teachers in Chinese history, emphasizing moral conduct in society and the importance of filial piety. On this day Confucius temples around the island hold a Grand Ceremony Dedicated to Confucius (祭孔大典) marked by loud drums as well as colorful costumes.

Tomb Sweeping Day
(清明節 *Chingmingjie)*
April 5
"Ching ming" means "clear brightness" in Chinese, so it should come as no surprise that this holiday falls during spring, a time of rebirth and renewal. During this time Chinese people return to ancestors' tombs to clear away weeds and plant new trees or flowers. Food is also offered at alters for the deceased. Traffic can become particularly intense during the days leading up to the Chinese Lunar New Year and on this day.

Women's Day
(婦女節 *Funujie)*
March 8
Women's Day is celebrated March 8 on Taiwan, as it is in many countries around the world, to acknowledge women's struggle for justice and equality. While Taiwan still remains a patriarchal society, women have made tremendous gains, obtaining leading roles in business and politics (Taiwan's two-term vice-president is Annette Lu, former governor of Taoyuan County). In addition, many colleges and universities now offer courses that deal specifically with women's issues. To learn more about women on Taiwan please see the section entitled, "Women On Taiwan" under "XY & Z (Useful Information) (很有用的信息)."

CHINESE OPERA (國劇)

Chinese opera dates back to 1790 when the emperor invited four troupes from China's Anhui Province to perform at the imperial court. The performance was a tremendous success and the art form sprung to life. There are four main roles: *sheng*, the male protagonist, *dan*, the female protagonist, *jing*, a splashy supporting male actor, and *chou*, a clown; different colors represent different personality characteristics. Characters with faces painted yellow and white tend to be cunning, the red-faced characters are moral and loyal, black-painted faces symbolize valorous characters, blue and green faces represent enterprising and rebellious characters, while actors with gold and silver-painted faces possess supernatural powers and often appear mysterious. Most Chinese operas are about important historical events or tales from Chinese history, and the art form has become a staple of Taiwan's folk arts and theatrical community.

Catch a performance at National Taiwan Democracy Memorial Hall's **National Theater** or at **National Dr. Sun Yat-sen Memorial Hall**. Free monthly performance guides and tickets are available at Caves, Eslite and Kingstone bookstores. Another option is to visit **National Taiwan Junior College of Performing Arts** (國立臺灣戲曲專科學校), Nei Hu Road, Section 2, #177 (台北市內湖路2段177號) (02) 2796-2666, the junior college is in Nei Hu, a thirty-minute ride on buses 247 and 267.

COMPUTERS (電腦)

For the latest and greatest in computers and software, you've landed on the right island. Taiwan boasts over eighty science-based industrial parks, with twenty more currently in the planning or construction stages. Many of the computer products sold in Taipei are produced locally at Hsinchu Science Park, an immense industrial park comprised of nearly three hundred firms in predominantly technology and electronics-related fields. Hsinchu is a little over an hour from Taipei by car or train.

In Taipei stop by **Nova**, Guanqian Road, #2 (台北市館前路2號) (02) 2381-4833, directly across from Taipei Main Station, adjacent to Shin Kong Mitsukoshi Life Building (台北車站新光三越旁). Open 11 am to 10 pm Monday through Friday, 10:30 am to 10:30 pm Saturday and 10:30 am to 9 pm Sunday. You may also find good bargains at nearby **K-Mall**, Taipei Main Station Exit 6, turn left, one block down on the left. Zhongxiao West Road, Section 1, #50, B2 (台北市中正區思孝西路1段50號).

By MRT take the blue line in the direction of Kunyang and exit at Zhongxiao Xinsheng

Station and walk one block south to reach Bade Road, Section 1. **Guanghua Market** (光華商場 *Kwanghua Shangchang*) is near the intersection of Xinsheng South Road and Bade Road at Bade Road, Section 1. The original Guanqhua Market, which opened on March 8, 1974, closed due to safety concerns, but you can still find many of the original vendors at a nearby location while construction for the new building is underway. Bade Road, Section 1 is known as "**computer street**" (電腦街 *diannao jie*). You'll need to speak Mandarin, have an interpreter or a local friend for the best deals. Visiting the area at night is not advisable.

International computer trade shows are held at Taipei World Trade Center and you'll spot several computer stores on Xinyi Road. **3C**, one of the largest electronics chains on the island, has a megastore at the intersection of Kuangfu South Road on Xinyi Road, Section 4, #375 (台北市信義路4段375號) (02) 2720-2289. You'll find everything from household appliances to digital cameras, PCs, laptops, printers and PDAs.

T Zone, a large chain with eight stores in Taipei, is another viable option, one is next to the Sheraton Hotel on Zhongxiao East Road, Section 1, #54 (台北市忠孝東路1段54號1樓, 湯城店) (02) 2392-2122. Call the T-Zone toll-free service hotline at 0800-231-688.

DANSHUI (淡水)

Once known as Huwei (滬尾), Danshui has become a must-see town. Be sure to saunter down **Danshui Historic Street** (淡水老街). Trinket shops and native food vendors also line the **Danshui River** (淡水河).

Fort San Domingo (紅毛城 *Hungmaocheng*), Zhongzheng Road, Lane 28, #1 (台北縣淡水鎮文化里中正路28巷1號) (02) 2623-1001 is a first-class relic built by the Spanish and later run by the Dutch after they expelled the Spanish from the island. Adjacent is the former British consular residence, from the comfortable (for its time) interior you can see that Western invaders once lived here in style. Open Tuesday through Sunday from 9 am to 5 pm, general admission costs NT $60 (U.S. $1.80), NT $40 for students. Closed Mondays, Chinese New Year's Eve and the first day of Chinese Lunar New Year. Red 26 (紅26) or 836 "Danshui Historic Sites" buses run to the fort; taxis are also an option, Passengers must add NT $30 to any fare that originates and ends in Danshui, so if the meter reads NT $100 you'd have to pay NT $130.

Hidden by woods, locals call **Huwei Fortress** "hidden fortress."

In the same vicinity as the serene green **Danshui Martyrs' Shrine** (淡水忠烈祠 *Danshui Zhonglietse*) is **Huwei Fortress** (滬尾砲台 *Huwei Paotai*). Also known as "Hobe Fort" and "Cannon Fortress," Huwei Fortress was constructed in 1886, one year after the Sino-French War, by Liu Mingchuan (劉銘傳), the first provincial governor of Taiwan. Open Tuesday through Sunday from 9 am to 5 pm, admission is NT $20, NT $15 for students and groups of 20 or more. Closed Mondays, Chinese New Year's Eve

and the first day of Chinese Lunar New Year. Zhongzheng Road, Section 1, Lane 6, #1 (台北縣淡水鎮中正路1段6巷1號) (02) 2629-5390. Accessible on the 836 "Danshui Historic Sites" bus that departs from Danshui Station.

Construction started on **Danshui White House** (小白宮 *Xiaobaigong*) in 1869 at a time when Taiwan was forced to open its ports to foreign trade. Danshui had flourished as a main trading port with the West, but the Japanese (1895 to 1945) made Keelung its main northern trading port in 1903. Danshui White House was once a residence for foreign customs officers, the official name is "Ch'ing Dynasty Chief Taxation Officer's Residence In Tamsui." Inside is a building model, fireplace, photos of Danshui (past and present) and information about Danshui a century ago--with bilingual explanations! Just outside is a Euopean-style courtyard. Adjacent to Danshui White House, across from Tamsui Wenhua Primary School, is a public park that offers a scenic view of Danshui River and Guanyinshan across the river on Bali. Danshui White House has a Western-style façade. Unlike the grand White House in Washington, D.C., however, locals refer to this house as "little white house," which appears much like a small European courtyard. Danshui White House is open Tuesday through Sunday 9 am to 5 pm, general admission is NT $40, NT $30 for students. Closed Mondays, Chinese New Year's Eve and the first day of Chinese Lunar New Year. To reach Danshui White House take the 836 "Danshui Historic Sites" bus, depart at Fort San Domingo and hike up past Alethia Unversity. Jenli (Truth) Street, #15, Danshui (淡水鎮真理街15號) (02) 2628-2865.

Red 26 (紅26) and 836 buses run from Danshui Station to **Fisherman's Wharf** (漁人碼頭) every twenty minutes. Discover a pleasant park with kite-flyers, artists, musicians, a sea wall, pristine pier, food and trinket shops and "Lover's Bridge," which often sparks new romantic memories.

Rev. George Leslie Mackay (馬偕 *Ma Jie*), a Canadian missionary born in Zorra, Oxford, Canada in 1844, had a profound influence on Danshui after arriving on Taiwan on March 9, 1872. He established Mackay Clinic (偕醫館), Taiwan's first Western medical clinic, and Tamsui (Tamkang) High School (理學堂大書院), in 1880. He also established Oxford College, now known as Aletheia University (真理大學 *Zhenli Daxue*), the first modern liberal arts college on Taiwan in 1882, and Tamsui Girls' School, the first school on Taiwan dedicated to women, two years later. This adventurous missionary lived by his motto, "Rather burn out than rust out." View photos and personal belongings of this once-beloved "black-bearded barbarian" at Tamsui Oxford Museum (牛津理學堂) at the original Oxford College building, Majie Street, #8 (台北縣淡水鎮馬偕街8號) (02) 2621-4043. Admission is gratis but call first. Mackay died from throat cancer on June 2, 1901, he, his family and close friends are buried just behind Tamsui High School on the school grounds on Zhenli (Truth)

Street (淡水鎮真理街), where his son later became the school's first principal. Mackay ordered that a wall be constructed between his tomb and the adjacent foreigner cemetery because he considered himself a Taiwanese. There are currently branches of Mackay Memorial Hospital (馬偕紀念醫院) around the island in Taipei, Danshui, Taitung and Hsinchu. Mackay Monument (馬偕雕像 *majie diao shang*) was erected in Dr. Mackay's honor on Zhongzheng Road.

Foreigner Cemetery (外僑墓園 *Waichiao Muyuan*) is where you'll find the graves of seventy-six foreigners that had passed away on Taiwan between 1867 and 1974. Max E. Hecht, the German architect who had supervised the construction of Huwei Fortress in 1886 was buried here, along with governers, merchants, missionaries, sailors and soldiers. Christians are buried on the eastern side, Catholics on the southern side, businessmen to the west and officers on the northern side of the cemetery. Some tombstones read, "Taihoku, Taiwan, Japan" for those that passed away during the Japanese period of colonization (1895 to 1945). Enter the cemetery from Tamsui (Tamkang) High School on Zhenli Street (淡水鎮真理街).

Fuyo Temple (福佑宮 *Fuyogong*), built in 1782, is one of the oldest Mastu temples on the island, explore it on Zhongzheng Road, #200 (台北縣淡水鎮中正路200號) (02) 2625-2084.

Danshui Night Market (淡水夜市) is on Yingzhuan Road (英專路) opposite Danshui Station.

The historic restaurant **Red Castle** (紅樓 *Honglo*) is atop Sanmin Street, Lane 2, #6 (台北縣淡水鎮三民街2巷6號) (02) 8631-1168.

To horseback ride or simply check out some beautiful imported horses, visit **Beach Country Riding Club** (綠野馬場馬術俱樂部), Danhai Road, Lane 280, Alley

33, #36 (台北縣淡水鎮淡海路280巷33弄
36號, 沙崙海水浴場旁) (02) 2805-8189.
Beach Country Riding Club rents horses for
special occasions and is a lively destination
for local kindergarten students. http://www.
horse-riding.com.tw.

If you're in the mood for a spot of tee (golf,
that is), you may be surprised to discover
that there are nearly seven dozen golf
courses on the island, one of which, **Taiwan
Golf and Country Club** (台灣高爾夫俱樂
部, 淡水球場), is in Danshui on Zhongzheng
Road, Section 1, Lane 6, #32 (台北縣淡
水鎮中正路1段6巷卅32號). A picturesque
park is adjacent to the golf course, so duck
if you see any incoming golf balls. Another
option is **New Danshui Golf Club** (新淡水
高爾夫球場), Pa-Sheh Road, #300 (台北縣
淡水鎮八勢路300號) (02) 2809-2466.

D ARTS (射鏢遊戲)

Darts, anyone? **The Chinese Taipei Darts
Organization**, Nanjing East Road, Section
2, #36, 9th Floor (台北市南京東路2段36號9
樓) (02) 2561-4242 sponsors tournaments
for die-hard dart players throughout the
year. If your dart-throwing skills aren't
up to par, perhaps they will be after a beer
and a few practice rounds at the The Pig
in Tienmu. You may fall in with some
interesting local lads should you join the fun.

D EPARTMENT STORES (百貨公司)

You'll find Sogo as well as resplendent
restaurants, cool cafés and unique
boutiques in "Dinghao," Zhongxiao East
Road, Section 4 (忠孝東路4段), by MRT
depart Zhongxiao Fuxing Station. Window
shop 'til you drop or give your wallet a
workout!

Asia World Department Store (環亞百貨
Huanya Baihuo) Nanjing East Road, Section
3, #337 (台北市南京東路3段337號)
(02) 2715-3777.

Breeze Center (微風廣場 *Weifeng
Guangchang*) At the intersection of Civil
Boulevard and Fuxing South Road, Breeze
Center combines upscale shopping, dining
and entertainment. Shop for name brand
products or unwind at Breeze Center's six-
theater movie complex. Fuxing South Road,
Section 1, #39 (台北市復興南路1段39號)
(02) 6600-8888 http://www.breezecenter.
com.

Core Pacific City (京華城 *Jinghuacheng*)
Referred to as "The Living Mall," Core
Pacific City is Asia's largest indoor mall, a
24-hour shopping extravaganza that boasts
coffee shops, restaurants, movie theatres,
and clothing stores. By MRT exit Dr. Sun
Yat-sen Memorial Hall Station, take bus
204, 605 or walk fifteen minutes. Bade
Road, Section 4, #138 (台北市八德路4段138
號) (02) 3762-1888 (service line)
http://www.cpcity.com.tw/welcome.htm.

Dayeh Takashimaya (大葉高島屋 *Dayeh
Gaodaowu*) In addition to super shopping,
Dayeh Takashimaya recently underwent
a makeover and darling, it looks fabulous.
The food court boasts Western, Indian,
Thai, Japanese and Chinese foods at
reasonable prices. A free shuttle bus runs
from across the overpass at Zhishan Station
to the department store every twenty to
thirty minutes. Zhongcheng Road, Section
2, #55, Tienmu (台北市忠誠路2段55號)
(02) 2831-2345.

D-Mart Department Store (德安百貨 *Dean Baihuo*) Chunggong Road, Section 4,
#180, Neihu (台北市成功路4段180號)
(02) 2796-0700.

East Metro Mall is an underground
shopping extravaganza that runs several
city blocks between Zhongxiao Fuxing and
Zhongxiao Dunhua MRT stations. Here
you'll find inexpensive accessories, meal
deals, upscale art and books. Enter at
Zhongxiao Fuxing Station. (02) 6638-0059.

Far Eastern Department Store (遠東百貨

Yuendong Baihuo) Baoqing Road, #32 (台北市寶慶路32號) (02) 2381-6088.

Hanshin Department Store (漢神百貨 *Hanshin Baihuo*) is within walking distance from Jingmei Station. Walk along Jingzhong Street and make a right onto Jingxing Road. Jingxing Road, #188, Wenshan District (台北市文山區景興路188號) (02) 2321-3456.

Idée Department Store (衣蝶生活流行館 *Ideé Shenghuo Liuxingguan*) is within walking distance from Zhongshan Station (Danshui line, one stop north of Taipei Main Station). Here you'll find an outstanding food court. Nanjing West Road, #14 (台北市南京西路14號) (02) 2564-1111. May be closing, call to confirm.

IKEA (宜家家居) See how furniture from the chain varies from your country or stop by for delicious Swedish meatballs. Dunhua North Road, #100, B1 (台北市敦化南路100號B1, 環亞購物廣場) (02) 2716-8900.

The Mall (遠企購物中心) Looking to make fashionable new friends? Searching for something snappy? The name says it all. By foot, Taipei Metro The Mall is a fifteen-minute walk from Technology Building Station. Dunhua South Road, Section 2, #203 (台北市敦化南路2段203號) (02) 2378-6666.

Miramar Entertainment Park (美麗華百樂園 *Meilihua Baileyuan*) in Dazhi, on the outskirts of Taipei, boasts fine shopping, dining, a modern cinema complex and Asia's second-largest ferris wheel that tops at eighteen stories above the city. A free bus runs to Miramar from Jiantan Station. Jinyehsan Road, #20, Dazhi (台北市大直敬業三路20號) (02) 2175-3456.

Miramar recently took over Warner Brothers Village cinemas in Tienmu. Check out the latest Hollywood hits and blockbuster movies from Asia. Zhongcheng Road, Section 2, #202 4F (intersection of Tienmu East and Tienmu West Roads) (台北市天母

美麗華 忠誠路2段202號4樓) (02) 2876-3300.

Ming Yao Department Store (明耀百貨 *Mingyao Baihuo*) Zhongxiao East Road, Section 4, #200 (台北市忠孝東路4段200號) (02) 2777-1266.

New York, New York (紐約 紐約) boasts name brands and chic boutique shopping less than a stone's throw from Warner Brothers Village. The Chinese restaurant on the top (seventh) floor is particularly good and prices are reasonable. Sungshou Road, #12 (adjacent to Warner Brothers Village) (台北市松壽路12號) (02) 8780-8111.

Shin Kong Mitsukoshi (新光三越百貨) is one of the largest department store chains on Taiwan. A new department store was recently erected in Tienmu on Tienmu East Road, #68 at the corner of Tienmu East Road and Zhongcheng Road (台北市天母東路68號; 天母東路, 忠誠路口) (02) 2875-6000.

The one with Topview Taipei Observatory is located directly across the street from Taipei Main Station: Zhongxiao East Road, Section 1, #66 (台北市忠孝西路1段66號) (02) 2388-5552. Another is on Nanjing West Road, #12 (台北市南京西路12號) (02) 2568-2868.

In the city's bustling Xinyi business district, just across from Warner Brother Village, the company recently finished erecting Shin Kong Mitsukoshi New Life Square (新光三越信義新天地) Songgao Road, #19 (台北市松高路19號) (02) 8780-5959 Sunggao Road, #12 (台北市松高路12號) (02) 8780-9966 Sungshou Road, #9 (台北市松壽路9號) (02) 8780-5959 Sungshou Road, #11 (台北市松壽路11號) (02) 8780-1000.

Shin Shin Da Chong Department Store 欣欣大眾百貨 Linshen North Road, #247 (台北市林森北路247號) (02) 2521-2211.

Sogo Department Store (Pacific Sogo)

(崇光太平洋百貨 *Taipingyang Sogo*) Zhongxiao East Road, Section 4, # 45 (台北市忠孝東路4段45號) (02) 2771-3171. Transfer to the blue MRT line heading in the direction of Kunyang. Exit the MRT three stops after leaving Taipei Main Station, at Zhongxiao Fuxing. Exit 4 will take you to this popular Sogo. A smaller Sogo is found on Dunhua South Road, Section 1, #246 (台北市敦化南路1段246號) (02)2777-1371, 2771-3171. Sogo recently opened a branch on the second floor of Taipei 101: Shifu Road #45, 2nd Floor (台北市市府路45號2F) (02) 8101-8111. Another Sogo is slated to open in Tienmu in 2008.

Sunrise Department Store (中興百貨 *Zhongxing Baihuo*) Fuxing North Road #15 (台北市復興北路15號) (02) 2731-2001.

Tongling Department Store (統領百貨 *Tongling Baihuo*) Zhongxiao East Road, Section 4, #201 (台北市忠孝東路4段201號) (02) 2752-2222.

Warner Brothers Village (華納威秀 *Wana Huishou*) This bustling shopping complex boasts clothing stores, restaurants, a large bookstore and seventeen massive modern movie theaters. Songshou Road, #18 (台北市松壽路18號) (02) 8780-1166, 8780-1166 Movie Theater: (02) 8780-5566.

Zoo Mall (動物園購物商場 *Dongwuyuan Gowu Shangchang*) After visiting the animals at the zoo you can act like one yourself—with your credit card! Zoo Mall is across from Taipei Zoo Station, next to the zoo on Xinguang Road, Section 2, #28, Wenshan District, Muzha (台北縣木柵新光路2段28號) (02) 8661-8811.

DESSERTS (甜點)

Taiwanese are known to nosh on finger foods (小吃 *xiao chi*), for a smattering of sumptuous selections stop by any night market. Dessert shops tend to offer ice

treats (刨冰 *bao bing*), such as red or green beans and the sweet gray taro vegetable (芋頭 *yu tou*) with shredded ice and flavored toppings. Taipei also boasts bounteous bakeries and cafés that serve delectable pastries and cakes. Here are a few savory suggestions:

North Pole Soft Ice Special Shop (北極綿綿冰 *Bei Ji*) If you're in Beitou, visit a fun dessert shop where Santa himself might delight on a cold sweet snack---the North Pole. Founded by the parents of current owner Lin Jien Yuen, this quaint ices/dessert shop has been frequented for over four decades. The soft homemade ices, which come in peanut, red bean, lemon, watermelon, and passion fruit flavors, are exceptional. Exit Xinbeitou Station and cross the street, it's at the intersection of Zhongho and Zhuhai streets, opposite Fuxing Park. Zhonghe Street #47 (在新北投中和街和珠海路交叉口, 復興公園斜對面) (02) 2891-2395.

With a motto of "pure, healthy and natural," **Guang An-Jie** (廣安偕) wins the prize for unique in-store decoration and culinary creativity. Mrs. Huang and her hard-working hakka family from Taoyuan founded the first Guang-An Jie on that street name with the last character for street (街 *jie*) in Chungli (中壢), Taoyuan. After meeting with success the family opened two more shops in Taipei, one in Tienmu and one in the food court of Idée department store. The art and decor of the Tienmu shop could be a featured exhibition at a modern art museum. Expect to find simple yet delicious dessert masterpieces that include honey yam brown-shaved ice, herbal jelly, purple rice porridge, sweet tofu pudding (豆花 *dou hua*) and natural teas. Your tongue won't be disappointed. Behind Shin Kong Mitsukoshi Department Store on Tienmu East Road, Alley 50, #20-9 (台北市天母東路50巷20-9號) (02) 2876-8583
Idée (衣蝶生活流行館) Nanjing West Road, #14, B1 (台北市南京西路14號,B1) (02) 2521-4831.

Idée Taoyuan:Zhongzheng Road, #19, Taoyuan (桃園市中正路19號).

To experience classic premium ice cream try **Häagen-Dazs**. There are currently twelve stores throughout the Taipei area, but unlike the West, the stores here appear fit for an emperor:
Tienyu Street, Lane 38, Alley 18, Tienmu (台北市天玉街38巷18弄1號) (02) 2874-5223
Dunhua South Road, Section 1, #173 (台北市敦化南路1段173號) (02) 2776-9553.

For upscale dessert gift items, try **Hsin Tung Yang** (新東陽). Founded in Taoyuan, Taiwan in 1967, there are now over twenty-five shops in the Taipei area alone. To bring something special to family and friends back home, a Hsin Tung Yang shop is on the third floor at Taiwan Taoyuan International Airport (台灣桃園國際機場三樓出境大廳) (03) 383-4696. You'll also find Hsin Tung Yang in several department stores.
Danshui: Across the street from Hwa Nan Bank (華南銀行) and down the road from Danshui Station, Jongshan Road, #28 (台北縣淡水鎮中山路28號) (02) 2622-9315
Shida: Heping East Road, Section 1, #218 (台北市和平東路1段218號) (Near National Taiwan Normal University) (02) 2365-6286
Shin Kong Mitsukoshi Department Store (Xinyi business district, near Taipei 101): Songshou Road, #11, B2 (台北市信義區松壽路11號B2) (02) 2722-7526
Shilin: Zhongzheng Road, #303 (台北市士林區中正路303號) (02) 2881-4467
Tienmu I: Dayeh Takashimaya Department Store, Zhongcheng Road, Section 2, #55, B1 (台北市士林區忠誠路2段55號B1) (02) 2831-7520
Tienmu II: Tienmu West Road, #26 (台北市士林區天母西路26號) (02) 2873-8286.

I-Mei (義美 E May) founded in 1934, is a bakery easily spotted by its pink and white logo. In addition to providing some of the finest baked goods on the island, the company also supplies bread and dairy products as well as fruit juices and cookies to international companies. There are over thirty I-Mei stores in Taipei alone. Although the chain is famous for its gourmet cakes, cookies, and other assorted delights, expatriates and locals alike are particularly keen on the soft ice-cream, which is outstanding and costs only NT $20 (US $.60) a cone. Here are a handful of I-Mei bakeries in convenient locations:
Beitou: Guangming Road, #132 (台北市北投區光明路132號) (02) 2891-3690
Shilin: Wenlin Road, #481 (台北市士林區文林路481號) (02) 2831-4482
Tienmu: Tienmu West Road, #42 (台北市天母西路42號) (02) 2871-2612
Danshui: Zhongshan Road, #11 (near Danshui Station and Hwa Nan Bank 華南銀行) (台北縣淡水鎮中山路11號) (02) 2623-2521.

Milkhouses (米哥烘焙坊) which prides itself on being "the best bakery in town," is a local bakery chain that offers outstanding birthday and wedding cakes as well as fresh pastries and sweet pudding desserts. Most are open from 6:30 am to 11:30 pm, but the ones in Shin Kong Mitsukoshi follow department store hours.
Beitou: Guangming Road, #158 (台北市北投區光明路 158 號) (02) 2898-2258
Shilin: Zhongzheng Road, #339 (台北市士林區中正路 339 號) (02) 2888-3558
Shilin (near Shilin night market): Da Tong Road, #82-1 (台北市士林區大東路 82-1 號,士林夜市圓環旁) (02) 2881-2505
Shin Kong Mitsukoshi: Songgao Road, #12, B2 (台北市信義區松高路12號地下2樓美食街) (02) 2723-0882, (02) 8789-1308
Shin Kong Mitsukoshi (across from Taipei Main Station):Zhongxiao West Road, Section 1, #66, B2 (台北市中正區忠孝西路1段66號地下2樓美食街) (02) 2371-4748.

We Care (惟客爾西點麵包坊) shows they care by providing fresh puddings, sweet cakes and pastries for Taipei residents. Here are four locations:
Zhongxiao: Zhongxiao East Road, Section 5, #370 (台北市忠孝東路5段370號) (02) 2722-3802
Gongguan: Roosevelt Road, Section 3,

#331 (台北市羅斯福路3段33 號)
(02) 2363-3824
Shilin: Zhongzheng Road, #210-1 (台北市士
林區中正路210-1號) (02) 2838-5162
Taipei 101: Jason's supermarket (Jason超市
側邊入口 台北市市府路45號B1)
(02) 8101-8286.

Discover delicious puddings and fine baked goods at local bakeries. Here are a few:

Kuoyuanye Foods (郭元益食品) (since 1867)
Danshui: Zhongzheng Road, #1 (淡水鎮中
正路1號) (02) 2620-6204
Shilin: Wenlin Road, #546 (台北市士林區文
林路546號) (02) 2831-3422
Gongguan: Roosevelt Road, Section 3, #236-2 (台北市羅斯福路3段236-2號)
(02) 2367-5861
Nanjing: Nanjing East Road, Section 5, #31 (台北市南京東路五段31號) (02) 2763-2507
Zhongxiao: Zhongxiao East Road, Section 5, #254 (台北市忠孝東路五段254號)
(02) 22758-3320.

Yuhuahsin Foods Company (御華興食
品公司) (since 1946) Songshan District, Jiaohe Street, #215 (台北市松山區饒河街
215號) (02) 2767-2086.

After downing delicious drinks and savory snacks at **OCoco** you may find yourself saying out loud, "Oh, Coco!" Or, you may simply smile like the rest of us. Founded in 1997, there are now over sixty OCoco stores in Taipei. Stop by the original OCoco's in Danshui Night Market.
Danshui: Chingshui Street, #14-1 (淡水鎮清
水街14-1號) (02) 8631-0491
New Beitou: Zhonghe Street, #27 (北投區中
和街27號) (02) 2893-3109
Shipai: Donghua Street, Section 1, #556 (北
投區東華街1段556號) (02) 2828-7232.

Sophisca Candy & Gift (菓風小舖) chain carries a variety of chocolate and candy delights. The colorful lollipop candy bouquets, each with a teddy bear key chain on top, make especially good gifts.

Core Pacific City Mall (京華城專櫃), Bade Road, Section 4, #138 (台北市八德路4段138
號, 京華城購物中心B2) (02) 3762-1726
Danshui: Zhongzheng Road, #135 (台北縣
淡水鎮中正路135號) (02) 8631-8706
Gongguan: (台北市羅斯福路4段50-1號)
(02) 2364-1449
Tung Hwa Street: Tung Hwa Street, #14 (台
北市通化街14號) (02) 2706-3984
Ximending: Wuchang Street, Section 2, #26 (台北市武昌街2段26號) (02) 2370-4740.

FORMOSA FUN COAST
(八仙樂園 *Bashien Leyuan*)

Formerly known as Formosan Water Park, **Formosa Fun Coast** (八仙樂園 *Bashien Leyuan*)) is on Bali, just across the river from Danshui. You can reach the water park by bus from Danshui Station. The park boasts water and children's rides, live performances, a restaurant and souvenir shops that are fully stocked with trinkets and t-shirts. By moped or car cross the bright red Guandu Bridge (關渡橋 *Kuandu Chiao)* that connects Bali and Guandu, the water park is just off of Xiping Gong Lu (西濱公路), the major road that runs through Bali. Open 9:30 am to 5:00 pm, 10 am to 5:00 pm during August, admission is NT $550/$490. Shaguchuen, #1-6, Bali, Taipei County (台北縣八里鄉下
罟村一鄰下罟子1-6號) (02) 2610-5200.

GOLF
(高爾夫球)

In urban areas, where vast green plots of land are hard to come by, golf is particularly expensive. Expect to pay upwards of US $100.00 for a round of eighteen holes.
In Danshui, play at **Taiwan Golf & Country**

Club (台灣高爾夫俱樂部, 淡水球場 *Danshui Gao Er Fu Chiu Chang*), Zhongzheng Road, Section 1, Lane 6, #32 (台北縣淡水鎮中正路1段6巷32號) (02) 2621-2211. A pristine park is adjacent to the golf course. If you've come to network this is where many visiting CEOs and dignitaries go for a round of both golf and beer during their stay. Three other fine Danshui golf courses are **New Danshui Golf Club** (新淡水高爾夫球場), Pa-Sheh Road, #300 (台北縣淡水鎮八勢路300號) (02) 2809-2466, **Ta Tun Golf & Country Club** (大屯高爾夫球場), Shangkong Road, #309 (台北縣淡水鎮商工路309號) (02) 2621-0388 and **Beitou Kuohua Golf & Country Club** (北投國華高爾夫俱樂部), Xiaopingding, #23-1 (台北縣淡水鎮坪頂里小坪頂23之1號) (02) 8626-1281.

GOLF DRIVING RANGE (高爾夫球練習場)

If you're looking to bone up on your swing, have fun hitting into a net just inches from a major highway at **New Ta Yeh Golf Practice Range** (新大業高爾夫球練習場), Dayeh Road, #306, Beitou (台北市北投區大業路306號) (02) 2894-0652. Golf balls cost NT \$150/basket. Clubs can be rented for NT \$50 per club, regardless of the duration of your practice session. Private lessons can be arranged with an instructor for upwards of NT \$800/hour. There is a small snack bar upstairs, but most patrons come here to work on their swing and not on their appetites. The driving range is located adjacent to a 24-Hour Wellcome Supermarket.

HELLO KITTY

Taiwanese girls (and many grown women) go crazy for this adorable little Japanese cat with big, bright eyes and no mouth. Most night markets sell Hello Kitty merchandise, but don't expect a warranty, some of it may

not be licensed by Sanrio®, the corporate parent of the famous kitty. Department stores and small boutiques are more likely to be carrying official merchandise. Brace yourself, you can now fly from Taiwan to Japan aboard EVA Air's Hello Kitty jet "with character-themed livery" (stewardesses don Hello Kitty aprons and ribbons), inflight Hello Kitty service accessories, Hello Kitty meals, and have access to EVA Air Hello Kitty duty-free shopping. Sounds like fun! Some may not be thrilled, however, with the thought of Rory, the yellow squirrel, frolicking on the plane's engine. In Taipei's Ximending shopping district there is also a popular Hello Kitty KTV. Here are the official Sanrio Kitty Shop stores in Taipei:

Guangfu: Guangfu South Road, #390-3 (台北市光復南路, 390-3號) (02) 2700-1628, 2703-2808

Minsheng: Minsheng East Road, Section 5, #95 (台北市民權東路5段95號) (02) 2753-4489, 2753-4028

Shilin: Zhongzheng Road, Lane 235, #12 (台北市士林區中正路235巷12號) (02) 2880-5158

Songchiang: Songchiang Road, #131 (台北市中山區松江路131號) (02) 2517-8628, 2502-5132

Tienmu: Tienmu East Road, #13 (台北市天母東路13號) (02) 2874-2111, 2876-9132

Ximending: Wuchang Street, Section 1, #41 (台北市武昌街1段41號) (02) 2312-1300, 2312-1443

Zhongxiao: Zhongxiao East Road, Section 4, Lane 16, #18 (台北市忠孝東路4段16巷18號) (02) 8771-0188, 2781-9236.

Sanrio Gift Palette offers a variety of Hello Kitty products, but is not as large as the Taipei City Sanrio shops. Sip tea on Hello Kitty china while admiring the famous Sanrio cat at a traditional teahouse just above the shop: Zhongzheng Road, #159, Danshui (台北縣淡水鎮中正路159號) (02) 2629-7648

Zhongzheng Road, #159, Floors 2 & 3, Danshui (teahouse) (台北縣淡水鎮中正路159號, 2, 3F) (02) 2629-7669.

HELLO KITTY KTV

This adorable Japanese cartoon cat and her friends appear everywhere on Taiwan, from promotions at large fast food chains to pencil and lunch boxes, book bags, slippers and shopping bags, and even on credit cards! If you simply can't get enough you can always sing at her very own KTV parlor on Hanko Street, Section 2, #51, Ximending (台北市漢口街2段51號) (02) 2314-7773.

HORSEBACK RIDING (騎馬)

On Taiwan, horses tend to be trained to suit all riders, including beginners. To experience the thrill of horseback riding, here are a few Taipei locations to saddle up. For a detailed list of riding clubs around the island visit http://www.OnTaiwan.com.

Taipei (台北市)

Across the street from the Guandu Temple, near Guandu Nature Park and the entrance to the Guandu Bikeway, is **KD Horse Field** (關渡馬場). This is not an expansive riding area as is the Beach Country Riding Club in Danshui; rather, here you'll find couples posing for wedding pictures and young children eager for pony rides. These beautiful ponies can be ridden three times around a circle for NT $100 or two can ride around the circle three times for NT $200. KD Horse Field is open from 8 am to 7 pm. (台北市北投區關渡里，對面關渡宮自然公園旁) (02) 2858-3131.

Taipei County (台北縣)

Beach Country Riding Club (綠野馬場 馬術俱樂部) is on the outer reaches of Danshui on Danhai Road, Lane 280, Alley 33, #36 (台北縣淡水鎮淡海路280巷33弄36號，沙崙海水浴場旁) (02) 2805-8189. A private riding class for forty minutes will set you back NT $2500 unless you purchase a package class deal in which prices drop to NT $1400 weekdays, NT $1800 weekends. Otherwise, every weekend you or your child can ride the ponies at the small circular horse riding area the company has set up behind Danshui Station, NT $100 to ride two times around the circle. At the ticket booth you can request a coupon to horseback ride for free at the Beach Country Riding Club, one coupon per person will get you ten to fifteen minutes of horseback riding on the house, or, in this case, on the saddle. http://www.horse-riding.com.tw

Omega Riding Club (澳美佳馬術俱樂部) Zhangchang Street, Lane 103, #45, Shiji, Taipei County (台北縣汐止市長江街103巷45號) (02) 2642-7760. Only fifteen minutes from Taipei's Xinyi district by car, the professional staff at Omega promises each guest a memorable experience. The owners are extremely friendly and outdoor barbeques are permitted on the premises. Open 9 am to 6 pm weekdays, 9 am to 9 pm weekends, riding here will set you back NT $2000 for forty-five minutes (private instruction included). Closed Mondays. Omega is a fifteen-minute cab ride (approximately NT $100) from the Shiji train station. Call in advance.

HOSPITALS (醫院)

Hospitals on Taiwan, like hospitals anywhere, aren't the most fun places to visit. Taipei hospitals are often crowded, particularly during the weekends. Most towns have small eye, ear, nose and throat clinics, and even without national health insurance, a visit to a clinic shouldn't cost more than NT $400 (US $12.00). Let's hope you won't need to visit any Taipei hospitals during your stay:

Adventist Hospital (大安醫院 *Taian Yiyuan*)
Bade Road, Section 2, #424 (台北市八德路2段424號) (02) 2771-8151
Air Force Hospital (空軍醫院 *Kongjun Yiyuan*) Jiankang Road, #131 (台北市健康路

131號) (02) 2764-2151

Cathay General Hospital (國泰綜合醫院 *Guotai Zongho Yiyuan*) Renai Road, Section 4, #280 (台北市仁愛路4段280號) (02) 2708-2121

Changgeng Hospital (長庚醫院 *Changgeng Yiyuan*) Dunhua North Road, #199 (台北市敦化北路 199 號) (02) 2713-5211

Mackay Hospital (馬偕醫院 *Ma Jie Yiyuan*) Zhongshan North Road, Section 2, #92 (台北市中山北路2段92號) (02) 2543-3535

National Taiwan University Hospital (台大醫院 *Taida Yiyuan*) Changde Street, #1 (台北市常德街1號.西址舊大樓門診住院服務) (02) 2312-3456

Veteran's General Hospital (榮民總醫院 *Rongming Zongyiyuan*) Shipai Road, Section 2, #201 (台北市石牌路2段201號) (02) 2875-7346

Yangming Hospital (陽明醫院 *Yangming Yiyuan*) Yusheng Street, #105, Shilin (台北市士林區雨聲街105號) (02) 2835-3456.

H OT SPRINGS (溫泉)

Experience at least one clean, modern and comfortable hot spring during your stay. Why? In addition to providing remarkable relaxation, natural hot springs are said to have therapeutic effects on the body. Green sulfur is acidic and is said to be beneficial for the treatment of rheumatism while white sulfur gives off that pleasant light egg smell in the Beitou area that subtly arouses olfactory nerves. White sulfur is said to help with ulcers, skin disorders, liver disease and diabetes. Ferrous sulfur, or sulfur that contains elements of iron, is said to help relieve strained nerves, arthritis and inflamed mucous membranes (so don't blow your nose too hard). Not surprisingly, most hot spring resorts emphasize the relaxation rather than the health benefits of their establishments.

Hot springs can be private (個人池 *gerenchi*) or public (公共浴室 *gonggong yushi* or 大眾池 *dachongchi*), and patrons bathe naked at the more traditional public hot springs that are separated by sex (male: 男 *nan*, female: 女 *nu*). Expect to find many elderly Taiwanese relaxing at traditional public hot spring baths. Swimsuits are required in the public bathing area at Spa World and at the outdoor hot springs at the Spring City Resort.

At most hot spring establishments, patrons are expected to shower prior to bathing, and it's a good idea to shower afterwards, as well. Observe posted guidelines regarding health, safety and bathing duration. In general, enter slowly, toe first and get used to the hot water, get out every fifteen or twenty minutes, relax and then re-enter. If you feel faint, get out of the water immediately. *Note: People with high blood pressure should be especially cautious when bathing in hot springs.*

In Taipei, the town of Beitou is famous for its new and recently renovated hot spring bathhouses, and New Beitou is where the most popular seem to be. Below you'll find some hygienic hot spring options:

Taipei (台北市)

Beauty Age Hotel (美代溫泉飯店 *Meidai Wenchuen Fandian*) Guangming Road, #281, Beitou (台北市北投區光明路281號) (02) 2898-6768. NT$1,000 (NT$1,200 during weekends).

Beitou Public Hot Springs (北投溫泉公共浴室 *Beitou Wenchuen Gonggong Yushi*) Across from Beitou Elementary School on Zhongyang North Road, Section 1, #12 (台北市北投區中央北路1段12號) (02) 2896-4996. This public Beitou springs bathhouse is popular with elderly residents. Open 24 hours, patrons bathe together nude separated by sex (NT $60) or in private springs (NT $200-300). Bring a towel and bottled water.

Hall Yard Resort (花月生活館 *Huayue Shenghuoguan*) boasts large private rooms with clean white sofas and natural hot spring baths, which comfortably fit two. Private hot spring baths are NT $1,000 (US $30.00) weekdays, NT $1,200 (US $36.00) weekends and holidays. Xinmin Road, Lane 1, #2.4, New Beitou (北投區新民路1巷2.4號) (02) 2893-9870. Undergoing renovation, call first.

Lengshuikeng (冷水坑) listed under "Taipei Guide to Mountain Climbing (台北登山指南)," boasts a public spring (swimsuits not permitted).

For a traditional spring experience try **Longnaitang** (瀧乃湯) Guangming Road, #244, Beitou (台北市北投區光明路244號) (02) 2891-2236. Beitou's oldest hot spring was established in 1907 during the Japanese occupation. The name means "small waterfall spring" and the crown prince of Japan bathed here during a visit in 1923. Patrons bathe naked separated by sex (NT $90). The water is quite hot so

enter slowly, take periodic rests and bring a towel and bottled water. Mr. Lin the owner speaks English and is happy to receive international guests.

Spa World (水都 *Shuidu*) is a modern resort that charges NT $600 (US $18.00) to bathe in the indoor public springs for two hours. Check for promotions. Guangming Road, #283, New Beitou (台北市北投區光明路 283號) (02) 2897-9060 http://spaspringresort.com.tw.

Many expatriates consider the splendid outdoor springs at **Spring City Resort** (春天酒店 *Chuntien Jiudian*) to be the best on the island, NT $800 (US $24.00) to bathe until 10 pm. The small but comfortable private indoor hot spring baths are open twenty-four hours and cost NT $600 (US $18.00) per person per hour. Yoya Road, #18, Beitou (台北市北投區幽雅路18號) (02) 2897-5555 http://www.springresort.com.tw.

You may be sweet on **Sweetme Hot**

Spring Resort (水美溫泉會館 *Shuimei Wenchuen Huiguan*) after a visit, the hotel is across from Xinbeitou Station on Guangming Road, #224 (台北市北投區光明路224號) (02) 2898 4506. A large private hot spring for two costs NT $1080/hour, shared spring pools (separated by sex) are NT $720. 7:30 am to midnight, open Fridays at noon. http://www.sweetme.com.tw.

In addition to the hot spring bathhouses listed above there's always New Beitou's **Millennium Hot Springs** (千禧湯 *Chianxitang*), public outdoor spring pools for the budget-minded. By foot it's five minutes from Xinbeitou Station on Zhongshan Road, #6 (台北市北投區中山路六號) (02) 2893-7014. NT $20 weekdays, NT $40 weekends, swimsuit required. Business hours are 8:30-11:30 am, 12 to 3 pm, 3:30 to 5:30 pm and 7 to 10 pm, adjacent to Beitou Hot Springs Museum.

In the Sa Mao Valley Hot Springs Area (紗帽山溫泉區), between Beitou and Tienmu, you may want to try **Tang Wu** (湯屋溫泉 *Tangwu Wenchuen*), Xingyi Road, #296-2 (台北市北投區行義路296號之2) (02) 2875-5808. NT $100/hour for a private bath (個人池 *ge ren chih*). Bring your own towel. Staff is pleasant but not bilingual.

Yangmingshan (陽明山)

In the rolling hills of Yangmingshan it doesn't get any better than this: **Landis Resort** (陽明山中國麗緻大飯店 *Yangmingshan Zhongguo Lizhi Dafandian*) Gezhi Road, #237 (台北市士林區陽明山格致路237號) (02) 2861-6661. Indoor springs are open 7 am to 10 pm and cost NT $1000 per person, individuals bathe nude, separated by sex. A small private nine-ping room with a spring will set you back NT $2500 weekdays, NT $3000 weekends.

The large hot spring pools are open from 7 am to 9 pm (NT $80) at **International Hotel** (國際大飯店 *Guoji Dafandian*), Hushan Road, Section 1, #7 (陽明山湖山路1段7號)

(02) 2861-6022.

Chianshan Park (陽明山前山公園 *Chianshan Gongyuan*) is down the road from Yangmingshan National Park at the intersection of Shamao Road and Jianguo Street. Here you'll find food and trinket vendors galore as well as older but free public hot springs. You'll find the springs on Jianguo Street, #1-9 (陽明山建國街1-9號).

Taipei County (台北縣)

Outside of Taipei, the aboriginal town of Wulai boasts the azure Nanshih River, where you'll find fun swimming and rafting activity as well as the largest waterfall on Taiwan. Wulai also boasts Dreamland (雲仙樂園 *Yunshian Leyuan*), a small amusement park within a resort open 8:30 am to 5 pm (NT $220/150 students) (02) 2661-6386. The cable car ticket comes included with the price of admission to Dreamland. A small train (NT $50) transports tourists through town to the cable car area.

Here are a few select Wulai hot spring bathhouses:

Cloud Spring Garden (雲頂溫泉行館 *Yunding Wenchuen Xingguan*) Xirouan Road, #45 (台北縣烏來鄉西羅岸路45號) (02) 2661-7755. People bathe naked in outdoor pools (NT $500, swimsuits not permitted), a private indoor spring costs NT $1200 for 1.5 hours.

Hall Yard Resort (花月溫泉館 *Huayue Wenchuenguan*) Wenchuen Street, #39 (台北縣烏來鄉溫泉街39號) (02) 2661-7779. NT $1500 for a large private room, NT $1200 for a small room. Note: Not affiliated with Hall Yard Resort in Beitou.

Pause Landis Hotel (璞石麗緻溫泉會館 *Pushi Lizhi Wenchuen Huiguan*) Yanti Road, #61 (台北縣烏來鄉忠治村壩堤路61號) (02) 2661-8000. NT $1800/hr for an indoor spring, $2500 for an outdoor spring. 10% discount for use not during weekends or holidays.

Spring Park Urai Spa & Resort (春秋烏來渡假酒店 *Chunchiu Wulai Dujia Jiudian*) NT $850 per private room (one person) or NT $1200 for a large room for one hour. A one-night stay will set you back around NT $14,000 (US $420.00). Yanti Road, #3 (台北縣烏來鄉堰堤3號) (02) 2661-6555.

You can always opt for the **free bathhouse** (烏來免費溫泉 *Wulai mianfei wenchuen*), across the bridge from Wulai Historic Street (烏來老街 *Wulai Laojie*), down the stairs on your left after crossing the road. Adventurous bathers take a dip in the river. When the author visited the sauna was closed for repairs. Swimsuits required.

Danshui (Taipei County) (台北縣淡水)

Star of Sea Spa Motel (淡水海中天溫泉飯店 *Danshui Haizhongtien Wenchuen Fandian)* Zhongzheng East Road, Section 2, #131 (台北縣淡水鎮中正東路2段131號) (02) 2809-9800 boasts upscale buffet meals and hot spring baths. Hot spring baths open at noon (NT $200 weekdays, NT $300 weekends). Since Star of Sea is located between Zhuwei and Hongshulin MRT stations and is not within walking distance, free shuttle buses run to the hotel about fifty meters from Zhuwei and Danshui MRT stations.

Jinshan (Taipei County) (台北縣金山)

Yangmingshan Tienlai Spring Resort (陽明山天籟溫泉會館 *Yangmingshan Tianlai Wenchuen Huiguan*) Mingliu Road, #1-7, Chonghe Village, Jinshan Township, Taipei County (台北縣金山鄉重和村名流路 1-7 號) (02) 2408-0000. In spite of its name, this spring resort is located in Jinshan (Gold Mountain), not far by car from Juming Museum. A spring for two is NT $1200/hr, a small private indoor room will set you back NT $400. The outdoor springs (swimsuits required) are NT $800, open 7 am to midnight.

Green Island (綠島)

For more information on the rare outdoor **saltwater hot springs** (旭溫泉 *shu wenchuen*) on Green Island (綠島 *Ludao*) please see the section entitled "Islands in the Strait (台灣本島)."

Antong Hot Spring Hotel (安通溫泉飯店 *Antong Wenchuen Fandian*) may not be convenient to reach (thirty minutes by foot from Antong Station) but these hot springs, built during the Japanese occupation, attract hordes from around the island and Japan. It's in Hualien County's quaint town of Yuli (玉里) on Wenchuen Road, #36 (花蓮縣玉里鎮溫泉路 36號) (03) 888-6108. One night will set you back NT $3600 (40% off during January, February, July and August), use of the hot springs is gratis for guests.

Ilan County (宜蘭縣)

Chuangtang Hot Springs Hotel (川湯溫泉養生館 *Chuangtang Wenchuen Yangshengguan*) boasts fifty clean, comfortable Western or Japanese-style rooms, outdoor hot spring pools, fine Eastern dining and 24-hour indoor hot spring baths. Chuangtang is in Chiaohsi Village, Ilan County on Chongshan Road, Section 2, #218 (宜蘭縣礁溪鄉中山路2段218號, 礁溪火車站旁) (03) 988-0606. From Chiaohsi Train Station (礁溪火車站) the hotel is a five-minute walk. Outdoor hot springs are open from 8 am to 1 am, NT $250 for adults, NT $220 for kids, or NT $150 for children 120 cm or under. Swimsuits required.

Pingtung County (屏東縣)

The former Emperor of Japan's brother honeymooned in Shichong (四重), Pingtung over a century ago, and visitors today can understand why the lure of relaxing in odorless and colorless hot springs continues to entice.

Jiahuan Hotel (四重溪合家歡大飯店) Wenchuan Road # No.253, Checheng

Township, Pingtung County (屏東縣車城鄉溫泉路253號) (08) 882-3111. With its European-style architectural design, it's hard to miss Jiahuan Hotel. Only hotel guests may bathe in the hot springs. Daily rates are NT $1800 weekends and holidays, NT $1,200 weekdays, includes breakfast. Cash only.

Sihjhongsi Hotel (四重溪溫泉大旅社) Wenchuan Road #4, Yuchuan Lane, Checheng Township, Pingtung County (屏東縣車城鄉溫泉村玉泉巷4號) (08) 882-1925, ext. 9. Boasts comfortable indoor and outdoor springs, a private indoor spring for two is NT $500 for 1.5 hours, NT $800 includes a bed to relax for three hours. Outdoor springs are complimentary for guests (swimsuits required). Daily rates start at NT $1200 (weekdays), NT $1800 (weekends and holidays), all rooms have hot springs, includes breakfast. Major credit cards accepted. Forty minutes by car to Kenting.

Taitung County (台東縣)

In addition to boasting aboriginal foods, clothing and culture, the eastern town of **Chihben** (知本) attracts tourists the world over with its indoor and outdoor springs. If you plan on experiencing the beauty of eastern Taiwan, a Chihben hot spring shouldn't disappoint. Upscale hot spring hotels are less than thirty minutes by foot from **Chihpen National Forest Recreation Area** (知本森林遊樂區), a pristine park (NT$100) and natural Taiwan trove that boasts footpaths and hiking trails that run for several kilometers.

Dong Tair Hotel (東台溫泉飯店) Longchuen Road, #147, Wenchuen Village, Pinan Township, Village, Taitung County (台東縣卑南鄉溫泉村龍泉路147 號) (089) 512-918 Ext. 2 (English). Relax at the outdoor spring across the street (NT $250/$150) open 9:30 am to midnight. Bring your own towel or rent one (NT $50), swimsuits are also available for purchase (NT $200-300/females, NT $100/males). Daily rates start at NT $2400 weekdays, NT $3200 weekends, breakfast is included. Major credit cards are accepted. All rooms have private hot spring baths. http://www.dongtair-spa.com.tw.

Hotel Royal Chihpen (知本老爺大酒店 *Chiben Laoyeh Dajiudian*) Wenchuen Village, Longchuen Road, Lane 113, #23 (台東縣卑南鄉溫泉村龍泉路113巷23號) (089) 510-666. This renovated five-star hotel boasts indoor and outdoor hot springs, a spa service, and elaborate dining that includes a Mongolian wok and Japanese teppanyaki grill. Daily room rates start at NT $6,800 plus a 10% service charge. Open 9 am to 11 pm, NT $350 to bathe in pools separated by sex, NT $800 for a private room. http://www.hotel-royal-chihpen.com.tw.

HSINCHU (新竹)
(Area Code: 03)
Population: 386,950

While Chicago is known in the United States as "the windy city," Hsinchu is referred to locally as Taiwan's windy city (風城 *feng cheng*) due to sudden gusts of wind that blow trinkets off of roadside tables and send baseball caps flying. Hsinchu, once called "Chu Chien," is famous for its abundant sea food and flavorful stir-fried rice noodles (炒米粉 *tsao mi fen*), which are usually dried by the sun before frying but may be dried by the wind, as well. Many Hakka people reside in this small northern city an hour from Taipei by train, bus or car. The Hakka are a tribe of people who migrated to the island a little over three hundred years ago from southern China. In addition to Mandarin, Hakka people speak the unique Hakka (客家 *Ke Jia*) dialect, which remotely resembles Cantonese. In Taipei, try some of their delectable dishes at Hakka House (咱厝邊大牛的店 *Za Tswo Bien*), on Renai Road, Section 4, Alley 266, Lane 15, #2 (台北市仁愛路4段15巷266弄2號) (02) 2707-0758.

Major Attractions

Hsinchu is relatively small compared with Taiwan's major cities (Taipei, Taichung and Kaohsiung) and the heart of the downtown area can be walked in a few hours. The scenic perimeter of the city, however, is far easier to navigate by car. Hsinchu boasts several respectable universities and a restored seventeen-kilometer coastline that includes cycling trails, scenic bird-watching areas and **Haishan Harbor** (海山漁港), a fishing harbor just southwest of the city. With its abundant blue fishing boats, large concrete anchors to prevent flooding and nearby "Sea Watching Stage" (海山漁港觀海平台), completed in 2004, the harbor and sea area has a look and feel similar to Danshui, sans the food vendors, trinket and coffee shops. From "sea stage" visitors can view enormous waves crashing upon the shore. Hsinchu City Government has also done an outstanding job of converting a former landfill into **Sea View Park** (看海公園), which boasts panoramic views of the ocean, Hsinchu Fishery Harbor and Hsinchu Sports Park to the north.

The oldest train station on Taiwan, **Hsinchu Train Station** (新竹火車站), was constructed during the Japanese occupation in 1913, the same year in which the museum in Taipei's 2-28 Memorial Peace Park was built. With its clock tower and unique European architectural style you may see this train station on local television commercials as well as in print advertisements.

Hsinchu Park (新竹公園) boasts a small zoo (新竹動物園), sports stadium (體育館), museum (博物館) and Confucian temple (孔廟) in one convenient downtown location (try finding these together in a park in the West!). If you appreciate carefully crafted works of glass art, you may appreciate **Hsinchu Municipal Glass Museum** (新竹玻璃工藝博物館). Once the residence for Japanese royalty, the museum is within walking distance from the historic train station. Make a right onto Zhonghua road

and then another right onto Dongda Road, the museum is down the road on the right. There are three exhibition halls, admission costs NT $50 per hall or NT $120 to enter all three. Open Monday through Thursday 9 am to 5 pm, Friday through Sunday 9 am to 8 pm. Dongda Road, Section 1, #2 (新竹市東大路1段2號) (03) 562-6091.

Construction started on **East Gate** (新竹東門), a Hsinchu landmark and Taiwan cultural relic, in 1826 and was completed in 1829. It was originally one of four gates built to protect the city, but the other three gates were torn down during the Japanese occupation. The plaza constructed in front of the gate is where young performers entertain curious onlookers during weekends. East Gate is at the intersection of Zhongzheng Street and Dongmen Road (新竹市中正街和東門路口).

Hsinchu boasts over a dozen traditional temples, many within walking distance from one another. One of the most popular city temples, **Musheng Temple** (母聖宮 Mu Sheng Gong), was built in 1974. Here residents worship Mu Sheng Niang Niang, the Mother Goddess of Heaven. Surrounded by trees, the hiking trail next to this exalted temple on a hill offers panoramic views of the Taiwan Strait. Dahu Road, #3 (新竹香山區朝山村大湖路3號) (03) 537-2955. Open 8 am to 5 pm.

Tienho Temple (新竹香山天后宮 Shangshan Tienho Gong), constructed in 1770, is one of the oldest temples on Taiwan dedictated to Matsu (湄州媽祖), Goddess of the Sea. Hsinchu fishermen often stop by to pray for health, safety and prosperity. Zhonghua Road, Section 5, Lane 420, #191 (新竹市香山區中華路420巷191號) (03) 537-4327.

Known as "Yule Theater" during the Japanese occupation and later "Kuomin Theater," **Hsinchu Municipal Image Museum** (新竹市立影像博物館) boasts a multi-functional audio visual room, an image relics exhibition, a movie hall, Byzantine air conditioners used when the theater first opened, and a movie gallery. The museum is within walking distance from the train station and is just down the road from East Gate. Open Wednesday through Sunday 9:30 am to noon, 1:30 to 5 pm and again from 6:30 to 9 pm, exhibit admission costs NT $80. Watching a movie at the theater will set you back an additional NT $100. Zhongzheng Road, #65 (新竹市中正路65號) (03) 528-5840.

Leo Foo Village (六福村 *Liufutsun*) was originally a small safari park (六福村野生動物王國 *yesheng dongwu wongguo*) that now includes children's rides, waterslides and Taiwanese who dress up in costumes to amuse children and their parents. Leo Foo Village isn't far from Taoyuan's Window on China so some visit both northern Taiwan tourist attractions in one day. Buses run to Leo Foo Village from both Jungli and Hsinchu bus terminals. In Taipei, buses (NT $100) run from Xingtian Temple (行天宮), Minchuen East Road, Section 2, #109 (台北市民權東路2段109號). By car take North Second Highway (北二高速公路 *Bei Er Gao*) towards Longtan, exit at Jiaoliudao and make a right, you should see signs for Leo Foo Village. The park is open 9 am to 4:30 pm Monday through Sunday. Hold onto your chopsticks, admission is a whopping NT $690 for adults, NT $630 for children. Guanshizhen, Renai Li, Gongzigong, #60 (六福村主題遊樂園, 新竹縣關西鎮仁安里拱子溝60號) (03) 547-5665.

Many computer products sold in Taipei are produced locally at **Hsinchu Science-based Industrial Park** (新竹科學工業園區), an impressive modern industrial complex established on December 15, 1980. Since its inception the government has invested over US $2 billion on upgrading the park's infrastructure and facilities, and this enormous investment seems to be paying big dividends. Nearly four hundred firms, predominantly in the electronics and information technology (IT)-related fields, have offices here. After work, local

businesspeople sometimes unwind at the pubs that have sprung up around the industrial park.

Aside from taking a bus, a faster mode of transport from Taipei to Hsinchu is the **Taiwan High-Speed Rail (THSR)**, Kaotie Si Road, #6, Chupei City, Hsinchu County (新竹縣竹北市高鐵七路6號) (02) 4066-5678. A one-way economy (standard) ticket from Taipei costs NT $290 and the trip takes around thirty minutes. The station is in Hsinchu County so you would need to take a bus or taxi from the HSR station to reach the city.

Hsinchu Hotels

The Ambassador Hotel (國賓大飯店) This upscale hotel boasts 257 rooms, a snazzy bar, Chinese and Italian restaurants, and 24-hour service. Rooms start at NT $7,500 a night. Zhonghua Road, Section 2, #188 (新竹市中華路2段188號) (03) 515-1111 http://www.ambh.com.tw.

The Howard Plaza Hotel, Hsinchu (新竹福華大飯店) boasts 125 luxury rooms and a modern fitness center with a pool. Business travelers will also be pleased to find a 24-hour business center, fine Eastern (Chinese and Cantonese) and Western dining and upscale shopping on the premesis. Rooms start at NT $5,600 a night. Zhongzheng Road, #178 (新竹市中正路178號) (03) 528-2323.

HUALIEN (花蓮)

(Area Code: 03)
Population: 109,324

The pristine green eastern side of Taiwan is a stark contrast to its modern urban sprawls. Here you'll find small towns, a comparatively lower cost of living, and some of the friendliest people you'll ever encounter. Hualien boasts two universities, a new amusement park with an ocean theme and an outstanding national park, which makes for an exciting weekend escape. The downtown area can be walked in under two hours, and the vibrant night market has pleasant vendors. Try (麻薯 *mwaji*), a famous Hualien food.

Major attractions

One of the most famous national parks not only on Taiwan but also in all of Asia is **Taroko National Park** (太魯閣國家公園 *Tairoga Guojia Gongyuan*). Created on November 28, 1986, Taroko National Park boasts towering mountains with peaks that reach over 3000 meters, steep gorges and the beautiful beryl Liwu River. Must-sees include Cingshui Cliff, Tiansiang, an Atayal aboriginal village, Swallows' Grottos, Tunnel of Nine Turns (resembles the Bat Cave and is not to be missed), Eternal Spring Shrine and Baiyang Trail, which runs for approximately two kilometers from the Atayal village of Tiansiang alongside the Waheier and Tachihjili streams. Most local hotels have brochures for half-day or full-day tour packages that start around NT $1000 and include lunch.

H
1
2
3
4
Hualien City
花蓮市
Scale-1:8200
Hualien County Stadium
花蓮縣立體育場
(花蓮巨蛋)
Hualien Baseball Stadium
花蓮棒壘球場
Jianguo Rd. 建國路
Taichang Rd. 大昌路
Eventide Market
黃昏市場
Jhonghua Rd. 中華路
Jhongshan Rd. Sec.2 中山路二段
Cihhuei Temple
慈惠堂
Jhongshan Rd.
Huedongsian Railway 花東線鐵路
To Taitung 往台東
Jifong Rd.

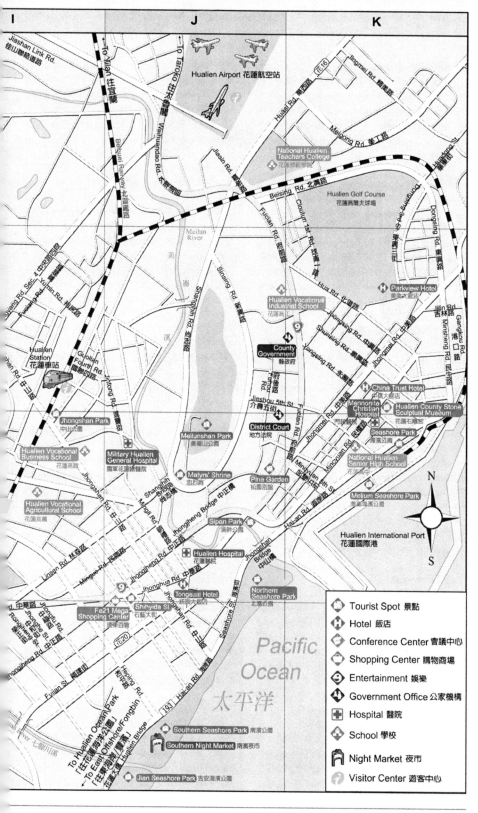

Hualien Airport 花蓮航空站

Jiashan Link Rd. 佳山聯絡道路

To Yilan 往宜蘭
To Taroko 往太魯閣

Beiyuan Railway Rd. 北迴鐵路
Waihuangdao Rd. 外環道路
Jiashin Rd. 佳新路

Huaai Rd. 華愛路
Jingmei Rd. 青美路

Meigong Rd. 美工路

National Hualien Teachers College 花蓮師院

Beising Rd. 北勝路
Fucian Rd. 府前路
Coulun 1st. Rd. 球崙一路
Hua Rd. 北濱路

Hualien Golf Course 花蓮高爾夫球場

Parkview Hotel 美侖大飯店

Hsinsing Rd. 新興路
Shangjin Rd. 商校街

Meihin River 美崙溪

Dongsing Rd. 東興路

Hualien Station 花蓮車站
Fushin Rd. 復興路
Fuyang Rd. Sec. 4 中央路四段

Guolian Fourth Rd. 國聯四路

Jintong Rd. 進豐街

Hualien Vocational Industrial School 花蓮高工

Gangkou Rd. 港口路
Minsheng Rd. 民生路

County Government 縣政府

Jilin Rd. 吉林路
Jhongmei Rd. 中美路

Shunsing Rd. 順興路

Jhongsan Rd. 中山路

Jhongshan Park 中山公園

Meilunshan Park 美崙山公園

Fucian Rd. 府前路

Hualien Rd. 華興路

China Trust Hotel 中信大飯店

Mennonite Christian Hospital 門諾醫院

Hualien County Stone Sculptural Museum 花蓮石雕館

District Court 地方法院
Jiesbou 5th. St. 介壽五街

Hualien Vocational Business School 花蓮高商

Military Hualien General Hospital 國軍花蓮總醫院

Matyrs' Shrine 忠烈祠

Seashore Park 海濱公園

Pine Garden 松園別館

National Hualien Senior High School 花蓮高中

Hualien Vocational Agricultural School 花蓮農校

Shangshin Bridge 尚志橋

Jhongjheng Bridge 中正橋

Sipan Park 溝仔尾公園

Minquan 4th. 民權四路

Melium Seashore Park 美崙海濱公園

Hualien International Port 花蓮國際港

Linsen Rd. 林森路

Jhongjheng Rd. 中正路

Hualien Hospital 花蓮醫院

Jhongshan Bridge 中山橋

Jhongsan Rd. 中山路

Jhonghua Rd. 中華路

Northern Seashore Park 北濱公園

Pacific Ocean 太平洋

Fe21 Mega Shopping Center 遠東百貨
Shihyida St. 石藝大街
Tongsuai Hotel 統帥大飯店

Seashore St. 海濱街
Haican Rd. 海濱路

Fujian St. 福建街
Heping Rd. 和平路

To Hualien Ocean Park 往花蓮海洋公園
To East Offshore/Fongbin 往東海岸/豐濱
花蓮大橋 Hualien Bridge

Southern Seashore Park 庫濱公園
Southern Night Market 南濱夜市

Jian Seashore Park 吉安海濱公園

	Tourist Spot 景點
	Hotel 飯店
	Conference Center 會議中心
	Shopping Center 購物商場
	Entertainment 娛樂
	Government Office 公家機構
	Hospital 醫院
	School 學校
	Night Market 夜市
	Visitor Center 遊客中心

I   J   K

N   S

If superior scenery summons, **Central Cross-Island Highway** (中橫公路) originates just beyond Taichung and winds over the Central Mountain Range (中央山脈) through Hualien's Taroko National Park before ending alongside the eastern coast of Taiwan.

East Hawaii Amusement Park (花蓮東方夏威夷遊樂園 *Hualian Dongfang Xiawaiyi Youleyuan*) boasts "lady boy" Thailand dancers and European acrobats. You'll also find touristy gift shops, a swimming area and rides. Adult tickets cost NT $350. Open 7:30 am to 6 pm. Shueiyuan Village, #1-9, Siouliu, Hualien County (at the end of Jianguo Road in Hualien City) (花蓮縣秀林鄉水源村1-9 號,花蓮市建國路底) (03) 857-0131 http://www.easternhawaii.com.tw.

Hualien Ocean Park (花蓮海洋公園 *Hualien Haiyang Gongyuan)* has a familiar theme for anyone that's ever visited San Diego's Sea World, there are eight theme zones with exhibitions, water rides, live performances, gift shops and eateries. Built by Hualien's upscale Far Glory Hotel, expect to see ads promoting the hotel at the park. Admission is steep (NT $890 for adults, not much less for kids) but so is the fun. Open Monday through Friday 9 am to 5 pm, 8:30 to 5:30 pm weekends. (花蓮縣壽豐鄉鹽寮村福德189號) Toll-free: 0800-801123 http://www.Hualienoceanpark.com.tw.

Hualien Hotels

Antong Hot Spring Hotel (安通溫泉飯店) The hot springs at this upscale hotel in Yuli (玉里鎮), Hualien County, were built in 1904 during the Japanese occupation. The hotel restaurant, which serves traditional Chinese dishes at NT $2000 to NT $8000 per table, is open from 11:30 am until 1 pm and again from 5:30 to 7 pm. Breakfast is NT $150 for adults, NT $80 for children. One night will set you back NT $3600 (40% off during January, February, July and August), springs are gratis for guests. Unfortunately, these hot springs are not easily accessable

without a car. By bus or train, Antong Hot Springs Hotel is approximately a half hour by foot after exiting Antong Station (安通站). Staff is not bilingual. Wenchuen Road, #36 (花蓮縣玉里鎮溫泉路 36號) (03) 888-6108 http://www.an-tong.com.tw.

Hualien Charming City Hotel (花蓮香城大飯店) This charming hotel in the heart of Hualien city boasts comfortable rooms, 24-hour free Internet access, complimentary coffee, tea, a hot water machine, a coffee shop and fine Eastern and Western dining. The basement exercise complex boasts ping pong tables, a baseball machine, dance machine and, on the second lower level, get ready to shake, rattle and roll--a KTV machine! Close to all major Hualien attractions, daily room rates start at NT $2100 (10% service charge already included) and include complimentary breakfast. Guoxing 2nd Street, #19 (花蓮市國興二街19號) (03) 835-3355 http://www.city-hotel.com.tw.

Hualien Chinatrust Hotel (花蓮中信大飯店) Located in the heart of the downtown area, weekday rates start at NT $3000, NT $3700 weekends. Complimentary breakfast is included. Hualien Chinatrust Hotel is under an hour from the entrance of Taroko National Park. Yongxing Road, #2 (花蓮市永興路2號) (03) 822-1171 http://www.chinatrust-hotel.com.tw.

Far Glory Hotel (花蓮遠來飯店) To feel as if you've entered the Victorian era rather than the Republic of China stay at Far Glory Hotel (formerly known as "Bellevista"). Rooms start at NT $6,600 per night. Shoufeng Township, Yanliao Village, Shanling #18 (花蓮縣壽豐鄉鹽寮村山嶺18號) (03) 812-3988 http://www.bellevista.com.tw

Grand Formosa, Taroko National Park (天祥晶華渡假酒店) It doesn't get more convenient than this. Built within Taroko National Park, Grand Formosa is a popular tourist spot for an afternoon tea and many tour companies stop here. Rooms start at

NT $3900 weekdays, NT $5100 weekends. In addition to fine dining, Grand Formosa, Taroko National Park boasts a palatial pool, full fitness center and great gift shop with impressive aboriginal art. Afternoon tea goes for NT $250 and includes a 10% service charge. Shoulin Township, Tianshang Road, #18 (花蓮縣秀林鄉天祥路 18號) (03) 869-1155.

Parkview Hotel (花蓮美侖大飯店) boasts friendly service, a public indoor spa and bathing area, outdoor pool with small overhead walking bridges, fancy fountains, an arcade complete with pool tables, and an adjacent golf course. Visitors can rent bicycles for an hour at a time to ride around the hotel premises. Be aware that at night you may be able to hear other guests' private pleasures through somewhat thin walls. Rooms start at NT $6000 per night, check for promotions. Linyuan #1-1 (花蓮市 民享里林園1-1號) (03) 822-2111 http://www. parkview-hotel.com.

The Hualien Visitor Center (花蓮遊客中 心, 觀光局東管處花蓮遊客中心) boasts a café and aboriginal goods, it's in Hualien's northcoast village of Shoufeng on Dakang, #5 (花蓮縣壽豐鄉鹽寮村大坑5號) (03) 867-1326. Open 8:30 am to 5 pm.

HYPERMARTS (大賣場)

Hypermarts, combination supermarket and outlet warehouses, sell everything from daily necessities to computers and electrical appliances. Hypermarts are particularly popular with expatriates and residents who deplete their supply of convenience store goods.

Two popular Taipei hypermarts are:

B&Q (特力屋, 士林店) Although you may not be inclined to make any major appliance purchases thousands of miles from home, this B&Q is one block north of Shilin Night Market. A free shuttle bus runs here from Jiantan Station. Jihe Road, #258 (台北 市士林區基河路258號) (02) 2889-1000 0800-008-007 (toll-free) http://www.bnq. com.tw.

There are currently forty-six Carrefour (家樂福 *Jia Le Fu*), "house of happiness and luck," hypermart stores on Taiwan. In Tienmu, Carrefour is one block north of Zhishan Station. Dexing West Road, #47 (台 北市德行西路47號) (02) 2833-8042.

On the way to Danshui you can spot a Carrefour in Zhuwei on Minchuan Road, #27 (台北縣淡水鎮民權路27號) (02) 2808-3536.

ILAN (宜蘭)
(Area Code: 03)
Population: 464,359

In northeastern Taiwan, daytrippers enjoy Ilan for its scenic views and proximity to the East China Sea. North of Hualien, Ilan is separated from Taipei and Taoyuan to the north and Taichung and Miaoli to the west by rugged mountains, which have helped to preserve the area's natural beauty. Ilan is known for its traditional temples, fresh fish, green gardens, fine fruit farms and pristine parks. Like Changhua, Ilan also boasts a tasty "cow tongue cookie" (牛舌餅) but these sweet treats are crunchy rather than soft.

Expatriates in nearby Taipei and Taoyuan sometimes visit during the weekends to enjoy the slower life pace. Ilan also hosts the Children's Folklore and Folk Game Festival (宜蘭國際童玩節) that attracts talented performers from around the world. From Taipei, Ilan is about two and a half hours by boat or train.

If traveling by car from Taipei you'll now be able to pass quickly through the Hsuehshan Mountain Range via the Hsuehshan Tunnel

(雪山隧道), a monumental government project that took over thirteen years to complete. The 12.9-kilometer tunnel, an important part of the 31-kilometer Taipei-Ilan Expressway, has both eastbound and westbound lanes and is the fifth-longest tunnel in the world.

A little over a hundred kilometers from Taipei on North Second Highway is **Beiguan Tital Park** (東北角管理處大里管理站), Ilan County, Toucheng Village (宜蘭縣頭城鎮) (03) 978-0727. Once a military outpost during the Ch'ing dynasty, discover unique rock formations, a historic temple, cannons nearly two centuries old and scenic views four hundred meters above sea level. Open daily from 8 am to midnight (free). Seafood vendors peddle a plethora of interesting edibles near the parking lot. Warning: High tides and crashing waves render water activities dangerous. Dayou Bus at Taipei Main Station runs to Beiguan, by train exit at Kueishan Station, it's a two-hour trip from Taipei.

To spend the night, standard rooms start around NT $2400 (breakfast included) at the upscale **Grand Boss Hotel** (伯斯飯店 *Baichee Fandian*), Yixing Road, Section 1, #366 (宜蘭市宜興路1段366號) (03) 931-2999. The hotel boasts a daily newspaper and mineral water, fine Western dining (open 24 hours) and free bike rental.

Another good option outside the city is **Chuangtang Hot Springs Hotel** (川湯溫泉養生館 *Chuangtang Wenchuen Yangshengguan*). The hotel (NT $2000/night) boasts fifty Western or Japanese-style rooms, outdoor hot spring pools and 24-hour indoor hot spring baths, as well as Eastern dining. Chuangtang is in Chiaohsi Village, Ilan County, Chongshan Road, Section 2, #218 (宜蘭縣礁溪鄉中山路2段218號, 礁溪火車站旁) (03) 988-0606. From Chiaohsi Train Station (礁溪站下車) the hotel is a five-minute walk.

INTERNET ACCESS (上網)

Most three to five-star Taiwan hotels provide complimentary Internet access for guests (call in advance to confirm). Internet cafés appear in virtually all areas of Taipei, and they're easy to spot after 4 pm from the hordes of students. If you're averse to cigarette smoke, be aware that many young patrons smoke while battling villains online. Most Internet cafés include a beverage gratis (usually cola, tea or juice) and charge around NT $100 (approximately US $3.00) per hour. For a list of island-wide Internet cafés visit http://www.OnTaiwan.com.

For free on-line Internet access, there are a handful of computers on the second floor of **Nova**, across from Taipei Main Station. Although there are signs above each terminal indicating a thirty-minute time limit, Nova becomes crowded during peak hours, and many Internet junkies feel no compunction exceeding the time limit. Arrive early when Nova opens at 11 am or expect to wait.

In the Shida area try **Net Coffee**, NT $40/hr, includes a beverage. Smoking/non-smoking sections. Shida Road, #119, B1 (台北市師大路119號B1) (02) 2364-9062. By MRT it's a three-minute walk from Taipower Building Exit 3.

McCafé, McDonald's' Asian answer to Starbucks, offers free Internet access as well as delicious bagels and beverages. The hot chocolate is especially good. Here are three Taipei McCafé locations:
Minsheng: Minsheng East Road, Section 3, #135 (Near the intersection of Minsheng East Road, Section 3 and Dunhua North Road) (台北市民生東路3段135號)
(02) 2713-0715
Tienmu: Tienmu East Road, #61-1, (Corner of Tienmu East Road and Zhongcheng Road) (台北市天母東路67-1號)
(02) 2873-2068
Zhongxiao: Zhongxiao East Road, Section

5, #289 (Corner of Zhongxiao East Road and Songxin Road) (台北市忠孝東路5段289號) (02) 2764-9488.

Aztec (戰略高手) is the city's largest Internet café chain, here you can write home and let the folks and friends know you're not only surviving your Taiwan adventure but are enjoying local delicacies such as stir-fried noodles, sweet gluttonous rice cakes and barbeque squid. Aztec is recognizable by its blue and white sign with a target on the logo:
Shilin: Wenlin Road #281 (台北市文林路281號1樓) (02) 2889-1414
Tienmu: Tienmu West Road, Lane 13, #9 (台北市天母西路13巷9號) (02) 2876-8008
Zhongxiao I: Zhongxiao West Road, Section 1, #50, 5th Floor (台北市忠孝西路1段50號5F) (02) 2370-8966 (near Taipei Train Station)
Zhongxiao II: Zhongxiao East Road, Section 4 (台北市忠孝東路4段64號1F, B1F) (02) 2771-6876, adjacent to Pacific Sogo and TGI Friday's.

▌SLANDS IN THE STRAIT ▌(台灣本島)

Islands in the Taiwan Strait, that is what they are... Well, at least Kinmen and Matsu are. If you're looking for hustle, bustle and hyped-up Hollywood kung-fu muscle you may be disappointed if you visit Taiwan's slower-paced outlying islands where historic sites and traditional Taiwanese culture prevails. While crime is virtually non-existant, it's always a good idea to have your wits about you.

Green Island   (綠島 *Ludao*)
A Snorkler's Paradise

If you're looking to relax while delving deeper into history, Green Island may be for you. Many find this serene, secluded island thirty-three kilometers southeast of Taitung to be a great place to unwind after a wired work week. Known as "Huo Shao" (baked wheat cake) during the Japanese occupation, perhaps for its once-barren sandy white appearance, the government planted trees around the island and officially changed the name to Green Island in 1949. Green Island, a small volcanic island with an odd, Louisiana-like shape, reaches approximately fifteen kilometers in length and has a road that winds 17.3 kilometers (10.8 miles) around its perimeter that can be walked in just under six hours.

On Green Island there are three villages where approximately 1,500 people reside, **Chungliao** (中寮村) in the north where the lighthouse and airport are located, **Nanliao** (南寮村), where you'll find the fishing harbor, and **Gungguan** (公館村), home to **Green Island Human Rights Memorial Park** (綠島人權紀念園區) and interesting natural volcanic rocks. **Huo Shao Mountain** (火燒山), the tallest mountain centrally located on the island, reaches 281 meters above sea level. Fishing has been and remains the main industry on the island, and aboriginal tribes thrived on Green Island without outside interference until the 1950s.

When the Nationalists arrived on Taiwan in 1949, Taiwan experienced a period of "white terror" in which martial law was imposed while dissodents were imprisoned, beaten and/or killed. On this placid island the government set up the "Freshmen Disciplinary Camp" (1951 to 1965) to lock up gangsters and "re-educate" political prisoners. The Camp later became a prison to house ferocious gangsters as well as minor offenders, many of whom were political dissenters, and was officially closed on Dec. 31, 2001. On the north coast of Green Island discover Green Island Human Rights Memorial Park (綠島人權紀念園區), home to **General's Rock** (將軍岩) and other large volcanic rocks, **Swallow Cave** (燕子洞), **Tsihang Temple** (慈航宮), **Niutou Mountain** (牛頭山) and **Chungliao** (中寮), where the first political prisoners ("Freshmen") arrived in 1951. Other Green Island tourist destinations include **Green Island Lighthouse** (綠島燈塔), **Nanliao**

Harbor (南寮漁港), where the creepy-looking but fun **Seaweed Ice Store** (海藻冰店) is, **White Sand Beach** (大白沙 *Dabaisha*), and **Pekinese Dog Rock** (哈巴狗岩) on the eastern side of the island. You'll also discover rare outdoor **saltwater hot springs** (旭溫泉 *shu wenchuen*) heated naturally by volcanic activity. Tourists bathe at all hours and sometimes stay to watch the sun rise. The only other natural saltwater hot springs in the world are located near Italy's Mount Vesuvius. Locals tell folk legends about the eerie rock formations and twisted banyan tree at the entrance of Black Ghost Cave.

After the island was put under the East Coast Scenic Area Administration in 1988 tourism began to flourish, and hotels, restaurants and equipment rental shops now dot the island. There are a handful of convenience stores and food markets on Green Island, to withdraw money there is an ATM machine in the Nanliao post office. The ferry from **Fugang Harbor** (富岡港) in Taitung to Green Island crosses at least once per day depending on weather conditions and holds up to two hundred and fifty people.

Taitung County Administration (台東縣綠島鄉公所) operates buses that run daily around the island, the fare is NT $100 for three days (089) 672-510.

Sungrong Hotel (松榮旅社), Yugang Road, #42, Nanliao (綠島鄉南寮村漁港路42號) charges around NT $1200 per night (089) 672-515. Another option is the Gungguan-based **Ludao Guomin Lushuh** (綠島國民旅舍), which somewhat resembles an older two-story Venice Beach, California apartment complex. The hotel is on Wenchuen (Hot Springs) Road, #56 (綠島鄉公館村溫泉路56號) (089) 672-314. For those that enjoy roughing it there are inexpensive (NT $300/night) campsites near the outdoor hot springs area (旭溫泉) and White Sand Beach (大白沙 *Dabaisha*).

Reaching Green Island by boat takes fifty minutes and may be an excellent experience for those who enjoy Indiana Jones-type adventures, but be warned that the rough Pacific seas often produce more than a couple of seasick passengers. Tickets cost around NT $300 and may be purchased at Fugang Harbor (富岡港) in Taitung. The first ferry departs Taitung at 8:30 am.

Flights to Green Island Airport (綠島機場) (15 minutes) cost approximately NT $700 for a one-way ticket and depart daily from the Taitung Fong Nian Airport (台東豐年機場) at 8:20 am, 11:55 am and 3:20 pm. The airport is located in Taitung on Minhang Road, #1100 (台東市民航路1100號) (089) 361-111. From Green Island to Taitung flights depart at 9:00 am, 12:50 pm and 4:15 pm, respectively.

For more information contact Green Island Travel Information Center (東管處綠島遊客中心) at (089) 672-026.

Kinmen (金門 *Jinmen*)
A Reason To Love Taiwan

Kinmen (金門) is far more than the location of a Taiwanese military base. **Kinmen National Park** (金門國家公園), Baiyu Road, Section 2, #460 (金門縣892金寧鄉伯玉路2段460號) (082) 313100, was established on October 18, 1995. The park boasts traditional villages with Ch'ing dynasty-style Chinese houses, fine fowl and battlefield monuments that include **Guningtou Battle Museum** (古寧頭戰史館) and **August 23rd Artillery Battle Museum** (八二三戰史館). Guningtou Battle Museum recalls the attack on Kinmen that took place on October 25, 1949 in which Nationalist forces held back around ten thousand Mainland Chinese troops. August 23rd Artillery Battle Museum commemorates the attack on August 23, 1958 in which Mainland China fired nearly five hundred thousand rounds of artillery at Kinmen, resulting in more than four hundred Taiwanese casualties. This Taiwanese victory is said to have prevented a full-scale invasion.

Inside Kinmen National Park you'll find eleven historical monuments and ancient **Beishan lion statues** (北山風獅爺) that are said to scare off evil spirits. It rains often during the summer, spring seems to bring an eerie rolling fog, and winter and fall tend to be cold. The weather may not be too hot (literally) but the interesting geology, fauna, flora, and ecology makes for an interesting excursion. Anthropologists in particular may appreciate a visit to Kinmen because there are traces of human habitation dating back nearly six thousand years.

Originally established as part of a military base in 1947, **Kinmen Airport** (金門航空站) (金門縣89146金湖鎮尚義機場2號) (082) 322-381 can be reached from Taipei (55 minutes), Taichung (55 minutes), Chiayi (50 minutes), Tainan (50 minutes) and Kaohsiung (1 hour).

The upscale **Taikin Hotel** (台金大飯店), Gaochang Road, #1 (金門縣金沙鎮高陽路1 號) (082) 353-888, is conveniently located within Kinmen National Park. Rooms start at NT $3,500/night. For overnight information contact Kinmen Youth Activity Center (082) 325-722. Kinmen County Transporation Tour Bureau (金門縣政府交通 旅遊局) can be reached at (082) 324-174.

Liuchiu Island (琉球嶼 *Liuchiu Yu*)
Paradise on the Sea

Liuchiu Island, known locally as "Paradise on the Sea" (海上樂園), is an ethereal escape from the rigors of city life. Unlike Taiwan's other islands, Liuchiu Island was formed entirely of coral deposits. Since the Chinese pronunciation of the island is the same as Okinawa, Japan, locals call the island "Small Liuchiu" (小琉球 *Hsiao Liuchiu*). Located within Dapeng Bay National Scenic Area (觀光局大鵬灣 國家風景區管理處), this quiet, 6.8-square kilometer island known for its fresh seafood can be walked in only a few hours. Like Green Island, Liuchiu Island boasts natural rock formations and unique snapshot

spots such as **Black Ghost Cave** (烏鬼洞) and **Meiren (Beautiful People) Cave** (美人洞), where even comedian Gilbert Godfried, recently voted the unsexiest man alive, may be allowed to visit (maybe). Locals tell folk legends about the eerie rock formations and twisted banyan tree at the entrance of Black Ghost Cave. Liuchiu Island also boasts the impressive **Lushan Temple** (靈山寺), **Chingen Garden** (親恩公園), an intimate **aquarium** (海底動物園 *Haidi Dongwuyuan*) and **White Lighthouse** (白燈塔) that offers serenity with its breathtaking view. Most visit to relax, swim or snorkel in the pure azure water, and local shops and hotels rent gear for water-related activities. Otherwise, feel free to read up on Liuchiu Island at the **local island library** (鄉立圖書館).

Liuchiu Island, or Hsiao Liuchiu, is also home to the "king boat ritual," a unique annual ritual that takes place at historic **Sanlong Temple** (屏東縣琉球鄉三隆宮) (08) 861-2297 every fall. A "king boat" is pulled around the island before it is burned at the waterfront to send the gods on a peaceful journey back to heaven.

The easiest way to reach Liuchiu Island is by public ferry (公營交通船) (08) 833-7493 or private ferry (民營交通船) (08) 832-5806 from Pingtung's **Tungkang Wharf** (東港碼 頭). Ferries begin departing at 7 am and leave at irregular intervals thereafter (call for schedule information); the last ferry departs around 6 pm. A one-way ferry ride typically takes thirty minutes and a roundtrip ticket costs NT $350 to NT $450.

Some Liuchiu Island hotels appear similar to the small cottages found on Balboa Island in Southern California. Although most people visit the island for only a few hours, try these hotels for a pleasant overnight visit:

Hsiao Liuchiu Hotel (小琉球大飯店) boasts outstanding ocean views from every window, scrumptious seafood at reasonable prices and a prime location, within walking distance from the wharf. Bikes are available for rent as is water-related activity gear. Rooms start at NT $1200/night (two people) weekdays, NT $1800 weekends. Minsheng Road, #43-2 (屏東縣琉球鄉民生路43-2號) (08) 861-1133.

Bailonggong Luguan (白龍宮旅館) rooms are NT $1200 for two people weekdays, NT $1500 weekends. Sanmin Road, #272 (屏東縣琉球鄉三民路272號) (08) 861-2536.

Accomodations are modest, much like a college dorm room, at **Fuxing Bing Guan** (復興賓館), but so are the prices. Rooms start at NT $1000 weekdays, NT$1200 weekends. Package deals that include transportation are available for an additional NT $300. Minsheng Road, #73 (屏東縣琉球鄉民生路73號) (08) 861-2617.

Coco Resort (椰林渡假村) boasts a friendly, accommodating staff. Guest rooms are modest but comfortable. Rooms for two start at NT $1800 weekdays, NT $2000 weekends. Minzu Road, #38-20 (屏東縣琉球鄉民族路38-20號) (08) 861-4368.

Matsu (馬祖)
I Left My Heart In... Matsu?

Looking for ultra-snazzy fast cars speeding down wide fast lanes, fast food and fast-talking salespeople that will try to convince you to fork over all of your hard-earned vacation money? Thankfully you shouldn't find any on Matsu (馬祖), a Taiwanese island named for the Taoist diety. Originally four quaint fishing villages, the island took on prominence after the Nationalists fled to Taiwan in 1949 and established a military base. Since Matsu was selected to become the first Taiwanese locale to have "three small links" (小三通), direct travel, mail and trade with China starting in January, 2006, the region turned its attention to Matsu to determine whether relations would improve across the Taiwan Strait. So far the

consensus seems to be that not much has changed, but three small links may be better than no links.

Matsu National Scenic Area (馬祖國家風景區) was established in 1999 and since then more tourists have been appreciating the area's traditional temples and relics that dot the landscape. Matsu's hilly terrain makes travel by car or moped seem daunting, so bring comfortable clothes, a good pair of sneakers or walking shoes, a hat and suntan lotion. Some expatriates have remarked that the fog, cool evenings, sudden gusts of wind and hilly terrain remind them of a Taiwanese San Francisco. Indeed, some of the views from Bi Mountain may jog Bay Area memories. Keep an eye on weather conditions (spring is often foggy with strong gusts of wind), and if you bring a camera be sure not to take pictures of military facilities or you may be taken as a spy. Matsu is an archipelago like Penghu with about seven thousand registered residents, but unfortunately for these residents, the hilly terrain makes trade, even with other areas of Taiwan, difficult. While visiting be sure to hike up to **Bi Mountain Viewing Point** (壁山觀景台) and explore **Biyung Memorial Park** (碧園), **Wusha Tunnel** (午沙坑道) and **Benli Beach** (坂里沙灘).

There are no international resort hotels on Matsu, but one of the larger establishments is **Captain Hotel** (船老大民宿 *Chuan Lao Daminsuh*), Daping Village, #72 (馬祖東莒大坪村72號) (083) 688-022. The hotel is clean and spacious, and the staff tries to be as helpful as possible. Captain Hotel has two locations so be sure to request a room at the newer one, opened in 2005. Single rooms go for around NT $1000 per night, NT $1,200 for two people. http://www.captain-hotel.com.

Like Kinmen, spring tends to be foggy, so flights may be delayed. Flights to Matsu fill quickly with government employees so purchase tickets early. In Taipei, Uni Air (立榮航空) (02) 2518-5166 flies from Songshan

Airport to the main **Matsu Nangang Airport** (馬祖南竿航空站) (50 minutes) from 6:50 am until 4:05 pm and from Matsu to Taipei from 8:05 am until 5:20 pm. Uni Air has three flights per day from Taipei to the smaller **Matsu Beigang Airport** (馬祖北竿航空站) (50 minutes) from 9:20 am until 5:10 pm and from Matsu to Taipei from 10:35 am to 6:30 pm. On Matsu the phone number for Uni Air (立榮馬祖) is (083) 626-511 (Nangang) or (083) 656-578 (Beigang). Once on Matsu, nine-passenger buses (NT $15) depart frequently from the airport from 6:20 am until 5:35 pm. Taxi fares start at NT $100 and from Matsu's **Fuao Port** you can take a commuter boat to other Matsu islets (Whitesand Port, Beigang, Chungchu Port of Dungyin, Menguo Port of Tungju, Chingfan Port of Hsiju) for NT $100.

Book two days before departure for **Taima Lun** (臺馬輪) (02) 2423-2423 (Matsu: 083-626-288), which departs from Keelung Harbor every other day. For reservations call (02) 2424-6868 (Matsu: 083-626-655). The one-way ride lasts approximately eight hours and departs from Gangxi Street, #16, 2nd Floor, East Pier 2. (基隆市港西街16號2樓, 西岸旅客碼頭2樓大廳侯船室). An economy ticket will set you back around NT $400.

The recently renovated **AP Vessel** (AP 鑑) (02) 2592-2244 also sails to Matsu, the government selects three sailing dates per month so call in advance to find out if the ship will be sailing during your stay. Tickets can be purchased at Keelung West Sixth Dock. Show up one hour before departure and bring identification. The number for AP Vessel in Matsu is (083) 622-417.

Orchard Island (蘭嶼 *Lanyu*)
The Dance of the Yami

Seventy-six kilometers off Taiwan's southeastern coast, Orchard Island was once "Red Head Island" because its northwestern mountain peaks resembled buring heads in the setting sun. Orchard Island boasts orchard fields, rare flora, fauna and the **Yami tribe** (雅美族). The Yami are known for their hand-carved fishing canoes and fishing expertise; their semi-subterranean homes, made predominantly of wood and stone, are built halfway into the ground to avoid excessive heat and typhoon damage. Since there are no high schools or colleges on Orchard Island, many inhabitants venture to cities on Taiwan (predominantly Taitung) for schooling and work. Those that remain tend to work in the hospitality industry.

Vibrant Yami festivals signify special occasions such as setting sail to a new fishing boat. **The Flying Fish Sacrifice** (飛魚祭 *Feiwuji*), the most important Yami festival, marks the beginning of flying fish season. During this ritual men don silver clothing and protective head garments, spread pig and chicken blood on outlying stones, light torches to attract flying fishes and perform a titillating tribal dance. The best place on Orchard Island to observe the Yami is **Langdau Village**. Anthropologist Hu Tai-Li (胡台麗) depicts Yami life on Orchard Island in her film, "Voices of Orchard Island." Hu won a Golden Horse Award for Best Documentary Film in 1993 and a Silver Plaque Award at the Chicago International Film Festival the following year. Be respectful when visiting, as Yami tend to be untrusting of outside influence.

Like Green Island, Orchard Island is rife with rocks formed by wind and sea erosion. Visitors are also intrigued by Yami art carved into the walls of **Wukung Caves**, as well. The local government, middle school and main bus station are in Yeyou Village, and the lighthouse just north of the village offers an impressive island view. **Kaiyuan Harbor** (開元港) is where the Kai Syuan Ke Yuen (凱旋客運) and Hsin Fa Hang Yuen (新發航運) ferries arrive from Taitung's Fugang Harbor (富岡港).

In Yuren (Fishermen) Village (魚人村) stop

by **The Epicurean** (無餓不坐) (yellow and purple exterior), dishes are simple but pleasing to the palate and average around NT $250. In addition to fantastic flying fish, the local delicacy, the restaurant/pub boasts Internet access, good brews and an invigorating view of the Pacific Ocean. Yuren Village, #77, Lanyu (台東縣蘭嶼鄉漁人村77號) (089) 731-623. Open 11:30 am until midnight.

Rooms start at NT $2000/night at **Orchard Island Hotel** (蘭嶼大飯店), Yeyou Village, #22 (台東縣蘭嶼鄉椰油村22號) (089) 732-032. A room for two at **Lanyu Hotel** (蘭嶼別館), Hongtou Tsun (Red Head Village), #45 (紅頭村45號) (089) 731-611 will set you back NT $1800. Mandarin Airlines (華信航空公司) flies to Orchard Island from Taitung (089) 362-669, its flights to the island are handled by Daily Air (德安航空公司) (089) 362-676 (7:30 am to 5:20 pm). Contact Orchid Island Administrative Office (蘭嶼鄉公所) (089) 732-009 for more information.

Penghu (澎湖)
A Romantic Getaway For Green Turtles And Humans

On Penghu (澎湖), sixty-four separate islands also known as "the Pescadores," you'll discover white sandy beaches, different species of birds, plenty of wild daisies, plants and traditional farm life. Experience plentiful peanuts and sumptuous sweet potatoes, historic temples and your friend and mine, the green turtle. These are no ordinary green turtles, some grow as large as 150 centimeters and weigh over 120 kilograms. You may spot these adorable "stone turtles" spawning on Penghu's pristine beaches.

Five Penghu lighthouses also attract visitors to the Penghu archipelago and tall banyan trees are a common sight. Fresh seafood is abundant on Penghu and you would be remiss not to try some. You can reach Penghu's **Magong Airport** (民用航空局馬公航空站) from Taipei (50 minutes), Taichung (30 minutes), Chiayi (30 minutes), Tainan (25 minutes) and Kaohsiung (35 minutes). By ferry it takes about four hours to reach **Magong Harbor** (馬公港) on Penghu (06) 926-4087 from Kaohsiung Harbor (高雄 七號碼頭) (馬公港) (07) 561-3866 and ninety minutes from Chiayi (嘉義布袋港) (馬公鎖港) (05) 347-7988. Once on Penghu you can fly from Magong to either Chimei (七美) (15 minutes) or Wangan (望安) (15 minutes). Uni Air (立榮航空) (06) 922-8999 flies to Magong Airport from Kinmen (35 minutes) (082) 324-481 for around NT $1040.

Baohua Hotel (寶華飯店) in Magong City has a reputation for cleanliness and friendly service, the hotel boasts a fine seafood restaurant, bar, café, and rooms that offer breathtaking harbor ocean views. Room rates are seasonal and start at NT $3,400 per night, the hotel is on Chong Cheng Road, #2 (澎湖縣馬公市中正路2號) (06) 927-4881.

The number for the Penghu National Scenic Administration (澎湖國家風景區) is (06) 921-6521.

JIUFEN (九份)

Jiufen (九份 *Chiu Fen*) is a mountainous village above Keelung, a major trading port and northern Taiwan city. "Jiu" in Chinese means "nine" and "fen" is a measure word meaning "item." At one point only nine families inhabited this small mountain village. When one of the villagers sojourned down the mountain to purchase something, he had to purchase nine items for each of the nine families, hence the unusual town name.

Once called "Little Hong Kong" due to a gold rush that sparked a flurry of excitement and thousands of settlers to the area in the late 1800's, the town's winding mountain roads, quiet coffee and tea shops, souvenir stores and art galleries provide a welcome respite. Buses run to Jiufen from Chung Lun Bus Station on Badeh Road, Section 2, the trip takes around two hours. Buses headed to Jinshan (金山) from Danshui Station stop at Keelung Bus Station, you can transfer across the street for the bus to Jiufen, altogether the trip takes an hour and a half to two hours, depending on traffic.

By train, make sure you exit at **Ruei (Ray) Fang** (瑞芳). You may also opt to exit the train at Keelung City Train Station to take a bus to Jiufen, but the fifty-minute bus ride through the city and up the winding mountain roads may tire you somewhat after taking the train. After you arrive in Rueifang you should see an intersection directly in front of the train station. Cross the street and walk slightly to your right, to the telephone pole on the corner. Here, on the corner, directly across from the OK convenience store, is where the bus stops every twenty minutes to pick up passengers traveling to Jiufen. The bus fare to Jiufen is NT $19 (US $.57) and the ride takes about twenty minutes. You can take a taxi from Rueifang, but be warned that these aren't metered fares and drivers typically charge a whopping NT $300 and up for the short ride.

Traverse Jiufen's famous Shuchi (Chee) Road (豎崎路), also known as "teashop street" (茶館街), a staircase with over three hundred steps lined with teashops and quaint galleries on either side. While Jiufen teashops regularly open and close, expect to find **Shanghai Teahouse** (小上海茶藝館 *Xiaoshanghai Chayiguan*), much of the 1989 hit movie "City of Sadness" was filmed here on Shuchi Road, #35 (台北縣瑞芳鎮豎崎路35號) (02) 2496-0852. Open 10 am to 8 pm, 10 am to 2 pm Sundays. Scenes were also filmed at the scenic teashop City of Sadness, Jingbian Road, #294-2 (台北縣瑞芳鎮九份輕便路294-2號) (02) 2406-2289.

Open 24 hours.

Jiufen Art Gallery, Jingbian Road, #131 (瑞芳九份輕便路131號) (02) 2497-9400, is open 10 am to 8 pm, admission is free and all are welcome. The gallery boasts a souvenir display area and teashop with scenic views.

Jiufen Gold Mining Museum (九份金礦博物館) (NT $100/80/60) Shipai Lane, #66 (台北縣瑞芳鎮九份頌德里石碑巷66巷) (02) 2496-6379. Open 9 am to 6 pm.

You can also delve into the area's history at **Gold Museum** (黃金博物園), Jinguang Road, #8 (台北縣瑞芳鎮金光路8號) (02) 2496-2800. Open 9:30 am to 5 pm Tuesday through Friday, until 6 pm weekends.

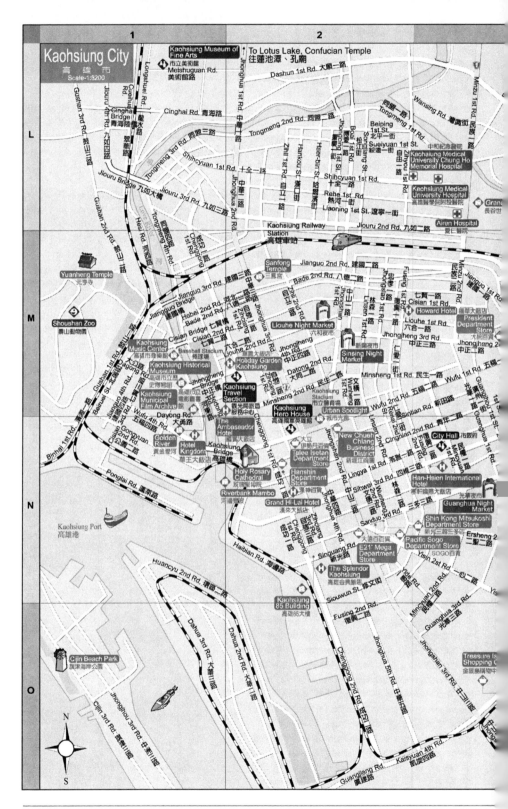

Kaohsiung City
高雄市
Scale-1:8200

1   **2**

Kaohsiung Museum of Fine Arts
市立美術館
Meishuguan Rd.
美術館路

To Lotus Lake, Confucian Temple
往蓮池潭、孔廟

Dashun 1st Rd. 大順一路

Cinghai Rd. 青海路

Cinghai Bridge
青海陸橋

Tongmeng 2nd Rd. 同盟二路

Beiping 1st St. 北平一街
Songjiang St. 松江街
Sueiyuan 1st St. 綏遠一街

中和紀念醫院
Kaohaiung Medical University Chung Ho Memorial Hospital

Shihcyuan 1st Rd. 十全一路

Shihcyuan 1st Rd. 十全一路

Rehe 1st Rd. 熱河一街

Kaohsiung Medical University Hospital
高雄醫學院附設醫院

Liaoning 1st St. 遼寧一街

Grand
長谷世

Kaohsiung Railway Station
高雄車站

Jiouru 2nd Rd. 九如二路

Airen Hospital
愛仁醫院

Yuanheng Temple
元亨寺

Sanfong Temple
三鳳宮

Jianguo 2nd Rd. 建國二路

Jianguo 3rd Rd. 建國三路

Jianguo Bridge
建國橋

Shoushan Zoo
壽山動物園

Hebei 2nd Rd. 河北二路
Bade 2nd Rd. 八德二路

Fusing 1st Rd.

七賢一路
Cisian 1st Rd.

Howard Hotel 福華大飯店

Cisian Bridge
七賢橋

Cisian 2nd Rd. 七賢二路

Liouhe Night Market
六和夜市

Liouhe 1st Rd.
六合一路

President Department Store
大統百貨

Kaohsiung Music Center
高雄市音樂館

Liouhe 2nd Rd.

Jhongheng 3rd Rd.
中正三路

Baseball Stadium
棒球場

Jhongheng

Kaohsiung Historical Museum
高雄市立歷史博物館

Holiday Garden Kaohsiung

Sinsing Night Market
新興夜市

Jhongheng Bridge
中正橋

Datong 2nd Rd.
大同二路

Minsheng 1st Rd. 民生一路

Wufu 2nd Rd. 五福二路

Kaohsiung Municipal Film Archive
高雄市電影圖書館

Kaohsiung Travel Section
觀光局旅遊服務中心

Kaohsiung Stadium
高雄體育館

Urban Spotlight
城市光廊

Wufu 4th Rd.
五福四路

Dayong Rd.
大勇路

Kaohsiung Hero House
高雄市英雄館

Sintian Rd. 新田路

City Hall
市政府

Binhai 1st Rd.

Golden River
黃金愛河

Hotel Kingdom

Kaohsiung Bridge
高雄橋

The Ambassador Hotel
國賓大飯店

New Chueh Chiang Business District
新崛江商場

Han-Hsien International Hotel
漢來大飯店

Holy Rosary Cathedral
玫瑰聖母院

Talee Isetan Department Store
大立伊勢丹百貨

Hanshin Department Store
漢神百貨

Guanghua Night Market
光華夜市

Riverbank Mambo
河畔曼波

Grand Hi-Lai Hotel
漢來大飯店

Shin Kong Mitsukoshi Department Store
新光三越百貨

Kaohsiung Port
高雄港

Ponglai Rd. 蓬萊路

Sanduo 3rd Rd.

Pacific Sogo Department Store
SOGO百貨

Ersheng 2
聖二

Singuang Rd.
新光路

E21' Mega Department Store

Huancyu 2nd Rd. 環球二路

The Splendor Kaohsiung
高雄金典酒店

Haibian Rd. 海邊路

Siouwun St. 修文街

Treasure Is Shopping C
金銀島購物中

Kaohsiung 85 Building
高雄85大樓

Fusing 2nd Rd. 復興二路

Cijin Beach Park
旗津海岸公園

Dahua 3rd Rd. 大華三路

Cijin 3rd Rd. 旗津三路

Jhonghou 3rd Rd. 中洲三路

Guangjiang Rd. 光榮路

Kaisyuan 2nd Rd. 凱旋二路

N

S

KAOHSIUNG (高雄)

(Area Code: 07)
Population: 1,238,925

Originally called "Dakou" (打狗), or "beat the dog" by the Takou tribe that had settled in the area before heading south to Pingtung, Kaohsiung boasts Taiwan's largest trading port and industrial center and the Kaohsiung Eye, a fantastic ferris wheel similar to the monumental one in Taipei. An elaborate MRT system should make city travel more convenient. The weather in Kaohsiung is typically calescent, sometimes grueling during the summer, so leave your sweater in Taipei.

Kaohsiung Railway Station Information Desk: (07) 237-5113

Major Attractions

Liuho Night Market (六合夜市) on Liuho 2nd Road (高雄六合二路) is a major tourist draw. Here you can sample everything from snake meat soup to stir-fried noodles and sweet papaya milk. The night market is about a fifteen-minute walk heading south on Zhongshan 1st Road (中山一路) from Kaohsiung train station.

Lotus Lake (蓮池潭) boasts Spring and Autumn Pavilions (春秋閣) with a statue of god of war Guan Gung towering above all who visit. You'll also find Dragon and Tiger Pagodas (龍虎塔) boasting magnificent works of art, and Confucius Temple (孔廟), Taiwan's largest, is the site of an annual September 28 Teacher's Day celebration.

Aquariums, pagodas and natural beauty awaits at Kaohsiung's largest lake, **Chengching Lake** (澄清湖), a valued local source of drinking water. The park is open from 6:30 am to 5:30 pm and costs NT $80 to enter. Inside you'll find Chengxing Pagoda (中興塔) that towers forty-three meters above tourists' flashing cameras and Cheng Ching Lake Ocean World (海洋奇珍園), a bomb shelter-turned-sea aquarium. Open 8:30 am to 5 pm weekdays and 8 to 5:30 weekends. Admission is NT $100/$70. City buses 60 and 70 run to Ocean World. Dapai Road, #32 (高雄縣烏松鄉大埤路32號) (07) 735-6166.

For business travellers, visit **Kaohsiung Business Exhibition Center** (高雄工商展覽中心), Zhongzheng 4th Road, #274 (高雄市鹽埕區中正四路274號) (07) 531-5555.

Founded in 1967, **Light of Buddah Mountain** (佛光山 *Foguangshan*), or Foguangshan Temple, attracts both curious tourists and devoted Buddhists the world over. Visible from several miles away, the golden Great Buddah statue towers thirty-six meters above four hundred and eighty smaller statues in Great Buddah Land. Inside are shrines, an art gallery, meditation, chanting and calligraphy halls, as well as a memorial park and museum. Children seem to enjoy the Walt Disney-meets-the-Buddah-type exhibits inside Pure Land Cave. The temple was closed to the public in May, 1997 but after a plea from President Chen and Kaohsiung officials reopened six days a week starting in 2001. Closed Mondays. Foguangshan Temple, Dashu Village, Kaohsiung County (高雄縣大樹鄉佛光山寺) (07) 656-1921 http://www.fgs.org.tw.

Chichin Island (旗津島), a nearby island with narrow roads and steep hiking paths, makes a fun adventure for daytrippers. On Chichin Island discover scenic Kaohsiung views, a historic lighthouse (旗津燈塔 *Chichin Dengta*) built by the British in 1883, (天后宮 *Tien Ho Gong*), a Matsu temple built in 1673, touristy but fun three-wheeled pedicab taxis and seafood vendors galore. Take city buses 1, 30 or 50 to the Chichin

ferry crossing, the island can be walked in a few hours.

Hikers enjoy **Longevity Mountain** (壽山自然公園), also known as "Shoushan Scenic Spot," a natural landmark that reaches nearly 360 meters at its peak in the southwest of the city. The service area, open 8 am to 5 pm, is on Wanshou Road, #350, Gushan District (高雄市鼓山區萬壽路350號) (07) 533-7095. Beware of wild monkeys in steeper areas, but say hello to the animals at **Shoushan Zoo** (壽山動物園) (NT $40/$20), open 9 am to 5 pm, gates close at 4:30 pm, closed Mondays and holidays http://www.kcg.gov.tw/~shoushan. **Yuenheng Temple** (元亨寺), originally built in 1697, is near the base of the mountain and can be reached by taking Kaohsiung city buses 19 or 43. Open 4 am to 9 pm. (高市鼓山區元亨街7號) (07) 521-3236. http://www.yhm.org.tw.

Kaohsiung's twelve-kilometer **Love River** (愛河), which looks similar to the Chicago River in certain areas, flows north to south to Kaohsiung Harbor. A journalist mispenned the original "Dakou River" name in June, 1949 and the more amorous-sounding name stuck. The government often sponsors events in West Riverfront Park (西河濱公園), a scenic walkway and popular snapshot spot for soon-to-be newlyweds. Large crowds gather here during Love River Lantern Festival (愛河夜光藝術節).

Seashore Park (海岸公園) boasts unique statues, an outdoor pavilion, and plenty of space to roam or spark a romance. Seashore Park is near the harbor so container ships are in view. Chichin 2nd Road, #1100 (高雄市旗津區旗津二路1100號) (07) 517-1500.

Opened in 1981, **Kaohsiung Culture Center** (高雄市立中正文化中心), Wufu 1st Road, #67 (高雄市五福一路67號) (07) 222-5136, often holds arts exhibitions and performances. The park's main entrance square has ample space for kite flying. On the Culture Center grounds you'll find people talking, relaxing, and enjoying the outdoors.

The Kaohsiung Museum of Fine Arts (高雄市立美術館), Meishukuan Road, #80 (高雄市鼓山區美術館路80號) (07) 555-0331 boasts local and international artist exhibits. Relax at the picnic area or by the picturesque pond. Open 9 am to 5pm, closed Mondays.

The Kaohsiung History Museum (高雄市立歷史博物館), Zhongzheng 4st Road, #272 (高雄市鹽埕區中正四路272號) (07) 533-0840, is open from 9 am to 5 pm, closed Mondays.

Discover local treasures and ancient artifacts at the **National Science & Technology Museum** (國立科學工藝博物), Chiuju 1st Road, #720 (07) 384-6471.

Kaohsiung has over 200,000 people of Hakka descent, learn more about Hakka history and culture at Taiwan's largest Hakka museum, **Kaohsiung Hakka Culture Museum** (高雄市客家文物館), inside Sanmin Park No.2 (三民二號公園) (07) 315-2136. The museum is reachable by Kaohsiung city buses 24, 92, or 301.

Baseball enthusiasts may want to check out Taiwan's largest baseball stadium built in Kaohsiung in 1999, home to the island's only **Baseball Museum** (棒球博物館), Dabi Road, #113 Niausung Shiang, Kaohsiung County (高雄縣鳥松鄉鳥松村大埤路113號) (07) 733-8602. The stadium and museum, reachable by city buses 70, 79, and 102, are outside the city so a visit may not be convenient if you are not a die-hard fan of the Chinese Professional Baseball League (CPBL).

Of course there's always **Kaohsiung Warner Village Cinemas** (高雄華納威秀) to catch the latest Hollywood or Asian action flick, it's in Kaohsiung's Lingya District on Sanduo 4th Road, #21, 13th Floor (高雄市苓雅區三多四路21號13樓, 大遠百購物中心) (07) 334-5566. An Eslite Bookstore (誠品書店, 遠百店) is on the 17th floor (07) 331-3102.

The two most common methods of reaching Kaohsiung from Taipei are plane or High-Speed Rail (HSR). By plane the trip from Taipei takes a little over an hour and a one-way economy ticket costs approximately NT $1500.

Kaohsiung International Airport (高雄國際航空站)
Chunshang 4th Road, #2, Kaohsiung (高雄市中山四路二號)
Domestic information counter: (07) 805-7630 (toll-free) 0800-090-108
Open from 6:30 am to 10 pm.
International information center: (07) 805-7631 (toll-free) 0800-090-108
Open from 5:30 am to 9:30 pm.

High Speed Rail (HSR) Zuoying Station (台灣高鐵, 左營站)
Kaotie Road, #105, Zuoying District, Kaoshiung City (高雄市左營區高鐵路105號) (02) 4066-5678. A one-way economy (standard) ticket from Taipei will set you back NT $1490 and the ride takes approximately two hours.

Kaohsiung Hotels

Ambassador Hotel (高雄國賓) There are 453 spacious rooms at this luxury hotel, with daily rates starting at NT $4,500. Minsheng 2nd Road, #202 (高雄市前金區民生二路202號) (07) 211-5211. http://www.ambassadorhotel.com.tw.

Evergreen Hotel (松柏大飯店) Room rates at this mid-range hotel range from NT $1480 to $3,200. Heping 1st Road, #219 (高雄市新興區和平一路219號) (07) 223-2251.

Holiday Garden (華園大飯店) This upscale hotel boasts 272 rooms, daily rates run from NT $3,800 to NT $4800. Liuhe 2nd Road, #279 (高雄市前金區六合二路279號) (07) 241-0123.

Kaohsiung Chinatrust Hotel (高雄中信大飯店) The Chinatrust Hotel chain tends to offer comfortable rooms in reasonably convenient locations, this hotel boasts 151 rooms with daily rates starting at NT $3,400. Daren Road, #43 (高雄市大仁路43號) (07) 521-7111.

The Grand Hotel (Kaohsiung) (圓山大飯店) Located just outside the city about thirty minutes from Kaohsiung International Airport, daily rates run from NT $2,400 to NT $4,400. Some rooms offer a picturesque view of Chengching Lake. Yuanshan Road, #2, Niaosong Township, Kaohsiung County (高雄縣鳥松鄉圓山路2號) (07) 383-5911.

KAYAKING (小艇)

Taipei boasts its own Adventure Kayak Club, Peixin Road, Section 1, #23, Xindian City (新店市北新路1段23號) (02) 2913-9752. Members have their own kayaks and equipment, but if you ask politely, they may lend you a boat and some gear. Members choose between river or sea outings, but most of the time the club navigates the azure Nanshih River in Wulai.

KEELUNG (基隆)

Population: 392,337

Once known as "Chicken Coop," (雞籠 *ji lung*), these Chinese characters were later changed to the same-sounding but far more fortuitous "land of wealth and prosperity" (基隆 *ji lung*). When you smell fresh fish, or if you see any jumping around outside the train window, you'll know you've arrived. New Yorkers who visit the area remark that Keelung has a feel much like Flushing in Queens, New York. The main section of the city is near Keelung Harbor while mountains surround the rest of the city. Clothing stores regularly offer discounts to attract shoppers. The town has a few Western fast food restaurants, comfortable cafés and ample traditional medicine, herb and teashops. Unfortunately, the harbor appears as if huge containers of coffee were hurled into the water, grinds and all. You may be able to find some interesting specimens floating around (or gasping for air) if you stare long enough.

Jiufen, a quaint mountain town, is a main attraction just outside the city. For more information please see "Jiufen (九份 *Chiu Fen*)."

Visitors would also be remiss not to visit **Miaoko** (基隆廟口), just outside Chingan Temple (慶安宮), about a fifteen-minute walk from the train station. Here you'll find everything from seafood delights like octopus tentacles and roasted squid to noodle vendors galore. The area is mostly empty during the day but becomes crowded after 5 pm, especially during weekends and holidays. The temple itself is also impressive.

In addition to boasting the largest natural port in the north, the second-largest harbor on Taiwan and a bustling night market that encompasses several city blocks, Keelung is also known for its unique parks. **Zhengzheng Park** (基隆中正公園), on the mountain just east of Keelung Harbor (基隆港東側山丘上) (02) 2420-1122, is where you'll find a statue of Guanyin, the goddess of mercy, towering nearly twenty-three meters above nearby food and trinket vendors. The park is open from 9 am to 5 pm. Remnants of gun emplacements that were built over a century ago also make for interesting excursions. **Seagate Fortress** (海門天險 *Haimen Tienxien*), literally "dangerous ocean gate," known locally as **Ershawan** (二沙灣砲台), was built in 1840 but the French nearly destroyed it during the Sino-French War in 1884. A few walls and cannons remain. Seagate Fortress is atop Ershawan Mountain, close to the eastern side of Keeung Harbor and reachable by Keelung city buses 101 or 103.

The British constructed **Shichiuling Paotai** (獅球嶺砲台), the highest gun emplacement in Keelung in 1884, but unfortunately the Japanese seem to have parted with the original cannons during their fifty-year occupation. Take Keelung city buses 201, 202, 205 or 501 to Ren 5st Road (仁五路), walk along Cheng 1st Road (成一路) and Shichiou Road (獅球路), the gun emplacement is about thirty minutes by foot.

Fairy Cave (仙洞巖 *Shandongyan*) got its unique name not because it was dedicated to a Disney princess but because many people converted to Buddhism here. Be mindful of people praying inside this narrow, dim cave, where Buddhist statues and interesting art line the walls. Keeung city bus 301 runs to the cave.

Keelung Ghost Festival (基隆中元祭), which takes place during ghost month (August), is also a major attraction. A parade several kilometers long runs from Zhongzheng Park to Chaolin Coastal Park (潮境公園), where floats stacked with lanterns are lit on fire and set out to sea to please the gods and appease ghosts. This ritual also seems to please tourists who turn out in droves to witness the event.

You can reach Keelung most easily by boarding a train at Taipei Main Station. From Taipei, the city is approximately fifty minutes by bus or train. Buses also head to Keelung from Danshui Station around 7 am and depart approximately every forty minutes thereafter. The sign in front of the buses say "Keelung → Jinshan → Danshuei" and signs on the back say "Taipei → Chiufen → Chinkuashih." These buses don't stop at Jiufen, you would need to transfer across the street from Keelung Train Station. From Danshui the fare is NT $150 for the hour ride.

The toll-free number for Keelung Bus Company (基隆汽車客運) is 0800-588-010. Keelung Tourist Information Center in on Gangsi (Gang Shee) Street, #1 (基隆市旅遊服務中心服務, 台港西街1號) (02) 2428-7664.

Two things you should know...

Taiwanese tend to be fervent about politics...

and Taiwanese youth clamor for the latest and greatest in overseas fashion fads.

KENTING NATIONAL PARK (墾丁國家公園)

Kenting National Park (墾丁國家公園), in sunny southern Pingtung, is one of the most popular tourist destinations outside of Taipei. Locals and expats often go for a pizza and cold brew at one of the pizza shops or pubs on Kenting Road and unwind on Kenting's pristine beaches.

Kenting is a major attraction that boasts green parks (Sheding Park, Longpan Park and the national park), Longluan Pond, Hengchun Farm, the Cyongma Historical Monument, white sandy beaches and Kenting Lighthouse. Spring Scream, an annual event that draws hordes of music and art enthusiasts, is a two-week extravaganza of live music and performances. Park headquarters are on Kenting Road, #596, Hengchun Town, Pingtung County (屏東縣恆春鎮墾丁路 596 號) (08) 886-1321. For more information visit http://www.OnTaiwan.com.

KTV
Your Own Private Karaoke Paradise

Taiwanese people are full of life, and they proudly express themselves through music, song and performance. One of their favorite pastimes is to get a group of friends together and visit KTV studios. Here, friends delight in singing the latest hits to videos playing on large screens while munching on local delicacies. Prices vary depending on when you visit, what you order and the quality of the KTV studio you frequent. Most studios typically charge between NT $100 to NT $200 per hour. After two or three hours of singing, large groups split the bill, so the cost works out to be quite reasonable.

Cash Box (錢櫃 *Chiangui*) and **Holiday** (好樂迪 *Haoledi*) are two large, reputable chains. Stay away from small karaoke bars in seedier areas, since prostitution is officially illegal these karaoke bars typically engage in other forms of entertainment. If a lady in a negligee invites you to join her "friends," don't frequent the establishment.

Cash Box (錢櫃 *Chiangui*)
Dunhua: Dunhua South Road, Section 1, #205, 2nd Floor (Zhongxiao East Road intersection) (台北市敦化南路1段205號2樓, 忠孝東路口) (02) 2731-6320
Zhongxiao I: Zhongxiao East Road, Section 4, #22 (Open 24 hours, across from Sogo Department Store) (台北市忠孝東路4段22號, SOGO百貨對面) (02) 2731-9090
Zhongxiao II: Zhongxiao East Road, Section 4, #160 (Open 24 hours, adjacent to Asia Pacific Hotel) (台北市忠孝東路4段160號, 亞太飯店旁) (02) 2771-5000.

Holiday (好樂迪 *Haoledi*)
Danshui: Zhongzheng Road, #650, Danshui (淡水鎮中正路250號) (02) 2626-6826
Shipai: Yumin 6th Road, #128, Shipai (Open 24 hours, near Shipai Station) (台北市北投區裕民六路128號, 近石牌捷運站,商城旁) (02) 2822-2168
Ximending: Xining South Road, #64 (Open 24 hours, Ximen Station Exit #6) (台北市西寧南路64號, 西門捷運站6號出口) (02) 2388-0768.

LANGUAGE STUDY (語言研究)

If you're serious about studying Mandarin there are a number of good options to choose from on Taiwan, many language programs here have a reputation for excellence. Here are two reputable learning institutions:

National Taiwan Normal University Mandarin Training Center (國立台灣師範大學國語中心) also known as "Teacher's College" (師大 *Shida*), is where many international students enroll to learn Chinese. You may want to arrange to audit a class or meet with admissions personnel prior to your arrival. Tuition runs NT $6000 (approximately US $180.00) per one-month term, or NT $18,000 (approximately US $540.00) per three-month semester. Some students supplement their income with English language tutoring jobs. Heping East Road, Section 1, #162, (台北市和平東路1段162號) (02) 2321-8457, 2391-4248 http://mtc.ntnu.edu.tw.

National Taiwan University (國立台灣大學) also known as "Taida" (台大), is the highest-ranked private university on Taiwan, and its **International Chinese Language Program (ICLP)** (台大國際華語研習所) has a reputation for rigor. Generally scholars and dedicated students of serious language study enroll here. Tuition costs US $3,500 per quarter. P.O. Box 13-204,Taipei, 106, Taiwan, R.O.C. (02) 2363-9123 http://ccms.ntu.edu.tw/~iclp/.

L AUNDROMATS
(洗衣店)

Many Taipei hotels offer laundry service. If you prefer to save money and visit a laundromat, you'll find 24-hour coin-operated laundromats conveniently located around town. Here are some locations for **Shia Peng Shee Yi Fang** (夏澎洗衣坊) laundromat:

Tienmu: Shipai Road, Section 2, #341 (台北市石牌路2段341號) (02) 2876-5253 (across from an OK convenience store).

Zhishan: Fuhua Road #155 (台北市士林區福華路155號) (02) 2821-1396 (near Zhishan Station, at the intersection of Lane 157 and Fuhua Road).
Beitou: Beitou Road, Section 2, #3 (台北市北投路2段3號) (near Beitou Station).
Danshui: Beixin Road, #19 (台北縣淡水鎮北新路19號) (centrally located and reachable by taking bus Red 23 (紅23).
Fuxing: Fuxing South Road, Section 2, Lane 148, #5 (台北市大安區復興南路2段148巷5號) (where Fuxing South Road meets Lane 148).
Minsheng: Sanmin Road, Lane 36, #6 (台北市三民路136巷6號) (02) 2876-5253 (near the intersection of Minsheng East Road and Sanmin Road. By bus the 505, 905 and 49 stop near the Sanmin Road laundromat).
Tienmu: Shipai Road, Section 2, #341 (台北市石牌路2段341號) (02) 2876-5253 (across from an OK convenience store).
Zhishan: Fuhua Road #155 (台北市士林區福華路155號) (02) 2821-1396 (near Zhishan Station, at the intersection of Lane 157 and Fuhua Road).

If you've headed to the far east for bargain prices on laundry services you may feel satisfied washing your wears at **Dong Dong Shee Yi Dian** (東東洗衣店), which can roughly be translated as the East East Laundry Shop (not to be confused with the West West Laundry Shop, probably in California). Dong Dong offers free detergent, dryer sheets, a wet wash and tumble dry as well as free clothes folding for the reasonable price of NT $100 per three (斤 *jin*) or less, or roughly US $3.00 for a load just under four pounds or less (1 jin is equal to 1.3228 pounds). Business travelers pay NT $170 to dry-clean a suit jacket, NT $80 for pants or NT $250 for a two-piece suit (top and bottom). Dong Dong is across the street from National Taiwan Normal University (Shida) on Longquan Street, #15 (台北市龍泉街15號) (02) 2363-5254.

In the same area, on Yongkang Street, **Yong Ji Gan Shee Shang Dian** (永吉乾洗商店) charges NT $200 for a load of four jin or less (soap is free) and NT $250 to dry-clean a two-piece suit. Yongkang Street, #50-1 (台北市永康街50-1號) (02) 2351-4057.

MARTYRS' SHRINES (忠烈祠)

Shrines are worshipping grounds that honor the war dead, they typically consist of a main hall that lists the names of fallen heroes and may hold memorial services. Built in 1969, **Martyrs' Shrine** (忠烈祠 *Zhong Lieh Tse*) resembles a Ming dynasty traditional castle and is easily spotted by its bright yellow and white façade. Taiwanese come here to pray for the 330,000 soldiers that died in wars with Japan and Mainland China after the fall of the Ch'ing dynasty, and historical pictures are on display. Stoic armed soldiers guard the shrine and there is a changing of the guard ceremony every hour on the hour until 4:40 pm. Open 9 am to 5pm, Martyrs' Shrine is located near The Grand Hotel in Shilin, Taipei on Bei An Road, #139 (台北市中山區北安路139號) (02) 2591-4162.

Aside from the impressive classic Chinese architechture found at the entrance, **Danshui Martyrs' Shrine** (淡水忠烈祠) seems more like a pristine park than a somber shrine and makes for a pleasant stroll. The upscale Om My Coffee Shop (不是咖啡館), Zhongzheng Road, Section 1, Lane 6, #31-1 (台北縣淡水鎮中正路1段6巷31-1號) (02) 2621-0306, boasts fine drinks and an outdoor lounge. This coffee shop/lounge bar (the Chinese name is "Is Not A Coffee Shop") is steps away from Huwei Fortress and the shrine. NT $250 "teatime" drink and cake specials start at 2 pm. The 836 "Danshui Historic Sites" bus runs from Danshui Station to the shrine.

MEDITATION (沉思)

In Taipei's placid Beitou district, **Nung Ch'an Monastery** (法鼓山農禪寺) holds free workshops in English every Sunday morning from 8:00 to 11:30 am. A discussion is held afterwards to enlighten curious attendees. Dayeh Road, Lane 65, #89, Beitou (台北市北投區大業路65巷89號) (02) 2893-3161 Ext. 608 http://www.ncm.org.tw.

Free meditation classes are offered Friday nights from 7:30 to 9:00 pm at **Taiwan Zen Buddhist Foundation**, Taan Zen Center, Xinyi Road, Section 3, #41-2 (across from Ta An Forest Park). (台北市信義路3段41-2號) (02) 2394-3225 Ext. 301.

MIAOLI (苗栗)

(Area Code: 037)
Population: 560,903

Centrally located just south of Hsinchu and north of Taichung on Taiwan's western coast, Miaoli is home to many people of Hakka descent, as reflected in the area's unique blend of arts and culture.

Major Attractions

Miaoli City Art & Culture Center (苗栗市藝文中心), Fuchian Road, #76 (苗栗市建功里府前路76號) (037) 331910, is a large ampitheater where both local troupes and international artists perform. Check to see if any interesting acts will be in town.

Those interested in the history, art and culture of making silk may want to pay a visit to **Taiwan Silk Industry Culture Center** (蠶業文化館), Gonguan, Guan Nan Village, #261 (苗栗縣公館鄉館南村261號) (037) 222-111. Open 9 am until 11:30 am and again from 1 to 4 pm. Admission is free but call in advance for an appointment.

Sanyi (三義鄉), a Miaoli town with a large Hakka population, is where you'll find a plethora of relics that can be seen in a few hours. The town is known for its woodcarving arts, and art enthusiasts may wish to partake in **Sanyi Woodcarving Festival** (三義木雕節), an annual event that draws thousands to this sleepy seaside town during October. Woodcarving artists display their wares in front of **Sanyi Train Station** (三義車站) (037) 872-018 and **Sanyi Old Mountain Line Shi-Liu-Fen Museum of Culture and History** (三義舊山線十六份文化館) in Sanyi's Fensing Village, #89 (三義鄉勝興村十四鄰勝興89號) (037) 870-435. The museum is open from 9 am to 5 pm, admission is NT $70.

Tunnel No.2 (二號隧道), constructed by the Japanese in 1905, is near the historic **Shengsing Train Station** (勝興車站). A popular Sanyi hiking destination is **Guandao Mountain** (關刀山), which is shaped like a Chinese saber and towers eight hundred and eighty-nine meters above sea level. The mountain, which divides Sanyi and Dahu, is where over two hundred and thirty plant species and unique bird species dwell in the lower areas of the mountain. **Longteng Bridge Remains** (龍騰斷橋), another tourist hot spot, was originally constructed nearly a century ago. The thirty-three meter bridge, once the highest on Taiwan, was severely damaged in the earthquake of 1935 and again in the September 21 earthquake of 1999. **Long Teng Waterfall** (龍騰瀑布) is a popular bathing spot for young people during the hot summer months; although not grand, the waterfall does invite tranquility.

West Lake Resort (西湖渡假村) in Sanyi's Sihu Village boasts a natural lake with a surrounding wooden walkway that covers ten hectacres just beside the resort. **Green Tunnel** (綠色隧道), which is not a real tunnel but a car lane carved through thick trees, starts at Miao Road #51 (苗51) and passes Provincial #13 Jianfeng Highway (陸橋銜接台十三線). Heading south it connects with Miao Road #52 (苗52). An immense bamboo forest is located on either side of the road.

Huoyan ("Dancing Fire") Mountain (火炎山) borders the towns of Sanyi and Yuanli, it towers over six-hundred meters above sea level and is said to resemble dancing fire at sunset. Since the land on this dense mountain cannot be cultivated, many indiginous plant species thrive here, including Chinese Red Pine and Oldham azalea. By foot, **Huoyan Mountain Eco-Museum** (火炎山生態博物館) is about a twenty-minute hike from **The Museum of Wood Sculpture** (木雕博物館).

Shendiao Village (神雕村), established specifically for woodcarvers to open studios and sell their wares, was a temporary home for internationally acclaimed Taiwanese superartist Ju Ming. In Shendiao Village, artists proudly display their creative passion.

The Museum of Wood Sculpture (木雕博物館), just north of Shendiao Village, is the only public museum on Taiwan that specializes in wood sculpture, and as such has become a center for the study and display of the craft. Just behind the museum is **Guangsheng April Snow Walkway (Tzuchi Walkway)** (廣盛四月雪小徑, 慈濟步道), which offers tranquility with its vast tea garden and Tung Oil trees.

Shuangtan Tourism Area (雙潭觀光園區) becomes foggy between March and May, thus it's referred to locally as "fog town." In Shuangtan Tourism Area purchase fresh fruits and vegetables produced locally at **Sanyi Fruit Farm** (三義鄉觀光農園).

Those interested in ceramic works may want to stop by **Miaoli Ceramics Museum** (苗栗陶瓷博物館), Gongguan, Funan Section, #212 & 213 (苗栗縣公館鄉福南段212, 213號) (37) 352-961. To learn more about the art of face painting on Taiwan, **Face Painting Culture Museum** (臉譜文化生活館) is nestled in Sanyi's Shuangliantan, #138 (苗栗縣三義鄉雙連潭138號). To learn more about Hakka people and culture stop by **Shangrila Hakka Museum** (香格里拉客家文物館), just a hop, skip and twenty-five minute bus ride from the Miaoli Train Station to Fenghu Village, Zaochiao Township, Rugushan, #15-3 (苗栗縣造橋鄉豐湖村1鄰乳姑山15-3號) (37) 561-369. The museum is located within the touristy but fun **Hakka Culture Village** (客家文化村) in Shangrila Paradise (香格里拉樂園), a resort and waterpark that boasts souvenier and coffee shops. Feel free to wear swim gear and slide down the steep red and yellow waterslides. Car enthusiasts may also wish to visit **Shangrila Auto Museum** (香格里拉古董車博物館), also inside Shangrila Paradise. http://www.shangrila.com.tw/.

Miaoli Hotels

West Lake Resort Hotel (西湖渡假大飯店) If you're looking for peace and tranquility outside the city, try West Lake Resort Hotel. Along with fine Eastern dining, standard rooms with twin beds come with refrigerators, mineral water and bathing amenities and start at NT $4000/night. A Winnie The Poo®-like theme park with hiking trails, a treehouse and large model dinosaurs is adjacent to the resort. Xihu, #11, Xihu Village (苗栗縣三義鄉西湖村西湖11號) (037) 876-699.

Suntong Hotel (三統大飯店) In Miaoli City, Suntong Hotel boasts sixty-four clean rooms on its nine floors. Rooms start at NT $1200/night for two people. Zhongzheng Road, #617 (苗栗市中正路617號1-9樓) (037) 325-959.

Miaoli Hotel (苗粟大飯店) Also in the city, Miaoli Hotel is like a clean motor lodge and charges approximately NT $1000 per night. Zhigong Road, #3 (苗栗縣苗栗市至公路3號) (037) 321-600.

From Taipei it takes about two and a half hours to reach Miaoli by bus or train. While the mountains of Miaoli offer picturesque views of the sea and towns below, passengers with weak stomachs may become ill due to the winding mountain roads and sometimes hasty nature of local drivers. For this reason, taking the train may be the safer choice.

For more information contact Miaoli County Tourism Association at (037) 363-108.

Monosodium Glutamate (MSG) (味精)

Much to the chagrin of some Western tourists, Taiwanese commonly add monosodium glutamate (MSG), a chemical used to enhance flavor, during the preparation of food. While Chinese restaurants in the West proudly display "We use NO MSG" to lure customers, here in the East, large containers of MSG make popular holiday gift items. Many ready-made foods, such as instant noodles, contain the chemical. While some feel no adverse reactions, other may develop headaches or experience hyperactivity or nausea. If you're allergic to the chemical, or would rather consume food without it, request that no MSG be added to your food. In Mandarin, MSG is (味精 *wei jing*). You shouldn't encounter a problem if you politely request, "I don't want MSG" (請不要加味精 *ching bu yao jia wei jing*) to the waiter or waitress. Another alternative would be to visit a hot pot restaurant and cook meat and vegetables in a boiling pot of water in front of you without adding the flavor enhancer.

MTV (No, Not The Music Video Channel)

If you spot an "MTV" sign in Taipei, it's probably not an ad for the music channel. On Taiwan, MTV studios are private rooms where friends delight in consuming local snacks while watching the latest blockbuster hits on a large screen TV. With the success of Blockbuster Video and a string of similar local movie rental chains, as well as the advent of DVD players, MTV studios are likely to become a cultural relic of Taiwan's past.

NAME BRANDS (名牌)

If you want to look like you just raided Madonna's closet, you'll find name brands at Taipei 101 and at many of Taipei's upscale department stores. Feel fabulous in Giorgio Armani, Gucci, Louis Vuitton, Moschino, and Polo Ralph Lauren:

Giorgio Armani

Renai Road, Section 4, #117 (台北市仁愛路4段117號) (02) 2777-3126. Giorgio Armani is also located in the Sunrise Department Store (台北中興百), Fuxing North Road #15 (台北市復興北路15號) (02) 2731-2001 Ext. 369 (Floor 2) for women's clothing, Ext. 385 (Floor 4) for men's.

Gucci

Dunhua South Road, Section 1, #246 (台北市敦化南路1段246號) (02) 2711-2043, 2711-5267. The main Gucci branch is on Zhongshan North Road, Section 2, #49-3, at the intersection of Zhongshan North Road and Changcheng Road, next to a Louis Vuitton clothing store. (台北市中山北路2段49-3號) (02) 2564-3234.

Louis Vuitton

is on the third floor of Taipei 101, on Zhongshan North Road, Section 2, #57-1 (台北市中山北路2段57-1號) (02) 2523-0753 in the trendy "Dinghao" area in section C of Mall 97 on Fuxing North Road, #97 (台北市復興北路97號1樓C座) (02) 2718-6128 and on Dunhua South Road, Section 1, #364 (台北市敦化南路1段364號) (02) 2705-1868.

If you're hungry for a fashionable bite of **Moschino** stop by the Pacific Sogo Department Store on Dunhua South Road or the Shin Kong Mitsukoshi department store in the Xinyi business district.

You'll find **Polo Ralph Lauren** at malls, including Taipei 101, ATT, Core Pacific City Mall, Far Eastern Department Store, Pacific Sogo, Breeze Center, and on Renai Road, Section 4, #115 (台北市仁愛路4段115號) (02) 2721-0114.

NANTOU (南投)
Population: 548,413

Centrally-located Nantou is adjacent to Hualien in the east, south of Taichung, west of Changhua and Yunlin, and north of Chiayi and Kaohsiung. With its mountainous terrain and abundant natural beauty, Nantou is referred to as the "Switzerland of Taiwan." Not merely a marketing ploy, Nantou offers cultural attractions and natural beauty, including the quaint town of Puli and the Sun Moon Lake area, popular for brief respites. Here you'll find aboriginal crafts, performances and a scenic lake getaway for honeymooning couples. Main industries include agriculture and fishing. During the fall there are hot springs festivals as well as a bamboo arts carnival and a pottery arts festival in November.

Nantou County Main Attractions

A famous Nantou County tourist attraction is **Sun Moon Lake** (日月潭), where hiking, biking and exploring the natural terrain are abundant. For camping information contact Sun Moon Lake Youth Activities Center (日月潭青年活動中心), Sun Moon Village, Zhongzheng Road, #101 (南投縣魚池鄉日月村中正路101號) (49) 285-0070. The dwindling aboriginal Thao tribe that live in Sun Moon Village ("Barawbaw" in the Thao language) place soil and grass on bamboo shafts and grow crops on the river. In August visitors bear witness to the Thao harvest ceremony. Sample Thao foods and purchase handmade Thao products at local village shops. http://www.sunmoonlake.gov.tw.

Sun Moon Lake Hotel (日月潭飯店) (台灣省南投縣日月潭名勝街11號) Daily room rates start at NT $1500. The hotel also offers packages for the touristy but fun "Culture Village" and sells tickets to use the hotel's spa facilities. (49) 285-5143 http://www.sunmoonhotel.com.tw.

The Lalu (涵碧樓大飯店) (南投縣魚池鄉水社村中興路142號) is where the wealthy go to play. Once a vacation respite for Chiang Kai-shek, The Lalu boasts the longest (60 meters) heated swimming pool on Taiwan, recreation facilities that include an aerobics room, tennis courts, a spa, steam room and sauna, meeting rooms, and for those that wish to read up on the former president or Sun Moon Lake, an impressive library. Bike rentals are also available to ride thirty-seven kilometers around the lake. During the winter, from Sunday through Thursday, a lakeside one-bedroom suite will set you back your typical gas allowance back home for a month, or NT $12,900 (US $387.00), and a Friday or Saturday night stay costs about one month's rent in Taipei, or NT $15,500 (US $465.00). Fine Eastern (Chinese and Japanese) and Western dining is available, and a complimentary breakfast is included. Zhongxing Road, #142 (49) 285-6888 http://www.thelalu.com.tw.

The quaint Nantou town of **Puli** (南投縣埔里鎮) boasts impressive Buddhist temples, an insect museum and **Puli Winery** (埔里酒廠酒文化館), Zhongshan Road, Section 3 #219 (南投縣埔里鎮中山路3段219號) (49) 290-1649. Puli Winery houses a factory, Wine Culture Museum and Puli Culture Museum. Visitors can visit the new exhibition hall to learn how local Shaohsing wine is produced. http://www.plwinery.com.tw.

Nantou and Puli became famous not only on Taiwan but also around the world when a disasterous 7.3 earthquake struck on September 21, 1999, killing thousands and destroying tens of thousands of buildings and homes. Some of these structures have not been rebuilt and there are areas where tourists can bear witness to the earthquake's destructive aftermath. Thankfully most of the region has now recovered.

NATIVE FOODS
(台灣食物)

Try Taiwan's delicious local ice dessert treat (刨冰 *bao bing*). After selecting three or four items, such as red or green beans, pineapple or wheat puffs, ice (冰 *bing*) is shredded and topped with strawberry, vanilla, chocolate or mango syrup. Bing is an especially popular snack during the spring and summer. Tea (*chicken*) eggs (茶葉蛋 *chayedan*) are found at night markets and 24-hour convenience stores, as are fried dumplings (煎餃 *chianjiao*, 鍋貼 *guotie*), shrimp dumplings (蝦餃 *shiajiao*) and fried leek dumplings (韭菜盒 *jiutsai ho*). Steamed, stuffed buns (包子 *baozi*) typically filled with pork, and steamed buns (饅頭 *mantou*) are sometimes consumed for breakfast. Stinky tofu (臭豆腐 *chou dofu*) is just as the name implies—stinky. It's also one of the more popular local snacks at night markets and touristy areas. Your nose can't miss it.

Plum drink (酸梅湯 *swanmeitang*) and the sweet yellow "jade" jelly drink (愛玉 *ai yu*) are found at most night markets. You may also find tofu pudding (豆花 *dou hua*), sweet sugar cane juice (甘蔗汁 *gan zeh zhi*), oyster omlets (蚵仔煎 *ou ah chien*), sweet gluttinous sesame balls (芝麻球 *zhi ma chiu*), and a slightly sweet black gooey substance made from grass that is usually cooked (燒仙草 *hsiao hsien tsao*). Doesn't sound appetizing? Try it!

Traditional breakfasts may include different kinds of congee (粥 *zhou*), such as sweet potato congee (地瓜粥 *digua zhou*) and seafood congee (海鮮粥 *haihsien zhou*), as well as the deep-fried bread stick (油條 *yo tiao*), onion pancakes (葱油餅 *tsongyobing*) and oven rolls (燒餅 *xiaobing*). Egg and vegetable soup (蛋花湯 *danhuatang*) is sometimes served with lunch or dinner.

Delicious homemade "shaved" noodles (刀削麵 *daoxiaomian*) are cut with a knife and cooked as you order them. For something sweet and natural, soybean milk (豆漿 *dou jiang*) makes for a popular breakfast drink. In Taipei County, Yongho (永和) is famous for its delicious soybean milk.

Exotic tropical fruits are abundant on Taiwan, stop by any day or night market or supermarket, such as Wellcome, to take a gander. While on Taiwan experience durian (榴槤 *liulian*), the evil green stinking cousin of the delicious pineapple. Other delectable edibles include ripe coconuts (椰子 *yehzi*), star fruit (楊桃 *yangtao*), which is said to help cure sore throats, Chinese pears (李子 *lizi*), which are round, sweet, yellow and unavailable in the West, fresh green and white guava (芭樂 *bale*), purple lichees (荔枝 *leezhi*), which come in delicious juice boxes at most 24-hour convenience stores, and fresh pineapples, oranges, tangerines, and bananas. Juice boxes are available at supermarkets and at 24-hour convenience stores, sample some of the outstanding juices that are available here. The lichees (荔枝) and green pumpkin (南瓜 *nangua*) drinks are particularly good.

You'll find plenty of green bean (綠豆 *lu dou*) and red bean (紅豆 *hongdou*) delicacies on Taiwan, typically served as a sweet soup for dessert or as sweet paste cake (豆糕 *dougan*). Sweet gluttonous rice balls (麻薯 *mwaji*) may be topped with peanut or sesame seed shavings. Mwaji typically costs NT $ 10 each or NT $100 for a box of ten.

Many road-side vendors sell steamed pork dumplings (小籠包 *xiaolongbao*), a popular local snack, and both young and old delight in tasting strawberries or cherry tomatoes (糖葫蘆 *tanghulu*) covered with a red candy coating. Sweet gluttonous pink or white rice balls (湯圓 *tangyuan*) are especially popular during Chinese holidays as they symbolize family togetherness. The dark purple taro root (芋頭 *yutou*) is a locally-grown vegetable found in many kinds of foods such as congee, hot pot dishes and soups, and even birthday and wedding cakes.

Fish meat rolled into balls (魚丸 *yuwan*), as well as roasted squid (烤墨魚 *kaoyoyu*) are found at most night markets. Another popular Taiwanese snack typically found in night markets and touristy areas is pig or chicken blood mixed with rice (豬血糕 *zhuxuegao*). The Taiwanese pronunciation is "di hway gway." Last but certainly not eaten least, glutinous rice dumplings wrapped in bamboo leaves (粽子 *zhongzi*) are typically consumed during the Dragon Boat Festival (端午節 *Duanwujie*).

When it comes to tantalizing tropical fruits and vegetable variety, Taiwan truly is a land of plenty.

Put away that hook, bait and pole, you'll find all the fresh
fish you need at Taiwan's traditional markets.

Fresh cut scallion anyone? They come in sizes large,
larger or too large to fit on the back of the moped.

I'm in the mood for duck, simply because you're near
me...

Traditional native foods at a traditional Taiwan market.

The popular **stinky tofu** (臭豆腐 *chou dofu*) snack is conveniently found at night markets and tourist attractions. Your nose can't miss it.

Tang Hu Lu (糖葫蘆) are strawberries or cherry tomatoes covered with a red candy coating. Also sold here are fresh green apples and ripened guava (芭樂 *ba la*).

Danshui Historic Street (淡水老街 *Danshui Lao Jie*) boasts native foods such as "iron eggs" (鐵蛋 *tie dan*), chicken eggs that are cooked until they become small, black, hard and chewy.

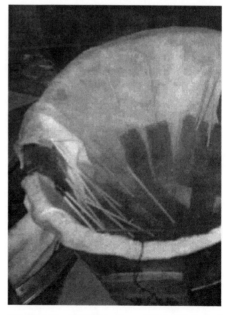

Zhu Shue Gao (豬血糕) is pig or chicken blood mixed with rice. Add hot spice or peanut shavings free of charge!

NATURAL & ORGANIC MARKETS (有機市場)

As Taiwanese become increasingly aware of issues that affect health and well-being, chemical-free foods, vitamins and other assorted health products have been growing markedly in popularity. Here are a few choice options for natural and organic products:

Green Village (綠色小鎮 *Luseh Xiaozhen*) is a natural and organic market that offers fresh fruits, vegetables, drinks, soups and snacks. Some boast small coffee shops that sell chemical-free cakes and organic coffees and teas.
Beitou: Zhonghe Street, #289 (北投店: 台北市北投區中和街289號) (02) 2891-6136
Chingnian: Zhonghua Road, Section 2, #431 (青年店: 台北市萬華區中華路2段431號) (02) 2307-1768
Hechang: Hechang Street, #75 (合江店: 台北市中山區合江街75號) (02) 2512-2609
Jingmei: Jinghua Street, #81 (景美店: 台北市文山區景華街81號) (02) 2935-3148
Shida: Taishun Street, #24 (師大店: 台北市大安區泰順街24號) (02) 2364-4858
Taida: Roosevelt Road, Section 3, Lane 283, #38 (台大店: 北市大安區羅斯福路3段283巷38號) (02) 2369-6206
Tienmu: Dexing East Road, #172 (天母店: 台北市士林區德行東路172號) (02) 2838-5760
Xinyi: Xinyi Road, Section 2, #1-4 (信義店: 台北市中正區信義路2段1-4號)
(02) 2391-2917 http://www.green-v.com.

Here are three **Organic and Natural House** (有機園地 *Yoji Yuendi*) Taipei locations:
Shipai: Rongminsan Road, #15 (石牌店: 台北市北投區裕民三路15號) (02) 821-1380
Songshan: Xinyi District, Hulin Street, #83 (松山店: 台北市信義區虎林街83號)
(02) 8787-2429
Tienmu: Tienmu West Road, Lane 13, #4 (天母店: 台北市士林區天母西路13巷4號)
(02) 2876-6609.

NEWSPAPERS (新聞)

There are currently three English dailies on Taiwan that cover breaking local news as well as important international events. Expatriates residing on Taiwan find these publications useful for finding jobs, language lessons or to chuckle at the latest comics:

The China Post
http://www.chinapost.com.tw
Taiwan News
http://www.etaiwannews.com
Taipei Times
http://www.taipeitimes.com

A popular web site for Taiwan employment, travel, housing and merchandise information is **http://www.OnTaiwan.com**.

Here are some Taiwan news sources:

Apple Daily
http://www.appledaily.com.tw
The Central News Agency
http://www.cna.com.tw
Common Wealth
http://www.cw.com.tw
The China Times
http://news.chinatimes.com
Next Magazine
http://twnext.atnext.com
The Liberty Times
http://www.libertytimes.com.tw
United Daily News
http://udn.com.

PINGTUNG (屏東)

(Area Code: 08)
Population: 900,199

While loud and lascivious Las Vegas may be known around the globe as the original "Sin City," the far smaller, calmer and quieter Pingtung is referred to locally as "Sun City." Taiwan's southernmost city, Pingtung is being marketed by the local government as "Coconut City" since many of the coconut trees planted by local officials along Chong Cheng Road, the city's main road, tower over twelve meters high. Pingtung is home to various aboriginal tribes, such as the Holo, Hakka, Paiwan and Rukai, which coalesce harmoniously. The terrain of Pingtung is unique in that it has a pristine west coast shoreline much like California, a mountainous eastern terrain akin to Vermount and the Hengchun Peninsula in the south where the sprawling Kenting National Park graces the tip of the island. Taitung borders most of northeastern Pingtung while Kaohsiung County borders most of the northwest. Liuchiu Island (琉球嶼 *Liuchiu Yu*), also known as "Small Liuchiu" (小琉球 *Xiao Liuchiu*), is located off the western coast of Pingtung and has become a popular destination for daytrippers. Information about Liuchiu Island is listed under "Islands In The Strait (台灣本島)."

Major attractions

Mintzu Road (民族路), five minutes by foot from Pingtung Railway Station, is where you'll find **Mintzu Road Night Market** (民族路夜市). Give your tastebuds a workout with native night market fare that includes chicken and duck delicacies.

Construction started on **Tzufeng Temple (Pingtung Matsu Temple)** (屏東 內埔 六堆 天后宮) in 1803. In the town of Neipu at the intersection of Zhongshan Road and Yungfu Road, a boisterous celebration to honor Matsu is held every year on her birthday, the 23rd day of the third lunar month (which usually occurs in March). You'll find the temple on Guang Tsi Road, #164 (屏東縣內埔箱內田村廣濟路164號). **Chang Li Shrine** (昌黎祠) next door is is dedicated to Han Chang-li (韓昌黎), a former Chaozhou, China governor who established more than a handful of learning institutions during his reign. Local students pray here for outstanding test scores, and the walls of the shrine become filled with examination ID cards just before the annual high school entrance examination. It is said that the higher students can place their exam ID cards on the prayer walls the higher their test scores will be, would you get the top grade?

Pingtung Confucius Temple (屏東市孔廟) is the site of a colorful ceremony every September 28, the eternal teacher's birthday. Built in 1815, this small historic temple is located on Shenli Road, #38 (屏東市勝利路38號).

Liyushan (*Liyu Mountain*) (鯉魚山) is a mud volcano that borders the Pingtung County towns of Wandan (萬丹) and Xinyuan (新園). This bizarre volcanic mountain sometimes spurts mud into the air for approximately eight hours at a time. Visit a spa for a facial, however, rather than smear volcanic mud on your face.

Santimen Aboriginal Culture Region (三地門原民文化區) encompasses the three mountainous aboriginal towns of **Santimen** (三地門), **Wutai** (霧台) and **Machia** (瑪家). Here you'll find **Aboriginal Culture Park** (原住民文化園區), Peiyei Village, Majia, Fongjin #104, Pingtung County (屏東縣瑪家鄉北葉風景104號) (08) 799-1219. Guests are invited (grabbed by the hand!) to join the spirited song and dance performances. Are you ready to tie the knot? Males with bad backs beware, you may find yourself dancing in a circle carrying a teen aboriginal female around in a chair on your back! Soonafter you'll share a spot of wine and discover that this ritual was actually part of a traditional Paiwan tribal marriage ceremony. A similar touristy but fun aboriginal culture park exists in Hualien.

The hidden **Dajin Waterfall** (大津瀑布) is in the village of Weiliao (尾寮村) in Santimen (三地門鄉). The mountainous Santimen area also boasts the popular **Feijia Air Sports Park** (屏東縣三地門鄉賽嘉航空園區) where adventurous locals and expatriates are fond of paragliding (飛行傘 *fei hsing san*) and hang gliding (滑翔翼 *hua hsang yi*). The park is three hundred meters above sea level, which makes for an outstanding view where strong gusts of wind may blow your new La New Bears cap off your head. For more information contact the Santimen County Government (三地門鄉公所) at (08) 799-1104.

Although the city may be small, Pingtung County covers an area of more than 2,700 square kilometers and is big on cultural life, as aboriginal galleries and historic museums dot the city and county. **The Taiwan Paiwan Carving Gallery** (台灣排灣族雕刻館) is on the fourth floor of the Cultural Affairs Bureau of Pingtung County (屏東縣政府文化局). Discover fine works of art from Taiwan's Paiwan aboriginal tribe. The Gallery is open from 9 am to 6 pm, closed Mondays and national holidays. Admission is free and all are welcome. Dalian Road, #69, 4th Floor, Pingtung City (屏東市大連路69號, 4樓) (08) 736-0331.

The Northern Paiwan Art and Culture Museum (北排灣族文物藝術館) in Chingshan Village may provide a welcome respite for those interested in learning about aboriginal art, culture and life on Taiwan. Minzu Lane, #46, Chingshan Village, Sandimen, Pingtung County (屏東縣三地門鄉青山村民族巷46號) (08) 796-4626.

View fascinating Buddhist works of art at **Pingtung Fo Guang Yuan Art Gallery** (屏東佛光緣美術館), Jianhua 3rd Street, #46, 3rd Floor, Pingtung City (屏東市建華三街46號3樓) (08) 751-2608 http://www.fgs.org.tw/fgsart.

You may better understand local history at **Local Art Museum** (鄉土藝術館), two small halls surrounded by a yard built in 1895 during the Ch'ing dynasty. Discover wonderful woodcarving, said to be the oldest art form in Chinese history, as well as paintings, pottery, calligraphy, washed pebbles and traditionally modeled windows. Tianliao Lane, #25, Pingtung City (屏東縣屏東市田寮巷 26 號) (08) 723-1637 http://www.cultural.pthg.gov.tw/museum/lam/EN/history/h1.htm.

Anthropologists and historians alike will be delighted by **Pingtung County Museum of Natural History** (屏東縣自然史教育館), Kending Road, #65, Hengchun, Pingtung County (屏東縣恆春鎮墾丁路65號) (08) 886-2564. Open Wednesday through Sunday, 2 pm to 10 pm. Admission is free and all are welcome.

Both locals and expatriates alike flock to Pingtung's **Kenting National Park** (墾丁國家公園), particularly during the spring and summer, to unwind for the weekend. Park headquarters are located on Kenting Road, #596, Hengchun, Pingtung County (屏東縣恆春鎮墾丁路 596 號) (08) 886-1321 For more information visit: http://www.OnTaiwan.com.

For more information on Pingtung County attractions contact Pingtung County Government (屏東縣政府) at (08) 732-0415.

Pingtung Hotels

Tapeng Bay Holiday Hotel (屏東大鵬灣大飯店) The fifty-eight comfortable rooms at Tapeng Bay offer Internet access (bring your own laptop). The hotel has an upscale seafood restaurant and free breakfast is included from 7 to 9:30 am. The hotel also boasts scenic views and is not far from the fishing harbor and Liuchiu Island. Rooms start at NT $1400/night. Zhongshan Road #59, Donggang, Pingtung County (屏東縣東港鎮中山路59號) (08) 835-3222. http://www.tpb.com.tw.

Ever Spring ECO-Farm (恆春生態休閒農場) boasts an enormous outdoor swimming pool, comfortable coffee shop and outdoor pavilion that offer breathtaking views, a small petting ranch and pristine green environment. Although comfortable, rooms appear somewhat out of date, akin to Snow White's dream bedroom circa 1980. Bathrooms are large and the staff, although not bilingual, is very accommodating. Room rates start at NT $3000 a night. Shanjiao Road #28-5, Pingtung County (屏東縣恆春鎮山腳路28-5號) http://www.ecofarm.com.tw.

Dachou Garden Hotel (大洲花園渡假山莊) Approaching Dachou Garden Hotel may jog memories of placid Lake George, New York. The hotel boasts rooms that are both modern, yet not pretentious, and spacious. The barbeque restaurant is open from 6 to 10:30 pm (NT $300 per person, children under 120 cm eat free). Karaoke costs NT $2000 if you wish to sing your heart out and is open from 8 am to 10:30 pm. Single rooms (two people) start at NT $1960 weekdays, NT $2520 weekends, rooms with two beds that sleep four for the same price are also available. Zhongshan Road, Lane 32, #1, Neipu Village, Pingtung County (屏東縣內埔鄉水門村中山路32巷1號) (08) 799-2055.

RADIO
(收音機)

International Community Radio Taiwan (ICRT) is an English-language radio station known for providing accurate local and international news on Taiwan. While the station tends to play popular Western selections it has come under scrutiny as of late for adding Mandarin pop songs into the play list. In Taipei and Kaohsiung the station can be found on 100.7 FM and in Taichung on 100.1 FM. http://www.icrt.com.tw.

RAFTING
(泛舟)

If you plan to visit Taiwan for more than a weekend, many adventurous expats take the train from Taipei to Rueisuei (瑞穗) in Hualian for rafting (泛舟 fanzhou) along the untamed Siouguluan River. By bus take the Fuli or Yuli lines in Hualien and exit at Rueisuei. The Rafting Center is located off Provincial Highway #9 in Rueisui on County Road #193. A rafting excursion will set you back around NT $1000, which includes lunch and insurance.

Rafting trips along the 25-kilometer stretch of the lower-lying section of the Siouguluan River typically take three to four hours, the trip makes for some sensational sightseeing of clear azure waters, steep gorges and white boulders near Rainbow Bridge; patrons typically stop for about half an hour at the aboriginal village of Cimei for lunch. For more information, contact: **Nan Sun Rafting Company (南山)** Guolian 1st Road, #81, Hualien (花蓮市國聯一路81號) (03) 833-9275 or **Pacific Rafting (太平洋)** Zhongshan Road, Section 1, #12, Rueisuei, Hualien (花蓮縣瑞穗鄉中山路1段12號) (03) 887-2822.

TAICHUNG
(台中)
(Area Code: 04)
Population: 1,032,778
City bird: Egret

Once home to the Pingpu tribe, Taichung was heavily influenced by the invading

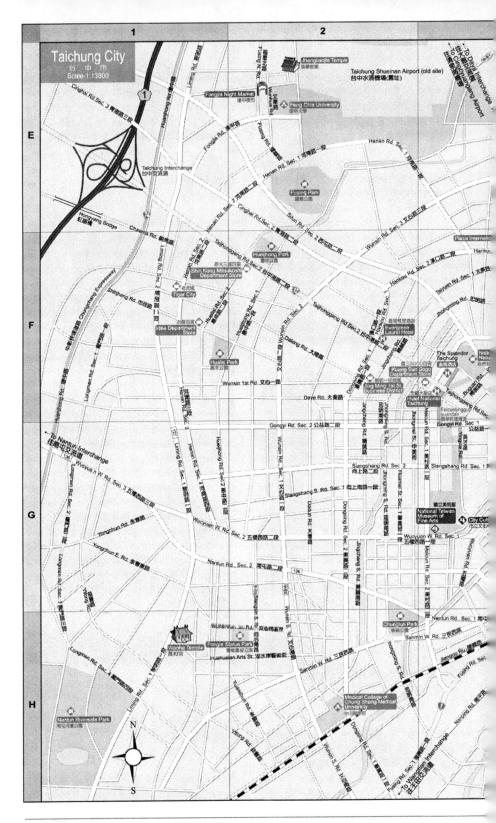

Taichung City
台中市
Scale 1:13500

1

Cinghai Rd. Sec. 3 青海路三段

Fonjia Rd. Sec. 2 逢甲路二段

Taichung Interchange 台中交流道

Hongyeng Bridge 紅陽橋

Chaoma Rd. 朝馬路

Shihgang Rd. 市政路

Liming Rd. Sec. 2 黎明路二段

Changcing Expressway 中彰快速道路

Henan Rd. Sec. 2 河南路二段 Cinghai Rd. Sec. 2 青海路二段

Taihonggang Rd. Sec. 2 台鴻港路二段

Shen Kong Mitsukoshi Department Store 新光三越百貨

Tiger City 老虎城

Idée Department Store 大遠百

Hyalai Park

Wunsin 1st Rd. 文心一路

Daye Rd. 大業路

Gongyi Rd. Sec. 2 公益路二段

To Nantun Interchange 往南屯交流道

Nantun Interchange

Wuyue n W. Rd. Sec. 3 五權西路三段

Yongchun Rd. 永春路

Yongchun E. Rd. 永春東路

Wucyuan W. Rd. Sec. 2 五權西路二段

Nantun Rd., Sec. 2 南屯路二段

Wunsinsi Jih Rd. 文心南路

Wanhe Temple 萬和宮

Fongle Statue Park 樂成雕塑公園

Hushuelan Arts St. 湖水岸藝術街

Nantun Riverside Park 南屯河濱公園

2

Jhangsiaojia Temple 張廖家廟

Fongjia Night Market 逢甲夜市

Feng Chia University 逢甲大學

Taichung Shueinan Airport (old site) 台中水湳機場(舊址)

To Daya Interchange 往大雅交流道
To Cinpuang Airport

Henan Rd. 河南路

Fusing Park 福星公園

Sihun Rd. Sec. 2 四維路二段

Wunsin Rd. Sec. 2 文心路二段

Plaza Internatio

Hankou Rd. Sec. 1 漢口路一段 Hankou Rd. Sec. 2 漢口路二段

Huejhong Park 華中公園

Taihonggang Rd. Sec. 2 台鴻港路二段

Dalong Rd. 大隆路

Tangyen Rd. Sec. 1

Cingming Rd. 精明路

Evergreen Laurel Hotel 長榮桂冠酒店

Boguan Rd.

The Splendor Taichung 金典酒店

Natio Natio

Dongsing Rd. Sec.

Kuang San Sogo Department Store 廣三SOGO百貨

Jing Ming 1st Business District

Hotel National Taichung

Feicuelhong Rd.

Gongyi Rd. Sec. 1 公益路一段

Meicun Rd. Sec.

Jhongming S. Rd.

Huamei St.

Jingcheng Rd.

Dadun Rd. 大墩路

Siangshang Rd. Sec. 2 向上路二段

Siangshang Rd. Sec. 1 向上路一段

Siangshang S. Rd. Sec. 1 向上南路一段

Jingcheng S. Rd. Sec.

National Taiwan Museum of Fine Arts 國立美術館

City Cul 市立文化

Wuciuan W. Rd. Sec. 1 五權西路一段

Nantun Rd., Sec. 1 南屯路一段

Chunjun Park 春社公園

Sanmin W. Rd. 三民西路

Sanmin W. Rd. 三民西路

Medical College of Chung Shang Medical University 中山醫學大學

To Wanfeng Interchange 往王田交流道

Nanong Rd. 南崗路

Fuhing Rd. 復興路

Dongsing Rd. Sec.

Yitong Rd. 一通路

N
S
E
W

E F G H

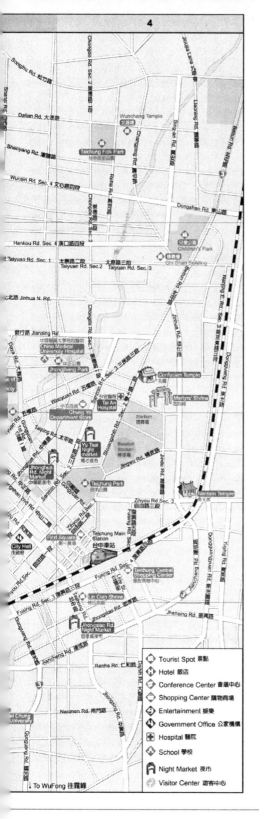

Dutch during the 1600s; unfortunately, most of the remnants of the Dutch occupation were destroyed by the occupying Japanese. Taiwan's third-largest city boasts a comfortable climate that makes visiting a famous European-style street, spacious parks, bucolic scenic areas and interesting museums, a pleasant experience. Taichung does not have an MRT system so getting around town may not be as convenient as Taipei. You may find that the city has a slower life pace compared with the capital, as well.

Major Attractions

Perhaps the most famous street in Taichung is **Jingming 1st Street** (精明一街), alternately known as "tea street," a European-style shopping district lined with coffee shops and cafés with spacious outdoor seating, as well as snazzy boutiques. Here you can find strange street urchins, peculiar performers and magnificent musicians hired by the city to perform during weekends and holidays. For a moment or two you may feel as if you're on the 3rd Street Prominade in Santa Monica, California rather than in Asia. Jingming 1st Street is nestled between Jingcheng Road (精誠路) and Jingming 2nd Street (精明二街), not far from Taichung Harbor Road (台中港路). http://www.jingming1st.com.tw.

Tunghai University (東海大學) makes for an interesting glimpse into the lives of hard-working young Taiwanese. Since it was founded in 1955 the university has grown into six colleges with over 15,000 students. Many successful professionals have graduated from this placid university, a North American alumni recently pledged a million dollars to the Tunghai University Endowment Fund. Cultural events are often held on campus and the university sponsors an annual arts festival that draws diverse crowds. Taichung Harbor Road, Section 3,

#181 (台中市西屯區台中港路3段181號)
(04) 2359-0121. http://www.thu.edu.tw.

Of course no Taiwanese city is complete without a lively night market, and the vast **Tunghai Night Market** (東海夜市), which encompasses several city blocks, is located adjacent to Tunghai University on Zhonggang Road, Section 3 (台中市中港路3段左轉遊園路).

National Taiwan Museum of Natural Science (國立自然科學博物館) boasts a 3-D IMAX theater as well as space and science centers, a Chinese science hall, botanical garden and one of the largest greenhouses in Asia. There are several eateries and cafés on the premises if you crave food, light snacks or beverages. Shops offer a variety of merchandise and entrance to the exhibition areas from 9 to 10 am on Wednesdays is free. General admission is NT $100/70 for the space theater, NT $100 for the science center, NT $20 for the science center and NT $20 for the greenhouse. By bus take Taichung Transit Company's 22, 27, 46, 47, 103, 106 or 135 or the Jen-you Transit Company's 22, 38, 45 or 125. Open 9 am to 5 pm, closed Mondays. Guanqian Road, #1, Taichung (台中市北區館前路1號) (04) 2322-6940 http://www.nmns.edu.tw.

Modern art lovers may marvel at some of the exhibits at National **Taiwan Museum of Fine Arts** (國立台灣美術館). Walk around the outdoor sculpture garden, explore works by some of Taiwan's finest artists and stop by the teacher resources center and arts library. The museum is open 9 to 5 pm, 6 pm on Saturdays and Sundays, closed Mondays. The information desk is open from 10 am to 4:30 pm, guided tours can be arranged by calling extention 327. Admission is free and all are welcome. Wuchuan West Road, Section 1, #2 (台中市西區五權西路1段2號) (04) 2372-3552 http://www.tmoa.gov.tw.

Established during the Japanese occupation

on October 28, 1903, **Taichung Park** (台中公園), also called Zhongshan Park in honor of Dr. Sun Yat-sen, boasts tennis courts, a soothing lake replete with lotus pads, a walking bridge, historic pavilions, and a boat-rental area. Leave your rod and bait in Taipei, fishing is not permitted. Inside this vast green park you'll also find a statue of Confucius as well as a separate statue of his famed horse. The main entrance to the park is on Gongyuan Road (台中市公路園) within walking distance from Taichung Train Station (台中火車站) and downtown shopping.

Taichung's **2-28 Memorial Park** (二二八紀念公園) is near the intersection of Taichung Road and Renho Road (台中路與仁和路交叉口附近). Every February 28 a memorial event is held during the evening, but most of the time this placid park is a welcome respite for weary citydwellers and their families.

If you're looking for fun and appreciate art the two coincide at **Fun Love Sculpture Park** (豐樂雕塑公園 *Fengle Gongyuan*). Founded in 1994, this well-known Taichung sculpture park boasts over fifty sculptures showcasing the works of renowned Taiwanese artists, a calming lake where locals sail model boats past interesting blue swirly statues, cool cafés and a stage where you can perform for complete strangers. You'll find the park where Yongchun Road meets Wenxin South Road (永春東路與文心南路).

Taste more than a smattering of Taiwanese food, art and culture at **Taichung Culture Folklore Park** (台中民俗公園). There's ample room to stretch your legs while exploring the scenic courtyard chock-full of colorful carp. The park boasts Folk Culture Museum, National Taiwan Folk Culture and Art Museum, and Folk Art Museum. Lushun Road, Section 2, #73 (台中市北屯區旅順路2段73號) (04) 2245-1310 http://www.folkpark.org.tw.

If you're traveling on business you may want to attend an event taking place at **Taichung World Trade Center** (台中世界貿易中心), Tienpao Road, #60 (台中市407天保街60號) (04) 2358-2271 http://www.wtctxg.org.tw.

Aside from catching a bus a popular method of transport from Taipei is the **High-Speed Rail (HSR)**, the ride takes an hour and a one-way economy (standard) ticket costs NT $700. Kaotie North Road, #8, Wurih Township, Taichung County (台中縣烏日鄉站區高鐵北路8號) (02) 4066-5678.

Taichung Hotels

Evergreen Laurel Hotel (長榮桂冠酒店, 台中) This luxury hotel boasts 354 spacious rooms and several fine eateries. Daniel Café (ext. 2893) is open from 6:30 am to noon, The Lobby Bar (ext. 2887) is open from 11:30 am to 1:30 am, Canton Palace (Cantonese) (ext. 2882) is open from 11:30 am to 2:30 pm for lunch and again from 5:30 to 10 pm for dinner. Chevalier teppenyaki & steakhouse (ext. 2875) is open from 11:30 am to 2:30 pm for lunch weekends only and from 5:30 to 10 pm for dinner, Formosa (seafood) (ext. 2862) and Evergreen Club (ext. 2862) are open the same times as Chevalier. The Gourmet Shop bakery (ext. 2173) is open from 10 am to 10 pm. Daily rates for two people start around NT $5,100. Taichung Harbor Road, Section 2, #6 (台中市台中港路2段6號) (04) 2313-9988.

Taichung Plaza International Hotel (通豪大飯店) This luxury hotel, a few blocks from Hotel National and National Museum of Natural Science, boasts Western and Chinese restaurants, a swimming pool, sauna, gym, and children's playroom. Daily room rates start at NT $ 2,900. Daya Road, #431 (台中市大雅路431號) (04) 2295-6789 http://www.taichung-plaza.com.

National Hotel (全國大飯店) is a five-star luxury hotel near the airport and major attractions. The hotel boasts several restaurants as well as an upscale coffee shop and lobby bar, a business center, concierge, currency exchange service, gift shop, outdoor swimming pool and manager on duty 24-hours to assist visitors. Room rates start at NT$ 4,700. Taichung Harbor Road, Section 1, #257 (台中市西區台中港路1段257號) (04) 2321-3111 http://www.hotel-national.com.tw.

Taichung Chinatrust Hotel (台中中信大飯店) Taiwan's Chinatrust Hotel chain typically provides comfortable accommodations in convenient locations. This one boasts 100 modern rooms with Internet access, a business center and Chinese restaurant on the first floor and a bar on the fifteenth so you can appreciate the city view while enjoying your cocktail. Room rates start at NT $2,220. Beitun District, Hozhuan Road (台中市北屯區后庄路306號) (04) 2425-5678.

TAINAN (台南)
(06 Area Code)
Population: 740,000
Dutch colonization period: 1624-1662
Original name: Anping (安平)

While Taipei may offer a glimpse into the future of Taiwan, Tainan, with over two hundred alluring ancient temples, offers a profound look into Taiwan's turbulent past. Originally called "Anping" (安平), Taiwan's modern history began in this comparatively placid southern city. Some of the most hospitable people you will ever meet live in Taiwan's fourth-largest city. In addition to its historic temples and landmarks, Tainan is famous for its outstanding native foods that include rice cakes, shrimp cakes, congee and glutinous rice dumplings wrapped in bamboo leaves (粽子 *zhongzi*), typically made during the Dragon Boat Festival (端午節 *Duanwujie*). Traditional teashops and restaurants are ubiquitous, it's never difficult to spot a delectable local dish.

Major Attractions

One of Tainan's most historic districts is

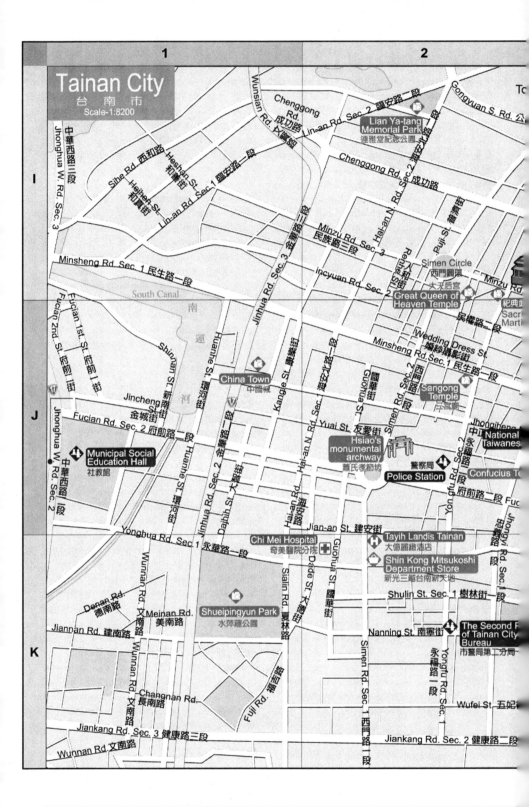

Tainan City
台南市
Scale-1:8200

Jhonghua W. Rd. Sec. 3 中華西路三段

Sihe Rd. 西和路

Heshan St. 和華街

Heihei St. 和緯街

Lin-an Rd. Sec. 1 臨安路一段

Wunsian Rd. 五賢路

成功路

Chenggong Rd.

Lin-an Rd. Sec. 2 臨安路二段

Chenggong Rd. Sec. 2 成功路

Gongyuan S. Rd. 公

To

Lian Ya-tang Memorial Park
連雅堂紀念公園

Minsheng Rd. Sec. 1 民生路一段

South Canal 南運河

Fucian 1st. St. 府前一街

Fucian 2nd. St. 府前二街

Shinnan St. 新南街

Huanhe St. 環河街

Jhonghua W. Rd. Sec. 2 中華西路二段

Jincheng St. 金城街

Jincheng St. 新南街

Fucian Rd. Sec. 2 府前路二段

Jinhua Rd. Sec. 3 金華路三段

Minzu Rd. 民族路三段

Renhe St. 人和街

Puji St. 普濟街

incyuan Rd. Sec. 2 慶佑路二段

Simen Circle 西門圓環
大天后宮

Great Queen of Heaven Temple

Minzu Rd. 民族

紀典亩

Sacri
Mart

Wedding Dress St. 婚紗攝影街

Minsheng Rd. Sec. 1 民生路一段

Renhe St. 人和街

Kangle St. 康樂街

Hai-an N. Rd. 海安北路

Yuai St. 友愛街

Guohua St. 國華街

Simen Rd. 西門路

Sangong Temple
慕宮廟

Jhongjheng 中正

National Taiwanes

China Town
中國城

Hsiao's monumental archway
蕭氏孝節坊

Jhonghua W. Rd. Sec. 2 中華西路二段

Municipal Social Education Hall
社教館

Huanhe St. 環河街

Jinhua Rd. Sec. 2 金華路二段

Dajih St. 大智街

Hai-an N. Rd. 海安北路

Jian-an St. 建安街

Police Station
警察局

Yongfu Rd. Sec. 2 永福路二段

Confucius Te

Fuc

Fucian Rd. Sec. 2 府前路一段

Chi Mei Hospital
奇美醫院分院

Guohua St. 國華街

Tayih Landis Tainan
大億麗緻酒店

Shin Kong Mitsukoshi Department Store
新光三越台南新天地

Jhongyi

Sec.

Yonghua Rd. Sec. 1 永華路一段

Sialin Rd. 夏林路

Dade St. 大德街

Shueipingyun Park
水萍塭公園

Shulin St. Sec. 1 樹林街一段

The Second F of Tainan City Bureau
市警局第二分局

Wunnan Rd. 文南路

Denan Rd. 德南路

Meinan Rd. 美南路

Jiannan Rd. 建南路

Fuji Rd. 福吉路

Simen Rd. Sec. 1 西門路一段

Nanning St. 南寧街

Yongfu Rd. 永福路一段

Wufei St. 五妃

Changnan Rd. 長南路

Jiankang Rd. Sec. 3 健康路三段

Jiankang Rd. Sec. 2 健康路二段

Wunnan Rd 文南路

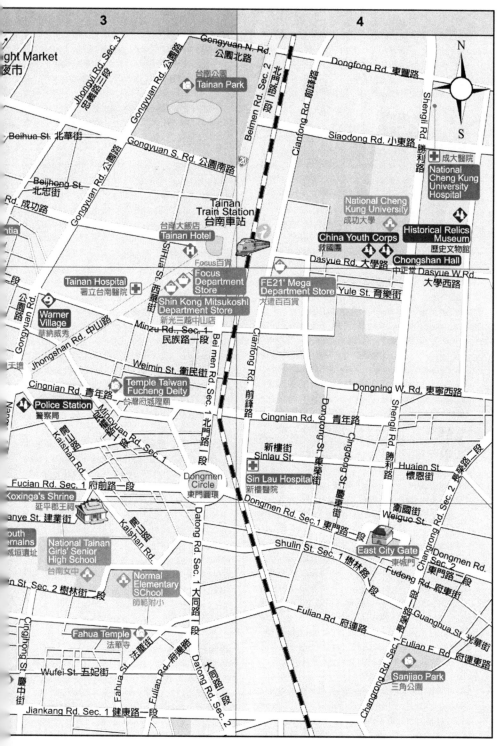

3

4

ght Market
夜市

Jhongyi Rd. Sec. 3 忠義路三段

Gongyuan N. Rd. 公園北路

Dongfong Rd. 東豐路

N

Beimen Rd. Sec. 2 北門路二段

Shengli Rd. 勝利路

台南公園
Tainan Park

Gongyuan Rd. 公園路

Beihua St. 北華街

Gongyuan S. Rd. 公園南路

Cianfong Rd. 前鋒路

S

Beijhong St. 北忠街

Siaodong Rd. 小東路

成大醫院
National Cheng Kung University Hospital

Rd. 成功路

Gongyuan Rd. 公園路

National Cheng Kung University
成功大學

Historical Relics Museum
歷史文物館

ntia

Tainan Train Station
台南車站

China Youth Corps
救國團

Chongshan Hall
中正堂

台南大飯店
Tainan Hotel

SiHua St. 西華街

Dasyue Rd. 大學路

Dasyue W Rd.
大學西路

Tainan Hospital
署立台南醫院

Focus百貨
Focus Department Store

FE21' Mega Department Store
大遠百百貨

Yule St. 育樂街

Warner Village
華納威秀

Shin Kong Mitsukoshi Department Store
新光三越中山店

Jhongshan Rd. 中山路

Minzu Rd. Sec. 1 民族路一段

Beimen Rd. Sec. 1 北門路一段

Cianfong Rd. 前鋒路

Weimin St. 衛民街

Dongning W. Rd. 東寧西路

Cingnian Rd. 青年路

Temple Taiwan Fucheng Deity
台灣府城隍廟

Cingnian Rd. 青年路

Dongcing St. 東慶街

Shengli Rd. 勝利路

Police Station
警察局

MingYuan Rd. Sec. 1 民生路一段

新樓街
Sinlau St.

Huaien St
懷恩街

Kaishan Rd.

Fucian Rd. Sec. 1 府前路一段

Sin Lau Hospital
新樓醫院

Koxinga's Shrine

Dongmen Circle
東門圓環

衛國街
Weiguo St.

anye St. 建業街

Dongmen Rd. Sec.1 東門一段

Dongmen Rd.

outh emains
成垣遺址

Datong Rd. Sec. 1 大同路一段

East City Gate
東城門

Changrong Rd. Sec. 2 長榮路二段

National Tainan Girls' Senior High School
台南女中

Kaishan Rd.

Shulin St. Sec. 1 樹林街一段

Fudeng Rd. 府東街

n St. Sec. 2 樹林街二段

Normal Elementary SChool
朗範附小

Fulian Rd. 府連路

Guanghua St. 光華街

Fahua Temple
法華寺

Fahua St. 法華街

Fulian E. Rd. 府連東路

Wufei St. 五妃街

Datong Rd. Sec. 2 大同路二段

Sanjiao Park
三角公園

Jiankang Rd. Sec. 1 健康路一段

Anping district (安平區) and it can be walked in under two hours. In Anping district you'll find Fort Zeelandia (Anping Fortress) (安平古堡), Eternal Golden Castle (Erkunshen Fortress) (二鯤鯓砲台), as well as historic buildings and temples.

The present site of **Chihkan Towers** (赤嵌樓) is where the Dutch started constructing Fort Provintia (台南建立赤崁城), known locally as "Tower of the Red-Haired Barbarians," or "Red Hair Tower," in 1653. The purpose of Provintia ("forever" in French) was for self-defense against a local uprising and its walls were once nearly thirty-six feet high to prevent such an occurance. Here the Dutch locally administered the operations for its Dutch East India Company (荷屬東印度公 *Helan Dong Indu Gongsi*). After Cheng Cheng-kung, or Koxinga (鎮成功), expelled the Dutch in 1661 he renamed the fort "Cheng Tien Fu Tai," (承天府治), "The Mansion Bestowed by Heaven." Some extraordinary historical items are here, which include stone turtle tables given to a local general by the Qianlong Emperor (1736 to 1796) for surpressing a local uprising. The emperor inscribed in both Manchu and Chinese dialects, making these tablets a rare find. Chihkan Towers are open 8:30 am to 5:30 pm daily and again from 5:30 pm until 9 pm. Admission is NT $50/$25. Mintsu Road, #212 (台南市民族路212號) (06) 220-5647.

Confucius Temple (台南孔子廟), completed in 1666, is the site of a colorful annual Teacher's Day celebration, which takes place every September 28. The temple is a reminder that, like the plaque hung in the main hall of the temple, Confucius will always be an "exemplary teacher forever." Open 9 am to 5 pm, Nanmen Road, #2, West Central district (台南市南門路2號).

Wu Temple (武廟 *Wumiao*), built in 1690, is one of the oldest temples on Taiwan dedicated to Guan Gong, the God of War. Yungfu Road, Section 2, #229, West Central district (台南市中區永福路2段229

號). According to Taoism, Guan Gong is the deity of business, loyalty, bravery and expelling demons. Two dragon statues protect the towering entrance, and a middle tower was built just outside the temple to protect it from fires. The temple, also called "Sacrificial Rites Martial Temple," is open from 9 am to 5 pm.

Unfortunately, most of the original **Fort Zeelandia (Anping Fortress)** (安平古堡), built by the invading Dutch starting in the 1620s, has been destroyed during Anping's turbulent history. However, the brick foundations, an aged wall, and some wall beams remain. Today you'll find a sixty-step cascading watchtower and observation rooms, which had been built by the Japanese in the early 20th century during their occupation. Cannons are also situated around the fort. Fort Zeelandia (makes you wonder how Ben Stiller came up with the movie name "Zoolander," doesn't it?) is open from 8:30 am to 5:00 pm and admission is NT $50/$25. Guosheng Road, #82, Anping district (台南市安平區國勝路82號) (06) 295-1504.

Eternal Golden Castle (Erkunshen Fortress) (二鯤鯓砲台), completed in 1876, was built by the French to guard against Japanese invasion. Ironically, fortress cannons were fired against invading French during the Sino-French War of 1884, and again in 1895 against the Japanese. This fort is called "Big Anping Fortress" by locals to distinguish it from Fort Zeelandia. Open 8:30 am to 5:30 pm, admission is NT $50/$25. Guangzhou Road, #3, Anping district (台南市安平區光州路3號) (06) 295-1504.

Koxinga Shrine (延平郡王祠) is a shrine that honors the spirit of Cheng Cheng-kung (鎮成功) (1624-1662), a Chinese warrior who expelled the Dutch from Taiwan. Cheng, known in the West as Koxinga (Koshinga), established Chinese schools, laws and customs, and built the first Confucian temple on the island. He had intended to build up a substantial army to overthrow the Manchus in China but died before his dream could be actualized. Admission is NT $50/$25. Koxinga Shrine is open 8:30 am to 5 pm and is on Kaishan Road, #152, West Central district (台南市開山路152號).

Constructed in 1664, Matsu, Goddess of the Sea, is honored at **Datienhou Temple** (安平開台天后宮) with a boisterous celebration on her birthday, which falls on the twenty-third day of the third lunar month (typically in spring). Inside you'll find stupefying stone scriptures, classic colorful patters, dragon-headed stone staircases and drum stones. 18 Yungfu Road, Section 2, Lane 227, #18 (台南市中區永福路2段227巷18號).

Tainan Xiaobei Night Market (小北觀光夜市) on Ximen Road (西門路) is about five long blocks from Tainan Train Station. In addition to the night market you can find all kinds of wonderful local delicacies around town.

Walk past structures that are over one hundred years old on "Taiwan's First Street," **Yenping Historical Street** (台南延平老街, 台灣第一街). No cars are permitted on this historic street, which was built in a narrow, curved fashion to prevent typhoon damage and invading pirates from plundering.

The normally quiet southern Tainan town of **Yanshui** (鹽水) brims with life during the Lantern Festival (元宵節 *Yuenxiaojie*), the fifteenth day of the first month of the Lunar Year, which marks the culmination of Chinese New Year. During this time, residents light thousands of Yanshui Beehive Firecrackers (鹽水蜂炮 *Yanshui Fengpao*) to chase away evil spirits and usher in a year of prosperity. "Yanshui Firecracker Festival" as it has come to be known takes place at the historic Wu Temple (武廟 *Wumiao*) (see above). After the sun has set, the gods have left the temple, and thunderous firecrackers, roaring bottle rockets and flaming fireworks fly everywhere, akin to

a festive war zone. Rather than run away, however, residents run into the firecracker frenzy! Locals believe that participating in the event will bring them prosperity, and businesspeople, in particular, turn out in droves. Those that choose to join the celebration take extreme precaution and wear helmets, boots, raincoats, facemasks, earplugs, goggles and towels to cover every part of their bodies or they may end up in local hospital emergency rooms, and every year participants do.

By car exit at the Xinying (Hsinying) Interchange (新營交流道) and take County Highway 172 (172縣道) to Wu Temple (武廟 *Wumiao*). By train and bus exit at Hsinying Station (新營站), cross the road and take Hsinying Ke Yuen (新營客運) bus to Yanshui. Not recommended for the faint-hearted.

Tainan Hotels

Abba Hotel (亞伯大飯店) In spite of its name, don't expect to find any members of the famous Swedish pop quartet crooning at this hotel minutes from Tainan Airport. The hotel boasts free Internet access for guests, fine Eastern and Western dining and a lobby bar. Rooms start at NT$ 1920 and include complimentary breakfast. Check to see if the hotel is running any promotions. Datong Road, Section 2, #617 (台南市大同路2段617號) (06) 268-6911 http://www.abba-hotel.com.tw.

Asia Emperor Hotel (亞帝大飯店) Disappointed you weren't born an Asian emperor? You may be treated like one at Asia Emperor Hotel. Rooms for two start at NT $1480. Breakfast is included. Dongmen Road, Section 3, #31 (台南市東門路3段31號) (06) 289-7360.

Premier Hotel (台南首相大飯店) This comfortable four-star hotel within walking distance from Tainan Train Station boasts a gym, laundry room and upscale restaurant, a recently remodled piano lounge, complimentary Internet access, icemakers and a microwave oven in the service center. Room rates run from NT $2,000 to NT $3,600, NT $3,200 for suites. Gongyuan Road, #128 (台南市公園路128號) (06) 225-2141 Toll-free: 0800-Premier (773-6437) http://www.premier.com.tw.

Tainan Hotel (台南大飯店) Directly across from Tainan Bus Station and within walking distance from department stores, Tainan Hotel is popular with expatriates on the go for its friendly bilingual staff and strict "no smoking" policy. Rooms include ADSL broadband connection, A/C, a fridge, hair dryer and complimentary slippers. Jade Restaurant buffet pleases pallets by offering fresh vegetables and local seafood, and patrons can dine indoors or outside by the pool. Unfortunately, Peacock Restaurant's piquant preparations are typically off-limits due to wedding receptions and banquets (crashing for Cantonese cuisine isn't advisable). Rates start at NT $2150 and include complimentary breakfast. Chenggung Road, #1, Tainan (台南市成功路1號) (06) 228-9101
http://www.hotel-tainan.com.tw

Department stores and **Tainan Park** (台南公園) are within walking distance from **Tainan Train Station** (台南火車站) (06) 226-1314. By train it takes between four to five hours to reach Tainan from Taipei, and one hour by plane.

Tainan Airport (台南航空站) (06) 260-1007 (press 3 for English service) is approximately twenty minutes from the downtown area, a one-way economy ticket from Taipei will set you back around NT $1,500 (US $45.00).

Alternatively you could opt for the **Taiwan High Speed Rail (THSR)** (台灣高鐵 *Taiwan Gaotie*), Gueiren Boulevard, #100, Gueiren Township, Tainan County (台南縣歸仁鄉歸仁大道100號) (02) 4066-5678. A one-way economy ticket from Taipei costs NT $1350 and the trip takes around an hour and a half.

Tainan HSR Station is approximately twenty minutes by car from downtown Tainan and buses run from the station to the city (NT $40/adult passenger). Taxis are also an option for around NT $300.

TAIPEI 101 (台北 101)

Ride the world's fastest elevator to the 89th floor observatory of Taipei Financial Center 101 (台北國際金融中心), **Taipei 101** (台北 101), a Taiwan landmark that towers at 508 meters, one of the tallest buildings not only on Taiwan but also in the world. The building elevator travels upwards at 1,010 meters (60.6 kilometers) per minute, and the world's largest wind damper, weighing 660 metric tons, is also on the 89th floor. In addition to companies that have rented office space in the skyscraper, swank shops and regal restaurants fill the bottom floors of the building for those that are hungry for lunch as well as luxury goods (the first five floors in the 106-floor Taipei 101 are underground). By MRT, transfer at Taipei Main Station for the Kunyang line and get off at Taipei City Hall Station. From there catch one of the free buses that go to Taipei 101. Taipei 101 is located in the Xinyi business district, a stone's throw from Taipei World Convention Center. Admission is NT $350 for adults, NT $320 for children, NT$300 for groups of 20 or more, and children under 70cm are admitted free. Shifu Road, #45 (台北市信義區市府路45號) (02) 8101-7777

http://www.tfc101.com.tw.

TAIPEI COUNTY (台北縣)

For Taipei residents, the pre-MRT stereotype of Taipei County was a dearth of cultural life combined with congestion. While Taipei's surrounding urban areas are still home to growing manufacturing facilities, that stereotype is changing with the advent of the MRT and careful urban planning on the part of Taipei County administrators. To the north of Taipei, ancient temples, pristine beaches and natural splendors of nature await, you may want to explore some of these more scenic Taipei County areas by car or bus.

Danshui (淡水) → Sanjhih (三芝) → Shimen (石門) → Jinshan (金山) → Wanli (萬里).

From Danshui (淡水), heading north on North Second Highway or Highway 2 (北二高速公路 *Beiergao*) you'll pass **North Coast National Scenic Area and Guanyinshan** (北海岸及觀音山國家風景區) before crossing **Datun River** (大屯河) and entering the northern town of **Sanjhih** (三芝). Here you can enjoy fresh chicken, watermelon, bamboo and mountain-grown yams. During the summer, Taipei surfers suit up and head over to Sanjhih's **Qianshuiwan (Cianshuiwan Beach)** (淺水灣) and, slightly further north, **White Sand Bay** (白沙灣 *Baishawan*). From here continue heading north to **Shimen** (石門), which means "stone gate," to experience fresh jelly, harvested peanuts, mountain-grown tea and steamed taro. After traveling about thirty kilometers stop along Highway 2 at **Shimen Cave** (石門洞), a natural gateway to the sea made of stone formed by years of wind and water erosion. Tourists explore the unique rock formations on the beach while locals work busily to sell fresh seafood. The lighthouse here stands at 14.3 meters above sea level and offers a fine view. Shimen is the northernmost village on Taiwan, and after passing this area you will begin heading south.

Further along Highway 2, **Temple of the 18 Nobles** (石門十八王公) appears on the right, a historic temple with fascinating folklore. Seventeen fishermen departed near this spot and were said to have drowned. Their loyal dog returned every night waiting for them to return. When they did not it is said that the dog jumped into the water and drowned. Locals were so moved when they heard this story they constructed a golden statue in the dog's image, and residents rub the statue for luck. The temple is said to bring great wealth, and ironically, has become a magnet for streetwalkers. At night the temple area becomes a carnal carnival of sorts.

After Shimen is **Jinshan** (金山) (Gold Mountain). **Jinshan Beach** (金山海灘) and **New Jinshan Beach** (新金山海水浴場) are summer hot spots for young couples and families, and annual surfing competitions held at Jinshan Beach attract several dozen participants and hundreds of onlookers. Acclaimed Taiwanese artist Ju Ming is from Taipei County. View his eclectic collection of sculpture works and hand-crafted creations at his expansive indoor and outdoor **Juming Fine Arts Muesum** (朱銘美術館), a few kilometers from downtown Jinshan. Juming Fine Arts Museum is listed under "Taipei Museum Guide (台北博物館指南)."

Lion's Head Mountain (獅頭山 *Shihtoushan*) is another popular Jinshan destination because of its natural beauty and preserved temples built inside caves and alongside the mountain. Contact Jinshan Youth Activity Center (金山青年活動中心), Chingnien Road, #1 (台北縣金山鄉菁年路1號) (02) 2498-1190 to rent water sports or camping equipment. Just beyond Jinshan is **Wanli** (萬里), best known for its pristine beaches and exclusive Howard Beach Resort Pacific Green Bay (太平洋翡翠灣福華渡假飯店 *Feicuiwan*). For more information please see "Beaches

(海邊)".

To learn more about Jiufen and Keelung please see the aforementioned sections. A kilometer past Jiufen on North Second Highway is **Jinguashi** (金瓜石), shuttle buses run from Jiufen to Jinguashi. Jinguashi was another mining village all but forgotten until November 2004 when Gold Ecological Park Museum, the former site of Taiwan Metal Mining Corp., was established. The number for Gold Ecological Park Tourist Information Center is (02) 2496-2800. Adjacent to the museum explore tunnels where minors had once toiled. If you're up for a steep hike scenic views awat at nearby Gold Zen Temple, built in 1897. The area boasts Japanese-style buildings nearly a century old as well as the refurbished Crown Prince Chalet, built for a visit from Japanese royalty that never materialized. In Jinguashi you'll also spot abandoned refineries and, a darker page from Taiwan's history books, Kinkaseki Concentration Camp, established by the Japanese during World War II. It is reported that over a thousand allied troops lost their lives here in untenable conditions before the end of the war. Jinguashi Police: (02) 2496-1528.

On Taiwan's northeast corner you'll spot **Cape Bitou** (鼻頭角) with its scintillating sea cliffs, coarse concave walls and rocks shaped like mushrooms and tofu. Taiwan boasts three capes where the Pacific Ocean meets the East Sea and Cape Bitou is one of them (the other two are Cape Fugui and Cape Sandiao). Geologists have discovered myriad fossils here. Of interest to tourists are the views from historic **Bitou Lighthouse** (鼻頭燈塔), which survived Allied bombing raids during World War II. Cape Bitou also boasts three scenic hiking trails, all 3.5-kilometers of which lead to **Bitou Fishing Village** (鼻頭漁村). Once you exit **Bitou Tunnel** (鼻頭隧道) you should spot the cape, as well as a vast parking lot, seafood restaurant, convenience shop and rest area.

Further along the highway, 87.9 kilometers, to be exact, is **Longdong Bay Park** (龍洞灣公園) (free), Kungliao Township, Taipei County (台北縣貢寮鄉) (02) 2490-9445, which boasts **Longdong South Ocean Park** (龍洞南口海洋公園) (02) 2490-2112 (fee). Along the coast you'll find a varied geological landscape and plethora of water activities that include diving, snorkeling and swimming. Avid Taipei rock climbers often train at Longdong Rock Climbing Area (龍洞岩場) along narrow catwalk passages and the ominous-sounding Crocodile Ridge (鱷魚稜). Open 8 am to 6 pm holidays and weekends, 8 am to 5 pm weekdays. The number for the visitor center is (02) 2499-1115.

Heading further south is **Cape Sandiao** (三貂角). When the Spanish landed on Cape Sandiao in 1626 they named it, ironically, "San Diego." Here you'll find a traditional fishing town (小漁村) and **Cape Sandiao Lighthouse** (三貂角燈塔) (02) 2499-1300. Open 9 am to 4 pm daily, closed Mondays. Continuing south, a hundred and fifteen kilometers from Taipei, is **Maoao Fishing Village** (卯澳漁村), another quiet fishing village dotted with historic temples, pagodas, stone buildings and banyan trees over a century old. Further south you should happen upon **Daxi** (大溪) and its lunar-shaped **Honeymoon Bay** (蜜月灣), where couples take seaside walks as the tide gently ebbs and flows. During the summer hordes of young people surf two to three-meter waves, play beach volleyball and make sand sculptures.

Further south is "Gold Sand Bay," **Jinshawan** (金沙灣), a narrow beach with more grass and rocks than sand. Those that want to camp, barbecue or play water sports head further south to the slightly larger **Fulong Beach** (福隆沙灘) (02) 2499-1211. The beach has become popular in recent years due to "Ho-Hai-Yan," a rock festival that rivals Kending's Spring Scream by drawing over twenty thousand animated fans to the annual event. Near Fulong is

Yanliao Seaside Park (鹽寮海濱公園) (02) 2490-2991 (NT $200/120), which boasts wooden pavilions, ancient pathways and water sports galore.

Aodi Harbor (澳底漁港) is a small fishing harbor on Taiwan's northeast corner south of Fulong. The quaint villages along North Second Highway are a fisherman's paradise.

A century ago, the cities of Taipei County were rustic faming societies made up of mostly aboriginal tribes. After the Nationalists retreated to Taiwan in 1949 the area met with a vast influx of Chinese immigrants, and during the 1950s and 1960s small manufacturing facilities began appearing. Taipei County has since become a Taiwanese melting pot of sorts as young people relocate from overseas and southern parts of the island for advanced schooling and settle in the area. Taipei County's fun town of **Wulai** (烏來) is home to the Atayal tribe, discover natural hot springs, cherry blossoms in full bloom during spring, bamboo shoots, millet cake and wine, plenty of roasted boar, trinkets, t-shirts and traditional aboriginal clothing. The town is only fifty minutes outside the city. To learn more about Wulai please see "Aboriginal Culture (原著民文化)."

Taipei County's **Yongho** (永和) is famous for sweet soybean milk (豆漿 *dou jiang*), several shops are near Dingxi Station. A five-minute walk from Yongnan Market Station is the venerable **Lehua Night Market** (樂華夜市), snack vendors crowd the outer perimeters but inside get your kicks on new shoes or find new digs that fit. In Tucheng City, **Taiwan Nougat Museum** (牛軋糖博物館) attracts young and old alike with nougat treats you can make yourself as well as an array of delicious displays. From Yongning Station it's a thirty-minute walk. Zichang Street, #31-2 (台北縣土城市自強街 31-2 號) (02) 2268-7222.

Boats may be rented in **Bitan**. Xindian, Taipei County.

Bitan is a three-minute walk from Xindian Station.

By MRT you can also more easily explore **Banqiao** (板橋), **Zhonghe** (中和) and **Xindian** (新店). **Banqiao Night Market** is a ten-minute walk from Fuzhong Station between Houpu Street and Nanya South Road. Banqiao also boasts **Jhueifong Circle**, a paved urban sprawl-turned-rollerblading park at Banqiao Station and **Lin Family Garden** (林本源園), a two-story house built in 1888. Lin Family Garden somewhat resembles Beitou Hot Springs Museum, a bridge and stream through the courtyard create a sense of nobility. The garden, a popular snapshot spot for local tourists, is on Ximen Street, #9 (台北縣板橋 市西門街9號) (02) 2965-3061. http://www. linfamily.tpc.gov.tw.

Zhonghe boasts **Xingnan Night Market** (興南夜市), three minutes from Nanshijiao Station, chill at an ice shop (over a dozen vendors), devour native foods or purchase a contrast of clothes. Zhonghe's hot and spicy Huaxin Street (中和華新街), a ten-minute walk from Nanshijiao Station, is also called "Thai and Burmese Street." Xindian is known for its bustling citylife, natural hot springs and locally-grown, slightly fermented Chinese green "baozhong" tea. Xindian also boasts **Bitan Special Scenic Area** (碧潭風景區 *Bitan Fengjing Chu*), Xindian Road, #207, 3F, Xindian City (台北縣新店市新店路207號3樓) (02) 2913-1184; "Green Lake" is a three-minute walk from Xindian Station. At this southern Taipei haven rent a boat to take in the area's green pastures, palatial pavilions, and natural cliffs, two to six people may rent boats for NT $100 (US $3.00) per person per hour.

Separate Banchiao and Tucheng MRT lines have recently opened. A traditional market is just across the street from Kunyang Station in Banchiao, and Muzha is home to **Taipei Zoo** (台北動物園) and **Maokong** (木柵貓空), tea plantations that provide a brief respite from urban life on Zhinan Road, Section 3.

TAIPEI DINING GUIDE
(台北餐廳指南)

When in Rome, do as Romans do...and when on Taiwan, eat as the Taiwanese do! It's nearly impossible to go hungry in Taipei, night markets stay open well after the sun has set and twenty-four hour convenience stores speck city streets. Stop by a convenience store to compare native foods with items sold in convenience stores back home. You may be surprised to find snacks such as seaweed, squid, pork or fish balls (fish meat rolled into balls) on a stick, rice balls with fish or dried pork wrapped in seaweed, dried squid, papaya milk and a variety of outstanding juice boxes.

You shouldn't have difficulty finding a spectacular spot for coffee talk, with the growing popularity of coffee as the social beverage of choice (some elderly folk now sip coffee during the evening rather than tea), coffee shops appear in virtually all areas of the city (which includes mountain areas, too!). And if you crave Western-style chicken and burgers, there are ample choices for those on the go.

For lunch or dinner, lower levels of most department stores have food courts that offer healthy doses of delectable dishes and prices are generally reasonable. Department store food courts may become crowded during peak hours so arrive early to beat the heat and get a seat. Hotels tend to offer fine dining, and for a sumptuous snack, try an "afternoon tea" between the hours of 2 to 4 pm. In addition to coffee, tea, juices and colas, delectable dishes such as dim sum and hearty vegetables are on tap. In particular, The Grand Hotel (圓山大飯店 *Yuanshan Da Fandian*) and Grand Formosa Regent (晶華酒店 *Jinhua Jiudian*) boast outstanding afternoon tea buffets.

Taiwanese like to eat Thai and other spicy foods, particularly during the winter. If you're not partial to spicy foods, make sure you tell the waiter in advance that you do not want the food prepared spicy. On Taiwan, "a little spicy" usually means the food will only burn a little hole in your tongue. In Mandarin, "not spicy" is "*bu la*" (不辣). There are a number of good restaurants on Fuxing North Road, near Zhongshan Middle School Station. There are also a variety of regal restaurants to choose from in Tienmu and near Shilin Station. Bear in mind that prices and restaurant formats change, so you may want to call in advance to find out if the delectable edibles you crave are still available.

Here are some fine Taipei cafés and eateries:

ARABIC

Ali Baba (阿里巴巴阿拉伯餐廳) on Xinyi Road, Section 4, #398 offers an array of exotic Lebanese and Syrian dishes. (台北市信義路4段398號) (02) 2706-9026.

BEIJING

If you're in the mood for upscale dining at a traditional Chinese restaurant, **Taoranting** (陶然亭) serves some of the best Peking duck on the island. The restaurant also boasts bounteous beef rolls and green onion pancakes. Fuxing North Road, #86, 2nd Floor (near the intersection of Fuxing and Nanjing East Road) (台北市復興北路86號2F) (02) 2778-7805.

If you crave some of the best Chinese food in town and are prepared to spend for it, **Shang Palace** (香宮) at Shangri-La's Far Eastern Plaza Hotel boasts choice Cantonese and sumptuous duck dishes prepared as if you were in Beijing. Dunhua South Road, Section 2, #201, 6F (台北市敦化南路2段201號 6F) (02) 2378-8888 (Ext. 5888).

CAJUN

If you want Cajun food prepared correctly you have to seek out a master, and thankfully you can find one in Taipei. The Chinese characters for **Cajun Master** (開心大師 Kaixin Dashi) mean "The Happy Master Chef," and after eating here your stomach may feel that way, too. The restaurant boasts a blissful blend of European, African and American food, and sumptuous seafood dishes. To try some delicious Cajun food, seek out the master on Henyang Road, #42 (台北市衡陽路42號) (02) 2382-6738.

CANTONESE

Although Taiwan isn't nearly as famous as Hong Kong for Cantonese food, there are ample choice Cantonese-style restaurants in Taipei.

Fulinmen (福臨門) restaurants, which offer some of the best Cantonese-style food on Taiwan, are conveniently located near MRT stations. The author strongly suggests thick rice noodles mixed with select beef and shaved onions (干炒牛河 gantsao niuhe) (NT $200), shrimp lightly wrapped in thin layers of noodle broth (鮮蝦仁腸粉 xian xiaren changfen) (NT $118), sliced beef topped with red and yellow peppers, ginger and onions (蠔油牛肉 haoyo niuroh) (NT $300) or sliced beef with Chinese broccoli (Jielan) vegetables (芥蘭牛肉 jielan niuroh) (NT $230). Refillable pots of pu-er tea (普耳茶 pu er cha) (NT $20) leave a smooth, slightly bittersweet aftertaste.

Nanjing: Nanjing East Road, Section 4, #186, 2nd Floor/1 (located at the Fuxing North Road intersection) (台北市松山區南京東路4段186號2樓之1, 光復北路口) (02) 2579-6862

New Beitou: Dayeh Road, #700 (Xinbeitou Station) (台北市北投區大業路700號, 新北投捷運站) (02) 2897-2211

Yonghe: Yonghe Road, Section 2, #116, 5th Floor (Tingxi Station, Exit 1) (台北市永和路2段116號5樓, 頂溪捷運站1號出口) (02) 8923-3656

Xindian: Beiyi Road, Section 1, #2, 2nd Floor (adjacent to Xindian Station) (台北縣新店市北宜路1段2號2樓, 新店捷運總站) (02) 2910-9777.

There are two locations for **Suntunglok Restaurant** (新同樂餐廳):
Dunhua South Road, Section 2, #34 (台北市敦化南路2段34號) (02) 2700-1818
Dunhua South Road, Section 1, Lane 232, #2 (台北市敦化南路1段232巷34號) (02) 2752-9797.

Hong Kong-based pop star Emil Chau (周華健 Chou Hua Zhen) recently opened a Cantonese-style chain, **Wakin's Kitchen** (粵華軒). The restaurant boasts shrimp rolls (杏香明蝦卷) and pork delicacies (香麻叉燒酥) (NT $92) as well as chicken, pork or beef set meals that include soup and rice (NT $130). Major credit cards are accepted.
Dayeh Takashimaya: Zhongcheng Road, Section 2, #55 (台北市忠誠路2段55號, B1)
Fuxing: Fuxing S. Rd, Sec. 1, #283 (台北市

復興南路1段283號2樓) (02) 2702-9988
Neihu D-Mart: Chenggong Road, Sec. 4,
#180, 9F, Neihu (台北市內湖成功路4段180
號, 德安百貨9樓) (02) 8792-8080.

FRENCH

As French language, dining and culture
gain ground amoung gourmands, you'll find
no shortage of fine French restaurants to
choose from in Taipei. You may find my
father, Monsieur Bob, dining at several of
them. Here are a select few:

Café Laurent is a café that offers appetizing
breakfast dishes, pastries and cakes, as
well as fine coffees and teas. There are six
branches in Taipei. Here are two popular
locations:
Tienmu: Zhongshan North Road, Section 6,
#764 (near Taipei American School) (台北市
中山北路6段764號) (02) 2875-5382
Renai: Renai Road, Section 4, #147
(intersection of Renai and Anho roads) (台
北市仁愛路4段147號) (02) 2721-2698.

The Taiwanese owner of **French Cuisine**
(法拉其 *Falechi*) won plenty of international
cooking contests, the restaurant's fine
French food tastes as if it were prepared at
a five-star hotel. Tienmu East Road, Lane
50, #27 (台北市天母東路50巷27號)
(02) 2874-7183.

Lin Chia-Yi's fluency in French is almost
as good as her fine French cooking. After
working as a Taipei chef for five years,
Ms. Lin decided to travel abroad to hone
her skills. She enrolled at two of France's
most prestigious cooking academies and
worked at two upscale restaurants in
Provence before returning to Taipei to follow
her dream and open **Jacques**, a French
café. Named after famous poet Jacques
Prevert, Ms. Lin finds that her own style of
cooking takes after the philosophy of Mr.
Prevert, simple yet poignant. Ms. Lin is also
a respected chef in the community, offering
French cooking classes. Try French-style
sandwiches, breads, and desserts at very

reasonable prices (NT $100 or less). After
a visit to Jacques, you may find yourself
saying, "C'est magnifique!" Zhongyi Street,
#30, Shilin, Taipei (opposite Taipei Municipal
Yu Nong Elementary School) (台北市士林
區忠義街 30號, 台北市士林區雨農國民小學
對面) (02) 2838-5767.

Le Bistro de L'Oliver (橄欖樹歐陸小館)
prepares dishes as if you were visiting the
French countryside. Weekday dinner sets
go for NT $690. Anho Road, Section 2,
#145 (台北市安和路2段145號)
(02) 8732-3726, 2377-8031.

Asiaworld's **Le ble d'or** (金色三麥) has
steadily been growing in popularity thanks
to the restaurant's original micro brewed
beers. Expect to spend between NT$ 400
(US $12.00) to NT$ 600 (US $18.00) per
person. Try the Hungarian beef stew or one
of the restaurant's fresh seafood dishes.
Dunhua North Road, #100 (環亞店北市敦化
北路100號) (02) 8712 8512.

Another **Le ble d'or** (金色三麥) is located at
Miramar Entertainment Park in Dazhi: (美麗
華百樂園, 台北市敬業三路20號5樓)
(02) 2175-3739.

Known for its provocative "provincial
cuisine," **Le Jardin** (馨亞美食坊) invites
guests to taste the foods of Provence in a
"delicate and romantic authentic French
setting." You may want to stop by before
checking out a baseball game, Le Jardin is
conveniently located across from Tienmu
Baseball Stadium. Closed Tuesdays.
Zhongcheng Road, Section 2, #170, Tienmu
(台北市士林區忠誠路2段170號)
(02) 2877-1778.

Every set at **Long Wall French Cuisine**
(長春藤餐廳 *Changchuenten*) is NT $230,
set meals include a fresh salad, sumptuous
soup, an exquisite entrée, flavorful fruit and
choice coffee or tea. You'll find fine eateries
on Yongkang Street, and this is one of them.
Yongkang Street, Lane 2, #11 (台北市永康
街2巷11號) (02) 2392-7533.

Maison Alexandre is a French deli in Tienmu known for its fine foods and wines, you'll find it near Taipei American School on Zhongshan North Road, Section 6, #764 (台北市中山北路6段756號) (02) 2876-1229.

Paris 1930, on the second floor of the Landis Taipei, serves traditional French cuisine such as roasted duck, healthy ginseng dishes, creamy tomato and butter soup, pan-fried fish and corn cakes. Food this good doesn't come cheap, patrons pay NT $2,500 to NT $3,500 per dinner set. Open for dinner at 6 pm, the last order is accepted no later than 9:30 pm. Minchuan East Road, Section 2, #41, 2nd Floor (台北市中山區民權東路2段41號) (02) 2597-1234.

Rich River (沅河靛 *Yuanhe Dian*) is a fine arts store in Taipei that also boasts a Chinese teahouse and French restaurant. Popular dishes include pig knuckle (NT $550), lamb chop (NT $550) and barbeque chicken (NT $450). Open Monday through Thursday, 11 am to 2 am and Friday through Sunday, 11 am to 3 am. Menus are offered in both Chinese and English, credit cards are accepted. Yongkang Street, Lane 14, #5 (near Xinyi Road, Section 2). (台北市永康街4巷5號) (02) 2341-5160, 2341-5305.

Round Table Teppanyaki, which boasts fine French-style teppanyaki served in an elegant atmosphere, also offers Japanese dishes. Valet parking is available. Dunhua South Road, Section 2, #128, B1 (台北市敦化南路2段128號B1) (02) 2700-8699.

Don't expect to encounter any of the Village People at **The Village** (小農莊 *Xiaonongzhuang*), the restaurant serves exotic French food in an elegant setting. Meals typically cost under NT $700. Tienmu West Road, Lane 13, #12 (台北市天母西路13巷12號) (02) 2873-1579.

GERMAN

Ready to make your tastebuds Sprechen Sie Deutsch? A fine choice for German cuisine is **Zum Fass** (香宜德國料理 *Shangyi Deguo Liaoli*), with its unique motto, "Speisen Wie Zu Hause," meaning "specials with the house." Too bad the delicious specials aren't on the house, the German and Swiss cuisine has a reputation for excellence. The restaurant has been on Taiwan for 26 years and recently relocated to a bigger, brighter, and more convenient location. Stop by for some classic German dishes. Xinsheng North Road, Section 1, #116-118 (台北市新生北路1段116-118號) (02) 2531-3815.

GREEK

If you can't make it to Greece, stop by **Greek Island** (希臘小館 *Xila Xiaoguan*) for a taste of some delicious authentic Greek food. Weekday set meals (beverage included) run from NT $180 to NT $280, NT $440 to NT $720 during weekends. Anho Road, Section 1, Alley 141, #9 (台北市安和路1段141弄9號) (02) 2704-2960.

Mediterranean Sea (夢見地中海美食坊) is another choice option for coffees, teas and a taste of Greece. Portions are somewhat small but prices are reasonable. Try the home-brewed fruit-flavored beer for NT $120. There are two locations, one is in the Shida area, the other is further downtown near National Taiwan University (Taida). Shida: Shida Road, Lane 83, #7 (台北市師大路83巷7號) (02) 2363-0336
Taida: Xinhai Road, Section 2, #159(台北市辛亥路2段159號) (02) 2736-8478.

INDIAN

Café India (寶來屋印度風味餐廳), a cozy Indian café that opened on August 15, 2004, offers a popular lunch buffet (NT $320 weekdays, NT $400 Saturdays and Sundays). The restaurant is open for lunch from noon to 2:30 pm and for dinner from 6 to 11 pm. KoQiang (Keh Chiang) Road, #30, Tienmu, near Tienmu Swimming Pool (台北市克強路30號, 近天母游泳池) (02)

2837-7365 http://www.cafeindia.com.tw.

Chef Deepak prepares authentic Indian dishes at **Himilaya Indian Restaurant** (西馬拉雅印度餐廳), Yenping North Road, Section 2, #97-1 (台北市延平北路2段97-1號) (02) 2555-5552.

There's never a shortage of fine curry dishes at **Hindustan Indian Cuisine** (興都斯坦印度餐廳) on Fuxing North Road, Lane 313, #43 (台北市復興北路313巷43號) (02) 2718-5608.

If you'd like to try an entirely Islamic-style of dining, **Kunming Restaurant** (清真昆明園) offers a variety of fresh Indian, Yu-Nan and halal foods. Fuxing North Road, Lane 81, #26 (台北市復興北路81巷26號) (02) 2751-6776.

Established on Taiwan over fifteen years ago, **Tandoor Indian Restaurant** (坦都印度餐廳) remains popular due to its mouth-watering weekend (Saturday and Sunday) buffet special. Set meals typically run between NT $300 and NT $400. Halal is also available. The restaurant is located between Hechiang and Longchiang streets. Hechiang Street, Lane 73, #10 (台北市合江街73巷10號) (02) 2509-9853 http://www.tandoor.com.tw.

Want to dine like royalty? **Taj Palace Restaurant** (嗒咭) serves exotic Indian food in a royal palace atmosphere. Songchiang Road, #270, 2nd Floor (台北市松江路270號) (02) 2567-2976, 2581-1436.

One of Taipei's most popular restaurants satisfying cravings for chicken tandoori is **The Spice Shop**, an Indian eatery on the road behind Miramar cinema complex. Tienmu East Road, Lane 50, Alley 10, #6 (台北市天母東路50巷10弄6號) (02) 2873-7775.

ITALIAN

For great Italian/American food, try **Capone's**.

Enjoy your meal while listening to live piano and jazz music. Fuxing North Road, #166-168 (台北市復興北路166-168號) (02) 2545-9365.

Galliano offers for fine Italian dining, wines, and live entertainment from 7 to 9 pm. Valet parking is available. Minsheng East Road, Section 3, Alley 25, Lane 113, #41 (台北市民生東路3段113巷25弄41號) (02) 2718-8289, 2514-8715.

Gino Italian Restaurant boasts a large Italian buffet and salad bar. Heping East Road, Section 3, #75 (台北市和平東路 3段75號) (02) 2736-7369.

Giorgio offers gourmet pasta and pizza at reasonable prices. Lunch specials start at NT $240. Renai Road, Section 4, #345 (台北市仁愛路4段345號) (02) 2731-7641.

Although **Italian Tomato** once served fine pasta dishes, the restaurant has since become a bakery in Beitou that offers only pastries and cakes. Daye Road #713, Beitou (台北市北投區大業路713號) (02) 2898-5229.

Italiano Risotto House offers only the finest Italian cuisine and wines. Tienmu East Road, Lane 50, #8 (台北市天母東路50巷8號) (02) 2873-7900.

L'Amico Restaurant offers traditional Italian dishes served as if you were in Italy. Expect to find a wide selection of fine imported wines, chilled U.S. beef and seafoods. Many couples, locals and expats alike, choose this restaurant for romantic dining. Valet parking is available. Minsheng East Road, Section 4, Lane 55, #10 (across from Citibank). (台北市民生東路四段55巷10號) (02) 2712-7190.

The chef of **La Giara**, "Maestro Antonio," creates with light and healthy ingredients so guests can keep fit. The restaurant combines modern chic and traditional Italian warmth. Fuxing South Road, Section 1,

#352, 2nd Floor (near Howard Plaza Hotel). (台北市復興南路1段352號) (02) 2705-0345.

Seats are hard to come by at either **La Pasta** location after 6 pm so arrive early. Prices are reasonable (NT $200 and up) and the seasoned pasta dishes keep hungry customers returning. Lunch runs from 11:30 am to 2:30 pm and dinner 5:30 pm to 9 pm. Tienmu East Road, #102, Taipei (台北市天母東路102號) (02) 2872-1738. Zhongcheng Road, Section 2, #14, Tienmu (台北市士林區忠誠路2段144號) (02) 2871-0304 http://www.lapasta.com.tw

Milan (米蘭) boasts sixteen varieties of noodles. Entrees are served for one or two people, and adding NT $150 per person will get each of you a drink, soup, salad and a slice of delicious cake. The restaurant can be reached by transferring at Taipei Main Station for the blue MRT line heading in the direction of Kunyang. Exit two stops after leaving Taipei Station at Zhongxiao Xinsheng Station. From exit 2, the restaurant is directly across the street. Zhongxiao East Road, Section 2, Lane 134, #6 (台北市忠孝東路2段134巷6號) (02) 2321-9301.

You may not find a taco at **Mr. Paco**, but you will, however, find delicious Italian food. Listen to live music every Friday evening. Renai Road, Section 4, Alley 4, Lane 345, #28 (台北市仁愛路4段345巷4弄147號) (02) 2773-6066.

Named after the Rialto bridge of Venice, Italy, **Osteria Rialto** offers authentic food prepared by an Italian chef with over thirty years of professional experience. The restaurant is around the corner from Capone's. Kuangfu South Road, Lane 260, #5 (台北市光復南路260巷5號) (02) 2778-1536.

Osteria Lido is the sister restaurant of Osteria Rialto and the fine Italian dishes served at this posh modern restaurant could be served at any five-star hotel. Sungshou

Road, #22, 2nd Floor (next to Warner Brother's Village) (台北市松壽路22號2F, 華納威秀旁) (02) 2758-7868.

The expatriate owner of **Papa Giovanni** (喬凡尼義大利餐廳) makes sure his customers are satisfied. Prices range from NT $500 to NT $1000, and specials include spaghetti with lobster and lamb rack with red wine sauce. Major credit cards such as Visa, Mastercard and American Express are accepted. Zhongxiao East Road, Section 4, Lane 6, Alley 120, #22 (台北市忠孝東路4段6巷120弄22號) (02) 2711-8720, 2711-8721.

Although the pasta dishes served at **Pomodoro** (蕃茄主義) taste as if you are aboard a luxury cuise ship, prices are quite reasonable. Spaghetti dishes start at only NT $75, and pudding desserts start at only NT $50. There is a minimum NT $300 charge for dinner. Dunhua South Road, Section 1, Alley 177, #47 (台北市敦化南路1段177弄47號) (02) 2772-0701 http://www.pomodoropasta.com.

Puro is an Italian coffee shop that offers delicious pastries, finger foods and coffees. Renai Road, Section 4, Alley 345, Lane 15, #4 (台北市仁愛路4段15巷345弄4號) (02) 2731-1232.

At **Trattoria** you'll find pastas, pizza, sandwiches, salads and fresh cheeses. Trattoria is located at two Eslite Books locations, at Taipei 101, and at Tienmu's Dayeh Takashimaya department store. Dunhua South Road, Section 1, #245, Floor G (誠品敦南店 台北市大安區敦化南路1段245號G樓) (02) 2775-5977 Ext. 616 Tienmu: Zhongcheng Road, Section 2, #188, B1 (台北市士林區忠誠路2段188號B1) (02) 2873-0966 Taipei 101: Shifu Road, #45, B1 (台北市信義區市府路45號B1) (02) 8101-8714 Dayeh Takashimaya: Zhongcheng Road, Section 2, #55, B1 Tienmu: (大葉高島屋, 台北市忠誠路2段55號) (02) 2836-2932.

The motto of traditional Italian restaurant

Tutto Bello is "everything is perfect," and from the soothing Italian opera music and fine cuisine it does indeed appear that the chefs are trying their best to ensure patrons have a delightful dining experience. Starters range from NT $240 to NT $450, soups include pumpkin cream with black truffle (NT $260) as well as Ligurian Seafood Soup (NT $280). The pasta dishes, which include linguine and angel hair pasta, range from NT $380 to NT $550. If you're in the mood for fine Italian food stop by and give Tutto Bello a try. Shuangcheng Street, Lane 25, #15 (next to Imperial Hotel). (台北市雙城街25巷15號) (02) 2595-1069.

JAPANESE

Due to its close proximity, Japan continues to have a strong influence on Taiwan, and in Taipei you won't have any trouble finding a quality Japanese restaurant to choose from. Shabu-Shabu hot pot restaurants are particularly popular with Taiwanese people during the winter.

The first **Azabu Sabo** (麻布茶房) opened in Tokyo on October 25, 1978, and within three decades twenty-five Azabu Sabo restauarants followed. The upscale chain arrived on Taiwan in 1999 and offers some of the finest Japanese eats, sweets and desserts in Taipei. Ramen noodle bowls start at NT $210 while tempura dishes go for NT $420. Afterwards try the red beans or green beans with ice and milk. The hot sweet potato a la mode also makes for an interesting snack. Most locations are open from 11 am to 11 pm, but the one in Ximending is open from 11:30 am to 10:30 pm and the one in the ATT department store is open Monday through Friday from 11:30 am to 10:30 pm and until 11pm on weekends.
Tienmu: Tienmu East Road, #59-1 (台北市天母東路59-1號) (02) 2876-1717
ATT Department Store: Zhongxiao East Road, Section 4, #218, 2nd Floor (台北市忠孝東路4段218號2樓) (02) 2778-7996
Ximending: Hanzhong Street, #116, 4th Floor (Ximen Station, Exit 6) (台北市漢中街116號誠品116號 4樓, 捷運西門站6號出口) (02) 2375-7246
Xinyi business district: Songshou Road, #22, 2F-2 (2nd Floor, Neo 19 complex) (台北市松壽路22號 2樓之2, Neo 19 營).

Aubergine (茄子咖哩 Chiezi Jiali), which means "eggplant curry," is a Japanese chain that offers fine "European-style" curry foods. The curry here is light, sweet and tangy rather than heavy. Choose how spicy you want your food prepared, from 1 through 5. "1" means not spicy while "5" means get ready to dive over the next table to down two pitchers of water. If you enjoy seafood try the seafood curry, you shouldn't be disappointed. Prices average between NT $250 to NT $350 (US $7.50-10.50) for set meals.
Gongguan: Roosevelt Road, Section 4, #85, 2nd Floor (台北市羅斯福路4段85號2樓) (02) 2366-1258
Nanjing: Nanjing East Road, Section 3, #285 (台北市南京東路3段285號) (02) 2717-1066
Tienmu: Zhongcheng Road, Section 2, #188, B1 (Eslite Books building) (台北市士林區忠誠路2段188號B1) (02) 2875-6389
Zhongxiao: Zhongxiao East Road, Section 4, #98, 3F (Across the street and one block east of SOGO) (台北市大安區忠孝東路四段98號3F) (02) 6638-6889.

Ben Teppanyaki is a Japanese tiebanxiao (鐵板燒), which borrows the traditional Japanese-style of cooking on a grill in front of patrons sans the theatrics. The upscale restaurant boasts well-trained chefs, an elegant atmosphere, and outstanding food. The restaurant also offers fine French and Chinese cuisine. Business lunches, which are offered between 11:30 am and 2 pm, go for NT $880. Dinner sets cost NT $1950.
Anho Road, Section 1, Lane 102, #2 (台北市安和路1段102巷2號) (02) 2703-2296.

If you're in the mood for spicy hot pot, **Buma Bula** (怖麻怖辣) is a popular Japanese hot pot chain. Pay one price for an all-you-can-eat buffet, which includes beef, pork or lamb, seafood, vegetables and ice cream. There are currently seven in Taipei, here are two:

Zhongxiao I: Zhongxiao East Road, Section 2, Lane 134, #2 (台北市忠孝東路2段134巷2號) (02) 2391-3407 (adjacent to Milan)

Zhongxiao II: Zhongxiao East Road, Section 4, Lane 194, Alley 1, #14(台北市忠孝東路4段194巷1弄14號) (02) 8773-8177 (opposite ATT dept store) http://www.bumabula.com.tw.

Some expatriates consider **Hadakoyama** (二子山拉麵) to be the best ramen noodle restaurant in Taipei. Entering feels as if you are leaving Taipei and stepping inside a small Japanese town where employees don traditional Japanese attire and patrons dine at the counter. Ramen noodle bowls run between NT $75 to NT $165 for a medium and NT $90 to NT $180 for a large. Specialties include barbeque pork green onion noodle ramen, lemon miso noodle soup, butter sweet corn noodle soup and samboo bamboo noodle soup. For those that enjoy spicy noodles, Hadakoyama offers spicy savia noodle soup ramen. Small dishes include shrimp hand roll salad (NT $55), Japanese pork chop (NT $80), fried dumplings (NT $60) and Japanese fried tofu (NT $45). The restaurant also serves beef bowls (NT $95 to NT $120) and pork bowls (NT $95). Korean dishes, including kimchi cold noodles (NT $140), are also available. There are currently two locations in the Tienmu area:

Tienmu East road, Lane 8, #89 (台北市天母東路8巷89號) (02) 2874-2367

Zhongshan North Road, Section 6, #738 (台北市士林區中山北路6段738號) (02) 2871-9331.

The Chinese name of **Japanese Food** (春日*Chuenre*) means "Spring Day," if you experience this traditional Japanese food during the spring, you may leave with fond memories of the restaurant's culinary creations. Daan Road, Section 1, #108 (台北市大安路4段108號) (02) 2731-4731.

Owned by a Japanese national, the chef of **Japanese Ramen** prepares jo jo ramen, an award-winning noodle. Try the ramen and discover why this noodle wins the prize. Daan Road, Section 1, Lane 83, #8 (台北市大安路1段83弄8號) (02) 2721-6688.

The heavenly helpings at **Japanese Zen Food** (本膳日本料理 *Benshan Huaishi Liaoli*) may bring you to a higher state of consciousness. Dunhua S. Rd, Sec 1, Lane 233, #2, 2F (台北市敦化南路1段233弄2號 2F) (02) 2773-7976.

Jiujinjia in Beitou, a small but crowded Japanese eatery, offers a taste of the authentic. Guangming Road, #195, New Beitou (台北市北投區光明路195號) (02) 2892-4127.

Tourists flock to **Lailai Ramen** during weekends, the service is slow but the noodles are worth noshing. Stop by if you have fifty minutes to spare. Wenchuen Road, #110, New Beitou (台北市北投區泉源路195號) (02) 2893-7958.

Mos Burger (摩斯漢堡) is a Japanese fast food chain with over sixty restaurants in the Taipei area. You may want to try the rice burgers with beef teriyaki.

Beitou: Zhongyang North Road, Section 1, #72 (opposite Beitou Elementary School) (台北市北投區中央北路1段72號) (02) 2896-0937

Danshui: Zhongzheng East Road, #35 (Opposite Danshui Station) (台北縣淡水鎮中正東路35號) (02) 2626-1487

Tienmu: Tienmu North Road, #85 (台北市天母北路85號) (02) 2871-1462.

No need to search through the forest to find **Red Woods**, a Japanese teppanyaki restaurant established in 1976. Business lunches are offered for NT $280. In addition to fine dining, the restaurant boasts a piano lounge for dessert and live entertainment. Valet parking is offered after 6 pm. Shuangcheng Street, #23-3 (behind Imperial Hotel). (台北市雙城街23-3號)

(02) 2591-1155, 2591-1156.

Established in Japan over five decades ago and on Taiwan in 1991, **Royal Host** (樂雅 樂 *Re Ya Re*) boasts excellent Eastern and Western cuisine and the best onion soup on the island. Set meals range from NT $250 to NT $498, most include soup, salad and a beverage. There are currently seven branches in Taipei:
Beitou: Beitou Road, Section 2, #9 (台北市北投區大業路452巷62號)(02) 2897-6248
Daan: Daan Road, Section 1, #73, 2nd Floor (台北市大安路1段73號2樓) (02) 2721-9038
Neihu: Minchuan East Road, Section 6, #491 (台北市民權東路6段491號)
(02) 2634-0663
Songchiang: Songchiang Road, #156-2, 2nd Floor (台北市中山區松江路156之2號2樓)
(02) 2542-9089
Taipei Main Station YMCA: Shuchang Street, #19 (台北市許昌街19號)
(02) 2371-3128
Tienmu: Tienmu East Road, #19, 2nd Floor (台北市天母東路19號2樓) (02) 2 2872-1622
Dunhua: Dunhua North Road, Lane 199, #9 (台北市敦化北路199巷9號) (02) 2546-1931.

A few decades ago, only the rich could enjoy sushi on Taiwan. Now, however, sushi on Taiwan costs less than in Japan, and eateries are springing up faster than spring rolls. **Sushi Express** (爭鮮迴轉壽司), with over thirty Taipei locations, is a chain that has capitalized on the food's popularity. Two or three sushi pieces are placed on a colored dish and put on a moving conveyer belt which hungry patrons pick up as they move by. Dishes typically cost NT $30 (US .90) each. Here are six locations:
Shilin: Zhongzheng Road, #230 (台北市士林區中正路230號) (02) 2838-4250
Nanjing I: Nanjing East Road, Section 2, #174 (台北市南京東路2段174號)
(02) 2508-2419
Nanjing II: Nanjing East Road, Section 3, #220 (台北市南京東路3段220號)
(02) 2771-5049
Ximending: Shichang Street, Section 2, #6 (台北市武昌街2段6號) (02) 2389-0259

Beitou: Chuenyuen Road, #12 (opposite Xinbeitou Station) (台北市泉源路12號, 全國電子旁) (02) 2895-3960
Yongkang: Yongkang Street, #2 (near Xinyi Road) (台北市永康街2號, 信義路口)
(02) 2392-5055.

Yoshinoya (吉野家 *Ji Yeh Jia*), a Japanese fast food chain recognizable by its orange and white logo with a drawing of a black bull's head in the center, offers chicken or beef set meals. Meals typically cost between NT $90 for a medium bowl of rice and meat or NT $125 for a large. There are over forty locations throughout Taipei. Here are five:
New Beitou: Guangming Road, #223-1 (台北市北投區光明路223-1號) (02) 2895-9268
Shilin I: Wenlin Road, #123 (台北市士林區文林路123號) (02) 2882-0896
Shilin II: Zhengzhong Road, #281 (台北市士林區中正路281號) (02) 2883-5309
Shipai: Shipai Road, Section 2, #79 (台北市石牌路2段79號) (02) 2826-3598
Zhongxiao: Zhongxiao East Road, Section 1, #174 (台北市忠孝東路1段174號)
(02) 2391-2566.

KOREAN

There are several Korean hot pot and barbeque eateries in the Tienmu / Shilin areas. You'll also find delicious barbeque and "Korean soul food" dishes at **Seoul Korean Bar-B-Q**. Zhongshan North Road, Section 1, Lane 33, #4 (台北市中山北路1段33巷4號) (02) 2511-2326.

MEXICAN

The décor of **Santa Fe Café** may not impress like the real Santa Fe, but the Mexican dishes are delicious. Chaozhou Street, #150 (台北市潮州街150號)
(02) 2394-2181.

There's always the touristy but popular **Tequila Sunrise** (佬墨日出) for Mexican food and margaritas at reasonable prices.
Tienmu: Tienmu East Road, #88 (台北市天母東路88號) (02) 2877-1118

Xinsheng: Xinsheng South Road, #42 (台北市新生南路42號) (02) 2362-7563.

Que Pasa receives high marks for hip ambiance but mediocre marks for pricy mixed drinks and set meals. You be the judge. Fuxing North Road, Lane 313, #32 (台北市復興北路313巷32號) (02) 2719-2600.

MONGOLIAN

If you're looking for a good **Mongolian Barbeque**, the restaurant name says it all! Meals cost NT $450 plus a 10% service charge. Nanjing East Road, Section 3, #176 (台北市南京東路3段176號) (02) 2711-4412.

There are also Mongolian woks at **Shann Garden** (禪園) in Beitou and at **Star of Sea** (淡水海中天 *Haizhongtien*), an impressive Chinese buffet in Zhuwei (both are listed below under "Taiwanese").

NORTH AFRICAN

North African Mood (北非心情 *Beifei Xinching*) is a Moroccan restaurant that serves traditional dishes such as Pita and Cous Cous. Pig lovers unite, the restaurant does not serve pork! Dunhua North Road, Lane 165, #1 (台北市敦化北路165巷1號) (02) 2713-3439.

PERSIAN

Persian Heaven is the first Persian restaurant on Taiwan. Set meals run the gamut from minced lamb to mixed vegetables and kababs and will typically set you back around NT $250 (US $7.50), a reasonable price for a wide assortment of culinary creations. Hochiang Road, Lane 61 #1 (台北市合江路61巷1號) (02) 2517-1603.

PORTUGESE

Hong Kong pop star Emil Chau (周華健) opened **Pinocchil** (木偶葡國餐廳 *Muohpuguo Tsanting*), a classy Portuguese restaurant, in 1998. The restaurant boasts a coffee shop on the first floor and Portuguese eatery one floor below that serves scrumptious barbeque dishes and exotic Macao foods. Daan Road, Section 1, #135 (台北市大安路1段135號) (02) 8773-0878.

PRAGUE

Prague (布拉格捷克餐廳, 日昇之屋 *Reshen Zhiwu*) is a traditional restaurant that also serves some Eastern dishes. Prague food is typically very sour, so some of the dishes have been altered a bit to fit local tastes. Changchun Road #410 (台北市長春路410號) (02) 2713-3439.

SHANGHAI

2046 presents fresh flavors in ambiance, design, drinks and food. While heliotrope and azure neon lights create an ultramodern essence, Chinese antiques on display add a retro-Chinese aura. 2046 offers an array of eats, from shrimp fried rice (NT $200) to Shanghai-style pork dishes (NT $250). Open 5 pm to 3 am, this exquisite pub/eatery is a seven-minute walk from Zhongxiao Dunhua Station. Zhongxiao East Road, Section 4, Lane 205, #4 (台北市忠孝東路4段205巷4號) (02) 2711-5589.

Yi Shang Garden (溢香園 *Yi Shangyuan*) boasts "new Shanghai dining" since 1979. The menu includes seaweed strips with pine nuts (NT $280), Shanghai-style fried rice (NT $25), and sweetened stuffed watterlilly roots (NT $220 small/NT $440 large) for starters, a sumptuous smattering of beef, pork, and poultry dishes (NT $200 to NT $390), and sweet delights that include taro mash with sweet bean toppings (NT $80). Yi Shang Garden is open from 11 am to 2 pm for lunch (2:30 on weekends) and from 5 pm to 9 pm for dinner. Tienmu East Road #41 (台北市天母東路41號) (02) 2871-7755.

SOUTHEAST ASIAN

Hungry for Southeast Asian cuisine? Try

Nanyang Meishi (南洋美食) in the lower level food court of the Eslite Books building in Tienmu, many palates have been pleased by the restaurant's native-tasting Southeast Asian dishes and hot pot meals. Prices are reasonable, expect to pay between NT $200 to NT $350 for set meals. Zhongcheng Road, Section 2, #188, B1 (台北市士林區忠誠路2段188號B1) (02) 2874-3165.

Spice Garden is a new Tienmu restaurant that offers exotic Southeast Asian cuisine. Set meals start at NT $250. Zhongshan North Road, Section 6, #762 (台北市中山北路6段762號) (02) 2871-6590.

SPANISH

The Living Bar offers great Spanish and Italian food and its own special house whiskey, "Shooting Decanter," to liven up the evening and make both local residents and international guests feel alive. Chingcheng Street, #18-1 (台北市松山區慶城街18號之1號) (02) 2546-5966.

For a variety of fine Spanish and Italian food, stop by **Edinburgh** (愛丁堡 *Aidingbao*). Expect something different, every two months the restaurant presents an entirely new menu. Lishui Street, #24 (台北市麗 水街1號) (02) 2391-9069.

SRI LANKAN

Owner and chef Damian Chee ensures that the food prepared at **Sri Lanka Restaurant** (蘭卡咖哩) tastes exactly as if it were prepared in Sri Lanka. In other words, if your taste buds tingle for spicy, savory foods you've found the right restaurant! Open for lunch from 11 am to 2 pm and for dinner from 5 to 9 pm, (closed Monday afternoons), curry dishes start at NT $185, and there are ample choices. Try yellow rice with chicken, fish or mutton curry, rice dishes that include spicy fried rice with minced meat, chicken or shrimp (NT $150), spicy fish head curry (NT $400), or vegetable curry starting at NT $100. Vegetable dishes include green

beans, lentil, green peas, potato, pumpkin, spinish, or pineapple (nothing wrong with throwing some fruit into the vegetable mix). Mixed vegetable curry and the mushroom with cashew nut curry each go for NT $110. You can also try devilled dishes from NT $200, palandy dishes from NT $230 or sambol dishes starting at NT $70. New dishes include poories with potato (NT $140) and plain poories for NT $65. Coconut cake goes for NT $80. There are ample soft and fruit drinks available (NT $40 to NT $70), as well as beer (NT $80 to NT $90). For an authentic taste of Sri Lanka, stop by today. Chongyi Street, #48, Shilin (near Yangming Hospital) (台北市士林區忠義街48號, 近陽明醫院) (02) 2832-0153.

SZECHWAN

Get it hot, hot, hot! (Szechwan Chinese-style spicy, that is).

The Black Modern Restaurant (現代啟示錄 *Shiandai Chishilu*) is a posh eating establishment that boasts choice, spicy Szechwan food. The restaurant comes alive at night as a DJ spins snappy songs from 9 pm to 12 am. Fuxing North Road, #323 (台北市復興北路323號) (02) 2545-4628.

Eating at **Chili Garden** is like eating a garden full of fresh hot chili peppers. Yum! The restaurant is not to be confused with the popular Western Chili's Grill & Bar. Renai Rd., Section 4, #25, basement (台北市仁愛路4段25號) (02) 2751-6525.

The spicy food food is good good at **Fufu** on Daan Road, Section 1, Lane 175, #14 (台北市大安路1段175巷14號) (02) 2702-4586.

Kiki, owned by Taiwanese singer Lan Shin Mei, offers some of the spiciest Szechwan in town. Get ready to down a pitcher of lemon water! Kuangfu South Road, Lane 280, #47 (台北市光復南路280弄47號) (02) 2781-4250.

Ningzhi Huoguo (寧記) serves spicy hot pot (火鍋 *huoguo*) soup meals, if you're looking to leave a lasting impression on your tongue and esophagus this is the hot, native flavorful food to try. Kuangfu South Road, Lane 200, #9 (台北市光復南路100巷9號) (02) 2772-1912.

SWISS

Some **Alpen Garden** shops have home decor, essential oils and bathing products, the following two boast epicurean eateries: Shin Kong Mitsukoshi department store, Hall A9, 4th Floor (新光三越A9館4F) (02) 8789 4426. Yongkang Street, Lane 14, #6 (台北市大安區永康街14巷6號) (02) 2341-2359 http://www.alpengarden.com.

Experience a lot more than cheese at Tienmu's **Ticino Swiss Restaurant**. This hidden haven for hedonistic gourmands boasts delectable dishes from Switzerland as well as rare Swiss wines and fine fondue finds. Chocolate fondue goes for NT $250 while cheese fondue goes for NT $500. Open for lunch from 11 am to 2:30 pm and again for dinner from 5:30 to 10 pm. Tienmu East Road, Lane 82, #2 (台北市天母東路82巷2號) (02) 2876-1101.

TAIWANESE

Aboriginal Stones (漂流木原住民餐廳 *Piaoliumu*) boasts live aboriginal singing Thursday and Saturday evening after 9:30 pm. Stop by for a wide selection of ambrosial aboriginal food. Roosevelt Road, Section 3, Lane 316, Alley 9, #4 (台北市羅斯福路3段316巷9弄4號) (02) 2365-7413.

The motto of **Ah Hong de Tsai** (阿鴻的菜) is "cooking with heart," and the fine fare taste as if the chef gives her all. In Beitou, this quaint red restaurant with traditional Taiwanese décor is worth a visit. Dayeh Road, Lane 452, #29 (opposite Beitou Station) (台北市北投區大業路452巷29號) (02) 2891-5206, 2897-5097.

Bafang Yunji (八方雲集食品公司), "eight way," with over three hundred locations, is a well-known chain that boasts more than eight ways to make delicious dumplings. The restaurants are nothing fancy but the food is delicious. At only NT $4 and $7 each, try the pork and vegetable dumplings (招牌水餃 *zhaopie shuijiao*) and shrimp dumplings (蝦餃 *shia jiao*). Menus are in Chinese so you may want to bring a local friend. Restaurants also offer soybean milk (豆漿 *dou jiang*).
Beitou: Guangming Road, #213 (台北市北投區光明路213號) (02) 2898-3881
Zhonghe Street, #299 (台北市北投區中和街299號) (02) 2897-9868
Zhongying South Road, Section 1, #132 (台北市北投區中央南路1段132號) (02) 2893-9001
Daan: Heping East Road, Section 1, #274 (台北市大安區和平東路1段274號) (02) 2362-8168
Heping East Road, Section 3, #85 (台北市大安區和平東路3段85號) (02) 2377-8686
Danshui: Beixin Road, #171 (台北縣淡水鎮北新路171號) (02) 2626-9396
Zhongzhong East Road, #49 (台北縣淡水鎮中正東路49號) (02) 2622-7720
Xinchun Street, #180 (台北縣淡水鎮新春街180號) (02) 2628-1515
Shipai: Shipai Road, Section 1, #91 (台北市北投區石牌路1段91號) (02) 2822-3636
Tienmu: Zhongcheng Road, Section 1, #35 (台北市士林區忠誠路1段35號) (02) 2838-7878
Tienmu East Road, #46 (台北市士林區天母東路46號) (02) 2876-3335
Zhongshan: Minsheng East Road, Section 1, #51 (台北市中山區民生東路1段51號) (02) 2567-4567.

If you crave mushrooms then **Baigu (Mushroom) Restaurant** (佰菇園) is for you! Each of the seven Taipei locations receives rave reviews from those with a taste for the exotic. Here are five locations:
Fuxing South Road, Section 2, #142 (台北市復興南路2段142號) (02) 2700-3671
Renai Road, Section 4, Lane 71, #17 (台北市仁愛路4段71巷17號) (02) 8773-3160

Minsheng East Road, Section 5, #60 (台北市民生東路五段60號) (02) 2753-0625
Tienmu I: Zhongcheng Road, Section 1, #91 (台北市忠誠路1段91號) (02) 2832-2146
Tienmu II: Zhongshan North Road, Section 7, Lane 63, #1 (台北市中山北路7段63巷1號) (02) 2876-6431.

Chef's Wine, Food and Teahouse (掌櫃酒菜茶館) may have a curious English name, but the dishes delight like Wang Chienming on the mound for the Yankees. The retro-Taiwan ambiance (established over five decades ago), local entrées (NT $250 and up), Chinese teas (NT $150) and drinks offer a fun introduction to Taiwanese dining culture. Open 5 pm to 3 am, smoking section. Jianguo South road, Section 1, Lane 252, #3 (台北市建國南路1段252巷3號) (02) 22708-0777.

Yang Li Hua, a Taiwanese opera star, owns **Chicken House** (雞家莊 *Jijiazhuang*). The restaurant offers Taiwanese-style and Hainan (China) dishes. Zhongshan North Road, Section 1, #11 (台北市中山北路1段11號) (02) 2541-8261.

China Pa (中國父 *Zhongguo Fu*) boasts "creative and exquisite" Chinese cuisine, healthy drinks and tea, wines and (classy or crassy?) cigars. You can hear live music daily from 9 pm to 12 am. Anho Road, Section 1, #145 (台北市安和路1段145號) (02) 2702-7011.

Owned by Taiwanese singer Chee Ching, savor spicy hot pot food served at **Chyiis Hot Chafer** (齊辣 *Chi La*). Zhongxiao East Road, Section 4, Lane 170, Alley 6, #7 (台北市忠孝東路4段170巷6弄7號) (02) 2711-5385, 2711-5391.

Local residents and expatriates alike are fond of watching native foods grilled before them on a tie ban shao (鐵板燒). Whereas "teppenyaki" meals in the West can easily set you back US $40.00 or more, set meal prices typically start at NT $120 (US $3.60) for rice, soup, meat and a vegetable (usually cabbage), bean sprouts or both. Some upscale restaurants may charge an additional 10% service charge. Otherwise there is no additional tax and no need to leave a tip; for additional information please see "XY & Z (Useful Information) (很有用的信息)." If you do not wish to have your meal prepared with spicy flavoring be sure to tell the chef you do not want spicy (不辣 *bu la*). Here are two terrific tie ban shao (鐵板燒) restaurants:

Big My (大嗖鐵板燒 *Damai Tiebanxiao*) is a teppenyaki chain on Taiwan famous for its inexpensive yet delicious eats. Most meals fall within the NT $90 to NT $120 range and include soup and a drink. A bowl of rice is an additional NT $10.
Tienmu: Tienmu North Road, #10 (台北市天母北路10號) (02) 2874-7769 (Tienmu West Road, Tienmu North Road intersection)
Minsheng: Sanmin Road #108-29 (台北市三民路108號之29) (02) 2768-3559 (near Sanmin Road and Minsheng East Road intersection).

Fuhua Tiebanxiao (福華鐵板燒) is a Danshui teppenyaki trove on Chingshui Street, #9-1 (北縣淡水鎮清水街9-1號) (02) 2621-8285. Portions are plentiful, menus are in Chinese. Open 11 am to 2 pm for lunch and 5 pm to 10 pm for dinner.

Your taste buds may take off at **Danshui Jichang** (淡水機場複合式餐廳), or "Danshui Airport," an upscale Chinese seafood restaurant conveniently located across the street from Hongshulin Station. Look for the purple-painted 737 airbus on the roof! Open 11:00 am to 2 am daily. Dishes start at NT $100 and guests pay depending on the number of dishes ordered. Zhongzheng Road, Section 2, #51-2 (台北縣淡水鎮中正東路2段51之2號) (02) 2808-2345.

There are branches of **Dintaifung** (頂泰豐) in Japan, Shanghai, Singapore, Hong Kong and U.S. The restaurant boasts delectable dumplings, sumptuous soups and various vegetables. Expect hordes of residents and international tourists, there's usually a thirty to forty-minute wait. Xinyi Road, Section 2, #194 (Xinyi Road, Sec. 2 and Yongkang Street intersection) (台北市信義路2段194號, 永康街口) (02) 2721-1890.

No, you're never gonna get it? Well, for NT $1000, NT $1200 or NT $1300 you'll get top-of-the-time gourmet Chinese cuisine at **En Vogue**, the staff prepares dishes for you and your party based on the amount you choose to spend. Fuxing North Road, #311 (台北市復興北路311號) (02) 2547-2588, 2547-2555.

Fang's Restaurant (方家小館 *Fangjia Xiaoguan*) boasts classic Chinese dishes. Snacks include steamed buns (NT $180 to NT $300), dumplings (NT $180 to NT $200), mango pudding (NT $60), and sweet mashed taro (NT $100). Cold dishes include Shanghai-style sliced pork (NT $256), asparagus with mayonnaise (NT $360), and spotted crab with wine and vinegar (NT $396). Seafood dishes run the gamut from steamed yellow fish (NT $496) and cod with minced soy beans, sour seeds or with brown sauce and onions (NT $576) to shrimps with tomato sauce, curry sauce, bean leaves, chili sauce, green peas, pineapple or with cashew nuts (NT $360 to NT $380). Fried eel with leeks (NT $366) and fried frogs (NT $396 to NT $436) are also available. There are also ample rice, noodle, beef, pork, chicken, casserole and vegetable dishes. Seats are hard to come by on weekends. Open 11 am to 2 pm for lunch (2:30 on weekends) and again from 5 to 9 pm for dinner. Tienmu East Road, #7 (台北市天母東路7號) (02) 2872-8402.

Not only fishermen enjoy the fine catches at **The Fisherman's Restaurant** (魚夫家飯 *Yufu Jiafan*), Yongkang Street, Alley 2, #12-1 (台北市永康街2弄 12-1號) (02) 2391-9473.

The family chef may be green with envy the choice Chinese and Western dishes are prepared so well at **Green House** (格林屋 *Gelinwu*), a restaurant owned by Taiwanese singer Chien Ying Jie. Dunhua South Road, Section 2, Alley 63, Lane 53, #2 (台北市敦化南路2段53巷63弄2號) (02) 2709-3430.

For good local Chinese eats you can always try **Guguyen** (姑姑筵). Near the night market on Liaoning Street, Lane 45, #5 (台北市遼寧街45巷5號) (02) 2752-6469.

Couples often hold wedding celebrations at **Haibawang** (海霸王) because the buffets and hot pot meals have a reputation for excellence.
Changan: Changan West Road, #287 (台北市大同區長安西路287號) (02) 2552-2205
Nanjing: Nanjing East Road, Section 5, #411(台北市松山區南京東路5段411號) (02) 2747-7835
Xining: Xining North Road, #7 (台北市大同區西寧北路7號) (02) 2552-7345
Zhongshan: Zhongshan N. Rd., Sec 3, #59 (台北市中山北路3段59號) (02) 2594-4737.

The Hakka are a tribe of people who live on Taiwan and speak the *Ke Jia* (客家) language, a dialect that remotely resembles Cantonese. Try some of their local dishes at **Hakka House** (咱厝邊大牛的店 *Za Tswo Bien*): Renai Road, Section 4, Alley 266, Lane 15, #2 (台北市仁愛路4段15巷266弄2號) (02) 2707-0758.

For spicy Taiwanese food eat healthy at **Healthy Hot Chafer** (天辣子 *Tien La Zi*), a local hot pot restaurant. Renan Street, Lane 23, #2 (台北市仁愛街23巷2號) (02) 2700-1313.

If the city leaves you feeling a bit too crowded, you can find a comfortable degree of **Human Space** (人性空間 *Renxing Kongjian*) at this fine local eatery. Human Space boasts heavenly hot pot meals for NT $150, NT $180 and NT $200, respectively. Roosevelt Road, Section 3, Alley 286, Lane 4, #1 (台北市羅斯福路3段4巷286弄1號) (02) 2365-5635.

You'll be welcomed at **Isabella's House**

(伊莎貝拉風情館 *Yishabeila Fengchingguan*), a quaint local eatery with an international flavor in Shilin one block from Shilin Station. The first floor offers a taste of England, on the second you'll find the placid setting of Bali, Indonesia and the third offers a glimpse of Prague. The seafood pasta meal is reasonably priced at NT $280 (US $8.60) while the pork, chicken and steak meals, which include a salad, range from NT $350 (US $10.50) to NT $450 (US $13.50). Add NT $100 or NT $150 for a beverage depending on the set you order. Open 11 am to 2 pm for lunch and 5 pm to 9 pm for dinner. Night owls flock to Isabella's House Monday through Friday from 12 am to 3 am and on weekends from 12 am until 5 am, bring your laptop for free Internet access. Zhongshan North Road, Section 5, Lane 505, #24 (台北市中山北路5段505巷24號) (02) 2883-3820.

If the wait is too long at Dintaifung, try **Kao's Snack Collection** (永康街高記 *Kao Ji*), a two-story traditional eatery that opened in 1950. Kao's boasts Taiwanese, Shang Hainese and Cantonese-style foods. Yongkang Street, #5 (near Xinyi Road, around the corner from Dintaifung). (台北市永康街5號) (02) 2341-9971, 2341-9984.

Noble Family Steak House (貴族世家 *Guizhu Shijia*), founded in Banchiao, Taipei County in 1995, is a steak house and buffet restaurant that now boasts over 180 branches. Although a tad pricier, the chicken, chops and steak are comparable to those offered by My Home Steak, and the one in Tienmu is located on the same road as its rival.
Beitou: Zhongyang South Road, Section 1, #76 (台北市北投區中央南路1段76號)
(02) 2896-9086 Open 10 am to 10 pm
Danshui: Zhongzheng Road, #84 (Danshui Historic Street) (台北縣淡水鎮中正路84號)
(02) 2626-1902 Open 11 am to 11 pm
Tienmu: Tienmu West Road, Lane 13, #9 (台北市士林區天母西路13巷9號)
(02) 2874-5091 Open 11 am to 10 pm
Ximending: Wuchang Street, Section 2,

#29, 2nd Floor (台北市萬華區武昌街2段29號2樓) (02) 2375-7890 Open 10 am to 11 pm.

My Home Steak (我家牛排 *Wojia Niupai*) wins customers for best local steaks at the lowest local prices. NT $120 (US $3.60) for a steak and pasta meal (includes salad bar, drinks and dessert) is hard to beat. The chain also serves chicken steaks with either rice or noodles and has moderate salad and dessert bars.
Beitou: Zhongyang North Road, Section 1, #78 (台北市北投區中央南路1段78號) (02) 2893-0954
Tienmu: Tienmu West Road, Lane 13, #13 (opposite Tienmu Elementary School) (台北市天母西路13巷13號) (02) 2873-5922.

My Humble House (寒舍食譜) is more trendy than humble, the restaurant is decorated with fine Chinese antiques and serves gourmet Chinese cuisine. Dunhua South Road, Section 1, #108, B1 (台北市敦化南路1段108號 B1) (02) 8771-9928, 8771-9929.

Barbeque restaurants, in which you select raw meats and vegetables and cook them on the table in front of you, are becoming increasingly popular. One good barbeque restaurant in Shilin is **Wuyen Xiaoroh** (無煙燒肉), Zhongshan North Road, Section 5, #678, Shilin (台北市中山北路五段678號1樓) (02) 2838-5848.

For a super spot to watch the serene Danshui sunset, **Red Castle** (紅樓 *Hunglo*) is a café/restaurant not far from Danshui Historic Street. You'll need to climb over a hundred steps up a narrow, winding alleyway, but the outstanding coffee and fruit drinks as well as chicken and pasta dishes are worth the trek. The waffles, however, would make good replacement hockey pucks. Sanmin Street, Lane 2, #6, Danshui (台北縣淡水鎮三民街2巷6號) (02) 8631-1168.

Sanshang Chaofu (三商巧福) means "three

owners" because this beef noodle chain with nearly forty locations was founded in 1983 by, you guessed it... The tag line for the chain, found on its napkins, is "The healthy, happy beef noodles chain," and your stomach may feel that way after you try a bowl. A beef noodles bowl, vegetable dish and drink typically go for NT $125. Chain restaurants are hard to miss from the orange sign with white Chinese characters. Menus are in Chinese.

Beitou: Beitou Road, Section 2, #13, B1 (台北市北投區北投路2段13號B1, 燦坤3C) (02) 2894-4218

Guting: Roosevelt Road, Section 2, #75 (古亭分店)台北市中正區羅斯福路2段75號) (02) 2363-8582

Minchuan: Minchuan West Road, #45 (台北市民權西路45號) (02) 2586-4023

Shipai: Shipai Road, Section 2, #118 (台北市石牌路2段118號) (02) 2825-0093

Shilin: Zhongzheng Road, #331 (台北市士林區中正路331號) (02) 2882-3706

Tienmu: Dexing West Road, #47, 2nd Floor (台北市德行西路47號2F) (02) 2833-9274.

Adjacent to Beitou Folk Arts Museum is **Shann Garden** (禪園), a traditional Chinese teahouse that boasts upscale dining, fine teas and a breathtaking view of New Beitou and the Guandu Plains. You may be surprised to learn that Shann Garden, built during the Japanese occupation in 1920, was once an "officer's club" for Japanese soldiers and later became a final respite for Japanese kamikazi pilots during World War II. Patrons can bathe in the outdoor hot spring for NT $250 or enjoy a Mongolian barbeque for NT $650 per person plus a 10% service charge. Open 11:30 am to 2:30 pm and again for dinner 5:30 to 9:30 pm. Youya Road, #24, New Beitou (台北市北投區幽雅路34號) (02) 2896-5700.

Owned by Taiwanese singer Pan Mei Chen, **Sir Duke** (加州主題餐廳) boasts live music and a variety of Eastern and Western cuisine. Anho Road, Section 2, #100 (台北市安和路2段100號) (02) 2701-7877.

Experience succulent spices at **Spice Chafer** (麻麻辣辣 Mama Lala), a Taiwanese hot pot restaurant. If you prefer less spicy food, request a little spicy (小辣shiao la) or not spicy (不辣 bu la) when you order. Fuxing South Road, Section 2, #191 (台北市復興北路2段191號) (02) 2700-2827.

Upscale Chinese buffet **Star of Sea** (淡水海中天 Haizhongtien) impresses with Asian dishes that include Hong Kong-style dim sum, Japanese sushi and fresh seafoods, fruits and vegetables. Or, choose fresh meats and vegetables to have cooked before you on a Mongolian wok. Breakfast is served from 7 to 10 am at a cost of NT $150 for adults, NT $120 for children between 111 and 140 cm Monday through Friday, NT $200/$150 weekends. Lunch runs from 11:30 to 2:30 pm for NT $480 adults, NT $300 for children Monday through Friday, NT $580/$350 weekends, and dinner will set you back NT $680/$400. Prices do not include a 10% service charge. Children under 110 cm eat free. Since Star of Sea is between Zhuwei and Danshui MRT stations and not within walking distance, free shuttle buses run near Zhuwei and Danshui MRT stations. Zhongzheng East Road, Section 2, #131 (台北縣淡水鎮中正東路2段131號) (02) 2809-9800.

Tingkuakua Fried Chicken (頂呱呱 Tingkuakua) is the Taiwanese equivalent of Kentucky Fried Chicken, the sweet potato fries and pizza rolls are worth a nosh. There are currently sixteen restaurants in Taipei, here are three in convenient locations:

New Beitou: Guangming Road, #218-2 (next to McDonald's) (台北市北投區光明路218-2號) (02) 2896-7065

Ximending: Kunming Street, #92-2 (台北市昆明街92之2號) (02) 2381-2037

Zhongxiao: Zhongxiao East Road, Section 4, #177 (台北市忠孝東路4段177號) (02) 2771-8652.

Tsway Yuen (翠園), also called "Yakiniku," is one of the best barbeque restaurants on the island. Lunch specials go for only NT $299 while dinners cost only NT $359 per person plus a 10% service charge, and meals are all-you-can-eat. For bountiful barbeque food in Danshui, stop by and give Tsway Yuen a try. Arrive early, the eatery fills quickly during peak dining hours. Menus are in Chinese so you may want to bring a local friend. Zhongzheng Road, Section 1, #3 (台北縣淡水鎮中正路1段3號) (02) 2805-6295.

If you hold your birthday party at **Traditional Taiwan Cuisine**, the owner will provide you with a large bowl of pig's leg with noodles, free of charge! Now that's a reason to celebrate. Fuxing North Road, #305 (台北市復興北路305號) (02) 2705-6999.

Zhuji (朱記) is highly regarded by locals for its outstanding beefcakes (the food, not the chefs), shredded pork soup with pickled mustard greens, and steamed dumplings. Renai Road, Section 3, #106 (台北市仁愛路3段106號) (02) 2702-9411.

THAI

Taiwanese people delight in savoring spicy foods, and Thai restaurants are becoming increasingly popular. Here are a few local favorites:
On Yongkang Street just behind National Taiwan Normal University (Shida), come hungry and leave happy at **Come Thai** (康泰小館). Traditional Thai rice and noodle dishes start at NT $100. Menus are in Chinese. Yongkang Street, #37-2 (台北市大安區永康街37-2號) (02) 2393-7537.

Orchard & Elephant (蘭花與象泰式料理 *Lanhua Yushang*) serves Thai cuisine as exotic as the restaurant's name. Salads include green papaya salad (NT $240), seafood salad (NT $280), beef salad (NT $280) and octopus salad (NT $280). Choice meat dishes include fried beef with celery (NT $280), Thai-style roast beef (NT $300), chicken and pork satay (NT $260), as well as fried lemon chicken legs with

chili (NT $280). Orchard & Elephant also offers shrip and fish cakes (NT $260 to NT $280) and flavorful soups such as mixed seafood soup (NT $350). Drinks include coconut juice and mango juice (NT $120) and the restaurant offers Thai-style mixed dessert (NT $100) and Thai style mixed ice (NT $100) as well as pumpkin pudding (NT $80 per slice, NT $600 to devour the entire cake). Your tongue won't be disappointed. Fuxing North Road, #307 (台北市復興北路307號) (02) 2712-8680.

Patara, which serves traditional Thai cuisine, is just down the road from the 24-hour Eslite bookstore on Dunhua South Road. Dunhua South Road, Section 1, Lane 247, #12 (台北市敦化南路1段247巷12號) (02) 2731-5288.

Owned by Taiwanese singer Wu Chi Lung, **PP Island** has a reputation for offering a variety of fine Thai dishes. Minsheng East Road, Section 5, #10 (台北市民生東路5段10號) (02) 2760-9617.

You may think you've arrived at the gates of St. Peter the food is so good at **Thai Heaven**. There are currently three locations in Taipei:
Heping: Heping East Road, Section 1, #53 (台北市大安區和平東路1段53號) (02) 2392-5969
Tienmu: Zhongshan North Road, Section 7, #59 (台北市中山7段59號) (02) 2871-3262
Yongho: Zhongshan Road, Section 1, #231, Yungho, Taipei County (永和市中山路1段231號) (02) 2925-0077
http://www.thai-heaven.com.

You just may cry when you eat Thai the food at **Thai Town Cuisine** is so flavorful. This very popular chain offers set meals in the NT $250 to NT $350 price range. Make a reservation or get there early. Renai Road, Section 2, #49 (北市仁愛路2段49號) (02) 2351-0960
Renai Road, Section 4, Alley 345, Lane 2, #5 (台北市仁愛路4段345巷2弄5號) (02) 2781-9148

Tienmu West Road, #116 (台北市天母北路116號) (02) 2826-4852.

Taiwanese star Gao Ming Jun owns **T.M. Palace**, a fine Thai restaurant.
Minsheng East Road, Section 5, #92 (台北市民生東路5段92號) (02) 2766-1777.

Very Thai is very good, as well. The sauces are all imported from Thailand. There are currently two Taipei locations:
Fuxing North Road, #319 (台北市復興北路319號) (02) 2546-6745
Nanjing East Road, Section 3, #146 (台北市南京東路3段146號) (02) 2751-6311.

TURKISH

For a fine taste of Turkey, **Istanbul Restaurant** (依斯坦堡餐廳) prides itself on being the "first and only" Turkish restaurant on the island. Relax and listen to traditional Turkish songs while perusing the unique imported instruments and ornaments that hang from the walls, adding a fine taste of Turkish culture to Taipei. Yanji Street, #242-3 (near the intersection of Xinyi Road, Section 4 and Kuangfu South Road) (台北市延吉街242之3號) (02) 2703-8968.

VEGETARIAN (素食)

You can distinguish local vegetarian restaurants throughout the city from the Buddhist sauvastika, or backwards swastika symbol, on the sign. Here are a few choice vegetarian restaurants to choose from:

Delve into a cornucopia of healthful organic dishes that range from Chinese and Korean to other international favorites at **The Art of Vegetarian Food** (回留 *Huiliu*). Drinks include fine teas. These two locations are within walking distance of one another: Xinyi Road, Section 2, Lane 228, #9 (台北市信義路2段228巷9號) (02) 2321-3069
Yongkang Street, Lane 31, #9 (台北市永康街31巷9號) (02) 2392-6707.

Easy House Vegetarian Cuisine (寬心園 *Jingxinyuan*) boasts natural foods in a natural setting. The restaurant offers healthful soups, salads and fruit dishes as well as noodles and vegetarian delights without the oils and emphasis on sodium. In addition to fresh teas, drinks and cakes, meals range from noodle dishes (NT $220 to NT $280) to set hot pot meals that come with rice (NT $360 to NT $420). Easy House makes choosing to eat healthy look easy. Open 11:30 am to 10 pm. Tienmu West Road, #9, 2nd Floor (above McDonald's) (台北市天母西路9號2樓) (02) 2874-5967.

After a stroll through a Taipei park you may feel healthier if you try the food at **Healthy Vegetarian House**, Daan Road, Section 1, #123 (台北市大安路1段123號)
(02) 781-8055.

In New Beitou, **Lienhua Vegetarian Restaurant** (蓮花 *Lienhua*) is a new restaurant that offers fine vegetarian cuisine or hot pot meals. Wenchuen Road, #110-2 (台北市北投區溫泉路110-2號)
(02) 2892-7611.

Adjacent to Lien Hua is **Lotus Café**, where you can ponder the will of Buddah while experiencing a variety of vegetarian dishes. Wenchuen Road, #110-1, New Beitou (台北市北投區溫泉路110-1號) (02) 2894-3945.

Become one with Buddha while enjoying your meal at the European-style **Vegetarian Buffet** (慈恩歐式素食自助餐 *Tse En Ohshi Sushi*). Along with serving great food, this popular local eatery plays an interesting array of spiritual Buddhist music. Anzhu Street, #30 (台北市安居街30號)
(02) 2378-6780.

Yoji Huayuan (有機花園) is a vegetarian buffet restaurant that offers healthful dishes at reasonable prices. Try a delicious bowl of vegetable soup with rice (NT $90) or a vegetarian pizza (NT $220). Minsheng East Road, Section 4, #103, 2nd Floor (台北市民生東路4段103號2F) (02) 2545-9338.

WESTERN

For flame-broiled fast food burgers, **Burger King** has several restaurants in town, here are two:
Hwaining Street, #36 (台北市中正區懷寧街36號) (02) 2388-5838
Chongqing South Road, Section 1, #86 (台北市重慶南路1段86號) (02) 2312-3188.

Chili's Grill & Bar is a fun place to grab a burger, soup, salad or fajita. The quesadillas are second-to-none. The first, Brobdingnagian restaurant in Taipei is adjacent to Warner Brothers Village. Another colossal Chili's recently opened at Miramar cinemas:
Songshou Road, Taipei, #22, 2nd Floor (台北市松壽路22號 2F) (02) 2345-8838
Zhongcheng Road, Section 2, #200 Tienmu (台北市忠誠路2段200號2樓) (02) 2875-4838.

Dan Ryan's Chicago Grill is a popular Western restaurant with a lively bar, to match. Dunhua North Road, #8 (台北市敦化北路8號) (02) 2778-8800.

European Town is a swank restaurant featuring fine international dining and interesting decor from Europe. Live music daily (pianist and violinist) from 8 to 9 pm. Dunhua North Road, Alley 155, #16 (台北市敦化北路155弄16號) (02) 2719-5242.

Where have all the flowers gone? Quite possibly to **Flower Land**! The theme of the restaurant is—you guessed it. Try the palatable pasta dishes and choice cappuccino. Zhongxiao East Road, Section 2, #132 (台北市忠孝東路2段132號) (02) 2393-4397.

G'day Café (晴西餐廳 *Chingxi Tsanting*) entices expatriates enrolled at National Taiwan Normal University (師大 *Shida*). Tourist trap or hip hashery? You be the judge. Xingan Street, #180 (台北市松山區興安街180號) (02) 2727-5927.

Gold In Tex fried chicken chain is pecking its way into the fried chicken fast food market, the chain's curly fries and trademark chicken are specked in department store food courts. Zhongcheng Road, #182, Shilin (near Shilin Station) (台北市士林區中正路182號) (02) 2831-9945.

Don't expect to find grandma in the kitchen of **Grandma Nitti's** (中西美食餐廳 *Zhongxi Meishi Tsanting*), this hash house has become a social hall for young people who disco dance until the sun rises. Some call it a tourist trap, try the homemade pancakes or waffles and decide for yourself. Shida Road, Lane 93, #8 (台北市師大路93巷8號) (02) 2369-9751, 2369-9752.

Jake's Country Kitchen (鄉香美墨餐廳 *Hsiang Shang Meimo Tsanting*), founded by owner Jake Lo in 1979, boasts finger-lickin' pizzas, chicken, burgers, fries, and mouth-watering Mexican food. Jake's offers free coffee refills and expats load up on their downhome, delectable homemade pies during the holidays. Zhongshan North Road, Section 6, #705, Tienmu (台北市中山北路6段705號) (02) 2871-5289.

Does **Hooters** really need an introduction? This American bistro boasts fine finger foods, set meals and fetching women in trademark orange Hooters wear. Open 11 am to midnight. Chingcheng Street, #18 (台北市慶城街18號) (02) 2716-5168.

You may not get a peck on the cheek, but the pizza is said to entice at **Kiss Pizza** (吉士披薩 *Zheeshi Piza*). This pizza and pasta house is particularly popular with students from nearby National Taiwan Normal University (師大 *Shida*). Yunho Street, #63 (台北市雲和街63號) (02) 2365-7792.

For Western fast food that's finger-licken' good, you can always go to **Kentucky Fried Chicken**, in Taipei alone there are over forty locations. Just don't lick your fingers off, as an early Chinese marketing campaign suggested. Here are three Taipei locations:

Shilin: Wenlin Road, #88 (Shilin Night Market) (台北市文林路88號) (02) 2881-1323
Tienmu: Tienmu East Road, #6-4 (台北市天母東路6-4號) (02) 2871-4607
Ximending: Chengdu Road, #87 (台北市成都路87號) (02) 2388-2712.

For muffins, coffee, tea and a whole lot more, **Lulu Bar & Restaurant** boasts "not only food... but fun and friends" with its dedicated employees. The pastries and cakes make a posh morning nosh. Minsheng East Road, Lane 113, #9 (台北市民生東路113巷9號) (02) 2713-2250.

The Malibu is a hoppin' café and bar where the food and drinks, which are served all day, are said to tantalize tastebuds. There are two locations:
Renai Road, Section 4, Lane 91, #5 (台北市仁愛路4段91巷5號) (02) 2776-4963, 2776-5120
Shuangcheng Street, Lane 25, #9 (next to Imperial Hotel) (台北市雙城街25巷9號) (02) 2592-8226.

Mary's Hamburger, which opened in 1979, is famous for its inexpensive but enjoyable eats. Zhongshan North Road, Section 6, #752, Tienmu (台北市中山北路6段752號) (02) 2871-4997.

McDonald's (麥當勞 My Dang Lao) You're kidding, right? Actually, some expatriates have remarked that they're curious to see a McDonald's menu in each country they visit to see how local tastes vary. You won't have trouble finding one.

My Place is a pub/grill where you can snack on Chinese, Western or Mexican food while watching live sports via satellite television. Shuangcheng Street, Lane 32, #3-1 (downtown in "the zone"). (台北市雙城街32巷3-1號) (02) 2591-4269, 2592-8122.

My Other Place is a fun Western-style restaurant/pub at the intersection of Minsheng East Road, within walking distance from Sherwood Hotel. This popular hangout has a reputation for piquant pasta dishes and delicious drinks. On Thursdays, ladies get a free margarita. Fuxing North Road, #303 (台北市復興北路303號) (02) 2718-7826.

For bagels, lox and cream cheese made like they are in my hometown, try **New York Bagels**, Yitong Street #28 (台北市伊通街28號) (02) 2507-5660. Yitong Street is near the intersection of Nanjing East Road and Jianguo North Road.
Or, visit a N.Y. Bagels Café at these convenient locations:
Renai Road, Section 4, #147 (Open 24 hours) (台北市大安區仁愛路4段147號) (02) 2752-1669
Xinyi Road, Section 5, #122 (Open 24 hours) (北市信義路5段122號) (02) 2723-7977.

The owners of **The Onion** (洋蔥 Yangtsong) must be crying tears of joy their Western-style restaurants have become such an immense success. Arrive early or call to reserve a table, otherwise you may cry yourself from the long wait. Tienmu North Road, Lane 9, #1, 3, 5, 7 (台北市天母北路9巷1,3,5,7號) (02) 2873-9992
Zhongshan North Road, Section 7, #31 (台北市中山北路7段31號) (02) 2874-5199.

If you crave pizza there's always **Domino's Pizza**® (02) 2882-5252 or **Pizza Hut**® (toll-free) 0800-231-927. There are simply too many branches to list (there are over sixty Pizza Hut restaurants in Taipei alone). On Taiwan, toppings are geared towards the local market, there's roasted squid on the seafood pizza, spicy Mexican pizza, and apple pizza. Domino's has a long-running, four-set special that has become especially popular. You may be surprised that typical fast food chains in the West appear like grand castles in the East. These two enormous Pizza Hut eateries boast bountiful salad bars:
Tienmu: Zhongshan North Road, Section 7, #156 (台北市中山北路7段156號) (02) 2875-2206

Zhongxiao East Road, Section 4, #333 (opposite Dr. Sun Yat-sen Memorial Hall, intersection of Kuangfu South Road) (台北市忠孝東路4段333號) (02) 2776-6600.

Pizzeria Rialto serves flavorful pizza and pasta dishes. Zhongshan North Road, Section 7, #116, Tienmu (台北市中山北路7段116號) (02) 2874-3269.

In Danshui you won't need your passport to enjoy Eastern and Western dining at **The Consulate** (領事館 *Lingshiguan*), across from Fort San Domingo. With its alluring orange ceramic tiles, upscale wine bar, unique Spanish decor, and elderly lady statue outside, The Consulate appears right out of a Spanish movie. In addition to a sumptuous smattering of Eastern and Western dishes that start at NT $250, the restaurant also offers coffees, teas, juice drinks as well as a relaxing view of Danshui River. Open 10:30 am to midnight. Zhongzheng Road, #257 (台北縣淡水鎮中正路257號) (02) 2622-8529.

Post 49 Bar & Grill is home of the local chapter of the American Legion. At Post 49 experience "Uncle Bob's" homemade pizza, prime rib dinners or stop by to play darts. The second floor boasts live music, a piano bar and karaoke while Club 49 on the third floor serves "authentic home-brewed German beers." Zhongshan North Road, Section 6, Lane 35, #31 (台北市中山北路6段35巷31號) (02) 2835-6491.

The pizza, pasta dishes and sandwiches served at **Round Table Pizza** taste superior here than they do back home. Here are three convenient Taipei locations: Nanjing East Road, Section 2, #60 (02) 2521-4472 Zhongshan North Road, Section 5, #685, Shilin (台北市中山北路5段685號) (02) 2834-0546 Zhongshan North Road, Section 7, Lane 14, #2, Tienmu (台北市中山北路7段14巷2號) (02) 2875-3361 (24 hours).

Ruth's Chris Steak House is an American bistro chain known for its exquisite and expensive steaks. Minsheng East Road, Section 3, #135, 2nd Floor (台北市民生東路3段135號2F) (02) 2545-8888.

Believe it or not, **Sizzler** (時時樂 *Shishile*) on Taiwan offers a wider selection of foods than its Western counterparts, and many expats comment that the food tastes better here, too. There are currently two towering Taipei locations:
Tienmu: Zhongshan North Road, Section 7, #113 (台北市中山北路7段113號) (02) 2873-0895
Xinsheng: Xinsheng South Road, Section 3, #2 (Opposite Daan Forest Park, at the Heping East Road intersection) (北市大安區新生南路3段2號) (02) 2365-6723.

Actors, DJs and movie stars frequent **South Train** (南方列車坊 *Nanfang Liechefang*), a quaint Danshui eatery that appears like the inside of an MRT car. The pasta, chicken mushroom dishes and desserts are delectable. Sweet corn chowder and a drink (coffee, tea or juice) are provided with entrees, which typically run under NT $200 (US $6.00). The restaurant is opposite Danshui Station on Boai Road, behind McDonald's. Boai Road, Lane 51, #1, Danshui (台北縣淡水鎮博愛路51巷1號) (02) 2629-2688.

The Stinking Rose (裝蒜 *Zhuangshuan*), a fun garlic restaurant, was established in San Francisco. There are also currently Stinking Rose restaurants in Los Angeles and Taipei. Don't expect to meet any vampires here! Fuxing North Road, #342 (台北市復興北路342號) (02) 2516-8880, (02) 2506-2727.

For ice cream, chicken, burgers or sandwiches, try **Swensen's** (雙聖 *Shuangshen*), the Western ice cream parlor/restaurant. Here are two popular locations: Renai Road, Section 4, #109 (台北市仁愛路4段109號) (02) 2772-6174 (24 Hours)
Tienmu: Zhongshan North Road, Section 7, Lane 14, #2 (台北市中山北路7段14巷2號) (02) 2875-3361 (Open 24 Hours).

You'll find plenty of Western-style sandwich restaurant chains in Taipei, these popular make-your-own-sandwich chains to appeal to healthful sensibilities for both local residents and expatriates on the go. Here are two local **Subber** chain locations:
Anho Road, Section 1, Lane 49, #25 (behind Ming Yao Department Store) (台北市安和路1段25號) (02) 8771-0272
Zhongshan North Road, Section 6, #476, Tienmu (台北市中山北路6段476號) (02) 2871-4855.

Or, "eat fresh" at **Subway**, the largest Western-style sandwich chain on the island. One is on B1 of the Taipei 101 Mall (Taipei 101), another is near Taipei Main Station on Hanko Street, Section 1, #57 (台北市漢口街1段57號1樓) (02) 2314-5725.

TGI Friday's, known in the West for its Mexican and Western food, pasta dishes, drinks and fun atmosphere, doesn't disappoint on Taiwan. The staff at each restaurant does an excellent job of making customers feel like every day is a Friday. There are currently seven Taipei locations:
Chongqing South Road, #94 (台北市重慶南路1段94號) (02) 2389-3579
Keelung Road, Section 2, #7 (near Taipei World Trade Center) (台北市基隆路2段7號) (02) 2345-2789
Miramar Entertainment Park: Jin Yeh 3rd Road, #22, 2nd Floor (美麗華店: 台北市敬業三路22號2樓) (02) 2175-3358
Dunhua North Road, #150 (台北市敦化北路150號) (02) 2713-3579
Ximending: Wuchang Street, Section 2, #72, 2nd Floor (台北市武昌街2段72號2樓) (02) 2388-0679
Zhongxiao East Road, Section 4, Lane 49, #2 (adjacent to Sogo Department Store) (台北市忠孝東路4段49巷2號) (02) 2711-3579.

Trader Vic's (偉克商人) serves exotic international cuisine for exotic international visitors such as you, and residents enjoy the upscale dining ambiance, as well.
Minsheng East Road, Section 3, #175, 7th Floor (台北市民生東路3段175號7F)

(02) 2545-9999.

Dining in Danshui (淡水餐廳/館)

There are a plethora of good cafés and eateries in Danshui. If you visit Fort San Domingo, referred to locally as "Red Hair Fort" (紅毛城 Hungmaocheng), a café that serves drinks, salads, pastas and finger foods is on the premises, and Western-style restaurants are directly across the street. Try **The Consulate** (領事館 Lingshiguan), Zhongzheng Road, #257 (台北縣淡水鎮中正路257號) (02) 2622-8529. The Consulate serves both Eastern and Western dishes that start at NT $250, as well as coffees, teas and juice drinks. Open 10:30 am to midnight.

For more traditional dining, stroll along Zhongzheng Road, **Danshui Historic Street** (淡水老街 Danshui Laojie). For noodle noshing and delightful dumplings try **Danshui Night Market** (淡水夜市) on Yingzhuan Road (英專路), directly across from Danshui Station. **Fuhua Tiebanxiao** (福華鐵板燒) is a terrific teppenyaki restaurant with reasonable prices in the Danshui night market on Chingshui Street, #9-1 (台北縣淡水鎮清水街9-1號) (02) 2621-8285. Open for lunch from 11 am to 2 pm and for dinner 5 pm to 10 pm. Menus are in Chinese.

Guobaobao (鍋寶寶) is a decent all-you-can-eat (lunch: NT $168, dinner: NT $199) hot pot restaurant near the night market. Guests are given a two-hour gorge period. You'll find it adjacent to McDonald's on Boai Street, Lane 51, #21 (淡水鎮博愛街51巷21號, 麥當勞旁邊) (02) 2625-9895.

For a romantic evening out, **La Cuisine** (香料廚房 Shangke Chufang) may provide a choice Italian escape. The restaurant is known for its fine pizza and pasta dishes. Lunch sets go for NT $180 and include a drink and dessert, dinner goes for around

NT $260. Open 11:30 am until 10 pm, 11 pm weekends. Zhongzheng Road, #332 (台北縣淡水鎮中正路332號) (02) 2626-5984.

South Train (南方列車坊 *Nanfang Liechefang*), mentioned above, boasts MRT car decor and a delectable dining experience. Boai Road, Lane 51, #1, Danshui (台北縣淡水鎮博愛路51巷1號) (02) 2629-2688.

For Western-style dining that boasts more than a great Danshui River view try **The River** (淡水河邊 *Danshui Hopang*). Upscale meals run from NT $370 to NT $890. In the yard behind the restaurant, be mindful of the coconut tree, coconuts sometimes surprise unsuspecting patrons (ouch!). The River is open from 11:30 am to 10 pm and is behind The White House on Zhenli Street, #15 (台北縣淡水鎮真理街15號旁) (02) 2625-6345.

Tsway Yuan (翠園) is a barbeque with unlimited servings on Zhongzheng Road, Section 1,#3 (台北縣淡水鎮中正路1段3號) (02) 2805-6293, lunch specials are only NT $299 and dinner costs NT $359. A 10% service charge is added. It's a reasonably low price for a big, magnificent meal but menus are in Chinese so you may want to bring a local friend.

Another good option is **Red Castle** (紅樓 *Honglo*), found atop Sanmin Street, Lane 2, #6, Danshui (台北縣淡水鎮三民街2巷6號) (02) 8631-1168. You'll have to climb over a hundred steps up a narrow, winding alley, but the frothy cappuccinos, light lattes, flavorful fruit drinks, as well as choice chicken and pasta dishes, are worth the trek. The round waffles, however, may inspire you to organize a game of street hockey.

Dining in Yangmingshan (Yangming Mountain)
(陽明山餐廳/館)

Patrons of **The Back Garden Fashion Café** (後花園) can sample Taiwanese cuisine while enjoying a beautiful view of Taipei City. Hwakang Road, Lane 59, #5-1, Shilin (台北市士林區華崗路59巷5號之1) (02) 2861-5567, 2862-2878.

You don't have to be Donald Trump to enjoy life at **The Top** (屋頂上). Formerly known as "Dong Shan Teahouse & Hotspring," (the antiquated hot springs have since been closed), The Top boasts a picturesque view of Taipei, heaping portions of Taiwanese, Cantonese and Southeast Asian foods, hot pot meals (NT $500 to $800) and barbeque dishes (NT $200 and up). Delectable desserts and fine finger foods impress even the most fickle customers. By bus take either the 109, 260, Red 5, 15, 303, or 111, it's a fifteen-minute walk down Kaishuen Road behind Chinese Culture University. The Top is open from 5 pm to 3 am Monday through Friday, 12 pm to 3 am weekends. Kaishuen Road, Lane 61, Alley 4, #33 (台北市陽明山凱旋路61巷4弄33 號) (02) 2862-2255.

Dining at **Forest Legend** (森林傳說 *Shenlin Chuanshuo*), a hidden mountain hashery, promises a breath of fresh air from the hustle and bustle of Taipei. Forest Legend boasts titillating Taiwanese and wonderful Western-style cuisine. Chingshan Road, #134-1 (台北市陽明山菁山路134號之1) (02) 2862-1355.

Pices (雙魚咖啡 *Shuangyu*) café serves choice coffee and tea along with light meals in two great locations. Taishun Street, Lane 38, #32, near National Taiwan Normal University (師大 *Shida*) (台北市泰順街38巷32號) (02) 2363-3457.

This one is set against the rolling hills of Yangmingshan: Chingshan Road, #134, Yangmingshan (台北市陽明山菁山路134號) (02) 2862-6898.

TAIPEI GUIDE TO MOUNTAIN CLIMBING (台北登山指南)

There have been publicized incidences of tourists getting lost in Taiwan's dense mountains, and as a result, one must now obtain a permit to climb Taiwan's more rugged terrain. However, feel free to explore hiking trails and pristine park areas around Taipei. Some paths run for several kilometers so it's a good idea to dress comfortably, bring bottled water, a camera and a snack. While you may feel the urge to explore unchartered terrain, there's a good reason why some areas are designated hiking areas and others aren't. Recently, one adventurous traveler went hiking, got lost and was stuck high atop a rugged mountain for three days. Had another tourist not brought a pair of binoculars and seen him, he may have met his fate up there amidst the sulfur pits and low-lying clouds. And that would have been a rather stinky way to die.

Without a car it may be difficult to reach some of Taipei's more remote mountain areas. For your convenience, areas are rated according to accessibility. 3 stars=easy to reach by bus, car, or moped, have a great time! 2 stars=no buses run to this area, so it may not be easy to access. If you have your heart set on going, inquire at the hotel or with local residents who are familiar with the area. 1 star=are you crazy?

At **Seven Stars Park** (七星公園 *Qixing Gongyuan*) (3 stars) view Guanyin Mountain on Bali across Danshui River along with picture perfect (depending on the weather) views of Danshui and Keelung Rivers. The seven mountain peaks, the highest of which reaches 1,120 meters (just over 3,739 feet), were formed centuries ago by lava spewing from the center of this now inactive volcano. This remote park is in an undisturbed natural setting, and Buddhists sometimes meditate at the wooden pagoda. A visit makes for a memorable experience. Take the MRT to Jiantan Station, then take the Red 5 (紅 5), 109 or 111 to the Yangmingshan Bus Terminal. Near Miaopu Bus Stop (苗圃車站) you'll find the trail that leads to the park.

For a wild workout hike three mountains in one day! Trails around **Carp (Liyu) Mountain** (鯉魚山) (2.5 stars), **Zhongyong Mountain** (忠勇山) (2.5 stars) and **Yuanjiejian Mountain** (圓覺尖) (2.5 stars) wind about five kilometers and take three and a half hours to walk. The mountains provide terrific Taipei views. From Kunyang Station take blue bus 27 (藍 27), 222, 240, 247, 267, 521 or 604 to Jinlong Temple (金龍寺), Neihu Road, Section 3, Lane 256, #2 (台北市內湖區內湖路3段256巷2號) (02) 2790-2604. The trail for Zhongyong Mountain (327 meters) starts across the street from the temple. After hiking for about two hours (3.1 kilometers) the trail runs into Carp Mountain (223 meters), this trail ends on Dahu Street (大湖街). By MRT depart at Zhongshan Junior High School Station and take brown bus 10 or Minibus 3 to Dahu Elementary School (大湖國小), transfer to bus 110, 278, 284, 287, 617, 620, 630, or 710 and exit at Dahu Park (大湖公園). From here would you need to walk to Dahu Street to climb Carp Mountain first, with the tail-end of the trail ending at Jinlong Temple.

If you hike to **Chingtiengang** (擎天崗) in Qichinshan (Seven Stars Mountain) (2.5 stars) you may discover not only natural beauty, but also grazing cows. As the author discovered a decade ago, the cows may stop grazing and stare curiously at hikers. Nowadays, however, they may chew the cud in more remote areas. The trail along Chingtiengang runs for several kilometers around the mountain.

You have to be in shape to hike **Dalunwei Mountain** (大崙尾山) (2.5 stars) and **Daluntou Mountain** (大崙頭山) trail (2.5 stars), Dalunwei towers 451 meters at its peak while Daluntou tops at 475 meters. In

Taipei's Shilin district, the steep trail winds 5.5 kilometers and most complete the hike in three hours. At Shilin Station take bus 255 or the 255 Interzone to Shuangxi Community Bus Stop 6 and walk along Zhongshe Road. Alternatively you could take Minibus 18 t o Bixi Bridge and walk along Zhishan Road until you reach the mountain trail.

Get your trunk in gear, **Elephant Mountain** (象山) (2.5 stars) awaits! Shaped like an elephant head that rises 183 meters above southeastern Taipei, Elephant Mountain makes for a fairly straightforward, unobstructed 2.4-kilometer hike. From Yongchun Station take bus 229 to Yongchun Senior High School (台北市永春高級中學) and continue walking towards Yongchungang Park (永春崗公園). If you pass Fude Temple on the left you'll hit Xinyi Road, Section 6, Lane 76, Alley 8 and will have gone off the hiking path (stairs). You should pass Jushi Park on the left and Yanshou Pavilion further on the left, which means you're on Xinyi Road, Section 5, Lane 150. You should find yourself on Xinyi Road, Section 5 in about .5 kilometers, or approximately twenty minutes. By MRT exit Taipei City Hall Station and take bus 32, 33 or blue 10 (藍10) to Xinyi District Administration Center, continue walking along Xinyi Road, Section 5, Lane 150.

Beitou's **Guizikeng** (貴子坑) (3 stars) boasts fresh air and scenic hiking trails. Make a right at Fuxinggang Station (Exit 1) to find Guizikeng Park (貴子坑公園), from here hike towards Guizikeng Xiaopingding Mountain (貴子坑小坪頂山), which towers 386 meters above Taipei at its peak. Along the way you'll see Guizikeng Camping Area, Soil and Water Conservation Learning Center and Budong Waterfall, a snapshot spot near Guizikeng River. The hike typically lasts around three hours. Contact Soil and Water Conservation Learning Center at (02) 2725-6631 for camping information.

An outstanding natural Neihu treasure is

Jiandaoshi ("Scissor Stone") Mountain (剪刀石山), also known as **Jinmian Mountain** (金面山) (2.5 stars). Although the mountain rises "only" 258 meters, it is perhaps the best location to get an unobstructed photo of Taipei 101 from the city's western side. The trail winds for about three kilometers and takes four hours to complete. From Taipei City Hall Station take blue bus 27 (藍 27) to Jinlong Temple, the bus stop is down the road from the temple. You should be near Neihu Road, Section 3, Lane 263 (台北市內湖區內湖路3段263巷), the trail begins at the bus stop for Jinlong Temple. Are you up for traversing two mountains in one hike? Hike **Mount Xiaojinmian** (小金面) (180 meters) before traversing over Jinmian. The trail stops at Takming College (德明技術學院), Huanshan Road, Section 1 (台北市內湖區環山路1段). Alternatively you could take blue 20 bus (藍 20) from Kunyang Station to Huanshan Road and start the hike at Takming College.

Find amazing fumaroles, natural springs (not suitable for bathing) and sulfur pits at **Lungfeng and Sulfur Valley** (硫磺谷) (3 stars), near the intersection of Beitou's Chuenyuen Road (泉源路) and Xingyi Road (行義路). Lungfeng Valley is just beyond the intersection of Chuenyuen Road and Xingyi Road, on the opposite side of the large four-way intersection. Yangmingshan (陽明山), once mined for its sulfur deposits, is home to some fantastic splendors of nature. A visit to these areas makes for a leisurely one to two-hour hike. By bus, take the 230, which runs from Beitou over Yangmingshan (陽明山) to Shilin (士林). Board the bus at Beitou Station or at the main bus stop across from Beitou's Taipei Fubon Bank. Make sure the driver knows where you want to go. Two small buses, Small 22 (小22) and Small 25 (小25), stop directly in front of Beitou Station. You can exit either of these buses at an intersection (the highest part of Chuenyuen Road) and walk about twenty minutes to reach Sulfur Valley.

Lengshuikeng (冷水坑) (3 stars) is referred

to as "milk pool" (牛奶池 niu nai tsi) by locals due to its milky white appearance. Lengshuikeng is a hot spring, but is not "hot" by local standards. Most natural hot springs, outdoors and undisturbed by man, have temperatures that reach between eighty and ninety degrees Celsius. Since the water here is only around forty degrees Celsius, the pool is considered a "cold water" (冷水 lengshui) natural spring. There is also a public spring here for bathing (swimsuits not permitted). By MRT and bus exit at Jiantan Station and take the Red 5 (紅5), 109 or 111 to Yangmingshan Bus Terminal, then take the small 108 bus that runs to Xiaoyoukeng and Lengshuikeng. The 108 departs every thirty minutes and runs from 7:30 am until 5 pm. For more information contact Lengshuikeng Tourist Service Center at (02) 2861-0036. The service center is open from 9:00 am to 4:30 pm, closed Mondays.

Atop **Datun Mountain** (大屯山 Datunshan) (2 stars) discover enchanting views of Keelung and Danshui River. Towering at 1092 meters, Zhufeng (大屯主峰) is the highest point on Datun Mountain, couples often take wedding pictures here, be sure to say, "Gongxi!" ("Congratulations!"). A cool fog settles most afternoons, so bring a light jacket. The mountain's southern and western sides are more difficult to traverse.

There is a small dye center at **Datun Nature Park** (大屯自然公園 Datun Ziran Gongyuan) (2 stars), if you're not fond of your new Armani suit ask the employees to turn it into something Jerry Garcia would have been proud to wear. After a dye demonstration, visit the gift shop. Visitors enjoy exploring the river area and walking across the wooden bridge. The natural surroundings are rife with towering trees, fascinating flowers and peculiar plants native only to Taiwan. For more information, contact Datun Nature Park Visitors Center at (02) 2861-7294, open daily from 9:00 am to 4:30 pm, closed Mondays.

Hike Datun Mountain's **Butterfly Flower Point** (蝴蝶花廊 Hudie Hualang) (2 stars), a scenic trail traversed by hikers and joggers, between April and October, that's when beautiful butterflies flutter in full view. On the western side of Datun Mountain is Er Zi Ping (二子坪), a natural setting where stones are placed over a pond (二子坪遊息區 Er Zi Ping Yo Chee Chu), the only man-made area around for miles. From here you can see the Taiwan Strait that divides Taiwan and Mainland China, as well as Danshui. The peak of nearby Datun Nature Park has been closed due to supposed military activities.

The southernmost range of Datun Mountain is **Mituoshan** (2 stars), which has since been renamed **Zhongzhengshan** (中正山) in honor of Chiang Kai-shek. You can arrive at this secluded mountain area by hiking from Beitou, but be aware that the path runs for miles around the towering mountain. Zhongzhengshan (646 meters) is higher than Zhuzihu (see below), so it can become quite cool during late afternoons.

There are many statues and temples dedicated to Guanyin, the Bodhisattva goddess of mercy, on Taiwan. **Guanyin Mountain** (觀音山 Guanyinshan) (2.5 stars) which towers 616 meters above sea level on Taiwan's Bali, is named in honor of the goddess, as well. Some expatriates are fond of hiking up the mountain and relaxing with a few cold beers once they reach the top. Enjoy your beers after you reach the top, however, so you don't end up on one of the mountain's eighteen smaller peaks. Be aware that it often rains during the afternoons high up in the mountain, so unless you enjoy wet trails you may want to hike during the morning. Watch out for the snakes. Buses run to Bali from Guandu Station and every half hour from Dacheng Street (大成路 Dacheng Lu) in Taipei, near North Gate (北門 Beimen). On Bali a free shuttle bus transports local passengers to the mountain from Tienho Temple (天后宮), across the street from Bali's wharf. For more information contact Guanyinshan Visitor Center at (02) 2292-8888.

Pingding Gujen (坪頂古鎮) (3 stars), built during the Ch'ing dynasty, is a 1.5-kilometer trail that runs from Pingjing Street to Neishuangxi (near National Palace Museum) and Shilin's Shenren Waterfall (聖人瀑布 Shenren Pubu). Stone steps enable people to more easily traverse the terrain. Fifteen minutes after leaving Pingjing Street you should arrive at a bridge, from here the road winds downward. View a variety of beautiful butterflies, as well as frolicsome fish and sprightly shrimp below the bridge. After exiting at Sanzi Road, Section 3, walk to Shenren Waterfall. While hikers once went for a dip, rocks and large stones have since fallen into the water. The Small 18 (小\18) bus takes passengers in Shilin to the waterfall.

Tienmu Old Road (天母古道 Shuiguan Gudao) (3 stars) was built over half a century ago during the Japanese occupation. Along this historic road, the Japanese constructed a water pipe that ran from Shilin to Shaomao Mountain. Thus, the path is also referred to as "Old Water Pipe Road" (水管古道 Shuiguan Gudao). The mountain road runs from Aifu 3rd Road, Lane 12, near Chinese Culture University (中國文化大學) to Zhongshan North Road, Section 7, Lane 232 in Tienmu (台北市中山北路7段232巷). The road is 2.6 kilometers long and takes about 1.5 hours to walk in one direction. There is a rest area along the way for hikers who want to relax, sip bottled water and take pictures. Further north of the hiking trail, heading in the direction of New Beitou, is the small but serene Cuifeng Waterfall (翠峰瀑布), which appears much like a stream out of Jurassic Park. You can start hiking from either direction, but most visitors start from Tienmu so they can catch a bus back to Taipei at the Tienmu bus circle upon their return.

Although **Tiger Mountain** (虎山 Hushan) (2.5 stars) may conjour images of the tiger trails that tower above Seattle, the one in Taipei (139 meters) is approximately one-sixth the size of the one in the U.S. pacific northwest (769 meters). Taipei's Tiger Mountain is part of Four Beasts Mountain (四獸山 Sihoushan), which includes Tiger Mountain (虎山) (139 meters), Leopard Mountain (豹山) (182 meters), Lion Mountain (獅山) (151 meters) and Elephant Mountain (象山) (183 meters). These mountain ranges are on the southeastern city border. Tiger Mountain trail begins from the tail-end of Xinyi business district (台北信義區), winds about 3.4 kilometers and takes three hours to hike if you don't trek Leopard Mountain, Lion Mountain, Elephant Mountain or hike up neighboring Nangang Mountain (南港山) (375 meters). From Houshanpi Station walk up Zhongpo South Road, make a left on Fude Street and then a right on either Lane 221 or Lane 251, near Fude Elementary School. By foot it takes about thirty minutes to reach the trail from Houshanpi Station. If you take Lane 221 you should pass Tiger Mountain's Fengtian Temple to the right and then Longshan Temple on the left, if you walk up Lane 251 you should pass Cihui Temple on the left. Mingshan Temple, Zhongyi Temple and Zhengguang Temple are high atop both hiking trails. Wear comfortable clothing, bring your camera and a bottle of water (or two).

Xiaoyoukeng (小油坑), the highest part of Qichinshan (2.5 stars), is a Yangmingshan range of rolling hills. The top of the mountain towers 1120 meters above Taipei and you're guaranteed to get a good workout. Xiaoyoukeng may be part of an inactive volcano, but steam rises from the Earth here year round. By MRT and bus, exit at Jiantan Station and take the Red 5 (紅5), 109 or 111 to Yangmingshan Bus Terminal (陽明山國家公園公車總站) and transfer to the small 108 bus which runs to Xiaoyoukeng and Lengshuikeng; the 108 departs every thirty minutes and runs from 7:30 am until 5 pm. For more information contact Xiaoyoukeng Tourist Service Center at (02) 2861-7024, the service center is open from 9:00 am to 4:30 pm, closed Mondays.

Xizikou Mountain (溪子口山), alternatively known as **Xianjiyan Mountain** (仙跡岩山), is more like a steep hill at 143 meters than a towering mountain in Taipei's Jingmei District (景美區). Xizikou Mountain's roads and rocky paths are popular with many local mountain bikers. From Jingmei Station on Roosevelt Road, Section 6, walk down Jingzhong Street, make a right onto Jingxing Road, pass Hanshin Department Store and continue to walk along Jingxing Road until you reach the entrance gate. The trail starts here and runs for approximately 3.5 kilometers. It takes around two hours to complete.

Discover phenomenal plant life, fantastic fauna, towering trees and marvellous mountain terrain at **Yangmingshan National Park** (陽明山國家公園 *Yangmingshan Guojia Gongyuan*) (3 stars). Scenic snapshot spots include a fantastic fountain, hiking trails, and a manicured flower clock that tells the accurate local time. You'll also discover puce pagodas and life-like monuments dedicated to significant figures in Chinese history, such as Sun Yat-sen and Ming dynasty laureate Wang Yang Ming (王陽明) (1472-1529). Yangmingshan National Park is a national cultural attraction and a visit is well worth your time. Reach the park by taking buses 301, 260, or Minibus 9 from Taipei, or bus 230 from Beitou. A free map of Yangmingshan is available at National Park Headquarters, Juzihu Road, #1-20
(台北市陽明山竹子湖路1-20號)
(02) 2861-3601.

The back of Chinese Culture University (中國文化大學) is **Yangmingshan Houshan** (陽明山後山) (3 stars), a tourist area that offers a picturesque Taipei view. Food vendors line the winding, steep road evenings to sell everything from roasted corn and stinky tofu to barbeque squid. Yangmingshan Houshan is usually lined with young couples. From the road below, just outside The Top (屋頂上), it appears as if everyone is staring at a movie screen. This famous road is located just above The Top, Kaishuen Road, Lane 61, Alley 4, #33 (台北市陽明山凱旋路61巷4弄33 號) (02) 2862-2255.

Yangming University (陽明大學 *Yangming Daxue*) (3 stars) is a medical college in Shipai. A good time to hike the steep campus road and surrounding hills is during early weekend mornings. Many hikers are fond of relaxing on Junjian Rock (軍艦岩), a powerful-looking fist-shaped rock nearly 186 meters above Taipei that juts out of the mountain and offers fantastic views of Shilin and Beitou on the right, Chinese Culture University directly across and the secluded Wellington Heights community below on the left. The entrance is about a fifteen-minute walk from Shipai Station along Donghua Street. Make a right at Lilong Road (立農街), the university is immediately on the left. Lilong Road, Section 2, #155 (台北市北投區石牌立農街2段155號) (02) 2826-7000.

Merchants flocked to **Yulu Gudao** (魚路古道) (2 stars), a winding road traversed over a century ago, to sell fish. Hikers will see the historic Jinbao Gate (金包里大道城門 *Jinbaoli Dadaochengmen*) and other ancient Chinese structures along this historic road (金包里大路 *Jinbaoli Dalu*). Yulu Gudao runs from Gold Mountain (金山 *Jinshan*) to Chingshan Road. You can also reach this road by hiking from Chingtiangang (擎天崗) to Tingbayen along Yangchinggong Road (陽金公路 *Yangching Gonglu*).

A Zhongho, Taipei County (台北縣中和市) hiking destination is **Honglusai Mountain** (301 meters) where Hongludi trail leads to **Yuantong Temple** (圓通寺) (2.5 stars). Do the mountains surrounding this tremendous temple built during the Japanese occupation appear like a classical Chinese chair? You be the judge. Hikers bow and pray at the traditional temples along the path; you'll also notice cherry blossoms in bloom if you visit during spring. Bring your camera, there are many scenic spots. The trail is a little over three kilometers and should take a little under two hours to trek. Exit at Jingan Station and take the free tourist bus to Yungtong Temple and Hongludi, the free shuttle bus runs every fifty minutes from Monday through Friday, thirty minutes during weekends. By bus take the 201, 241, 242, 243 or 344 and exit at Yuantong Temple.

Has work got you going bananas? Then make like an ape and head over to **Monkey Mountain** (猴子山) (3 stars) for some great climbing action. **Zhinan Temple** (指南宮), Wanshou Road, #115 (台北市文山區萬壽路115號) (02) 2939-9922 may be a tad far from the heart of Taipei, but the ancient temples and shrines along the path give the trail a historical life of its own. The three-story Zhinan Temple was built in 1890 and has become the center of religious life for countless Taiwanese, blending Buddhism, Daoism, and Confucianism. Also known as "Temple of a Thousand Steps," you'll need to climb over 1,200 steps to reach the temple. Along the way you'll be greeted by stone dragon pillars. Just outside the temple are picturesque views and a camping ground; inside is a tremendous temple dedicated to Confucius that bears his sculpture. One god worshipped here, Lu Dong-bin (呂洞賓), was unsuccessful in his attempts to woo his dream lover, Ho Hsien-ku (何仙姑), the only female of the Eight Immortals. Therefore, legend has it a visit by couples leads to breakups. This section of Zhinan Road is known as **Maokong Tea Road** (台北市文山區指南路, 貓空), you should pass Jade Emperor Hall and Dacheng Hall and find many traditional tea houses alongside the road. Former President Lee Teng-hui sojourned to this area often to relax. Although the road continues, stop, relax and then and head back at **Taipei Tea Promotion Center** (台北市鐵觀音包種茶研發推廣中心), Zhinan Road, Section 3, Lane 40, #8-2 (台北市指南路3段40巷8-2號) (02) 2234-0568. From either Muzha Station

or Taipei Zoo Station walk to the trailhead at Zhinan Road, Section 3, Lane 33 (台北市指南路3段). Or, take brown bus #11 or the 236, 237 or 282 to National Chengchi University (國立政治大學), known for its outstanding political science department, and take Zhinan bus 3 or 6 and exit at the stop for Zhinan Temple. A skytrain from Taipei Zoo with stops at Zhinan Temple and Maokong (final stop) should make travel to the area more convenient.

Zhuzihu Lookout Point (竹子湖觀景平台 *Zhuzihu Guangjing Pingtai*) (3 stars) comfortably seats a hundred, but it seems as if this popular area receives nearly three times as many visitors during holidays and weekends. Students and couples flock here to enjoy the view of Chinese Culture University to the left, Datun Mountain to the right, Taipei City and the Keelung and Danshui Rivers below. Visit on a clear day or night for the best views. The exotic white calla lily (海芋 *hai yu*), which costs approximately NT \$100 a bunch, is in season between November and May. At Zhuzihu, nosh on sumptuous sunflowers, red ripe tomatoes and other flavorful fruits and vegetables. You'll also find farmhouses, teashops and florists about twenty-five minutes down the road by foot. You can reach Zhuzihu by car or moped from the fork in the road in Yangmingshan (at 7-Eleven and Starbucks, down the road from the entrance of Yangmingshan National Park) heading in the direction of Gold Mountain (金山 *Jinshan*). From here Zhuzihu Lookout Point is about a fifteen-minute moped, car or bus ride. The Small 9 (小9) bus which departs Beitou Station and stops near Yangmingshan National Park also runs to Zhuzihu.

TAIPEI GUIDE TO NIGHT MARKETS (台北夜市指南)

Didn't think an exciting nightlife was part of traditional Taiwanese culture? Think again! There are over five hundred night markets on Taiwan, and these boisterous street carnivals could encompass a city block or several city streets. The literal translation of night market is "night city" (夜市 *yeh shi*), most towns have their own small day/night markets, but a few Taiwan districts, such as Shilin, have immense night markets that have become international tourist attractions. At some night markets you'll find fresh fish, fruit and vegetable vendors during the day that become packed evenings with vendors hawking a multitude of wares. For your convenience, day/night markets are rated according to location, quantity of goods and variety of products. 5 stars=outstanding, 4 stars=very good, 3 stars=good, 2 stars=decent but nothing spectacular, usually not advisable to visit at night, 1 star=doing laundry is more fun than a visit here.

After sunrise traverse **Beitou Day Market** (北投市場) (3 stars), walking distance from Beitou Station, where locals bargain over fresh fruits, exotic vegetables, and inexpensive clothing. A visit here provides an interesting perspective of how traditional Taiwanese culture persists in a thriving, modern Asian city. **Beitou Night Market** (北投夜市) (2 ½ stars), where you'll find standard night market fare, tends to be less thrilling than its daytime counterpart. If you're hungry, however, food vendors line the night market and Guangming Road (光明路) until well after the sun has set.

Danshui Night Market (淡水夜市) (4 stars) on Yingzhuan Road (英專路), opposite Danshui Station, tantalizes tastebuds with terrific traditional Taiwanese drinks and scrumptious snack foods. Bargain hunters haggle for accessories, shoes, caps and clothing. Avoid the students on mopeds heading to Tamkang University up the hill.

Head to **Dihua Street** (迪化街) (3½ stars) for delicious dried foods, which include mushrooms, fruits and watermelon seeds, as well as items for prayer, such as incense and ghost money. If you're just aching for herbs, tea leaves or traditional Chinese medicine, you can find them here, any time of year. Residents flood the area during Chinese Lunar New Year, weekends and holidays. On historic Dihua Street you can't miss Xiahai City God Temple, listed under "Taipei Temple Guide (台北寺廟指南)." Dihua Street is one of Taiwan's oldest traditional markets, it's in historic Dadaocheng (大稻埕), northwest of Taipei Main Station and listed under "Taipei Historic Sites (台灣歷史上的地方)." From Shuanglian Station Exit 2 it's a twenty-minute walk or four-minute cab ride (NT $70-80). Note: due to prurient activity it may not be advisable to visit the area at night.

To reach **Huaxi Street Night Market** (華西街夜市), otherwise known as "Snake Alley," (3 stars), hop on the MRT heading in the direction of Xinpu and exit at the second stop, Longshan Temple Station. You won't need to change trains to reach Snake Alley, it's around the corner from Longshan Temple. You may have visited the temple and nearby area in the morning, but the large, indoor night market really comes alive in the evening. That's when locals begin dining on delicacies that may have been crawling or slithering around only moments earlier.

Jingmei Night Market (景美夜市) (2 stars) is a smaller, more traditional Taipei night market. Bargain for a variety of inexpensive foods, accessories and clothing. The night market is a five-minute walk from Jingmei Station.

Opposite National Taiwan University, (台大 *Taida*), the highest-ranked private university on Taiwan, is **Gongguan** (公館) (3 ½ stars), a large shopping area with an eclectic flavor akin to Ximending. This is a fun area to nosh native foods and bargain hunt. By MRT, take the green line towards Xindian and exit at Gongguan, five stops after Taipei Main Station. The large shopping area is outside Gongguan Station, between Roosevelt Road, Section 4, and Dingchou

Street.

To visit a smaller, more traditional Taipei night market, **Liauning Street Night Market** (遼寧街夜市) (2 ½ stars) is a good choice for inexpensive light snacking and backpacking. The night market, which runs for about a hundred meters between Changan East Road and Chung Hsing High School (長安東路與中興高中之間), is a fifteen-minute walk from Nanjing East Road Station.

Linjiang Street Night Market (臨江街觀光夜市) (2 ½ stars), walking distance from Taipei World Trade Center, is an ordinary street lined with vendors by day that later becomes a bustling pedestrian hot spot. The night market, between Xinyi Road, Section 4 and Keelung Road, Section 2, is a ten-minute walk from Daan or Liuzhangli Station.

Ningxia Street Night Market (寧夏街夜市) (2 ½ stars) is comparable in size and stature to Liauning Night Market, it's also one of Taipei's less-crowded, more traditional night markets. By MRT the night market is a ten-minute walk from Zhongshan Station.

Riaohe Tourist Night Market (饒河夜市) (3 stars), at the intersection of Bade Road, Section 4 and Fuyuen Street, is in an older part of town, across the street from Songshan Train Station. Venders sell succulent snacks and typically offer bargain deals, so bone up on your haggling skills. Items tend to be slightly cheaper here than at more touristy night markets. When here check out "Wufenpu," listed below. It's hard to imagine that until only a decade ago vast rice paddy fields dotted Songshan district, formerly known as "Xikou." From Taipei City Hall Station the 203, 276, and 311 buses run to Songshan. By MRT exit at Houshanpi Station, the night market is a fifteen-minute walk.

If you're in Beitou or Tienmu and crave a traditional snack, the lively **Shipai Night Market** (石牌夜市) (3 stars) on Yumin 1st Road (裕民一路) has vendors that may grill, fry, boil or roast that local delicacy you yearn for. Those in the mood to croon can visit the enormous Holiday KTV. The night market is only a few blocks from Shipai Station.

Where do students from National Taiwan Normal University (師大 *Shida*) go to shop, eat and hang out? They cross Heping East Road and walk two blocks to **Shida Night Market** (師大夜市) (4 stars). On Shida Road you'll find cool cafés and really good local restaurants as well as pubs and nightclubs (Roxy Jr., Underworld, and Blue Note thrive in the area). Expect to see excited expats and hordes of young people. The night market is between Shida Road and Longquan Street.

A visit to **Shilin Night Market** (士林夜市) (4 ½ stars) is a must, there's simply no substitute for the Shilin Night Market experience. During the weekends, unregistered vendors crowd the middle of the walkway hawking food items, trinkets and clothing. While this may add to the selection of imitation goods to choose from, it makes walking through the crowded night market an even more memorable experience. You may need a strong stomach to try some of the fried food court delicacies. Visit this famous night market in its original, frenzied form. Shilin Night Market is between Wenlin Road and Datong Road, Danan Road and Xiaobei Street. By MRT, exit at Jiantan Station.

Shuangcheng Street (台北市雙城街) (2 ½ stars) isn't a night market, per se, it's a once-thriving area where you can find decent pub grub and drinking holes. Shuangcheng Street and the adjoining narrow streets make up "the zone," or "the combat zone," from the era when U.S. soldiers were stationed on Taiwan. After the U.S.'s withdrawal in 1979, the area lost a lot of reputable businesses and has become somewhat of a red light district.

Community leaders are working aimlessly to turn the area into a center of cultural, rather than carnal, activity, and an annual summer block party is making an impact. Will it be enough to turn the area into a more unadulterated, thriving entertainment district, such as Ximending? That remains to be seen. In the meantime, a handful of pubs offer karaoke and decent happy hour specials.

If you're in the mood to snack on local delicacies while strolling through a traditional night market, **Southern Airport Night Market** (南機場夜市 *Nanjichang Yeshi*) (2 ½ stars) may be for you. You'll find it on Zhonghua Road, Section 2 (台北市中華路2段), between Lane 305 and Lane 309.

Tunghua Street Night Market (通化街夜市) (3 stars) is a bustling night market in central Taipei between Tunghua Street and Lingchiang Street (臨江街). You'll find numerous native foods between Lingchiang Street and Keelung Road (基隆路). *Chingdao Douzhang* (青島豆漿), Tunghua Street, #73 (台北市大安區通化街73號) (02) 2708-6149 sells some of the best soybean-based products in town, seating is limited so get your soybean milk and onion cake to go. For a Taiwanese hamburger try *Shijia Shibao* (石家割包), Lingchiang Street, #104 (台北市大安區臨江街104號) (02) 2738-1773, in business for over five decades. The unique urban wear on Tunghua Street attracts "Tai ke" youth dressed as if they had just attended a Chinese punk rock concert.

Wufenpu (五分埔) (3 stars) is a famous Taipei discount garment district near Riaohe Tourist Night Market where vendors from other night markets are said to purchase their wares. You'll literally find bags full of discount clothing at bargain prices, but quality may be questionable. By MRT depart at Houshanpi Station (five-minute walk), by train exit Songshan Station and cross the street.

Ximending (西門町) (4 ½ stars) isn't a day or night market, per se, but an afternoon or evening here makes for a truly memorable eating, shopping, and people-watching experience. The area is usually packed with young people eager to check out the latest fashion imports from Europe, America, and Japan. Transfer at Taipei Main Station for the blue line bound for Xinpu and exit at the first stop, Ximen Station (西門站).

Yongkang Street (永康街) (4 stars) is lined with fine eateries that boast coffee, tea and gourmet foods. Yongkang Street, not far from National Taiwan Normal University (師大*Shida*), runs perpendicular to Xinyi Road, Section 2. For delectable dumplings, Dintaifung, the New York Yankees of dumplings restaurants, is located here.

TAIPEI HISTORIC SITES
(台灣歷史上的地方)

Dadaocheng (大稻埕), an overlooked, underrated section of northwest Taipei, was once the wealthiest city on Taiwan during the time of Liu Ming-chuan (劉銘傳), Taiwan's first provincial governor. Tea, cloth, silk and rice were heavily traded, and residents once dried harvested rice outside North Gate (北門 *Beimen*). Dadaocheng is getting a reconstruction makeover with the addition of a modern coffee square. However, the area's cultural heritage is kept alive by local food vendors and teashops. On Dihua Street (迪化街) you'll find a variety of herbs, teas, spices and dried foods, which the district is famous for. Depending on the current, boats sail from Dadaocheng Wharf to Guandu (NT $150), the wharf is a twenty-five minute walk from Shuanglian Station Exit 2.

Fort San Domingo (紅毛城 *Hungmaocheng*) in Danshui has been classified as a first-class relic by the Ministry of the Interior. In layman's terms, that means it's worth checking out. The Dutch conquered Fort San Domingo from the Spanish in 1641;

today locals refer to "Fortress of the Red-Haired Barbarians," or "Red Hair Fort," in reference to the former Dutch settlers. Once inside, visitors can enter the site of the former British consulate, adjacent to the fort. The consulate was established in 1867, and much of the original furniture and interior remains intact. This small fort is a major Danshui cultural attraction, and for only NT $60 a visit is well worth your time. Fort San Domingo is open 9:00 am to 5 pm and is reachable by foot (a twenty-minute walk from Danshui Station) or on bus Red 26 (紅26) from Danshui Station. Zhongzheng Road, Lane 28, #1 (台北縣淡水鎮文化里中正路28巷1號) (02) 2623-1001.

In spite of rapid reconstruction, renovation and revitalization, Taipei boasts historic houses that have not been bulldozed in the name of progress. **Chenyueji Historic Estate** (陳悅記祖宅), Yenping North Road, Section 4, #231 (台北市延平北路4段231號), built in 1807, is a third-grade cultural relic in Taipei's Datong district (大同區). Also known as "Teacher's Residence" (老師府), this ancestral home-turned-memorial house is dedicated to Chinese scholar Chen Yue-ji. Inside the courtyard are ornate offices, spacious halls and a pavilion. **Chienmu House** (錢穆故居), Linxi Road, #72, Shilin (台北市士林區臨溪路72號) (02) 2880-5809, managed by nearby Soochow University, commemorates the contributions of Ch'ien Mu, a former Beijing University professor and founder of Hong Kong's New Asia College. Open 9 am to 5 pm Tuesday through Sunday, closed Mondays and national holidays. From Jiantan Station take bus 304 to Soochow University. **Gu Xian-Rong** (辜顯榮), a wealthy merchant from Lukang, Tainan, built a tremdous Taipei residence, even by modern standards, nearly a century ago. Although his historic estate is now Xingrong Kindergarten, the building, which resembles the New York Public Library, stands a few blocks from Dadaocheng Wharf on Guisui Street, Lane 303, #9 (台北市大同區歸綏街303巷9號). **Huang Family Old House**, Heping East Road, Section 2, Lane 76, #4 (台北市大安區和平東路2段76巷4號), is a traditional Chinese house built by the Huang family from the Fukian, Changzhou Province. The large (for its time) dwelling, built in classical Ch'ing dynasty fashion, has a u-shape roof. **Lin Antai Historic Home** (林安泰古厝), Binjiang Street, #5 (台北市中山區濱江街5號) (02) 2598-1572, built in 1783, provides unique snapshot spots as the inside rooms and courtyard are open for guests. From Yuanshan Station cross Zhongshan North Road, it's a brisk twenty-five minute walk. **Linyutang House** (林語堂故居), Yangde Boulevard, Section 2, #141 (台北市仰德大道2段141號) (02) 2861-3003, stores manuscripts and other relics from once-famed writer Lin Yu-tang. With its Western décor and glazed tiles, inside is a curious confluence of Chinese artifacts nestled within a singular Spanish architectural design. When he passed away at age 82, Mr. Lin was buried near the backyard courtyard in April, 1976. Open 10 am to 9 pm. From Jiantan Station take bus 260, 303, or Minibuses 15 or 16 and depart at Yongfu. Built in 1876, **Yifang Old House**, Keelung Road, Section 3, Lane 155, #128 (台北市基隆路3段155巷128號), is a traditional Chinese house made of stones and bricks where a family surnamed Chen once housed guns to ward off robbers. With its Ch'ing dynasty Chinese architecture and u-shaped roof, Yifang Old House is a classical contrast from the nearby conflux of modern skyscrapers.

If you're interested in ancient architecture, **Xuehai Academy** (學海書院 *Xuehai Shuyuan*) is the site of what would be the oldest school in Taipei. Opened in 1843 during the Ch'ing dynasty, the academy was originally used as an office/dormitory for military officers and government officials working in the Taipei area. After 1847, Xuehai Academy became a public school, and has since become a shrine. Huangho South Road, Section 2, #93 (台北市萬華區環河南路2段93號).

After exploring Longshan Temple, you may want to traverse nearby **Mengjia Historic Street** (艋舺老街 Mengjia Laojie). Walk from Longshan Temple to Xiyuan Road, Section 1 to find Buddhist shops and traditional Chinese stores that sell hand-made embroidery works. Although many shop owners aren't fluent in English, they're glad to explain to tourists how to make traditional Chinese embroidery.

In times past, there were five gates in which one could enter Taipei City. Built in 1879, **North Gate** (北門 Beimen), also referred to as Chengen Gate, stands at the intersection of Zhongxiao East Road and Boai Road (台北市忠孝西路與博愛路口). If you take a bus, the gate will be in full view at downtown Beimen Station. Unfortunately, the other four historic gates have been destroyed in the name of economic progress.

Old Taipei Railway Station (鐵路局), outside North Gate (北門 Beimen), was constructed during the Ch'ing dynasty. In 1919, the station was reconstructed by the Japanese in its current form, in a traditional 19th century British-style. The site of the former station is at the intersection of Yenping North Road, Zhongxiao West Road and Zhonghua Road (延平北路,忠孝西路和中華路交叉口).

Guiling Road (台北市桂林路 Guiling Lu), one section of Mengjia Historical Street, has an impressive history. In decades past, Wanhua Police Station was a storage facility for rice and other grains. You'll find Chinese traditional medicine, paper, and Buddhist shops here (台北市萬華區桂林路).

Over three centuries ago, **Guiyang Street** (台北市貴陽街) was a bustling area for purchasing Chinese potatoes, that's why Guiyang Street is referred to locally as "potato street" (蕃薯街 fanshujie). During the Japanese occupation, Guiyang Street became a seedy red light district, with brothels lining each side of the street. Thankfully, previous mayors peeled away

profligates and the area has continued to clean up.

The Presidential Office Building (總統府 Zongtongfu) was built between the years 1912 and 1919. The original building was built during the Japanese occupation but much of the original European design was destroyed during WWII and rebuilt in its original form soon thereafter. Chiang Kai-shek occupied the building in 1950, and since that time, the building has been used as the official office of the President of Taiwan. Thankfully, the building's European design remains intact today. From Topview Observatory of Shin Kong Life Tower, the building appears like the Chinese character for sun (日 re). The Presidential Office Building is on Chongqing South Road, #122 (台北市中正區重慶南路1段122號). Don't expect a full five-floor tour, however, the president is busy. **Taipei Guest House**, built during the Japanese occupation between 1899 and 1901, is used for state banquets and hosting foreign dignitaries. It's on Ketalagan Boulevard adjacent to the Presidential Office and is open to the public for viewing and tours once every two months (June, August, October, December, February, and April).

It's hard to imagine that a traditional teahouse could be a historical site but **Wistaria House** (紫藤廬茶館 Tzutenglu Chaguan), named for the three wisteria trees planted in the spacious outside courtyard, continues to draw curious tourists. Customers sit on tatami mats and discuss art, life, and politics, much the way they had during the 1950s when Taiwan was under martial law and citizens met to discuss prospects for democracy. Light snacks include dried fruits and watermelon seeds (NT $200 to NT $300) while over a dozen fine teas are available (NT$200 to NT$350). Xinsheng South Road, Section 3, Lane 16, #1 (台北市新生南路3段16巷1號) (02) 2363-7375, 2363-9459 http://wistariahouse.com.

TAIPEI HOTEL GUIDE
(台北飯店指南)

Although over two hundred hotels dot this impressive Asian city, some smaller budget hotels may cater to "working women." To ensure you have a pleasant stay, you may wish to reside at one of Taipei's finer three to five-star hotels. Hotel rates are seasonal, so expect higher rates during peak travel months. Most hotels charge a 10% service charge but include a continental or buffet breakfast, have a business center or offer free Internet access (inquire before you book). Many upscale Taipei hotels also offer "teatime" between 2 and 4 pm, which people frequent for coffee talk, tea tasting, delectable desserts or perhaps a buffet meal. To contact a hotel from abroad, dial your country's international calling code followed by Taiwan's country code (886), Taipei's area code (02), and leave out the zero when dialing. From the United States, to dial Chinatrust Executive Suites, Beitou one would dial 011 886 2 2893-0911.

Upscale (Traveling In Style)

The Ambassador Hotel (國賓大飯店 *Guobing Dafandian*), a five-star hotel near Shuanglian Station, boasts an outdoor swimming pool (not open year round) as well as a fitness center, sauna, and upscale Eastern and Western dining. Daily room rates start around NT $4500 (US $135.00)/night plus 10% service charge. Complimentary breakfast is included. Check to see if any promotions are being offered. Zhongshan North Road, Section 2, #63 (台北市中山北路2段63號) (02) 2551-1111 http://www.ambh.com.tw/.

Brother Hotel (兄弟大飯店 *Shongdi Dafandian*) Oh brother, where art thou? Probably relaxing at this luxury four-star hotel! Single rooms go for NT $4,300 (US $129.00) to 4,800 (US $144.00)/night. The hotel boasts fine Japanese, Taiwanese, Cantonese, French, Italian and teppenyaki

dining, a bar and lounge, and a conference room. Near Nanjing East Road Station, Nanjing East Road, Section 3, #255 (台北市南京東路3段255號) (02) 2712-3456 http://www.brotherhotel.com.tw.

Ceaser Park Taipei (台北凱撒大飯店 *Taipei Kaisha Dafandian*) is directly across from Taipei Main Station, so getting around shouldn't be a problem. Ceaser Park boasts an impressive health club and upscale Japanese restaurant. Guests relax in comfortable lounge chairs after a dip in either of the two whirlpools on the roof garden. Superior rooms start at NT $7,200 a night. Zhongxiao West Road, Section 1, #38 (台北市忠孝西路1段38號) (02) 2311-5151 http://www.caesarpark.com.tw/.

Evergreen Laurel Hotel Taipei (長榮桂冠酒店 *Changrong Guiguan Jiudian*) This five-star hotel boasts meeting and banquet rooms, exquisite dining, and a spa. Standard single rooms start around NT $5800 (US $174.00) and go up to NT $7,000 (US $210.00)/night. Songchiang Road, #63, near Nanjing East Road Station. (台北市松江路63號) (02) 2501-9988 http://www.evergreen-hotels.com.

Far Eastern Plaza Hotel (遠東國際大飯店 *Yuandong Guoji Dafandian*) This five-star hotel offers more than panoramic views of the city. Near Liuzhangli Station and upscale Taipei department stores, restaurants, bookstores and night life, Asian pop stars often hold press conferences here to promote their latest recordings. The hotel has a popular afternoon teatime where movers and shakers often meet to mingle. Standard double rooms start around NT $9600. Dunhua South Road, Section 2, #201 (台北市敦化南路2段201號) (02) 2378-8888 http://www.feph.com.tw.

Ferrary Hotel (台北華麗飯店 *Taipei Huali Fandian*) No, it's not the Ferrari Hotel although you may feel as if you own one if you stay here (NT $4200/ night). Walking distance from Huaxi

Street and Ximending, Ferrary Hotel boasts fine Eastern and Western dining (complimentary breakfast for guests), Internet access, a laundromat, and gym. Near Ximen Station. Kangding Road, #41 (台北市康定路41號) (02) 2381-8111 http://www.f-hotel.com.tw.

Fortuna Hotel (富都大飯店 *Fudu Dafandian*) This five-star hotel boasts an exquisite coffee shop, upscale lounge, Fortuna Grill, a revolving restaurant offering 360-degree views (now reserved only for banquets), and Dragon Court, an outstanding Cantonese-style restaurant. Single rooms start at NT $2660. Near Minquan West Road Station on Zhongshan North Road, Section 2, #122 (台北市中山北路2段122號) (02) 2563-1111 http://www.taipei-fortuna.com.tw.

The Grand Hotel (圓山大飯店 *Yuanshan Dafandian*) Once owned by Madame Chiang Kai-shek, this five-star hotel with a classic Chinese façade featured in the Ang Lee classic, "Eat Drink Man Woman" is a distinct Taiwan landmark. Visit The Grand Hotel restaurants for choice cuisine, or stop by the café for piquant pastries, coffees and teas. At night relax at the 60's Bar and enjoy your drinks while listening to some great tunes (or shake, rattle and roll on the dance floor). The hotel provides a free shuttle bus from nearby Yuanshan Station. Rates vary depending on whether you want a room inside or outside with a scenic view of Taipei. Check the hotel web site for rates and promotions. Zhongshan North Road, Section 4, #1 (台北市中山北路4段1號) (02) 2596-5565 http://www.grand-hotel.org.

Grand Formosa Regent (晶華酒店 *Jinhua Jiudian*) During your stay you may encounter a touring pop star (it's good enough for Japanese pop duo Puffy and Michael Jackson...) Restaurants serve outstanding Eastern and Western cuisine while a three-piece orchestra performs. The Business Center is first-class, offering Internet access, typing, photocopying and

fax services (are also available at many 24-hour convenience stores), and business card printing. Safety deposit boxes are also available upon request. Rates start at NT $8000/night plus a 10% service charge. Breakfast not included. Near Zhongshan Station. Zhongshan North Road, Section 2, #41 (台北市中山北路2段41號) (02) 2523-8000 http://www.grandformosa-taipei.com.tw.

Grand Hyatt Taipei (凱悅大飯店 *Kaiyue Dafandian*) This five-star hotel, within walking distance of Warner Brothers Village and Taipei World Trade Center, boasts outstanding eateries including Ziga Zaga, an exquisite Italian restaurant by day and hopping disco at night. Ziga Zaga is not for the faint-hearted, businesspeople are known to unwind at the bar and get into the groove on the dance floor. Rooms start at NT $6000 per night. Near Taipei City Hall Station, Sungshou Road, #2 (台北市忠孝東路3段8號) (02) 2720-1234 http://www.taipei.hyatt.com.

Holiday Inn Asiaworld Taipei (假日大飯店 環亞台北 *Jiare Dafandian Huanya*) Formerly known as Asia World Plaza Hotel (環亞大飯店 *Yazhou Dafandian*), this enormous four-star hotel, adjacent to Asia World Department Store, provides ample choices for dining and shopping. The hotel boasts a heated indoor swimming pool, conference room, business center, and fitness center. Single "business" rooms start at NT $4179 weekdays, NT $4,850 weekends. Includes continental breakfast. Near Nanjing East Road Station. Dunhua North Road, #100 (台北市敦化北路100號) (02) 2715-0077, 2713-8383.

Howard Plaza Hotel (福華大飯店 *Fuhua Dafandian*) Near Zhongxiao Fuxing Station, the comfortable rooms in this fine four-star hotel are decorated in elegant Chinese fashion. Howard Plaza Hotel boasts a full fitness center, business center and fine international dining in an upscale location. NT $4700 and up. Renai Road, Section 3,

#160 (台北市仁愛路3段160號)
(02) 2700-2323 http://www.howard-hotels.
com.

Imperial Hotel (華國大飯店 *Huaguo Dafandian*) Formerly known as Imperial Inter-Continental Hotel, this five-star hotel fit for a king is minutes from MRT stations and Shilin. Inside is a gym, sauna, massage, games room and sportswear shop. If it's good enough for the Australian Chamber Orchestra... There are several eateries to choose from, which include an international buffet and Cantonese cuisine, and an upscale bar, popular with many long-term expatriates. Imperial Hotel is near Shuang Cheng Street, "the combat zone," where it's easy to find a good watering hole. Standard single rooms start at NT $4399 (US $132.00). Linshen North Road, #600 (台北市林森北路600號) (02) 2596-5111 http://www.imperialhotel.com.tw.

Le Petit Sherwood Taipei (台北小西華飯店 *Taipei Xiaoxihua Fandian*) Located in a trendy shopping area just around the corner from Far Eastern Department Store, this sixty-two room hotel boasts excellent Western dining and attentive service. Standard single or double rooms start around NT $6000 (US $180)/night. Dunhua South Road, Section 1, #370 (台北市敦化南路1段370號) (02) 2754-1166.

Les Suites, Taipei (台北商館 *Taipei Shangguan*) are two luxury boutique hotels that promise a comfortable respite for weary business travelers. Standard rooms have a queen-sized bed and come equipped with a large TV, DVD player, coffee maker, minibar, hot water pot (for tea), and standard bathroom amenities. Guests also enjoy a complimentary deluxe buffet breakfast. Room rates start at NT $4999.00 (approximately US $150) per night. There are two Les Suites hotels in Taipei, one is on a quiet street near the intersection of Nanjing East Road and Fuxing North Road, the other is in the upscale Daan district near Taipei 101, World Trade Center and Warner

Brothers Village.
Chingcheng: Chingcheng Street, #12 (台北市慶城街12號) (02) 8712-7688
Daan: Daan Road, Section 1, #135 (台北市大安路1段135號) (02) 8773-3668
http://www.suitetpe.com.

Miramar Garden Taipei (美麗信花園酒店 *Meilixin Huayuan Jiudian*) boasts two hundred spacious rooms, an outdoor swimming pool, spa, sauna, and gym. The hotel is the first to be leased with the government under a build, operate and transfer (BOT) plan in which the property must be returned to the government after fifty years. Book your stay now before bureaucrats make you do paperwork and wait on long lines. Rooms start around NT $4,200 (US $126.00)/night. Near Zhongxiao Xinsheng Station. Civil Boulevard, Section 3, #83 (台北市市民大道3段83號) (02) 2500-6465 http://www.miramargarden.com.tw.

Rebar Holiday Inn Crowne Plaza Taipei (力霸皇冠大飯店 *Libahuangguan Dafandian*) boasts a prime location from which to visit National Dr. Sun Yat-sen Memorial Hall, Warner Brothers Village and Taipei World Trade Center. Call for rates and availability. Standard single rooms start around NT $4550 (US $136.60). Near Nanjing East Road Station. Nanjing East Road, Section 5, #32 (台北市松山區南京東路5段32號) (02) 2763-5656.

The Landis Taipei (亞都麗緻大飯店 *Yadu Litzi Dafandian*) You know where fashion sits, don't you? This luxury five-star hotel formerly called "The Ritz" offers a complementary fresh fruit basket and daily newspaper. The hotel boasts outstanding Eastern and Western dining (Paris 1930 for fine French cuisine), as well as a sauna and jacuzzi. Superior room rates start at NT $8000 (US $240.00). Near Minquan West Road Station. Minchuan East Road, Section 2, #41 (台北市民權東路2段41號) (02) 2597-1234 http://www.landistpe.com. tw.

Hotel Royal Taipei (老爺大酒店 *Laoye Dafandian*) This five-star hotel near Zhongshan Station in northern Taipei boasts four restaurants and two bars, so guests can choose from a variety of Chinese, Japanese or Western foods and snacks. Facilities include a health club, sauna, and rooftop swimming pool. Rooms start at NT $4500 (US $135.00). Zhongshan North Road, Section 2, #37-1 (台北市中山北路2段 37-1號) (02) 2542-3266 http://www.royal-taipei.com.tw.

Sheraton Hotel Taipei (台北喜來登大 飯店 *Taipei Xilaitun Dafandian*) recently completed a three-year, US $60 million renovation in time for President Chen's son's wedding. Enjoy the swimming pool, health club, squash courts, gym, sauna, 24-hour medical center, barber shop and beauty salon, as well as postal and currency exchange services. There's also a drug store, safety deposit box, florist (if you're in the mood for romance), and valet parking, for those adventurous enough to rent a car. The hotel offers upscale Chinese, Western and Japanese dining, shopping arcades (shops within the hotel that sell luxury imported goods), a full business center, a golf center and airport transport service. Standard rooms start around NT $4,800. Zhongxiao East Road, Section 1, #12 (台北市忠孝東路1段12號) (02) 2321-5511 http://www.starwoodhotels. com/sheraton/search/hotel_detail. html?propertyID=956.

The Sherwood Taipei (台北西華飯店 *Xihua Fandian*) attracts hordes of gourmands with its fine French grill, international buffet and Chinese restaurant, as well as a classy bar for those who choose to sip their martinis in style. Bring your bathing cap, goggles and trunks, the hotel has a heated indoor swimming pool. Standard single rooms start at NT $5,600. Near Zhongshan Junior High School Station, Minsheng East Road, Section 3, #111 (台北市民生東路3段111號) (02) 2718-1188 http://www.sherwood.com. tw.

The Tango (台北柯旅天閣 *Kelu Tienge*) You ready to tango? This ultramodern five-star hotel in the heart of Xinyi business district offers complimentary breakfast and a daily newspaper. Rooms start at NT $6200. Near Yongchun Station. Zhongxiao East Road, Section 5, #297 (台北市忠孝東路五段297號) (02) 2528-8000 http://www.thetango.com.tw.

United Hotel (國聯飯店 *Guolien Fandian*) Simple yet elegant, this upscale hotel is a three-minute walk from Dr. Sun Yat-sen Memorial Hall Station in Xinyi business district. In addition to boasting business and fitness centers, guests relax in the sauna after working out on the top floor health club. Enjoy dinner on the second floor or relax at the Copper Bar where the whiskey promises to make you feel like gold. Standard rooms start at NT $7800 (US $234.00)/night. Guangfu South Road, #200 (台北市光復南路200號) (02) 2773-1515 http://www.unitedhotel.com.tw.

Mid-Range
(Comfortable And Accomodating)

Ambiance Hotel (喜瑞飯店 *Xirei Fandian*) At the intersection of Changan East Road and Xinsheng North Road is Ambiance Hotel, which prides itself on being avante-garde, comfortable, and functional. Standard rooms, which start around NT $2,600 (US $72.00), come equipped with CD/DVD players, minibars, tea kettles, and high speed Internet access. Guest services include laundry/dry cleaning, currency exchange, room service, photocopy/fax, postal/courier, and car service. The hotel also boasts Ambiance Lounge, a café that offers breakfast and light dining from 7 am to 10 pm daily. Check for promotions. Changan East Road, Section 1, #64 (台北市中山區長安東路1段64號) (02) 2541-0077 http://www.ambiencehotel.com.tw.

Charming City Hotel (香城飯店 *Shangcheng Fandian*) As the name implies, this charming hotel is within walking distance to Warner Brothers Village and Taipei World Trade Center. Expect charming city service along with clean, comfortable accommodations. Standard rooms run from NT$3,100 (US $91.00) to NT $3,600 (US $108.00). Those on a budget could stay on the basement floors for NT$1,400 (US $42.00). Xinyi Road, Section 4, #295 (02) 2704-9546 (台北市信義路4段295號) Toll-free 24-hours: 0800-021-112 http://www.city-hotel.com.tw.

Cosmos Hotel (天成大飯店 *Tiencheng Dafandian*) At this three-star hotel, conveniently located near Taipei Main Station, standard single rooms run from NT $3,200 (US $96.00) to NT $3,600 (US $108)/night. Rooms are clean and the staff is known for its hospitality. Zhongxiao West Road, Section 1, #43 (台北市中正區忠孝西路1段43號) (02) 2361-7856 http://www.cosmos-hotel.com.tw.

Golden China Hotel (康華大飯店 *Kanghua Dafandian*) Just a notch below five-stars, this comfortable four-star hotel boasts a swimming pool, gym, fine dining, a conference room and full business center. Standard rates start around NT $3000 (US $90.00). Songchiang Road, #306 (台北市松江路306號) (02) 2521-5151 http://www.golden-china.com.tw.

Leofoo Taipei (六福客棧 *Liufu Ketsan*) Looking for a comfortable hotel conveniently located near Nanjing East Road Station? Three-star Leofoo Taipei, which boasts a conference room, business center and upscale dining, may be for you. Standard room rates start at NT $2,500. Changchun Road, #168 (台北市中山區長春路168號) (02) 2507-3211 http://www.leofoo.com.tw/hotel.

San Want Hotel Taipei (神旺大飯店 *Shenyan Dafandian*) Want a comfortable stay sans hassles? Try San Want Hotel, a four-star hotel near Zhongxiao Dunhua Station, near department stores, Dr. Sun Yat-sen Memorial Hall, Taipei City Hall,

Warner Brothers Village and Taipei World Trade Center. Rates start at NT $4,200 (US $126)/night. Zhongxiao East Road, Section 4, #172 (台北市忠孝東路4段127號) (02) 2772-2121 http://www.sanwant.com.

Season's Garden Executive Suites (四季軒 *Xilichuan*) Less than a twenty-minute walk from Taipei World Trade Center, Season's Garden Executive Suites boasts a health club that includes a sauna and weight room, twenty-four hour cable TV and VCR, a laundry room and comfortable rooms with daily rates that start at NT $2,800. Guests also receive a complimentary breakfast at the hotel restaurant. Anho Road, Section 2, Lane 181, #10 (台北市安和路2段181巷10號) (02) 2378-5668.

Young Men's Christian Association (YMCA) International House

If you're a single person out for a singularly good time it's always fun to stay at the YMCA (according to the Village People). In Taipei the YMCA is near Taipei Main Station so you can easily hail a cab, hop on a bus or the MRT and shuttle off to other parts of the city. Royal Host on the first floor tends to satisfy even the most voracious appetites. Single rooms for singles (one person) start at NT $1,800, NT $2,200 for two. Safety deposit boxes are available on first floor, and self-service coin-operated laundry machines are available on the seventh. You must be a member of the YMCA to reside so non-members must pay NT $200 (US $6.00) to join for a year. Hsuchang Street, #19 (台北市許昌街19號) (02) 2311-3201, 2331-2924 http://www.ymcataipei.org.tw.

HOTELS (Beitou) (飯店, 北投)

While there are older, relatively inexpensive hot spring hotels to choose from in Yangmingshan, Internet access is hard to come by and most personnel are not bilingual. The four Beitou hotels listed below should make for a pleasant stay:

Hall Yard Resort (花月溫泉館 *Huayue Wenchuenguan*) offers complimentary breakfast as well as fine amenities such as shower caps, a comb, razor, towels, bathing lotion, moisturizer, shampoo and mineral water. Spring rooms are spacious and have a couch to relax between bathing sessions. In addition, there is a separate shower area. Hall Yard charges NT $1000 (US $30.00) per room per hour and a half. During national holidays the price increases to NT $1,200 (US $36.00). From Beitou Station take bus Small 22 (小22), the bus stops three minutes by foot from Hall Yard Resort. Guests can walk from Xinbeitou (New Beitou) Station but the resort is a fifteen-minute walk up steep Xinmin Road. Rooms start at NT$4,800 (US $144.00)/night. Xinmin Road, Lane 1, #2.4, Beitou, Taipei (台北市北投區新民路1巷2.4號) (02) 2893-9870. Undergoing renovation, please call first.

Chinatrust Executive Suites, Beitou (中信商務會館 北投館 *Zhongxin Shangwu Huiguan, Beitou Guan*) One word sums up Chinatrust Executive Suites, Beitou: Ideal. Expect to find comfort and quality in a convenient location. The hotel boasts a fitness center on the top floor with scenic views, as well as a laundromat on the eighth. Guests also receive a complementary fruit basket and newspaper daily, as well as a continental breakfast at Royal Host, which offers exceptional American or Japanese-style meals in a casual dining atmosphere. The Ethernet Internet connection in your room may be hit or miss but you can access the computer on the thirteenth floor, gratis. While doing laundry, relax and enjoy your morning coffee with fantastic views of Beitou's Datun Mountain (the main mountain range of Yangmingshan), neighboring Shipai and Shilin districts, and, off in the distance, Taipei City. NT $2400 (US $72/night) weekdays, NT $3000 (US $90.00) weekends and holidays. Beitou Road, Section 2, #9, Beitou, Taipei (台北市北投區北投路2段9號) (02) 2893-0911 http://www.chinatrust-hotel.com.

Spring City Resort (春天酒店 *Chuntien Jiudian*) This luxurious five-star hotel five minutes up the mountain from Xinbeitou Station makes for a great getaway. Near Yangmingshan National Park, Spring City Resort boasts two outstanding restaurants, stunning outdoor hot springs (most have whirlpools), and clean, comfortable indoor springs. Many contend that the hot springs at Spring City Resort are not only the best in Taipei, but also the best on Taiwan. Standard room rates begin around NT $7,000 (US $210.00)/night. The outdoor springs (NT $800) are open from 9 am to 10 pm, the indoor springs (NT $600/person/hour) are new and comfortable but the bathing room is small. Youya Road, #18, Beitou, Taipei (台北市北投區幽雅路18號) (02) 2897-5555 http://www.springresort.com.tw.

Sweetme Hot Spring Resort (水美溫泉會館 *Shuimei Wenchuen Huiguan*) Another new addition to Beitou's hot spring resort hotels, Sweetme has a reputation for offering fine cuisine and serenity. For guests that would like to be treated like Julius Caesar, the hotel boasts sixty-nine new rooms and hot springs that reflect "the nobility of the ancient Roman Empire." The hotel is located in New Beitou adjacent to New Beitou Park, across the street from Xinbeitou Station and a stone's throw from Beitou Hot Springs Museum and Ketagalan Culture Center. Rooms start at NT $5,600 (US $168.00) for a standard double. Guangming Road, #224 (台北市北投區光明路224號) (02) 2898-3838 http://www.sweetme.com.tw.

HOTELS (Danshui) (飯店, 淡水)

Hotel RegaLees (福格大飯店 *Fuke Dafandian*) boasts a café on the first floor, saunas and a coffee shop on the fourth, business centers one story above, a VIP room on the seventeenth floor and a buffet on the top floor. The buffet, billed as an "Italian restaurant," disappoints with its minimal selection of mediocre foods. Aside from cold cuts, no Italian dishes are to be found (most dishes are Asian). Many may contend that the decent view does not make the buffet worth the NT $600 adult price (plus 10% service charge). Room rates start at NT $3,600 (US $108.00)/night. Shuifu Road, #89, Danshui (台北縣淡水鎮學府路 89 號) (02) 2626-2929 Ext. 8890 http://regalees-hotel.network.com.tw/inst.asp.

Hotel Solar (萬熹大飯店 *Wanxi Dafandian*) If you stay at this three-star hotel you're paying for convenience, not luxury. Opposite Danshui Station and behind a bus terminal, Hotel Solar was a magnet for traveling golfers over two decades ago. NT $2500/night seems high considering breakfast is not included. A Mos Burger Japanese fast food restaurant is downstairs and guests are a stone's throw from Danshui Historic Street, the night market and major Danshui attractions. Accomodations are modest, the staff speaks a modicum of English, and non-smokers may have difficulty staying in some rooms. Zhongzheng East Road, #35 (台北縣淡水鎮中正東路35號) (02) 2621-3281 http://hipage.hinet.net/Hotel_Solar.

The Fisher Hotel (淡水漁人碼頭旅館 *Danshui Yuren Matou Luguan*) Rooms may be small but expatriate guests have remarked that they are indeed comfortable. The Fisher Hotel is within walking distance from Danshui's famed Fisherman's Wharf and is a short bus ride from other notable Danshui attractions. Guests receive a complimentary buffet breakfast with both Eastern and Western-style dishes. Room rates typically fall between NT $1820 to $3,000, depending on season. Zhongzheng Road, Section 2, Lane 22, #8 (淡水鎮中正路2段22巷8號) (02) 2805-8886 http://www.fisherhotel.com.tw.

Danshui Chinatrust Hotel (淡水中信大飯店 *Danshui Zhongxin Dafandian*) is in Hongshulin (紅樹林), a town just south of Danshui that got its name from the mangrove tree that grows in the area. The hotel is on Zhong Zheng East Road, a main thoroughfare that runs north to south from Danshui to the Guandu/ Beitou area. Danshui Chinatrust Hotel boasts seventy-five rooms and a scenic view of Danshui River and Guanyin Mountain. Guests enjoy complimentary high-speed Internet access, a daily newspaper, and breakfast. Take the MRT to Hongshulin Station, cross the street and walk about three minutes. Zhongzheng East Road, Section 2, #91 (台北縣淡水鎮中正東路2段91號) (02) 8809-1111 http://www.chinatrust-hotel.com.

See's Revert Hotel (觀海樓旅店 *Guanhai Loluguan*) boasts a second-floor buffet restaurant with fine Eastern and Western dining, breathtaking views of Danshui River, Guanyin Mountain and close proximity to Danshui and Hongshulin. Standard rooms for two people, which may be somewhat small, start around NT $2,300/night. Staff isn't bilingual and the hotel is not within walking distance to MRT stations. Zhongzheng East Road, Section 1, #129 (台北縣淡水鎮中正東路1段129號, 登輝大道口) (02) 2629-1117 http://www.sees.com.tw.

Star of Sea Motel (淡水海中天溫泉飯店 *Danshui Haizhongtien Wenchuen Fandian*) It's hard to imagine that only a decade ago this hot springs motel was a popular children's arcade. Adjacent to the motel, the upscale Star of Sea buffet boasts impressive Asian dishes. In addition to Hong Kong-style dim sum, Japanese sushi and heaping portions of native foods which inclue fresh seafoods, exotic fruits and cooked vegetables, guests select fresh meats and vegetables to have cooked on a Mongolian wok. Breakfast is served from 7 to 10 am, NT $150 (US $4.50) adults, NT $120 (US $3.60) children between 111 and 140 cm Monday through Friday, NT $200/$150 during weekends. Lunch runs from 11:30 to 2:30 pm, NT $480/$300 Monday through Friday, NT $580/$350 on weekends, and dinner will set you back NT $680/$400. Prices do not include a 10% service charge. Children under 110 cm eat free.

To stay at the motel, rooms start at NT $3000/night for a single bed (one to two people) and NT $5000/night for double beds (one to four people), which is somewhat high considering that the motel appears more like a motor inn than an upscale resort. The motel boasts a three-lane pool, hot spring fountain pools and private hot spring baths. Personal hot spring baths open at noon and cost NT $200 weekdays and NT $300 weekends. Since Star of Sea is between Zhuwei and Hongshulin MRT stations, free shuttle buses run to the motel about fifty meters from Zhuwei and Danshui MRT stations. Zhongzheng East Road, Section 2, #131 (台北縣淡水鎮中正東路2段131號) (02) 2809-9800 http://www.newsos.com.tw.

HOTELS (Tienmu)
(飯店, 天母)

Feeling Hotel (花翎汽車旅店 *Hua-Ling Chiche Ludian*) If you plan to visit Tienmu, Beitou and Yangmingshan, you may feel good about the low-key Feeling Hotel. In the heart of Tienmu, one block south of Taipei American School, this quaint hotel is within walking distance (less than half a block) to restaurants, cafés, and buses that run to MRT stations (Shilin or Shipai). Many guests spend the day in the city and relax in the mountains at night. Feeling Hotel is similar to a simple yet convenient Motel 6. Standard rooms, which typically go for NT $1680 (US $51.00), have desks, air conditioning and cable television. Zhongshan North Road, Section 6, Lane 728, #2 (near Taipei American School). (台北市中山北路6段728巷2號) (02) 2873-5511 http://www.feelinghotel.com.tw.

HOTELS (Yangmingshan)
(飯店, 陽明山)

Yangmingshan is rife with older hot springs hotels, but without Internet service, a bilingual staff, Western dining or continental breakfast, international guests may not be satisfied. Yangmingshan is also a particularly popular respite on weekends and holidays.

Hotel International (國際大旅館 *Guoji Daluguan*) If you dare to experience Yangming Mountain as an elderly local might, you may enjoy your stay at Hotel International. Since 1952, Hotel International has been offering guests rooms to relax while they explore nearby mountain terrain. Both Japanese rooms with tatami mats or rooms with beds are available. The hotel restaurant serves traditional Chinese dishes such as sweet sliced beef (NT $220), spring rolls (NT $200) and chicken soup (NT $250), unlike the kind your mother used to make. Rooms with two beds start at NT $2310. The hotel also offers a traditional Chinese foot massage (NT $500/thirty minutes, NT $1000/hour). From 7 am to 9 pm, patrons may bathe nude in large hot spring pools (NT $150) separated by sex. By bus the 230 and Small 9 (小9) depart from Beitou and stop near the hotel. From Jiantan Station take the Red 15 (紅15) bus. Hushan Road, Section 1, #7, Yangmingshan, Taipei (台北市北投區陽明山湖山路1段7號) (02) 2861-7100 http://www.ihhotel.com.tw.

Landis Resort (陽明山中國麗緻大飯店 *Yangmingshan Zhongguo Dafandian*) Looking for luxury in Yangmingshan? This five-star resort with forty-seven rooms offers exquisite eateries in a lovely mountain location. The resort boasts hot spring pools, an outdoor spring swimming pool, and a full fitness room. Landis Resort also boasts two fine restaurants that offer luscious local cuisine as well as international dishes, and a café to unwind with a choice cup of coffee or tea. Rates are seasonal and start at NT $7,000 (US $210.00)/night. For an additional NT $500 (US $15.00) upgrade to a Deluxe Room with a hot spring bath. By bus, take the 260 to Hotel China. Or, from Jiantan Station take the Red 5 (紅5) to Hotel China. Each bus stops within walking distance. Gejr Road, Yangmingshan, Taipei (台北市士林區陽明山格致路237號) (02) 2861-6661 http://www.landisresort.com.tw.

TAIPEI MUNICIPAL CHILDREN'S RECREATION CENTER (兒童育樂中心)

Taipei Municipal Children's Recreation Center (兒童育樂中心 Ertong Yule Zhongxin) is a ten-minute walk from Yuanshan Station. However, it may be a good idea to take a cab due to the arcane location of the entrance, just under a major highway. Admission is NT $30/$15. Inside are large slides and kiddie rides (NT $20/each) galore. Inside Children's Science Exhibition Hall is a computer recreation area and exhibits on light, colors, gears, and the Earth, including water circulation, atmospheric structure, water ecosystems, pollution, recycling, and space exploration. Admission to Science Exhibition Hall is NT $50/$30 for students. Zhongshan North Road, Section 3, #66 (台北市北市中山北路3段66號) (02) 2593-2211 http://www.tcrc.gov.tw/Amusem%7e1.htm.

Space Theater (太空劇場 Taikong Juchang) shows films about underwater and space exploration (NT $100/$50). Get your friends together because groups over thirty receive a 30% discount. Children's Recreation Center is open 9 am to 5 pm, closed Mondays, Chinese New Year's Eve and the first day of Chinese New Year. The Recreation Center becomes crowded (and noisy!) during weekends. Zhongshan North Road, Section 3, #66 (台北市北市中山北路3段66號) (02) 2593-2211.

By MRT exit Yuanshan Station and walk to Dunhuang Road or Jiuchuen Street to find the main entrance on Zhongshan North Road. By bus take the 21, 26, 40, 203, 208, 216, 218, 220, 224, 247, 260, 266, 277, 279, 280, 287, 288, 290, 303, 304, 308, or 310.

TAIPEI MUSEUM GUIDE (台北博物館指南)

Aristotle wrote, "The aim of art is to represent not the outward appearance of things, but their inward significance." On Taiwan you can find space to contemplate the mysteries of humanity, the essence of life or simply stop in to appreciate some outstanding works. Find out what life is truly like on the other side of the world. Lose yourself in a Taiwanese museum and discover new horizons of self-expression. Many museums also have parks on the premises so you can get that cappuccino to go and stroll after having your fill of history and culture for the day.

Learn about Taiwan's military history and prowess at Armed Forces Museum (國軍歷史文物館), the museum is clean and the government intends to keep it that way, no smoking, chewing gum (betelnut included), eating or drinking is permitted, and all bags must be checked at the first-floor counter. Admission is free and all are welcome. Open 9 am to 4 pm Monday through Saturday, closed Sundays and national holidays. Guiyang Street, Section 1, #243 (台北市貴陽街1段243號) (02) 2331-5730. http://museum.mnd.gov.tw/wwwroot/eng_index.htm.

Beitou Folk Arts Museum (台灣民俗北投文物館), originally a Japanese officers club built in 1913, displays pictures, paintings and artifacts from both residents and aboriginal tribes. Learn about some of the customs of the indigenous peoples of Taiwan and view interesting relics of their past. Stop by the souvenir shop on your way out to purchase prismatic postcards and handmade gift items. Open Monday through Friday 9 am to 5 pm, 9 am to 7:30 pm Saturdays and Sundays. Visit Shann Garden next door for fine barbeque, ambiance and traditional teas. Please call first as this historic museum may be undergoing renovation. Youya Road, Beitou District, #32 (台北市北投區幽雅路32號) (02) 2891-2318.

Beitou Hot Springs Museum (北投溫泉博物館 *Beitou Wenchuen Bowuguan*) Once a main respite for Japanese soldiers during Japan's fifty-year occupation of Taiwan, Beitou Hot Springs Museum informs visitors of local life as it were. Discover rare crystallized stones and actual hot springs used by Japanese soldiers built in 1913. The museum is within walking distance from New Beitou Station and admission is free. You will need to remove your shoes and wear slippers (provided) to enter. Zhongshan Road, #2, New Beitou (台北市北投區中山路2號) (02) 2893-9981.

Chang Foundation Museum (鴻禧美術館 *Hongximei Shuguan*) houses artifacts similar to the National Palace Museum, except these ancient Chinese treasures belong to the prestigious Chang family. The museum is within walking distance from Zhongxiao Xinsheng Station. Tours are offered in either English or Chinese, but you'll need to call to arrange one. Open Tuesday to Sunday, 9 am. to 4:30 pm. Renai Road, Section 2, #63 (台北市仁愛路2段63號) (02) 2356-9575.

Kids big and small love **Children's Art Museum of Taipei** (蘇荷兒童美術館). Founded in 2003 by art enthusiast Lin Chien-Ling (林千鈴), the museum displays creative works by aspiring local artists (children), and some paintings and plaster works are truly impressive! Groups of six or more are invited to call and arrange for a class. The museum often holds free events and promises a fun morning or afternoon for the entire family. Open Tuesday through Sunday 10 am to 5:30 pm, closed Mondays. Reservations are suggested a week in advance for group tours of fifteen or more. Tienmu West Road, Lane 50, #20, B1 (台北市天母西路50巷20號B1) (02) 2872-1366 http://www.artart.com.tw.

Children's Museum of Transportation (兒童交通博物館 *Ertong Jiaotong Bowuguan*) in Chinese is "Children's Traffic Museum." As if the traffic in Taipei weren't bad enough,

now children have the opportunity to study it formally! Kidding aside, the museum opened on July 1, 1981 and includes a children's play area and transportation park, which boasts bumper cars, spinning teacups and electric cars. Put the pedal to the metal, it's great fun for kids and adult kids alike! Open Tuesday through Sunday 9 am to 5 pm. Dingzhou Road, Section 3, #2 (台北市中正區汀州路3段2號) (02) 2365-4248 http://www.kidspark.com.tw.

Discovery Center of Taipei (台北探索館) is a relatively new (opened in 2002) exhibition hall at Taipei City Hall that explores Taipei's past, present and future. There are four floors, Taipei Impressions Hall is on the first, Special Exhibitions Hall is on the second, City Discovery Hall is on the third, and "Dialogue With Time" Hall, which chronicles Taipei's development and history, is on the fourth. Discovery Theater, a 114-seat multi-projection theater with a slow revolving floor is also on the fourth floor. Current short films, each fifteen minutes in length, are "Historical Journey: The History of Taipei", "Present: City Life" and "Future: My Dream City." If you can snag a seat before a local student does the movies make for an entertaining experience. A suggested tour would be to go from the first floor to the fourth and explore the different halls on the way down, which legislators may do between meetings. Open Tuesday through Sunday 9 am to 5 pm, closed Mondays and national holidays. Admission to the Center and theater are free. Shifu Road, #1 (台北市市府路1號) (02) 2757-4547 http://www.discovery.taipei.gov.tw/english.

Fire Safety Museum of the Taipei Fire Department is open from 9 am to 12 pm and again from 2 to 5 pm except for national holidays and is located in the Neihu Administration Building on Chenggong Road, Section 2, #376 (台北市內湖區成功路2段376號) (02) 2791-9786. Admission is free and all are welcome. If you're in Neihu and are looking for something different you shouldn't feel burned by a brief visit.

Danshui now boasts a quaint **Fishball Museum** (魚丸博物館), although display descriptions are in Chinese it may be fun to stop by. Zhongzheng Road, #117, Danshui (台北縣淡水鎮中正路117號) (02) 2629-3312.

Grass Mountain Chateau (Yinhe Hall) (草山行館 *Caoshan Xingguan*), once a Yangmingshan residence of Chiang Kai-shek, is now a charming café. In addition to Yinhe Hall's somewhat pricy coffee, tea and pastries, discover photos and other cultural relics of the president's past. Open 9 am to 5 pm, admission costs NT $20. The adjacent café is open 10 am to 11 pm. From Jiantan Station take bus Red 5 (紅5) to the last stop. May be undergoing renovation, call first. Hudi Road, #89, Yangmingshan (台北市北投區湖底路89號) (02) 2862-1911.

Established in 1971, **Hwa Kang Museum** (華岡博物館) on the Yangmingshan campus of Chinese Culture University (中國文化大學) boasts three floors of ancient Chinese ceramics, compelling Chinese paintings and calligraphic works, Chinese folk arts and woodblock prints. Folk arts and handicrafts classes are often held here for students. Open 9 am to 4 pm Monday through Friday, closed weekends, summer/winter vacations and national holidays. By bus take either the 280 from Taipei Main Station or the 6 from Shilin Station. Admission is free and all are welcome. Huakang Road, #55, Yangmingshan, Taipei (台北市陽明山華岡路55號) (02) 2861-1801 Ext. 17608.

Insects Science Museum (昆蟲科學博物館 *Kuenchong Kexue Bowuguan*), inside Chenggong Senior High School, boasts fifty thousand non-living insects. Museum hours are 9 am to 4 pm, closed Sundays and holidays. Be mindful of the students. Jinan Road, Section 1, #71 (成功高中昆蟲博物館又稱蝴蝶館, 台北市中正區濟南路1段71號) (02) 2396-1298.

Juming Fine Arts Museum (朱銘美術館 *Zhuming Meishuguan*) captivated art enthusiasts the world over upon its

opening on September 19, 1999. This Taiwan trove deep in the rolling hills of Gold Mountain (Jinshan), Taipei County is where you'll find fourteen outdoor display areas. The most popular, especially during spring and summer, is the "water area," where both children and adults splash around in Swan Lake (天鵝池 *Tienertsi*).

The museum, which boasts an impressive gift shop, bookstore and café, is open 10:30 am to 5:00 pm daily, closed Mondays. Large rocks with zippers, "Living World Series" New York City dweller sculptures and "Tai Chi Series" tai chi boxing-inspired rock creations especially impress. Buses (fee) from Taipei Fine Arts Museum in Shilin run weekdays (excluding Mondays) at 8:40 am and again at 1:10 pm and operate more frequently on Saturday and Sunday. Shi-shi-hu, #2, Jinshan (台北縣金山鄉西勢湖2號) (02) 2498-9940 http://www.juming.org.tw.

Ketagalan Culture Center (凱達格蘭文化中心) is dedicated to the preservation of aboriginal language and culture on Taiwan. Floors four through seven hold performances and language/culture classes, while the first three floors house an impressive collection of native art works. Admission is free and all are welcome. Opposite Xinbeitou Station. Zhongshan Road No. 3-1 (台北市北投區中山路3之1號) (02) 2898-6500.

At **Kuoyuanye Museum of Cake & Pastry** (郭元益糕餅博物館) learn about this historic company and Chinese cake culture (NT $80). Tours are in Chinese and available for groups only (call first). From Shilin Station Exit 1 turn right at Wenlin Road overpass. Wenlin Road, #546 (台北市士林區文林路546號) (02) 2831-3422.

Lin Liu-Hsin Puppet Theatre Museum (林柳新紀念偶戲博物館) was founded by Dr. Paul C.F. Lin and Dr. Robin Ruizendaal, eye exhibitions or patronize puppet workshops to learn how to create these peculiar prismatic puppets. International troupes are invited to perform and Taiyuan Puppet Theatre Company regularly performs at the museum's Nadou Theatre. Tickets cost NT $120/$80. From Shuanglian Station bus Red 33 (紅33) runs to Xining North Road. Lin Liu-Hsin Puppet Theatre Museum is near historic Dihua Street and Minsheng West Road on Xining North Road, #79 (台北市西寧北路79號) (02) 2556-8909 http://www.taipeipuppet.com.

The Mayor's Residence Arts Salon (市長官邸藝文沙龍) is the former Taipei mayor residence-turned-café. Enjoy sandwiches and tea after viewing historic pictures. Open 9 am to 11 pm. By MRT depart Shandao Temple Station. Xuzhou Road, #46 (台北市中正區徐州路46號)

(02) 2396-9398.

Miniatures Museum of Taiwan (袖珍博物館 *Shojen Bowuguan*) is the largest miniature museum in Asia and the second largest in the world. Discover over two hundred hand-made miniature works, each built with fine attention to detail. The museum is open Tuesday through Sunday 10 am to 7 pm, closed Mondays and holidays. Admission is NT $120/$90. Get your friends together, groups with 25 or more are offered a 10% discount. By bus take the 41, 52, 202, 203, 205, 257, 276, 288 or 298 to Chung Shan Girls High School. Jianguo North Road, Section 1, #96, B1 (台北市中山區建國北路1段96號B1) (02) 2515-0583.

The Mongolian and Tibetan Cultural Center (蒙藏文化中心) is hidden near National Taiwan Normal University on Chingtien Street, Lane 8, #3 (台北市青田街8巷3號) (02) 2351-4280. Taiwan's only professional Mongolian and Tibetan Cultural Center boasts an exhibition area displaying artifacts, a reading room, a lecture hall, a conference room and a prayer hall. This quaint museum is open 9 am to 12 pm and again 2 pm to 5 pm Monday through Saturday, closed Sundays. http://www.mtac.gov.tw.

Museum of Drinking Water (自來水博物館 *Zilaishui Bowuguan*) is inside Taipei Water Park. Here you'll find a garden, nursery, hiking and sculpture areas, an exhibition area, children's play areas, and Gongguan Purification Plant. Inside the museum are photos and equipment relevant to Taiwan's water supply history. This scenic park is a hot spot for couples to take wedding photos. July 1 to August 30 single adult tickets are NT $150 (same price for married couples), NT $120 for students and NT $70 for seniors and children taller than 90 cm, under 90 cm enter free. During other seasons tickets cost NT $100, NT $80 and NT $50 for seniors. By MRT take the Xindian line to Gongguan Station Exit #4 and find the intersection of Dingzhou Road and Siyuan Street, the entrance is on Siyuan Street, #1 (台北市中正區思源街1號) (02) 8369-5145, 8369-5096 http://waterpark.twd.gov.tw/english/museum/museum.htm.

Founded in November, 2001 by an iconoclastic Buddhist monk, **Museum of World Religions** (世界宗教博物館 *Shijie Zongjiao Bowuguan*) implores all to "respect all beliefs, embrace all peoples" and "cherish every life." Entering the small, dimly-lit museum on the seventh floor of a Yonghe, Taipei County department store is a zen-like experience in itself. Admission is NT $150 for adults. Zhongshan Road, Section 1, #236, 7th floor, Yonghe City, Taipei County (7th Floor of the Pacific Department Store). (台北縣永和市中山路1段236號7樓) (02) 8231-6699 http://www.mwr.org.tw.

The impressive 620,000 artifacts "for all people under heaven" at the **National Palace Museum** (故宮博物 *Gugong Bowuyuan*) run the gamut from ancient musical instruments and art to wine vessels and pottery. These treasures were carefully removed from Mainland China by truck, railway, and boat before the Civil War. Sensational souvenir shops are on the first and third floors while visitors relax at an upscale café on the fourth. Adult admission is NT $150 (US $4.50). Zhishan Garden (至善公園) is adjacent to the museum, admission is only NT $10 (US $ .30) and makes for a pleasant stroll. By MRT depart Shilin Station Exit 1, on Zhongzheng Road take the 304, 255, Minibuses 18 or 19, or the Red 16 (紅16). Zhishan Road, Section 2, #221, Shilin, Taipei (台北市士林區至善路2段221號) (02) 2881-2021 http://www.npm.gov.tw.

Established in 1958, the architecture for **National Taiwan Science Education Center** (國立科學教育館 *Guoli Taiwan Kexue Jiaoyuguan*) is modeled after Tien Tan, an area to pray to Buddhist gods, in Beijing. Open 9 am to 5 pm Tuesday to Sunday. Get there early, after 4:30 pm the guard at the door won't let you in, no matter how much you plead. Shichang Road, #189, Shilin (台北市士林區士商路189號) (02) 6610-1234 http://www.ntsec.gov.tw.

Puppetry Art Center of Taipei (台北偶戲館) is another good option for learning more about Taiwan's puppet theater (NT $100/80/60). If you like song, dance and colorful visual imagry, Song Song Song Children's & Puppet Theatre puts on puppetry masterpieces that delight both children and adults. Open 10 am to 5 pm daily, closed Mondays. Civil Boulevard, Section 5, #99, 2-4F (next to Core Pacific City, "The Living Mall") (台北市松山區市民大道5段99號 2-4F) (02) 2528-7955 http://pact.org.tw.

Shihsanhang Museum of Archaeology (十三行博物館) boasts sui generis archeological findings and a roof that resembles a whale's tail. Conquer your acrophobia, from the glass walkway on the top floor view exhibits four floors below. The Red 13 (紅13) bus runs to the museum from Bali or Guandu Station. Bowuguan Road, #200, Bali, Taipei County (台北縣八里鄉博物館路200號) (02) 2619-1313 http://www.sshm.tpc.gov.tw.

Learn about Taiwan's nine aboriginal tribes and view ancient artifacts, weapons, textiles and clothing at **Shunyi Museum of Formosan Aborigines** (順益台灣原著民博物館 *Shunyi Taiwan Yuenzhumin Bowuguan*). The basement boasts a distinct display on ancient religious life. Videos are shown at 11 am and again at 1, 3 and 5 pm. Open 9 am to 5 pm, closed Mondays. Admission is NT $150, but guests can receive a 10% discount by bringing an admissions ticket from the National Palace Museum. By bus, take the 213, 255, 304, or small 18 or 19 to the National Palace Museum. Zhishan Road, Section 2, #282, Shilin. (台北市士林區至善路2段282號) (02) 2841-2611.

At **Suho Memorial Paper Museum** (樹火

紀念紙博物館 *Suho Jinianzhi Bowuguan*) learn more about the history of paper, view handmade paper from around the world and learn games children on Taiwan play with paper. Then, have fun by making paper yourself! By MRT, transfer at Taipei Main Station for the blue line heading toward Kunyang, the museum is a ten-minute walk from Zhongxiao Xinsheng Station. Changan East Road, Section 2, # 68 (台北市長安東路2段68號) (02) 2507-5539 http://www.suhopaper.org.tw/english/default.htm.

View unparagoned paintings and atypical art created by local and international artists at **Taipei Fine Arts Museum** (台北美術館 *Taipei Meishuguan*). Exhibits are ever-changing and continually entice. Open 10 am to 6 pm Tuesday through Sunday, closed Mondays. Zhongshan North Road, Section 3, #181, Shilin (台北市中山北路3段181號) (02) 2595-7656 http://www.tfam.gov.tw.

With state-of-the-art facilities and a wide variety of exhibits, **Taipei Astronomical Museum** (台北市立天文科學教育館 *Taipei Shili Tienwen Kexue Jiaoyuguan*) promises to quench your thirst for knowledge about astronomy and space exploration. The first floor boasts one of the largest IMAX domes in Asia. Tickets (theater & museum) are NT $100/$50. Open Tuesday through Sunday 9 am to 5 pm, Saturday from 9 am to 8 pm, closed Mondays. Jihe Road, #363, Shilin (behind Shin Kong Hospital) (台北市士林區基河路363號) (02) 2381-4551 http://www.tam.gov.tw/eng/intro.htm.

Taipei 2-28 Memorial Museum (台北二二八紀念館) commemorates the victims of the February 28, 1947 incident, please see "2-28 Incident (二二八 *Er Er Ba*)." Katagalan Boulevard, #3 Taipei (台北市中正區凱達格蘭大道3號) (02) 2389-7228 http://228.culture.gov.tw/web/web-eng/museum/museum-2.htm.

Taipei Film House, also known as "The Spot" (SPOT 台北之家), is a thinking person's coffeehouse where art, literature and culture flourish. Once the site of the American consulate on Taiwan, this refurbished manor managed by director Hou Hsiao-hsien (侯孝賢) boasts an Eslite bookstore, gallery, winery lounge, and café with spacious indoor and outdoor seating. Adjacent to the bookstore, an air-conditioned movie theater showcases independent and international films (NT $220 non-members, NT $170 members). If you're looking for a hip spot for coffee talk where avant-garde meets trendy, try Taipei Film House. Zhongshan North Road, Section 2, #18 (Zhongshan Station, Exit 4) (台北市中山北路2段18號, 捷運中山站4號出口旁) (02) 2511-7786 http://www.spot.org.tw.

Discover alluring Hakka art, books that beckon and nectareous native foods at **Taipei Hakka Culture Museum** (客家文化會館 *Kejia Wenhua Huiguan*), Xinyi Road, Section 3, Lane 157, #11 (台北市大安區信義路3段157巷11號) (02) 2702-6141. Open 9 am to 9 pm Tuesday through Friday, 9 am to 5 pm weekends, closed Mondays. Admission is free and all are welcome.

The site of the former Taipei City Government Hall became **Taipei Museum of Contemporary Art (MOCA)** (台北當代藝術館) on May 27, 2001. The museum boasts local and international exhibitions, an enticing eatery and broad bookstore. An audio guide, guided tours and workshops are available. No packages or coats may be carried inside. Open Tuesday to Sunday 10 am to 6 pm, closed Mondays. General admission is NT $50, children under 6, the elderly and disabled persons enter free. By MRT exit Zhongshan Station, the museum is about a ten-minute walk. Changan West Road, #39 (台北市大同區長安西路39號) (02) 2552-3720 http://www.mocataipei.org.tw.

Don't go postal, there's plenty to see in Taipei! Unravel the historical mysteries of the postal service on Taiwan at **Taipei Postal Museum** (郵政博物館), open 9 am to 5 pm Tuesday through Sunday, closed Mondays and national holidays. Zhongyang South Road, Section 2, #45 (台北市中正區重慶南路2段45號) (02) 2394-5185 http://www.post.gov.tw/post/internet/y_postmuseum/index_all.htm.

At Taipei Fine Arts Museum stop by the adjacent **Taipei Story House** (台北故事館). Built in 1914, "Yuanshan Villa," once owned by wealthy tea merchant Chen Chao-chun, details historic Taipei life. Chen once hosted dignitaries, tea merchants and business people from abroad, and it is believed that Dr. Sun Yat-sen had once visited. The first floor boasts a quaint gift shop and an upscale teahouse operated by Taipei Landis Hotel, open Tuesday through Sunday 10:30 am to 10:30 pm (02) 2596-1898. During weekends a line forms longer than a stretched piece of melted taffy because only thirty guests are permitted inside at one time. Open Tuesday through Sunday 10 am to 6 pm, closed Sundays, admission is NT $30, NT $20 for students and groups of 10 or more, children under 110 cm, seniors and disabled persons enter free. Turn off your cell phone when entering and call in advance to find out if traditional musical performances will be held in the outside garden. For guided tours call (02) 2587- 5565 ext. 19. Zhongshan North Road, Section 3, #181-1 (台北市中山區中山北路3段181-1) (02) 2587-5565 http://www.storyhouse.com.tw.

Taiwan National History Museum (國立歷史博物館 *Guoli Lishi Bowuguan*), built in 1955, has a classical Chinese façade. On the first floor you'll find Chinese artifacts and one floor up is an art gallery almost as colorful as the author. Admission is NT $20, students and the elderly pay NT $10. Open 10 am to 6 pm, closed Mondays. Nanhai Road, #49 (台北市南海路49號) (02) 2361-0270 http://www.nmh.gov.tw/nmh_web/english_version/info/info_001.cfm.

Learn about the history and art of tea making at **Taiwan Pinglin Tea Museum** (坪林鄉茶業博物館), Shuisong Qikong, #19-1, Pinglin, Taipei County (台北縣坪林鄉水鑊凄坑19-1號) (02) 2665-6035. Admission is NT $100/$50. Open daily 9 am to 6 pm, after 5 pm visitors are not admitted. Open until 7 pm Sundays. The easiest way to reach the museum from Taipei is by bus, which takes an hour and a half. Buses run to Pinglin (坪林) from the insurance building (公保大樓 *Gongbao Dalo*) near Taipei Main Station.

Taiwan Provincial Museum (台灣博物館), built by the Japanese in 1908, is the oldest museum on Taiwan. Don't be fooled by the grand Greek columns and Western façade, inside are alluring aboriginal artworks, artifacts, handicrafts, an herbal display and native clothing (nothing you'd find at The Gap). Operating hours are Tuesday through Sunday, 9 am to 5 pm, closed Mondays and holidays. Within walking distance of Taipei Main Station. Hsuzhou Road, #48 (台北市徐州路48號) (02) 2397-9396.

A visit to **Taiwan Storyland** (台灣故事館) is a pure slice of Taiwanicana. Experience what life was like on Taiwan four decades ago (circa 1965) by perusing a bookstore, general store, hot spring display area, classroom, pub, theater display area, cafeteria, and Japanese-style eating hall. In the center of this Taiwan trove are traditional carts used by food vendors, a snack shop and a furnished living room. A drug store, photo shop and barbershop are also indicative of the era. NT $250/150/100, in the K-Mall basement, Taipei Main Station Exit 6, turn left, one block down on the left. Zhongxiao West Road, Section 1, #50, B2 (台北市中正區忠孝西路1段50號B2) (02) 2388-7158.

Model ships from the 15th to 20th centuries are on display at **Tamkang University Maritime Museum** (淡江大學 海事博物館). The third floor boasts a globe, library, and audio-visual room, one floor up is a control room closed for repairs when the author visited. On the lower level is an

AC generator, engine control console, a switchboard, steam turbine engine, lubricating pump, rudders, pumps and ventilators. Maritime enthusiasts may appreciate a visit. Open 9 am to 5 pm Tuesday through Sunday including holidays, closed Mondays, the day after national holidays, Dragon Boat Festival, Mid-Autumn Festival and winter vacation. By bus the 27 runs from Danshui Station to Tamkang University, the museum is on campus near the terminal. By foot the museum is a thirty-minute hike. Admission is free and all are welcome. Yingzhuan Road, #151, Danshui (台北縣淡水鎮英專路151號). (02) 2621-5656 Ext. 2618.

Tittot Glass Museum (琉園水晶博物館 *Liuyuen Shuijing Bowuguan*) is a hidden treasure for those that enjoy glass artwork and making their own glass art creations. This small gem of a museum founded in 1999 by Heinrich Wang (王俠軍 *Wang Hsia Jun*) offers glass blowing demonstrations and workshops. In addition to Wang's fine glass artworks, which have been displayed around the globe, you'll also find a brilliant crystal collection that dates back to the Eastern Chou dynasty. Guandu Station Exit 2, walk south toward Beitou. Zhongyang North Road, Section 4, Lane 515, #16 (台北市北投區中央北路4段515巷16號) (02) 2895-8861 http://www.glass.com.tw.

Yangming Villa (陽明書屋), the largest residence owned by former president Chiang Kai-shek, occupies 1000 square meters on fourteen hectares of land. A reclusive villa hidden within woods, tranquil surroundings include plum blossom trees as well as a pond. Inside you'll witness Chiang's taste for upscale Chinese furnishings, view portraits of the former leader as well as Dr. Sun Yat-sen and see clothes worn by the former president as well as ornate dishes used by the former first couple. The second floor veranda offers a picturesque view of Danshui and Keelung Rivers, Shamao Mountain to the east and Datun Mountain to the west. Open 9:30 am to 4:30 pm Tuesday through Sunday, *visitors are only permitted inside the villa at 9 am and 1:30 pm.* Admission is NT $50. At Jiantan Station the 304 and Minibuses 18 and 19 run to the villa. Zhongxing Road, #12, Yangmingshan (台北市北投區陽明山中興路12號) (02) 2861-1444.

If you're interested in pottery, sojourn to **Yingge Ceramics Museum** (台北縣立鶯歌陶瓷博物館). Yingge, an hour from Taipei City by car, is a town famous for its outstanding pottery, and the museum exhibits fine local works. Guided tours are offered 10 am to 3 pm, call in advance or register at the front desk. Audio tours are also available. Stop by the souvenir shop to pick up unique local pottery. The museum, open Tuesday through Friday, 9:30 am to 5:00 pm, closed Mondays and weekends, is a fifteen-minute walk from Yingge Train Station. Wenhua Road, #200, Yingge, Taipei County (台北縣鶯歌鎮文化路200號) (02) 8677-2727.

Yuyu Yang Digital Art Museum (楊英風美術館) showcases the singular sculptures and lifescape creations of Yang Ying-feng (楊英風) (1926-1997), a former professor from Ilan. The artist brought his art to life, and his art may add color to yours, as well. Chongqing South Road, Section 2, #31 (台北市重慶南路2段31號) (02) 2396-1966.

TAIPEI PARKS GUIDE (台北公園指南)

Taipei's lush green parks provide a welcome respite from the rigors of city life. Parks are popular destinations for family outings, especially during weekends and holidays, and for couples to take wedding pictures. Some parks boast singular statues, sculptures and fountains while others may house geological goldmines or ponds teeming with colorful fish. For a detailed list of parks around the island check out http://www.OnTaiwan.com.

Close to Yangmingshan National Park,

near the intersection of Shamao Road and Jianguo Street, is the small but charming **Chianshan Park** (陽明山前山公園 *Chianshan Gongyuan*). Here you'll find a pristine lake, natural scenery, and a public hot spring. Merchants line the road selling everything from bamboo to a light purple herbal pancake (山藥 *shan yao*), Consider bathing in the free Japanese-style spring, swimwear isn't permitted so if you're embarrassed to disrobe in front of strangers you may prefer a private bathhouse instead.

Daan Forest Park (大安森林公園 *Daan Shenlin Gongyuan*) is to Taipei what Central Park is to New York City, live concerts and other exciting events such as political rallies are often held here. Four main roads surround the park, Xinsheng South Road (新生南路) (west), Heping East Road (和平東路) (south), Jianguo South Road (建國南路) (east), and Xinyi Road (信義路) (north).

Dajia Riverside Park (大佳河濱公園) Taipei's second-largest park, is an expansive preserve (410,000 square meters) alongside Keelung River in historic Dadaocheng (大稻埕) district. During weekends residents fly kites, ride bicycles or jog near the river. Within walking distance from Dadaocheng Wharf (大稻埕碼頭).

The original name of **2-28 Memorial Peace Park** (二二八和平公園 *Er-Er-Ba Hoping Gongyuan*) was Taipei New Park, the name was officially changed in February, 1996. By MRT exit 1 of NTU Hospital Station leads to Shangyang Road, #2 (台北市襄陽路2號). To learn more about the 2-28 incident see "2-28 Incident (二二八 *Er Er Ba*)" under "XY & Z (Useful Information) (很有用的信息)."

Huashan Culture Park (華山藝文特區) was once the site of the Jianguo Brewery, the city did a fine job of turning an antiquated warehouse into a performance arts center. Residents now view arts exhibitions or see theater, dance or musical performances here. Open 9 am to 6 pm (inside), 9 am to 10 pm (outside). By MRT exit Zhongxiao

Xinsheng Station. Bade Road, Section 1, #1, 2F (台北市八德路1段1號2F) (02) 2392-6180.

Hell Valley (地熱谷 *Di Ruh Gu*) is a sulfuric pond that appears much like a wide witch's cauldron. Local residents once boiled eggs in the water, but complaints from local hospitals that children were burning their hands led the town to erect a fence around the edge of pond. Thankfully, visitors can still experience the eerie beauty of the park. A Buddhist alter, stream and natural waterfall create the impression that Taipei's own Hell Valley may not be so hellish after all. Hell Valley is a ten-minute walk to the end of Zhongshan Road from Xinbeitou Station. Entrance is free, and after a visit here you can tell your friends you've been to hell and back—literally! Open Tuesday to Sunday, 9 am to 5 pm, closed Mondays. (地熱谷, 台北市北投區中山路底) (02) 2888-2117.

Explore nature trails, bird watching cabins, a stream, marsh, and an indoor nature center at **Guandu Nature Park** (關渡自然公園 *Guandu Ziran Gongyuan*). Exotic birds seem to migrate every time expatriates visit. Admission is NT $50 for adults and children, students and senior citizens pay NT $30. Kids under 90 cm are admitted free. Open 9 am to 6 pm weekdays, 9 am to 6:30 pm weekends. Guandu Road, # 55, Taipei (台北市關渡路55號) (02) 2858-7417.

Opposite Guandu Temple, adjacent to Guandu Wharf is **Guandu Riverside Park** (關渡水岸公園), a snapshot spot for biking, strolling, and viewing the Guandu Bridge and one section of the "Blue Highway," Danshui River. A popular bike pathway winds around the protected marsh area of Guandu Nature Park. Local residents sometimes hold weddings here in the parking lot across from the temple.

Lingshan Park (關渡宮靈山公園 *Lingshan Gongyuan*) is on the mountain behind Guandu Temple, view Bali to one side and

Guandu Plains and Taipei to the other, as well as intricate temple rooftop designs and impressive temple artwork. A small barbeque area is popular for family outings and infatuated young couples walk around at night.

Meilun Science Park (美崙科學公園), adjacent to Taipei Astronomical Museum, boasts half-courts for shooting hoops and is divided into separate children's play areas. Dataphobes may wish to stay away from the math & physics area. From Shilin Station exit 1 walk for ten minutes down Zhengzheng Road and and make a right onto Jihe Road. Meilun Street, #190, Shilin (台北市士林區美崙街190號)
(02) 2861-6533.

Nanhai Botanical Garden (南海學園 *Nanhai Xueyuan*), built by the Japanese in 1921, was originally a government hall. An education center was added to the park in 1945. Today you'll find history, science and art museums here. Nanhai Botanical Garden is in front of Jienguo Junior/Senior High School (成功高中).

New Beitou Park (新北投公園 *Xinbeitou Gongyuan*) boasts a roller blading rink and serene grounds that include a river and fountain. Elderly residents often dance here early mornings, if you can start the day early you may learn a new move or two. This quaint park is just across the street from Xinbeitou Station.

In 1996, **Shilin Chiang Kai-shek Official Residence** (士林官邸 *Shilin Guandi*), one of many mansions Chiang Kai-shek built on the island, was opened to the public. Today, visitors stroll past flower gardens, a large fountain, and pavilion on the park grounds. Security stands in front of the former general's official residence, guarding what is said to be relatives, but no one seems to know for certain. Open Monday through Friday 8:30 am to 5 pm, 8:30 am to 7 pm weekends. The park is a ten-minute walk from Shilin Station. By MRT depart

Shilin Station Exit 2 (Wenlin Road). Walk down the alley adjacent to the My Island swimming pool, Zhongshan North Road, Section 5, Lane 505 (台北市中山北路五段505巷). Cross Zhongshan North Road, the entrance will be about a hundred meters up on your right. Zhongshan North Road, Section 5, Lane 460, #1 (台北市中山北路五段460巷1號) (02) 2881-2912.

In the city's southwestern section discover **Taipei Botanical Garden** (台北植物園), founded over a century ago in 1896. Today the botanical garden boasts eight hectares and nearly two thousand unique plant species. Display areas include an ethno-plants garden, a glass house, Plants of Chinese Classical Literature, as well as Buddhism Garden with its lavish lotus pond and a "touch and feel" plant exhibition. Professors often visit to research ecological structure as well as environmental physiology and ecophysiology. Taipei Botanical Garden is half a kilometer from the Presidential Office Building off Boai Road, not far from Taiwan National History Museum. By MRT depart Xiaonanmen Station, exits 3 or 4. Nanhai Road, #53 (台北市南海路53號)
(02) 2303-9978.

Taipei Water Park (自來水園區 *Zilai Shuiyuanchu*) boasts the Museum of Drinking Water and has eight sections, Mist Garden (the entrance area), a nursery to view colorful flowers, Guanyin Hill Hiking Area, Pipe Sculpture Area with a shower area, Water Distribution Material Exhibition Area, Water Country Garden (a wet play area for children), and the Gongguan Purification Plant. July 1 to August 30 admission is NT $150, NT $120 for students and NT $70 for seniors and children taller than 90 cm, children under 90 cm enter free. Otherwise tickets are NT $100, NT $80 and NT $50 for seniors. By MRT take the Xindian line to Gongguan Station, Exit 4 and walk to the intersection of Dingzhou Road and Siyuan Street. Siyuan Street, #1 (台北市中正區思源街1號) (02) 8369-5145,

8369-5096 http://waterpark.twd.gov.tw/english/guide.htm.

Play tennis, baseball, golf, roller blade or swim at **Taipei Youth Park** (青年公園 *Chingnian Gongyuan*). Musical concerts are often held at the large outdoor area. Shuiyuen Road, #199 (台北市萬華區水源路199號).

Expatriates with children often bring the kids to play on the swings, monkey bars and slide at **Tienmu Park** (天母公園 *Tienmu Gongyuan*), top of Zhongshan North Road, Section 7 in Tienmu (台北市中山北路7段). Not convenient if you're not in the area. **Tienmu Sports Park** (天母運動公園 *Tienmu Yundong Gongyuan*) is behind Tienmu Baseball Stadium, opposite the Eslite bookstore building on Zhongcheng Road, here you'll find a jogging track as well as tennis (fee) and basketball courts (free).

Wang Xiuqi Sculpture Park is an outdoor art gallery where singular stone sculptures depict mainly family themes. Xinan Road, #168 (台北市士林區新安路168號) (02) 2861-2168. Off Yangde Boulevard in Shilin.

Xinsheng Park (新生公園), Xinsheng North Road, #105 (台北市新生北路105號), is between Xinsheng North Road, Section 3 and Binjiang Street on one side and Minzu East Road and Songjiang Road on the other. Young people relax at Xinsheng North Park at night to watch planes taking off and landing at Taipei Songshan Airport (台北松山機場).

Yangmingshan National Park (陽明山國家公園 *Yangmingshan Guojia Gongyuan*) changes ever-so-slightly from season to season, but its quintessential beauty remains. The mountain is an inactive volcano, which explains the hot springs and natural volcanic topography in certain areas. During early spring (February through April) a flower festival is held at the park, where visitors delight in viewing cherry blossoms. You may find snow on Qichinshan (Seven Stars Mountain) and Datunshan, the highest parts of the mountain, during winter. Hike the nature trails around the mountain and park area. By bus the 230, 260, 303, Small 6 (小6), Small 9 (小9) and Small 15 (小15) run to Yangmingshan National Park, Zhuzihu Road, #1-20 (台北市陽明山竹子湖路1-20號) (02) 2861-3601 http://www.ymsnp.gov.tw/html/engnew/index.htm.

Yeliu (野柳 *Yeh Liu*) ("Wild Willows"), called "Yeliu Scenic Area" in Chinese, beckons with rare rock formations and striking hiking through the Datun mountain range. The "Queen's Head" rock in most Taiwanese tourist literature is here, follow the flashes, it's usually surrounded by hordes of tourists. You'll also find rocks shaped like a candle, an elephant trunk, a mushroom, tofu and dragon's head. Geologists visit Yeliu to examine erosion, land flow, fossils, rocks and minerals. Open 8 am to 5 pm (NT $50). Yeliu also boasts Ocean World (野柳海洋世界), an aquariam that delights with sea turtles, colorful coral, fine fish and an outdoor seal show (NT $350/$300) (02) 2492-1111. Buses run to Yeliu from Keelung, Danshui and Taipei City. A bus ride from Taipei takes 1.5 hours, fifty minutes from Danshui. From Taipei, Danshui or Keelung take Taichi Express Bus heading to Jinshan (金山) and depart at Yeliu (野柳站). Gangdong Road, #167-1, Yeliu (台北縣萬里鄉207 野柳村港東路167-1號) (02) 2492-6516.

Behind Yangming Hospital in Shilin, **Zhishan Cultural and Ecological Garden** (芝山岩文化史蹟公園) makes for a brief albeit pleasant perambulatory experience (NT $50/$20). Prehistoric artifacts include Zhishan yen (rock) (芝山岩) that date back over six thousand years, ancient pottery, "optoelectric games" (computer games) and an anchor studio for future broadcasters. In the park area are various species of plants, insects (butterflies), frogs and birds. The park hill ascends 51.5 meters and traces of rice farming (stalks) from centuries ago have been unearthed here. Exhibits are in

Chinese so you may learn more if you visit with a local friend. Open Tuesday through Sunday 9 am to 5 pm. Yusheng Street, #120 (台北市雨聲街120號) (02) 8866-6258.

Zhishan Garden (至善公園) is a serene park adjacent to the National Palace Museum (故宮博物院). Admission is only NT $10 (US $ .30). From Shilin Station exit 1 take the 304, 255, or the minibuses 18 or 19, or Red 16 (紅16) on Zhongzheng Road. Zhishan Road, Section 2, #221, Shilin (台北市士林區至善路2段221號) (02) 2881-2021.

After a two hundred meter hike up **Zhishanyen** (芝山岩) discover historic Huiji Temple (惠濟宮), built in 1752, which pays homage to the goddess of mercy Guanyin, amoung other gods. Scenic Zhishan Park is nearby. Zhicheng Road, Sec. 1, Lane 326, #26 (台北市士林區至誠路1段326巷26號) (02) 2831-1728.

Adjacent to Taipei Fine Arts Museum is the fine **Zhongshan Arts Park** (台北市中山藝術公園), where couples calmly coalesce around an ultramarine pyramid, singular sculptures, wondrous watercolor exhibits, a tranquil lake and a manicured, malachite meadow. By foot the park is a ten-minute walk from Yuanshan Station.

TAIPEI PUB GUIDE (台北PUB指南)

If you prefer to relax with a cool brew rather than a cool rendition of Brahms, the Taipei pub scene is for you. Taipei is rife with hip pubs and funky dance clubs, and each pub has an entirely different ambiance. Bear in mind, however, that while there are smoking and non-smoking sections at most restaurants, there are no sections set aside for non-smokers in most Taipei drinking establishments. In fact, you'll typically find that cigarettes are sold at the bar while attractive young ladies hawk cigarettes and beer. Bring I.D. and call in advance to find out if a hot pub is open the evening you wish to chill. Also note that Taiwanese men

are not fond of foreigners hitting on their close female friends and girlfriends. On Taiwan, as with any situation that involves raging hormones, fermones and alcohol, it's best to walk away rather than get into an altercation. If you don't go looking for trouble, it shouldn't go looking for you. Also, some pubs are all-you-can-drink for the price of admission. Remember to drink responsibly while having fun.

Across Roosevelt Road and a few blocks down from 45 Pub, a lively crowd usually frequents **@Live** to bust out fresh moves and rock the dance floor. Expect ample expats. Open 9 pm to 4 am, NT $350 cover during the week, NT $500 Fridays and Saturdays. Heping West Road, Section 1, #15, 3F (台北市和平西路1段15號3F) (02) 2396-3155.

Got the blues, baby? You will if you chill at **Blue Note** (藍調). For NT $300, NT $350 Friday and Saturday, take in smooth live blues from 7 pm to 1 am. Since 1974 Blue Note has been a Taipei mainstay for great jazz and blues, it's on the corner of Roosevelt Road, Section 3 and Shida Road. NT $200 cover Sunday and Monday. Roosevelt Road, Section 3, #171, 4th Floor (台北市羅斯福路3段171號4樓) (02) 2362-2333.

There may not be dancing at **Brown Sugar**, but if you've a sweet spot for jazz this snappy bar packs out fast weekends. Live music from 9:30 to 12:30 am. NT $480 cover Fridays and Saturdays, $300 Monday to Thursday. Doors close at 2 am. Jinshan South Road, Section 2, #218 (台北市金山南路2段218號) (02) 2322-4677.

Carnegie's is loud, touristy and fun, the kitchen of this rock and roll restaurant and bar stays open until 10 pm. Women drink free champagne on Wednesdays. Anho Road, Section 2, #100 (台北市安和路2段100號) (02) 2325-4433.

Hardly ugly, **Coyote**, on the twelfth floor of

the Core Pacific Mall, welcomes an upscale clientele who come to relax after an arduous day of shopping. Popular and touristy, NT $350 cover Monday through Thursday, NT $500 Friday and NT $600 Saturday, add 10% each night. Drink prices run from NT $200 to that-must-be-SOME-drink! Bade Road, Section 4, #138, 12th Floor (next to Plush at Core Pacific Mall) (台北市八德路4段138號, 京華城購物商場12樓).

Expect to find only party animals roaming **Farmhouse Pub** (田莊), locals and expatriates are fond of the friendly service and live music. The pub is located in the "combat zone," or "the zone," an area of town where expat soldiers and sailors used to get their kicks. The animals come out at 7:30 pm, but the barn really rocks around 10 pm. NT $250 cover weekdays, NT $500 weekends. Shuangchung Street, Lane 32, #5 (台北市雙城街32巷5號) (02) 2595-1764.

Expat students from NTNU (師大 *Shida*) pack out **45 Pub** after class. This fun British-style pub has no cover charge and it's a cool, downhome place. Heping East Road, Section 1, #45, 2nd Floor (和平東路1段45號2樓) (02) 2321-2140.

Fresh is a fun Western-style gay pub with no cover. There are three floors, a funky room to chill on the first, a dance floor and enormous bar on the second, and a balcony on the roof. Stop by for good conversation and drinks, or dance to techno and trance on the second floor. Jinshan South Road, #7, 2nd Floor (Shida area). (台北市金山南路7號2F) (02) 2358-7706.

For Latin music try **Hips** (formerly Barrio), Dunhua South Road, Section 2, #227, B1 (Corner of Heping East Road) (台北市敦化南路二段277號B1) (02) 2378-9955.

Expect a squeeze of something **Juicy** from DJ Orange (Chang Chen Yue), a Taiwanese pop star who owns this trance/hip hop/disco club and occasionally rocks out as a DJ. Xinyi Road, Section 4, #107-2 (台北市信義路4段107-2號1F) (02) 2704-7700.

Snazzy **Light Bug** (光蟲) lounge in Warner Brothers Village packs patrons who light up each other's eyes with their trendy digs. Cover charge varies. Songshou Road, #18, B1 (台北市松壽路18號B1) (02) 2345-2778.

Luxy, Taipei's second-largest dance hall, has become a magnet for young house and hip-hip aficionados. Covers run from NT $350 to NT $800 depending on the evening. Zhongxiao East Road, Section 4, #201, 5th Floor (台北市忠孝東路4段201號5樓) (02) 2772-1000.

Don't expect to find didactic ministers at **Ministry of Sound (MoS)**, a slammin' dance hall with three floors, a bang-up bar and a rockin' restaurant. If you dig live DJs, strobe lights and clubbing, get ready to have nothin' but a good time! International hip-hop stars and guitar wizards grace the grand stage. Since MOS is in Neihu you may need to cab it back to your hotel. Weekly cover charges range from NT $350 and up. Lequn 3rd Road, #310 (台北市內湖區樂群三路310號) (02) 8502-1111.

For a fresh dose of retro remixes and jumping jams try **Mint**, a trendy Taipei disco house. Located in the lower level of Taipei 101, Mint boasts an enormous bar, flashing L.E.D. displays, glassy thermoplastic furniture typically used by artists and a futuristic illuminated dance floor. Entering Mint may take a few Mint-pressed greenbacks out of your pocket (after exchanging them for New Taiwan dollars, of course), NT $800/men, NT $600/women cover Fridays and Saturdays, NT $500 Sunday through Thursday. The cover charge includes one menu drink. Wednesday is ladies' night. Shifu Road, #45, B1 (台北市信義區市府路45號B1樓) (02) 8101-8662.

The upscale clientele that frequent **Plush** enjoy life the way the club name implies. The restaurant is open 11 am to 9 pm, open

9 pm to 4 am. NT $350 weekdays, NT $700 cover at the door weekends. Core Pacific Mall, Bade Road, Section 4, #138, 12th Floor (台北市八德路4段138號12F) (02) 3762-1600.

The ambiance at **Riverside Music Café** (河岸留言) may not soothe nerves the way the outstanding view from New York's own Riverside Park might, but you can still chill and hear good live music from 9:30 to 11:30 pm. NT $250 cover. Roosevelt Road, Section 3, Lane 244, #2, B1 (台北市羅斯福路3段244巷2號B1) (02) 2368-7310.

Room 18 is a posh discoteque at Warner Brothers Village that attracts a younger crowd with money to burn. With glowing neon wall lights, dance floor smoke machines, green laser lights that shoot out from the DJ booth, and both hip local and international DJs, the atmosphere inside Room 18 is Taipei meets Sex & The City. Taiwan celebrities and celebutantes often stop by to make an impression. Bottled beers start at NT $250. Wednesday, Friday and Saturday 10 pm to 5 am, 4:30 am Wednesdays. No cover Monday, Tuesday and Thursday, Wednesday is ladies' night, NT $500/men, NT $700 across the board Friday and Saturday nights. Closed Sundays. Songshou Road, #22, B1 (Neo19 building) (台北市松壽路 22 號 B1) (02) 2345-2778.

Roxy Vibe may be the best rock and roll dance pub in Taipei, DJs cranks out a great mix of 70's, hip-hop and heavy/alternative and the crowd knows how to bust a move. Take off the tie, it's party time! Jinshan South Road, Section 1, #155, B2 (台北市金山南路1段155號B2) (02) 2341-0642 http://www.roxy.com.tw/new.

Roxy 99, adjacent to Brown Sugar, boasts great drinks and alternative music. From Roxy 99 (NT $300 cover, includes one drink), many patrons stumble down to Roxy Vibe to dance the night away, the perfect end to a perfectly intoxicating evening. Jinshan South Road, Section 2, #218, B1

(台北市金山南路2段218號B1) (02) 2351-5970.

Looking for a casual place to play darts, foosball or hear jukebox jams? **Roxy Jr. Café** is a cool hangout (open 24 hours) near Shida, the menu also offers a variety of Chinese and Western fare. Shida Road, Lane 80, #1 (台北市 師大路 80巷1號) (02) 2366-1799.

Being bad never felt so good! **Saints & Sinners** (都會館) sports bar, which boasts a 100-inch TV, airs live sporting events from around the globe. Enjoy a variety of Thai, Chinese or Western cuisine or hang out and play foosball or air hockey. Ladies drink free margaritas on Wednesdays, so in fairness the men enjoy free beers and spirits on Thursdays. Anho Road, Section 2, #114-116 (near Far Eastern Plaza Hotel). (台北市安和路2段114-116號1樓) (02) 2739-9001.

If you're looking for a sports venue to chill with some cold brews and a fun crowd while watching live international sports, stop by **The Brass Monkey** (銅猴子). You'll find "The Monkey" on Fuxing North Road, #166 (台北市復興北路166號) (02) 2547-5050. http://www.brassmonkeytaipei.com.

Enjoy a cold one and become one yourself--literally! Located at the intersection of Dingzhou and Shida roads, the frozen atmosphere inside **Ice Bar** (烈火賓館) is lit with florescent lights, creating a true winter wonderland in the middle of Taipei. Bottled beers and martinis go for NT $150. Leave the plastic at the hotel, credit cards are not accepted. Dingzhou Road, Section 3, #2 (台北市中正區汀州路3段2號) (02) 2364-4974.

Known as "The Pig & Whistle" in the Hsinchu and Kaohsiung locations, **The Pig** (犁榭), a classic Tienmu British-style pub, boasts live pop music 9:30 pm to 12:30 am weekdays, 9:30 pm to 1:30 am Fridays and Saturdays, and Latin music on Sundays

9 pm to 12 am. Expect to hear "Hotel California" early in the set, Taiwanese go absolutely crazy for this classic Eagles song. NT $500 cover charge on Fridays and Saturdays, NT $400 Sunday through Thursday. Tienmu East Road, #78 (台北市天母東路78號) (02) 2874-0630.

At The Grand Hotel, **The 60s Bar** (圓山大飯店 60s 年代) is a happening hot spot to revel in a fun bygone era rather than bust a move at one of Taipei's dynamic new millenium discos. Admission will set you back NT $600 plus a 10% service charge. Zhongshan North Road, Section 4, #1 (台北市中山區中山北路4段1號) (02) 2886-8888.

If you're looking for fun you may find it at **The Source**. Located one block north from @Live, Taipei residents interested in meeting members of the same sex not only come for the drinks, but they also come here to dance. Guling Street, #66 (台北市牯嶺街66號) (02) 3393-1678, 3393-1789.

The Tavern is a sports pub that boasts a variety of good beers, finger foods and a prime location near the Hyatt Hotel and Taipei World Trade Center. Keelung Road, Section 1, Lane 380, #5 (台北市基隆路1段380巷5號) (02) 8780-0892.

The Wall Live House is another hip joint for indy live music near National Taiwan University (Taida), touring Asian and Western acts sometimes rock the lounge out. Admission typically costs NT $300 to NT $400 and includes a drink. Roosevelt Road, Section 4, #200, B1 (台北市文山區羅斯福路4段200號B1) (02) 2930-0162. By MRT, The Wall is about a ten-minute walk from Gongguan Station, Exit 1.

If you're into loud hip-hop, **TU** is for you! The dance floor fills before bands slam the stage Thursday through Sunday. NT $200 cover Thursday, Saturday and Sunday, NT $300 Fridays. Fuxing South Road, Section 1, #249, B1 (台北市復南路1段249號B1) (02) 2704-7920.

Discover another world where alternative is the norm! Many bands at **Underworld** (地下社會 *Disha Shihui*) could be experimenting with the effects of beer on the body while playing music. Definitely a Frank Zappa meets Yoko Ono experience. Follow the loud, eerie noises to Shida Road, #45 B1 (台北市師大路45號B1) (02) 2369-0103.

Students hang at **Watersheds**, a fun jazz pub behind the fire station on Xinyi and Anho roads. Wenchang Street, #123 (台北市文昌街123號B1) (02) 2707-6121.

Many local acts get their start at **Witch House** (女巫店), a throwback to the 1960's era of the United States. The café features a variety of musical acts, as well as purposeful poets and touring theater troupes. There's an open mike night for aspiring poets the first Monday of the month, and an open mike night for musical acts the third Monday of the month. If you have something to say, get up and say it! Xinsheng South Road, Section 3, Lane 56, #7 (台北市新生南路3段56巷7號) (02) 2362-5494.

Experience the flavor of the era at **Zeitgeist Live House**, a rock club where live bands punk out during weekends. NT $250 cover. Zhongxiao East Road, Section 2, #122, B1 (台北市忠孝東路2段122號B1) (02) 2394-3004, (02) 2367-7475.

Guys leave ties on and dress to impress, **Ziga Zaga** is where businesswomen let their hair down. Grand Hyatt Hotel, Songshou Road, #2 (台北市松壽路2號) (02) 2720-1234 ext. 3198 or (02) 2720-1200 ext. 3435.

TAIPEI SEA WORLD (Fin's Life Taipei) (台北海洋生活館)

Looking for an alveolate Taipei aquarium? You won't find one here. While there are tropical fish and mantra rays, the highlights seems to be two large electric eels, a few enormous crabs from the waters of Kenting in southern Taiwan and a walkway to view sharks. This pint-sized aquarium delights children, but if you can't squeeze a visit into your schedule don't feel too disappointed. You could complete your tour in twenty minutes, thirty if you play with the unfortunate starfish and sea urchin that are groped by hyperactive toddlers all day in the outdoor exhibit area. Admission is a whopping NT $480/$430, free for children under two. Some hotels offer discount tickets (NT $350). Jiantan Station exit 1. Open 9 am to 10 pm daily. Jihe Road, #128, Shilin, Taipei (台北市士林區基河路128號) (士林夜市旁,捷運劍潭站1號出口) (02) 2880-3636.

TAIPEI TEMPLE GUIDE (台北寺廟指南)

The story behind **Cheng Huang Temple** (城隍廟 *Cheng Huang Miao*) intrigues. Years ago, Cheng Huang was a lone ghost haunting the ocean. Like Casper, he was considered a good ghost because he harmed no one. Therefore, according to Buddhist scriptures, Buddha decided to make him a deity. Taiwanese pay homage at this temple constructed in his honor in 1861. The Japanese destroyed the original temple, but after the occupation ended, the temple was rebuilt. Locals pray here for good weather, health and success. Wuchang Street, Section 1, #14 (near Chongqing South Road, Section 1 and Poai Road). (台北市武昌街1段14號) (02) 2361-5080.

Ciyou Temple (松山慈祐宮) remains the center of religious life for many in Taipei's Songshan district, the entire area lights up during goddess Matzu's birthday as her statue is carried through a litany of firecrackers. Near Songshan Night Market on Bade Road, Section 4, #761 (台北市八德路4段761號) (02) 2766-9212.

Confucius Temple (台北市孔廟) was built in 1879. After the Japanese occupied

Taiwan, this magnificent temple was destroyed. In 1925 a Taiwanese group started rebuilding the temple, but due to a lack of funds, work wasn't completed until 1939. Chinese people pray to Confucius because they hold a deep respect for his teachings. The temple is a ten-minute walk from Yuanshan Station. To learn more about Confucius, please see the section under "XY & Z (Useful Information) (很有用的信息)" entitled, "Religion On Taiwan." Dalong Street, #275 (台北市大龍街275號) (02) 2585-2728.

The main Buddha inside **Dalongtong Baoan Temple** (大龍峒保安宮) is Bao Shen Da Di, a doctor while he was mortal, so people pray here for health. The temple was built in 1805 and, with three huge halls, captivating carvings and prominent paintings, is the third-largest temple in Taipei. If you'd like to pray to many Buddhas at one time, there are thirty-seven Buddhas inside! Hami Street, #61, Datong District (intersection of Jiuchuen Street) (台北市哈密街61號) (02) 2595-1676. Baoan Temple is a ten-minute walk from Yuanshan Station.

Fuyo Temple (福佑宮 *Fuyo Gong*), built in 1782, is one of the oldest Mastu temples on the island. Don't expect the two elderly temple attendants to answer your inquiries, however, they seem to be napping every time expatriates visit. Fu Yo Temple, on Danshui Historic Street, is open 5 am to 9 pm. Zhongzheng Road, #200, Danshui. (台北縣淡水鎮中正路200號) (02) 2625-2084.

If you're headed to Danshui stop by historic **Guandu Temple** (關渡宮), Zhixing Road #360 (台北市北投區知行路360號) to say a quick prayer to Matsu, goddess of the sea, among other gods. Behind the temple is elaborate artwork featuring three buddahs, the gods of life, money and luck, protected by a tiger on the left and a dragon on the right. You can spot this elaborate artwork, as well as intricate temple rooftop designs, from Lingshan Park (關渡宮靈山公園), a park that overlooks Bali to one side and Guandu Plains and Taipei to the other. Enter or exit the temple through a cavernous tunnel that boasts prayer alters, Buddhist god statues and remarkable religious artwork. To read up on Taiwan's temples (most material is in Chinese) visit the adjacent Guandu Temple Library. Patrons frequent Guandu Food Court to buy roasted peanuts, dried squid, stinky tofu and live turtles. The temple, said to be the oldest on Taiwan, was originally built in 1661 and is a fifteen-minute walk from Guandu Station. By bus the Red 35 (紅35) departs from Guandu Station Exit 1 and runs to the temple.

The small but revered **Ji-ing Temple** (景美集應廟), established in 1867, is a third-class relic on Taiwan. Ji-ing Temple was built during the Ch'ing dynasty and makes for a unique snapshot spot if you're perambulating Jingmei Night Market. Jingmei Street, #37, Wenshan District (台北市文山區景美街37號).

Longshan Temple (龍山寺 *Lungshan Shi*) was built in 1738 but a devastating earthquake in 1815 all but destroyed it. The temple was rebuilt but leveled by a tremendous storm in 1867; it was rebuilt again, but while residents were inside praying for peace, a scourge of hungry white ants devoured most of the wooden structure and foundation of the temple in 1919. The temple was slightly redesigned and rebuilt in 1920 and remains in this form today. During WWII the temple was bombed, but to the amazement of residents, the statue of the goddess of mercy Guanyin remained intact, and some hid under the statue for safety. In 1953, the temple was rebuilt again with its original design. Enter the grand temple gates to find a waterfall, ponds, a golden urn for burning incense and magnificent traditional Chinese architecture. The city government recently commercialized the area under the temple for traditional businesses such as fortune-telling and facial hair removal. Guangzhou Street, #211 (台北市廣州街211號)

(02) 2302-5162.

Mengjia Chingshui Temple (艋舺清水巖) was built in 1787. There are sixty-three Mengjia Chingshui temples on Taiwan, but this is by far the biggest and most famous. In 1817 the temple was rebuilt, and the historic sign outside the temple was written by Guang Shu, a Ch'ing dynasty (1644-1911) emperor. The temple houses many 18th and 19th century Chinese artifacts. Kangding Road, #81 (台北市康定路81號).

Wanhua district's **Qingshan Temple** may be small in pings but is vast in history. Built over a century ago to honor Zhang Gun, a victorious general during the Three Kingdoms period, the elaborate interior entrances as does the warriors at the gates who seem to watch patrons with "Mona Lisa" eyes. Near Huaxi Street Night Market (Snake Alley). Guiyang Street, Section 2, #218 (台北市萬華區貴陽街2段218號) (02) 2382-2296.

Sanyu Temple (三玉宮) is a historic Buddhist temple at the intersection of Zhongshan North Road, Section 6 and Tienmu East Road and Tienmu West Road. People pray here to Matsu (湄洲媽祖), goddess of heaven, the seven statues of celestial beings (七尊大神像 *chee shen da zhen zhu*), the god of farming (神農大帝 *Shennong Dadi*, also referred to as 五穀先帝 *Wu Guh Shen Di*), as well as other gods. The temple was built over two hundred and forty years ago when thousands of people, mostly farmers, immigrated from China's Fujien and Chuenchou provinces. It was moved to its current location and formally opened in January, 1979. Tienmu East Road, #6 (台北市士林區天母東路6號) (02) 2871-3000.

Tiande Temple (天德宮), near Shilin Night Market past the end of Jiantan Road (fifteen-minute walk), is a singular shrine in Sanjiaodu Riverside Area (三腳渡碼頭). The shrine, built on a platform supported by steel poles, is raised to ensure that over four-dozen gods do not endure flooding after typhoons. Open 6 am to 6 pm. (02) 2356-0222.

In Ximending explore **Tienho Temple** (天后宮 *Tienho Gong*), the temple had been moved by the Japanese and was rebuilt after the Japanese occupation. Today, the temple is within walking distance from the heart of the shopping area, it's across the street and down the block from Ximen Station. Guang Shu, a former Ch'ing emperor of China, donated the sign that hangs at the entrance of the temple. Chengdu Road, #51, Ximending (台北市成都路51號) (02) 2331-0421.

On historic Dihua Street you can't miss **Xiahai City God Temple** (台北霞海城隍廟), a temple built in 1859 that becomes one of Taipei's livelist, especially during holidays. A main god at this Daoist temple is Yue Xia Lao Ren (月下老人), the god of love. Singles pray to this old man under the moon to find their dream lovers while married couples pray for healthy children and to remain sweethearts forever. After a brief visit you may find the love you've been searching for. Dihua Street, Section 1, #61 (台北市迪化街1段61號) (02) 22558-0346, 2558-6146.

The Buddha inside **Xingtian Temple** (行天宮), Minchuen East Road, Section 2, # 109 (台北市民權東路2段109號) (02) 2503-1831, (02) 2502-7924 is called "*Kuan Shen Di Zhuen*," or Guan Gong (關公). Guan Gong was a famous soldier who lived during the Three Kingdoms (220-280 AD) period in China. After he died he became immortalized in the eyes of the Chinese, who admired him for emerging victorious after every battle. Locals pray to Guan Gong for safety, health and prosperity. There are five entrances to this enormous temple, but only on very important religious holidays will all five doors be opened. The god typically receives offerings from over 20,000 people daily, with over five times

as many during religious holidays. In the underground walkway, fortune-tellers predict futures (算命 *suanming*), but for a price.

If you long to see one of Taiwan's oldest Taoist temples, a visit to **Zhinan Temple** (指南宮) makes for a titillating Taipei adventure. Zhinan Temple is referred to as "Temple of a Thousand Steps" because visitors must climb over a thousand steps to reach the temple. The temple is located atop Monkey Mountain in Muzha, and you may feel like one yourself after the steep hike. On clear, sunny days, the temple offers particularly scenic Taipei views. Be warned, however, that the temple and small adjacent park become crowded during weekends. Zhinan Temple is near Taipei Zoo. From Taipei Main Station take the blue MRT line towards Kunyang, transfer at Zhongxiao Fuxing and head to Taipei Zoo, or take bus 236, 237, or Zhinan buses 1 or 2. Make sure the driver knows your final destination, some buses run to the zoo but not to the temple. Wanshou Road, #15, Taipei (台北市萬壽路115號) (02) 2939-9922.

TAIPEI ZOO (台北動物園)

Taipei Zoo (台北動物園 *Taipei Dongwuyuan*), a large zoo even by Western standards, is an enjoyable way to spend the afternoon (NT $60/30). It's a wonder you won't find Dorothy and her friends on the yellow brick road outside the bears exhibit, at the zoo you'll find a lot more than lions, tigers and bears (oh my!). The elephants sometimes appear a bit unnerved by the crowds, and the lions and tigers may keep to themselves.

At the outdoor bear exhibit, tourists delight in viewing huge grizzly bears snoozing in the sun. Both adults and kids alike seem to go bananas at the outdoor monkey area, where monkeys swing from trees, push one another off a small man-made island into the surrounding water or pick and eat the

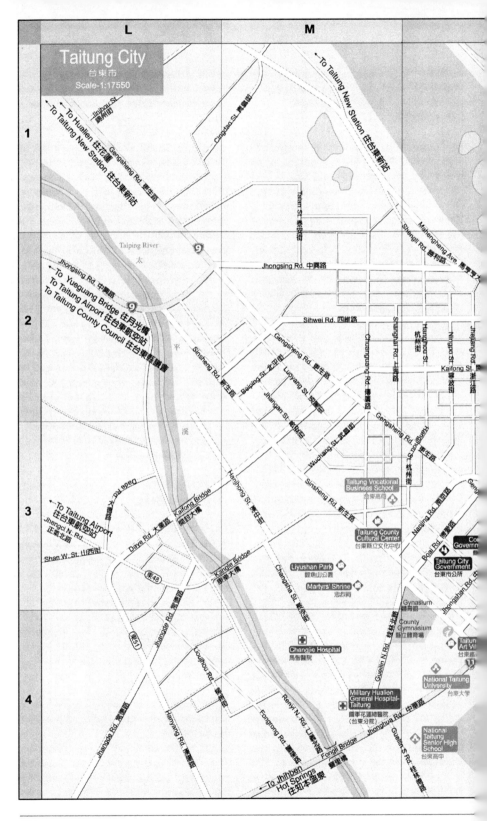

Taitung City
台東市
Scale-1:17550

L **M**

Jinhou St. 錦洲街
Cingdao St. 青島街
Gengsheng Rd. 更生路
To Taitung New Station 往台東新站
To Hualien 往花蓮
To Taitung New Station 往台東新站
To Taitung New Station 往台東新站

Taian St. 泰安街
Mahengsheng Ave. 馬亨亨大道
Shengli Rd. 勝利路

1

Taiping River
太

Jhongsing Rd. 中興路
To Yueguang Bridge 往月光橋
To Taitung Airport 往台東航空站
To Taitung County Council 往台東縣議會

Jhongsing Rd. 中興路

Jhongsing Rd. 中興路
Sihwei Rd. 四維路

Gengsheng Rd. 更生路
Beijing Rd. 北平路
Luoyang St. 洛陽街
Sinsheng Rd. 新生路
Jhangan St. 長安街
Wuchang St. 武昌街

Shanghai Rd. 上海路
Hangzhou St. 杭州街
Ningpo St. 寧波街
Zhejiang Rd. 浙江路
Kaifong St. 開封街
Chuanguang Rd. 傳廣路

Gengsheng Rd. 更生路

2

平

溪

Dade Rd. 大德路
Sinsheng Rd. 新生路
Hanghong St. 康中街
Kaifong Bridge 開封大橋
Kangle Bridge 康樂大橋
Changsha St. 長沙街

Hangzhou St. 杭州街

Taitung Vocational Business School 台東高商

Nanjing Rd. 南京路

3

To Taitung Airport
往台東航空站
Jhengci N. Rd.
正氣北路
Shan W. St. 山西街
Dave Rd. 大業路
Jhangde Rd. 彰德路

Taitung County Cultural Center 台東縣立文化中心

Boai Rd. 博愛路

Taitung City Government 台東市公所

Cou Governm

Jhongshan Rd. 中山路

Liyushan Park 鯉魚山公園
Martyrs' Shrine 忠烈祠

Gynasium 體育館

County Gymnasium 縣立體育場

Taitun Art Vil 台津鐵...

4

Jhangde Rd. 彰德路
Loupou Rd. 樓埔路
Hanyang Rd. 漢陽路
Renyi N. Rd. 仁義北路
Fongrong Rd. 豐榮路
Changjie Hospital 馬偕醫院
Guelin N. Rd. 桂林北路

Military Hualien General Hospital-Taitung 國軍花蓮總醫院（台東分院）

Jhongnua Rd. 中華路
Guelin S. Rd. 桂林南路

National Taitung University 台東大學

National Taitung Senior High School 台東高中

Fongli Bridge 豐里橋
To Jhihben Hot Springs 往知本溫泉

insects off one another (yum!). Don't forget to visit the indoor Nocturnal House to learn about bats and other creatures of the night. At the indoor Butterfly House and Garden, even the butterflies don't seem to mind the tourists fluttering about. It's advisable not to make too much noise at the bird exhibit, however, or the young zookeepers may lock you up, as well. Open 8:30 am to 5 pm daily, closed Chinese New Year's Eve. After giving your legs a workout at the zoo give your credit card a workout at the adjacent two-story Zoo Mall. By bus take the 236, 237, 258, 282, 291, 294, 295 or 611 to Taipei Zoo. By MRT transfer at Taipei Main Station for the blue MRT line that runs toward Kunyang, transfer at Zhongxiao Fuxing Station for the Muzha line. Exit at the last stop. Xinkuang Road, Section 2, #30, Wenshan District, Muzha, Taipei County (台北市文山區新光路2段30號) (02) 2938-2300 http://english.taipei.gov.tw/zoo/index.jsp.

TAITUNG (台東)

(Area Code: 089)
Population: 127,000

On the southeastern coast of Taiwan, Taitung boasts National Taitung Univeristy (國立台東大學), a downtown shopping area and **Chipen** (知本), a quaint town famous for its natural hot springs (知本溫泉). Amis (阿美族) aboriginal people thrive on Taiwan's eastern side and coastal plains areas, you may find Amis wares here. In case of an emergency, the number for the Taitung Police Department is (089) 322-034.

Taitung boasts **Taitung County Museum of Natural History** (台東縣自然史教育館).Chonggong Town, Jihuei Road, #16 (台東縣成功鎮基翬路16號) (89) 851-960 ext.501. The inside of the museum appears somewhat like a community college science lecture hall, with wall-size posters and rows of exotic exhibits in glass cases. Open 8 am to 5 pm.

Examine Neolithic artifacts that were once used by the Austronesian-speaking peoples that had lived on Taiwan at **The National Museum of Prehistory** (國立臺灣史前博物館), Bowuguan (Museum) Road, #1 (台東市豐田里博物館路1號) (089) 381-166. The museum is close to the Beinan (卑南) archeological exploration area.

Butterfly and insect enthusiasts may be enthused by a visit to **Waan Butterfly Eco-Park** (萬安蝴蝶生態園), Waan Village, Neighborhood 1, #5-2 (台東縣池上鄉萬安村1鄰5之2號) (89) 862-371.

Once part of a strategic military base, **Taitung Fengnian Airport** (台東豐年機場) resembles Tallahassee Airport in Florida, it's on Minhang Road, #1100 (台東市民航路1100號) (089) 362-530. Far Eastern Air (遠東航空 *Yuendong Hangkong*) (089) 390-388 and Uni Air (立榮航空 *Lirong Hangkong*) (089) 362-626 fly from Taipei to Taitung (50 minutes) and from Taitung to Taipei with early departures starting between 7:00 and 8:00 am. A one-way ticket will set you back around NT $2000. Mandarin Air (華信航空 *Huaxin Hangkong*) (089) 362-669 flies from Taichung to Taitung (1 hr 5 minutes, NT $2311) and from Taitung to Orchard Island (蘭嶼 *Lanyu*) (30 minutes, NT $1408) and Green Island (綠島 *Ludao*) (20 minutes, NT $1091). The number for the Taitung Airport service desk is (089) 361-111.

Taitung Hotels

Naruwan (娜路彎大酒店) This upscale "aboriginal" hotel boasts aboriginal art, an outdoor hot spring bath and salt water swimming pool, shopping arcade, and theater for touristy but entertaining aboriginal dance performances. Single or double rooms start at NT $6,000 plus a 10% service charge. Lianhang Road, #66 (台東市連航路66號) (089) 239-666 http://www.naruwan-hotel.com.tw.

Hotel Royal Chihpen (知本老爺大酒店) Located in the heart of Chihpen hot springs village, this five-star hotel boasts indoor and outdoor hot springs, a spa service, and elaborate dining that includes a Mongolian wok and Japanese teppanyaki grill. Rates start at NT $6,800 plus a 10% service charge. Longchuen Road, Lane 113, #23 (台東縣卑南鄉溫泉村龍泉路113巷23號) (089) 510-666 http://www.hotel-royal-chihpen.com.tw.

Taitung Bus Station (台汽台東車站)) is on Hsinsheng Road, #93 (台東市鐵花里5鄰新生路93號) at the intersection of Hsinsheng Road and Kuangming Road. King Bus Company (國光客運台東站 *Guoguang Keyyuen*) service desk in Taitung is (089) 322-027.

From Taichung: Just across the street from Taichung Train Station is Taichung Bus Station, Jianguo Road, #174 (台中市中區建國路174號), King Bus Company (國光客運台中站 *Guoguang Keyuen*) (04) 2222-2830 buses run to Taitung often.

From Taipei: King Bus Company is near Taipei Main Station on Zhongxiao West Road, Section 1, #173 (台北市中山區忠孝西路1段173號) (02) 2311-9893. A one-way fare will set you back NT $350. Tour bus companies are on Chengde Road (台北市大同區承德路) two blocks north of Taipei Main Station, ticket prices may be higher but the trip includes a complimentary movie.

TAOYUAN (桃園)
(Area Code: 03)
Population: 1,871,474

The aboriginal Pingpu tribe had cultivated Taoyuan for thousands of years prior to the arrival of Han Chinese that migrated from China's Fujian and Guangdong provinces during the Ch'ing dynasty (1644-1911). After their arrival the new Chinese immigrants planted an abundance of peach trees and the area became known as "Tao Zi Yuan"

(桃子園), or Peach Garden. You may have to search for quite some time to find a peach garden in the area today; located halfway between Taipei and Hsinchu, Taoyuan has become a major Taiwan business center and northern industrial work zone.

Taoyuan boasts Jungli Industrial Park and Pingjen Industrial Park, two of Taiwan's largest science-based industrial parks. Over 450 companies are based in Jungli Industrial Park while Pingjen Industrial Park boasts over 150. Many of Taoyuan's industrious labor force of nearly 800,000 are employed at these modern industrial parks.

Taiwan Taoyuan International Airport is located here, Taoyuan is called the "door to Taiwan" and Taiwan's gateway to the world. Although not considered one of Taiwan's great tourist destinations, there are some interesting sites around town.

Major Attractions

Aside from the impressive international airport, Taoyuan boasts **Chung Cheng Aviation Museum** (中正航空科學館), you'll need to take the free shuttle buses to the museum from the airport hotel or from either terminal. Open in 1981, the museum boasts aviation exhibitions and aircraft replicas. Admission is NT $30 for adults, NT $20 for children and NT $15 for groups. Open 9 am to 5 pm (no admittance after 4:30 pm), closed Mondays (03) 398-2677.

The 16.5-kilometer **Shimen Reservoir** (石門水庫), the largest reservoir not only on Taiwan but also in the Far East, was constructed in 1964 to prevent flooding after typhoons. The reservoir has become a popular tourist attraction for its pristine scenery.

Taoyuan Martyrs Shrine (桃園縣忠烈祠) was originally a Shinto shrine built by the Japanese in 1938 and its original architecture was left largely intact. The shrine is comprised of a main hall, a worshipping hall, a "pilgrim path," an enormous front gate, a washing well and a stone lantern. In case you're curious about the washing well, visitors were required to wash their hands and mouths before praying. Chonggong Road, #200 (桃園市成功路200號).

Loud, colorful festivals are held at **Taoyuan Confucius Temple** (桃園孔廟) every September 28, Teacher's Day, to honor Confucius on his birthday. Without a car the temple is not easy to reach, it's near Chonggong Road, Section 3 (桃園縣成功路3段), make a right at Taoyuan High School (桃園高中), the temple is down the block. For assistance contact the Taoyuan Cultural Affairs Bureau (桃園縣文化局) at (03) 332-2592.

The Taoyuan Museum of Chinese Furniture (桃園縣中國家具博物館) displays traditional Chinese furniture and a traditional furniture how-to display. You'll find the museum on the third floor of the Cultural Affairs Bureau of Taoyuan County Government on Shianfu Road, #21 (桃園市縣府路21號) (03) 332-2592.

Taoyuan County's **Tahsi** (大溪) is famous for its soft and sweet bean curds. Stop by *Huangrexiang Douchian* (黃日香豆干本店), Heping Road, #56 (大溪鎮和平路56號) (03) 388-2055 or Da Fang Food (大房豆干), Zhongzheng Road, #46-48 (桃園縣大溪鎮中正路46-48號) (03) 388-3457 to experience why locals prefer Tahsi bean curd.

If you find yourself with time and a few extra NT dollars before your departure you may want to stop off at **Tai Mao** (台茂), a shopping mall in Luzhu on Nankan Road, Section 1, #112 (桃園縣蘆竹鄉南崁路1段112號) (03) 311-1234.

Jungli (中壢), also spelled "Chung Li," is a Taoyuan County town approximately fifty minutes southwest of Taipei by bus or train.

Think Jungli is small? The town boasts eighteen primary schools, seven junior high schools, five senior high schools, and seven colleges and universities, as well as a large Hakka population and a flourishing arts culture. There are two Sogo department stores (太平洋SOGO百貨中壢元化店, 中壢中央新館) and ample pubs for a fun night out. Many bands hone their skills and build up a fan base here while trying to make it big in Taipei. Jungli isn't far from Shimen Reservoir (石門水庫), Window on China (小人國) and Leo Foo Village (六福村 *Liu Fu Tsun*) so the town may be included in area package tours.

Taoyuan County Fine Arts Museum (Jungli Arts Hall) (桃園縣立文化中心藝術館, 中壢藝術館) boasts a concert hall, lecture hall, meeting room, rehearsal space and an exhibit room. Open 8 am to 5 pm, closed Mondays, the last Tuesday morning of every month and national holidays. Jungmei Road, #16, 2nd Floor, Jungli (near Zhongzheng Park and Jungli Train Station) (桃園縣中壢中美路 16 號2F, 火車站附近) (03) 425-8804.

For great deals on computer products stop by the Jungli branch of **Nova** on Zhongzheng Road, #389 (中壢市中正路389號) (03) 402-8686.

The high altitude (300 to 400 meters above sea level) and flat terrain of **Lungtan Village** (龍潭鄉), just northeast of Jungli, creates a fertile environment for tea cultivation. Over sixty percent of Lungtan Village is Hakka, which makes for some interesting arts shows, food tasting and religious ceremonies. There are over a half dozen traditional temples here as well as traditional family villas built during the Ch'ing dynasty. Four tourist tea farms are open to the public. Window on China (小人國) miniatures park is also located here, unless you know the roads, driving may not be safe as an eerie fog rolls in most mornings and evenings but clears during the afternoon. To learn more visit http://www.OnTaiwan.com.

Taoyuan Hotels

Chungli Business Hotel (中壢大飯店) boasts a meeting center, gym, laundry facilities, Internet access (bring your own laptop), a free continental breakfast and a karaoke bar on the first floor. The hotel is a five-minute walk from the train station and a twenty-five minute car ride to the airport. Room rates start at NT $2200 per night, check the web site for promotions. Yenpin Road, #645, 4th Floor (opposite Chungli Elementary School) (桃園縣中壢市延平路645號4樓, 中壢國小正對面) (03) 422-5871 http://www.chungli-business-hotel.com.tw.

Chuto Plaza Hotel (住都大飯店) Taoying Road, #398 (桃園縣桃鶯路398號) Approximately 3.5 kilometers from Taoyuan Train Station, the hotel boasts 128 comfortable rooms, fine Chinese dining, fitness and business centers, 24-hour room service, free breakfast and parking as well as airport limo service. Single room rates start at NT $4200 per night. (03) 376-6177 http://www.chuto.com.tw.

By bus, **Aloha** (阿囉哈客運公司) (02) 2550-8488, (0800) 043-168 (toll-free) offers 24-hour service to Taoyuan and a Taipei bus departs every twenty minutes. In Taipei the company is at the intersection of Beiping West Road (國道客運總站北平西路口). Aloha also offers service to Hsinchu, Taichung, Chiayi, and Kaohsiung.

Alternatively you could take the **Taiwan High-Speed Rail (THSR)** (台灣高鐵 *Taiwan Gaotie*) from Taipei to Chungli City, Taoyuan County, the ride takes twenty minutes and a one-way economy (standard) ticket costs NT $160. Kaotie North Road, Section 1, #6, Chungli City, Taoyuan County (桃園縣中壢市高鐵北路1段6號) (02) 4066-5678.

TEA STATION

In Maokong and Nangang relaxation
Begets a Taiwan tea sensation
For placid mountain contemplation
Depart the skytrain at Tea Station.

Although coffee seems to be the beverage of choice amoung Taiwanese youth, brewing tea (泡茶 *pao cha*) and tea drinking remain a cornerstone of traditional Taiwanese culture. In addition to Taipei Zoo, Muzha, Taipei County boasts **Maokong** (木柵貓空), a steep enclave where traditional teahouses provide a brief respite from urban life on Zhinan Road, Section 3. This section of Zhinan Road is known as **Maokong Tea Road** (台北市文山區指南路, 貓空). The area can now be readily accessed without a car or moped by riding the **Maokong Gondola**, a new tram lift that opened in July, 2007. The gondola stops at Taipei Zoo Station, Zoo Precinct Station, Zhinan Temple Station and Maokong Station, making a visit to this once-remote area more convenient. Tickets for the gondola can be purchased at Zoo Precinct Station.

Former Taiwan President Lee Teng-hui prevented many illegal teashops from being closed since he enjoyed relaxing in the area. Be warned that some teashops have KTV machines where locals may get carried away with their crooning. Maokong is also a popular area for hiking, perhaps so visitors can readily get away from star-struck KTV crooners.

Visit a tea garden to experience tantalizing local teas and learn more about Taiwan's traditional tea culture, at tea gardens you may smell the sweet fragrance of osmanthus plants. While osmanthus was once used to flavor jasmine tea, Taiwanese now make separate sweet osmanthus teas and delicious drinks. Over a century ago, Taiwan brides brought osmanthus and pomegranate plants to their husbands to symbolize that offspring would prosper and that she would produce an abundance of offspring, respectively. While this custom is no longer prevalent, residents continue to enjoy the sweet osmanthus fragrance and the beverages it produces. It tends to be cooler at tea plantations, which are typically between two to three-hundred meters (or higher) above sea level.

In the late 1800s, tea merchants flocked to Taipei's Dadaocheng district to export teas abroad. **Wang's Tea** (有記名茶), founded in 1890, continues to use the same ancient techniques for selecting, roasting and producing the finest teas for export and local consumption. Admission is free and all are welcome. Chongqing North Road, Section 2, Lane 64, #26, Datong district (台北市重慶北路2段64巷26號) (02) 2555-9164 http://www.wangtea.com.tw.

A popular respite for Maokong hikers is **Taipei Tea Promotion Center** (台北市鐵觀音包種茶研發推廣中心), Zhinan Road, Section 3, Lane 40, #8-2 (台北市指南路3段40巷8-2號) (02) 2234-0568. Open Tuesday through Sunday 9 am to 5 pm, closed Mondays, call first. Tour a tea plantation, learn tea ceremony techniques and taste Tieguanyin tea (木柵鐵觀音), a major tea produced here. By MRT depart Wanfang Community Station and take Minibus 10 to Maokong. A skytrain from Taipei Zoo with stops at Zhinan Temple and Maokong (final stop) should make travel to the area more convenient.

Nangang, on Keelung River's southern basin, means "south port," and tea was once heavily exported from here. Today, Nangang still boasts serene spots to sip tea. Many tea gardens are open to visitors on Jiuzhuang Street (舊宗路), although you'll also find a handful on lower Nanshen Road (南深路). Over forty companies cultivate tea in the area. Stop by a local tea garden or **Nangang Tea Processing Demonstration Center** (茶業製示範場), Jiuzhuang Street, Section 2, #336 (台北市南港區舊宗路 2段336號) (02) 2783-1343 to sample Baozhong tea (包種茶), a local favorite. Open 9 am to 4 pm. By bus the 205, 212, 276, 281, 306 and 605 run to the area, at Nangang Station Minibus 5 runs to the tea plantations. By MRT depart at Kunyang Station, local buses run to the center.

Learn more about the history and art of tea making at **Taiwan Pinglin Tea Museum** (坪林鄉茶業博物館), Shuisong Qikong, #19-1, Pinglin, Taipei County (台北縣坪林鄉水簀淒坑19-1號) (02) 2665-6035. Admission is NT $100/$50. Open 9 am to 6 pm, after 5 pm visitors are not admitted, open until 7 pm Sundays. Travel information is listed under "Taipei Museum Guide" (台北博物館指南)."

Taipei County's placid tea plantation town of **Shiding** (石碇) holds an annual fall Meiren Tea Festival at the town square (台北縣石碇鄉), participants learn how tea is produced while listening to soothing live music. For inquiries call (02) 2733-3972 ext. 13.

In Taipei there are ample opportunities to try Taiwan teas as teahouses dot the city and many hotels host "tea time" between 2 to 4 pm. In addition to fine pastries and cakes, buffet meals may also be offered.

Channel Tea (一茶一坐 *Yi Cha Yi Zuo*) is a modern Chinese teahouse that offers a wide selection of teas, as well as hot or cold fruit drinks. Here are three Taipei locations: Main store: Zhongxiao East Road, Section 4, #201 2nd Floor (台北市忠孝東路4段201號2F) (02) 8773-8778
Zhongxiao II: Zhongxiao East Road, Section 1, #100 (台北市忠孝東路1段100號) Songshou Road, #12, Xinyi District (台北市松壽路12號) (02) 8780-8818.

Many enjoy the traditional drinks at **Hsieh Lan** (謝籃), a quaint Chinese teahouse. Zhongshan North Road, Section 2, #85 (台北市中山北路2段85號) (02) 2561-7711.

Don't expect to find any little bears in **Little Bear Forest** (小熊森林 *Shiao Shong Shen Lin*), it's a quaint Taiwanese teahouse on Dunhua South Road, Section 1, Lane 177, #25 (台北市敦化南路1段177 25號) (02) 2772-5550.

The Rose Garden (古典玫瑰園 *Gu Chu Mei Gui Yuen*) resembles an English countryside teahouse in urban Taipei. Dunhua Road, Section 2, Lane 81, #55 (台北市敦化北路2段81巷55號) (02) 2700-2958.

Shann Garden (禪園) is a traditional Chinese teahouse that boasts upscale dining, fine teas and a breathtaking view of New Beitou and the Guandu Plains. Adjacent to Beitou Folk Arts Museum, Youya Road, #24, New Beitou (台北市北投區幽雅路34號) (02) 2896-5700.

Relax in **Southern Comfort** (南方安逸 *Nan Fang An Yi*) at this Western-style Taipei teahouse. Jinhua Road, Lane 199, Alley 1, #6 (台北市金華街199巷1弄6號) (02) 2395-2199.

Founded in Gangshan, Kaoshiung in 1953, **Ten Ren** (天仁茗茶) has grown to become the largest tea company not only on Taiwan but also in the world, with over 120 retail shops worldwide. In addition to its Ten Ren Tea shops, the company owns Ten Ren Tea Culture Foundation and Luyu Tea Art Center, Ten Fu Group, which runs eight companies and five processing plants, and the popular Cha For Tea restaurant chain with branches in Toronto, Los Angeles, Sydney, Malaysia and Japan. Stop by a Cha For Tea restaurant for choice Chinese teas and food, and pick up some fine tea on the way out.
Danshui: Zhongzheng Road, #242 (台北縣淡水鎮中正路242號) (02)2621-0200 (10:00 am to 10 pm)
Dunhua: Dunhua South Road, Section 1, #331 (台北市敦化南路1段331號) (02) 2705-9789 (11 am to 11 pm)
Fuxing: Fuxing North Road, #152 (台北市復興北路152號) (02) 2719-9900 (7:30 am until 11pm)
Henyang: Henyang Road, #62, 2nd floor (台北市衡陽路62號2樓) (02) 2312-2828 (11:00

am to 11 pm) (Historic façade; tea lovers should be titillated by the spacious store)
Nanjing: Nanjing East Road, Section 2, #146 (台北市南京東路2段146號)
(02) 2507-8199 (11 am to 11:30 pm)
Zhongshan: Zhongshan North Road, Section 5, #555 (台北市中山北路5段555號)
(02) 2888-2929 (11 am to 11 pm).

Taipei Tea Merchants Association can be reached at (02) 2555-7598 or 2555-2962.

THEATERS & MEMORIAL HALLS (劇院與紀念館)

When it comes to theater, Taipei boasts some of the finest artists and musicians in the world. Pamphlets promoting upcoming performances are available at MRT stations and bookstores throughout the city, and tickets may be purchased at these bookstores, as well.

Open 10:00 am to 7:30 pm, **Taipei Artists Village (TAV)** (台北國際藝術村) provides a unique art and cultural exchange between Taiwanese and international artists. TAV hosts dance performances as well as contemporary art exhibitions. Beiping East Road, #7 (台北市北平東路7號)
(02) 3393-7377 http://www.artistvillage.org.

The National Theatre
The National Concert Hall
The Recital Hall
The Experimental Theatre
The aforementioned concert halls are located at:
National Taiwan Democracy Memorial Hall (國立臺灣民主紀念館) The National Theatre typically features lively ballet and modern dance, as well as Peking Opera performances. The National Concert Hall showcases local young piano and violin virtuosos, as well as classical musicians and choirs from around the world. Pick up a free Monthly Program Guide at any major bookstore, such as an Eslite, Kingstone, or Caves. For more information please see "National Taiwan Democracy Memorial

Hall (國立臺灣民主紀念館)" from Day 1. Zhongshan South Road, #21 (台北市中山南路21號) (02) 2341-9898.

Zhongshan Concert Hall is named in honor of Zhong Shan, Dr. Sun Yat-sen. Yenping South Road, #98 (台北市延平南路98號) (02) 2381-3137.

Guiling Street Avant-Garde Theater (牯嶺街小劇場) was once a police station, nowadays the theater promises to arrest with its positively progressive opera, drama and dance performances. Stop by the classy café/souvenier shop on the top floor. The theater is a ten-minute walk from CKS Memorial Hall Station. Guiling Street, Lane 5, #2 (台北市牯嶺街5巷2號) (02) 2391-9393 http://www.ifkids.com.tw/theatre.

National Dr. Sun Yat-sen Memorial Hall (國父紀念館) was built in 1932 in the style of a traditional Chinese castle, experience a drama, music, dance or arts performance here. The theater seats 2,626 people. A sweeping green city park surrounds the memorial hall, providing parents a paved, pristine play area to bring the kids, with ample space to roller blade as well as fly kites. You'll find no shortage of food, beverage and trinket vendors inside the park. Renai Road, Section 4, #505 (台北市信義區仁愛路4段505號)
Memorial Hall: (02) 2758-8008
Theater: (02) 2234-3351.

National Taiwan Arts Education Center (國立臺灣藝術教育館) was established by the Ministry of Education to promote the interaction between human life and art. Fine dramatic works, dance and traditional Chinese music and opera performances are held here. Nanhai Road, #41 (台北市南海路47號) (02) 2311-0574 http://www.arte.gov.tw.

Novel Hall for the Performing Arts has an intriguing history. Originally founded as "Danshui Drama Club" in 1897 during the Japanese occupation, the dramatic works performed during this era were questionable. The theater was bombed during World War II but later rebuilt and dedicated in 1997 by Dr. Jeffrey Koo, Honorary Chairman and Chairman of China Trust Commercial (CTC) Bank. Today Novel Hall is where outstanding works are performing by some of Taiwan's greatest composers. Songshou Road, #3-1 (信義區 松壽路3之1號) (02) 2722-4302 http://www. novelhall.org.tw.

Taipei Cultural Center (台北市立社會教育 館), also known as Social Education Hall-Metropolitan Hall, opened in January, 1964. Taipei Cultural Center boasts distinct dance and drama performances, see one while you're in town! From Nanjing East Road Station take bus Brown 9 or Brown 10 and depart at Taipei Arena. Bade Road, Section 3, #25 (台北市八德路3段25號) (02) 2577-5931 http://www.tmseh.gov.tw.

Although **Taipei International Convention Center** (台北國際貿易中心) isn't a theatre, per se, musical acts and spicy girls attract attendees to vendor display areas. If you have time, stop by to see how vendors promote products at Taipei trade shows. You may find some good bargains at vendor booths, as well. Xinyi Road, Section 5, #1 (台北市信義路五段1號) (02) 2723-2535.

The Red Playhouse (紅樓劇場) (also known as "Red Theater") was built during the Japanese colonization period in 1908. It originally housed a traditional market and later a playhouse and movie theater. Photos of vendors selling their wares and some of the items that were sold decades ago are on display on the first floor. A recent renovation has sparked renewed interest in the theater, where today you can watch unique dance and theater performaces while enjoying an afternoon tea. Chengdu Road, #10, Ximending (台北 市萬華區成都路10號) (02) 2311-9380.

TOILETRIES (盥洗用具)

Forgot to pack your toothbrush? Not to worry, most 24-hour convenience stores carry toiletries and other daily necessities. Hong Kong-based **Watson's** (屈臣士 *Chuchengshi*), a drugstore chain established in 1828, has stores on Hong Kong, Macau and Taiwan as well as in China, Singapore, Malaysia and Thailand. The chain is easily spotted by its trademark blue sign and red logo. Watson's carries everything from pain relievers and vitamin pills to towels, hygiene products, packets of tissues or wet tissues, and even underwear. If you can't find a Watson's you can always stop in a **Cosmed** (康是美藥妝店 *Kangshimei*) drugstore, the Chinese name means "health is beautiful." There are over seventy Cosmed stores in Taipei and the store seems to appear in the few areas where Watson's is not:

Watson's (屈臣士)

Beitou: Huanggang Road, #8 (near Beitou traditional market) (北投店 台北市北投區礦 港路8號) (02) 2897-8578
Danshui: Yingzhuan Road, #46 (Danshui night market) (淡水店 台北縣淡水鎮英專路 46號) (02) 2623-7815
Guting: Roosevelt Road, Section 2, #100 (古亭店 台北市中正區羅斯福2段100號)

(02) 2364-6276
Jingmei: Jingyu Road, #195 (景美店 台北市
文山區景興路195號) (02) 2935-0607
New Beitou: Guangming Road, #223, 223-1
(opposite New Beitou Park) (北投店 台北市
北投區光明路223,223-1號) (02) 2896-4701
Shilin: Zhongzheng Road, #285 (士林店 台
北市士林區中正路285號) (02) 2883-0443
Tienmu 1: Tienmu North Road, #6 (台北市
士林區天母西路6號) (02) 2875-5036
Tienmu 2: Tienmu East Road, #32 (台北市
士林區天母東路32號) (02) 2874-7501
Xinyi: Songshou Road, #22-24(信義店 台北
市松壽路22-24號) (02) 8786-2122
Yongkang: Xinyi Road, Section 2, #251
(永康店 台北市中正區信義路2段251號)
(02) 2351-1500
Zhongxiao: Zhongxiao East Road, Section
4, #128 (忠孝店 台北市忠孝東路4段128號)
(02) 2752-9455, 2752-9418.

Cosmed (康是美藥妝店)

Beitou: Guangming Road, #29, 31 (北投店
台北市北投區光明路29, 31號)
(02) 2895-0155
Danshui: Shuifu Road, #11 (淡水店 台北縣
淡水鎮學府路11號) (02) 2625-0552
Mingde: Mingde Road, #88 (明德店 明德路
88號) (02) 2823-7226
Yongchun: Zhongxiao East Road, Section
5, #361, 363 (永春店 忠孝東路五段361, 363
號) (02) 2748-4243
Yongji: Yongji Road, Lane 30, #104 (永吉店
台北市永吉路30巷104號) (02) 2742-0941
Yongkang: Yongkang Street, #7-2 (永康店
台北市永康街7之2號) (02) 2391-6291
Zhongxiao: Zhongxiao East Road, Section
3, #226 (忠孝店 台北市忠孝東路3段226號)
(02) 2711-7274.

TOPVIEW TAIPEI
(新光摩天展望台)

Topview Taipei Observatory is on the top
floor of what was once the tallest building
in Taipei, Shin Kong Mitsukoshi Life Tower
Building. The building is directly across
the street from Taipei Main Station and is a
landmark taxi drivers use to navigate around
the city. Discover 360-degree views of
Taipei, a full-scale model and history of the
observatory, view photos of dignitaries who
have visited, or purchase t-shirts and other
assorted souvenirs. Enjoy piquant pastries
or sip coffee, tea or cocoa at the Topview
Café. The Observatory is a superb spot
to visit either day or night, but try to stop
by on a clear day or evening for a better
view. Open daily 11 am to 10 pm, 11 pm
on Saturday, admission is a reasonable NT
$160 for adults, NT $80 for children 100 cm
and above. Zhongxiao West Road, Section
1, # 66 (opposite Taipei Main Station) (台北
市忠孝西路1段66號) (02) 2388-6130
http://www.topview.com.tw.

TOURIST INFORMATION
(旅遊訊息)

A popular web site for Taiwan employment,
travel, housing and merchandise information
is http://www.OnTaiwan.com.

Another good reference is the Taiwan
Government Information Office:
http://www.gio.gov.tw.

**Taiwan Taoyuan International Airport
Tourist Service Center** (中正國際機場旅
客服務中心) (03) 383-4631. Open 7 am to
11:30 pm at the lobby entrance of Terminal
1. A twenty-four hour monorail and a free
shuttle bus that runs from 5:20 am to
1:10 am transports passengers between
terminals 1 and 2.

**Tourism Bureau Ministry of
Transportation and Communications**
(交通部觀光局) Zhongxiao East Road,
#290, 9th Floor (台北市忠孝東路4段290號9
樓) (02) 2349-1500.

Travel Information Service Center (觀光
局旅遊服務中心) Dunhua North Road, #240
(台北市松山區敦化北路240號)
(02) 2717-3737.

Taiwan Visitor Association (台灣觀光協會)
Minchuan East Road, #9, 5th Floor (台北市

民權東路2段9號5樓) (02) 2594-3261.

Taichung Travel Section (觀光局旅遊服務中心, 台中服務處收) Gancheng Street, #95, Nantun District, Taichung (台中市南屯區干城街95號) (04) 2254-0809, toll-free: 0800-422-022.

Tainan Travel Section (旅遊服務中心, 台南服務處) Minchuan Road, Section 1, #243, 10th Floor, Tainan (台南市權路1段243號10樓) (06) 226-5681, toll-free: 0800-611-011.

Kaohsiung Travel Section (旅遊服務中心, 高雄服務處) Zhongzheng 4th Road, #235, 5th Floor-1, Kaohsiung (高雄市中正四路235號5樓) (07) 281-1513, toll-free: 0800-711-765.

Taipei Visitor Information Centers

Beitou Station (捷運北投站旅遊服務中心) (Right-side, 10 am to 4 pm) Guangming Road, #1 (北市光明路一號 捷運北投站入口左側) (02) 2894-6923.

East Metro Mall (東區地下街旅遊服務中心) (#4-2, 10 am to 5 pm) Daan Road, Section 1, #77 (台北市大安路1段77號地下街4-2) (02) 6638-0059.

Jiantan Station (捷運劍潭站旅遊服務中心) (Right-side exit, 10 am to 6 pm) Zhongshan N. Rd, Section 5, #65 (台北市中山北路5段65號入口右側) (02) 2883-0313.

Taipei Main Station (台北車站旅遊服務中心) (1st Floor, West Side, 8 am to 5 pm) Beiping West Road, #3 (台北市北平西路3號台北車站1樓大廳西北側) (02) 2312-3256.

Taipei Songshan Airport (松山機場旅遊服務中心) (Lobby, 8 am to 4 pm) Dunhua North Road, #340-9 (敦化北路340之9號松山機場入境大廳) (02) 2546-4741.

Ximen Station (捷運西門站旅遊服務中心) (10 am to 5 pm) Baoqing Road, #32-1, B1 (Exit 5) (台北市寶慶路32-1號B1, 5號出口) (02) 2375-3096.

TRAFFIC TIPS (Or, "Invasion of the Mopeds!") (交通安全)

You won't need to travel to a Disney theme park to experience thrills and spills, simply walk down a busy Taipei street to experience it live.

Forget Everything You Know

Do you remember the slogan "Forget everything you know" from the movie "Vanilla Sky?" Well, that pretty much applies to the traffic regulations in Taipei. It often seems as if everyone is colorblind, or just blind, in general. Some people turn right when the light is red (it's against the law), make a u-turn when a sign in the middle of the road explicitly forbids it, or, if it's convenient, drive a car or ride a moped or motorcycle the wrong way down a one-way street. It's a wonder direction signals were even installed in the cars sold on Taiwan as few people seem to use them.

Only a decade ago, bus drivers were notorious for causing accidents and steadily increasing the fatality rate as buses weaved in and out of traffic as if the driver forgot he were responsible for the three dozen lives behind him. The construction of bus lanes throughout the city has led to a marked decrease in traffic fatalities over the past decade.

The Surreal Life

The traffic in Taipei can best be described as "surreal," it's like being in a live video game, and crossing many city streets is an adventure in and of itself. Drivers put the pedal to the metal as pedestrians j-walk, children and adults peddle bicycles, venders push carts and elderly citizens peddle three-wheeled, slow-moving carts. The way some young people drive, as if the Grand Prix had been moved to the streets of Taipei, it wouldn't be a bad idea for minors to spend a day watching videos of families grieving for loved ones killed in traffic fatalities before licenses were administered. Thankfully, Taipei City Government has been broadcasting public service announcements as of late, reminding people that they're not always behind the wheel of a car.

Cabbies On Crack

Cab drivers, in particular, are known for their creative driving techniques. It's possible The Ramones were inspired to write their underground hit "Cabbies on Crack" after a brief stop in Taipei; however, the drivers were probably chewing and hyped up on the legal, addictive betelnut rather than crack. The penalty for trafficking illegal drugs in Taiwan is death, and the police are particularly harsh on offenders who are caught using illicit products.

As a word of caution, you never know what kind of business your cabbie may be involved in during the wee hours of the night (and it's certainly best not to ask him). If you're unhappy with how he's driving, it's best to get out of the cab at the next traffic light and hail another cab rather than get into an altercation. Taiwanese taxi drivers have a reputation for being easily provoked, especially if they're chewing betelnut, which acts as a stimulant and makes them particularly excitable.

Those with non-Asian features can anticipate at least three to five honks a day from taxi drivers hungry for business from those unfamiliar with the capital's streets. This is not to say drivers are out for foreigner (外國人 waiguoren) blood; on the contrary, cab drivers here seem far more honest than those in other countries. Most won't drive twenty kilometers when you only need to go two minutes from where you are.

Cab Fares

Fares are reasonable when compared with fares in other international cities. From 6 am to 11 pm a Taipei taxi costs NT $70 (US $2.10) for the first 1.5 kilometers and NT $5 (US $.15) every two hundred and fifty meters thereafter. From 11 pm until 6 am the fare is the same but the meter runs faster. Traveling the same distance in a taxi in Manhattan, Tokyo, or Paris typically costs three times as much. For fares that start and end in Taipei some companies charge NT $10 for "trunk service" or for telephone booking. For taxi rides that originate and end in Danshui, which include the neighboring towns of Hongshulin and Zhuwei, you will need to add NT $30 to the fare, presumably to prevent cab drivers from playing musical prices. Due to rising gas prices, taxi and public transportation fares may be increasing, for updates check http://www.OnTaiwan.com.

Don't Tip

Tipping, as is common in many Western countries, is not the norm on Taiwan. If you attempt to tip, the driver will likely hand you back the extra few NT, assuming you paid too much for the fare. This also applies to restaurants. At upscale dining establishments a 10% service charge is typyically included in the bill, and this is considered the tip. As an aside, you may also be surprised to find that the service provided at most restaurants is truly outstanding. What's even more surprising is that employees provide this outstanding service without expecting any sort of additional compensation. In the individualistic West, for instance, restaurant patrons often go ignored because a waiter or waitress does not service other areas. On Taiwan, however, the communal spirit prevails, resulting in truly outstanding service at no additional cost to the customer. For additional information please see "XY & Z (Useful Information) (很有用的信息)."

The MRT: A Favorable Alternative

If you decide against using a taxi to reach your destination, the Mass Rapid Transit

(MRT) railway system (捷運 *jieyun*) is a favorable alternative. The MRT is clean, quick and comfortable, fares vary depending on how far you need to go but are reasonable. If you're traveling into the city, the main line runs from Danshui to Taipei Main Station. At Taipei Main Station you can transfer to separate lines that run from Taipei Zoo in Muzha, Taipei County, to Zhongshan Middle School, at the intersection of Fuxing North Road and Minchuan East Road. Many visitors walk to Warner Brothers Village for shopping and entertainment from Taipei City Hall Station.

If you have time to wait for a bus, which can take anywhere from five to thirty-five minutes, the fare is NT $15 per adult, NT $12 for registered students, and NT $8 for children and the elderly. If you're a student, be sure to being your Student ID card for discounts on everything from movie and theatre tickets to bus fares.

You may want to purchase an Easy Card as opposed to single fare MRT tickets. An Easy Card is a magnetic stored value card that may be used at MRT stations and on buses. The transaction is quick and convenient and you may return the card at any MRT station to receive a refund for the unused stored card value.

Passengers pay the fare while boarding or leaving the bus according to the red sign above the driver. If you can't read Chinese, observe the other passengers to determine when to use your Easy Card or put your coins into the fare box. It's a good idea to have your money ready before the bus arrives in case you have to pay while getting on—the last thing you need is a crowd of impatient local commuters behind you as you fumble for change!

Invasion of the Mopeds

Don't even think about renting a car and driving around town, most people in Taipei drive like they're looking for a bathroom after drinking an entire pot of coffee. If you find yourself in this kind of situation, try a Western-style fast food restaurant or any MRT station if you prefer to use a toilet with a lid as opposed to a squat toilet. Also, finding a parking space is more difficult than finding a hamburger without mustard on it, not to mention that Taipei traffic jams can be mind-numbing, particularly during Sundays and holidays. For those unfamiliar with traffic on Taiwan, get ready for "the Taiwanese moped experience." Even if you're from a big city, nothing can prepare you for the seeming onslaught of motorcycles and mopeds that race into the intersection seconds before the light turns green and weave through cars like schools of restless fish in a crowded sea. Holidays in Taipei look frighteningly like the filming of a sci-fi thriller, "Invasion of the Mopeds."

Beethoven's Ice Cream Symphony

And what's that dulcet music you hear at night? Is it the ice cream man? I'm afraid not! You'll be disappointed if you had run outside in nothing but your new **Taipei In A Day** t-shirt hoping to purchase ice cream. While ice cream trucks play soothing music to attract young customers in the West, garbage trucks play Beethoven's "Fur Elise" to attract both young and old alike to dispose of their trash here in the East.

For those traveling to the East for the first time, trash collection on Taiwan is something of an amusing spectacle. Large yellow garbage trucks slowly creak to a stop on the side of the road and blast Beethoven out of speakers on top of the truck for everyone within a half-mile radius to hear. Suddenly, residents from across the street to several blocks away come running with their garbage, in government-mandated trash bags purchased at convenience stores and supermarkets, to toss into the compactor.

Although traffic jams in Taipei may sometimes make you feel sleepy, it shouldn't be a nightmare to reach your final destination. Most Taiwanese are friendly towards international guests and will help you if you're in need of assistance. Study a map of the main roads and landmarks to familiarize yourself with Taipei (start by taking a look at the maps in **Taipei In A Day**), practice asking for directions in Chinese, bring a portable dictionary, and if you can, a colleague or friend who can speak Mandarin. If you don't get into an altercation with a taxi driver, you should have an oh-so marvelous time!

VALUABLE EXPRESSIONS (有用的措辭)

Social dining and drinking are central to Taiwanese culture. Taiwanese often welcome guests by holding up a glass filled with an alcoholic beverage and saying, "Huanying!" (Welcome!). You are then expected to hold up your glass and say, "Xie xie!" (Thank you!). Each uses both hands to take a small sip, and holds the glass back up in the air facing the other afterwards.

If you're at a social gathering it's common to hear "cheers!" or "bottoms up!" (乾杯 *gan bei*). The expression literally means "dry cup" so if you shout, "Gan bei!" you and your compatriats are expected to finish what's in your glass. (In other words, be careful what you shout out!) If you finish your drink expect it to be refilled immediately.

Daily Conversation (會話 *Hui Hua*)

Hello! (你 好! *Ni hao!*)
How are you? (你好嗎? *Ni hao ma?*)
Very well, and you? (很好,你呢? *Hen hao, ni ne?*)
Thank you! (謝謝! *Shieh shieh!*)
You're welcome! (不客氣! *Bu keh chee!*)
Cheers! (乾杯! *Gan bei!*)
Happy New Year! (新年快樂! *Xinnian kuaile!*)
Excuse me (to ask a question) (請問 *Ching wen*…)
Excuse me (to walk past someone) (借過 *Jie guo*)
I'm sorry (對不起 *dui bu chee*)
Not spicy (regarding food preparation) (不辣 *bu la*)
A little spicy (小辣 *xiao la*)
I want spicy (我要辣 *wo yao la*)
May I have a beverage? (飲料, 好嗎? *Yinliao, hao ma?*)
Can you speak English? (你會說英文嗎? *Ni hui shou yingwen ma?*)
The bathroom does not have toilet paper (洗手間沒有衛生紙 *sheeshoujian meiyo wei sheng zhi*)
The bathroom does not have soap (洗手間沒有肥皂 *xishoujian meiyo feitsao*)
(I/we) don't want (any), thank you. (不要,謝謝! *Bu yao, shieh shieh!*)
Small (小 *xiao*)
Medium (中 *zhong*)
Big (大 *da*)
A lot (很多 *hen duo*)
A little (一點 *yi dian*)
Please don't add MSG (請不要加味精 *ching bu yao jia weijing*)
I like (it/this) (我喜歡 *Wo xihuan*)
I don't like (it/this) (我不喜歡 *Wo bu xihuan*)

The food is delicious! (好吃! *Hao chi!*)
Are you full? (你吃飽了嗎? *Ni chi bao le ma*)
I'm full! (我吃飽了! *wo shi bao le*)
Strange (奇怪 *cheeguai*)
Strange smell (奇怪的味道 *cheeguai de weidao*)
Vegetarian (素食者 *Su shizhe*)
I am a vegetarian (我吃素 *Wo chi su*)
How much money (does this cost)? (多少錢? *Duoshao chian?*)
Too expensive! (太貴! *Tai gway!*)
(A little) cheaper, okay? (便宜一點, 好嗎? *Pianyi yi dian, hao ma?*)
Allergy (過敏 *guoming*)
I am allergic (我有過敏 *wo yo guoming*)
May I please have the bill? (賬單, 好嗎? *zhang dan, hao ma?*)
Bitter (苦 *ku*)
Bowl (碗 *wan*)
Chopsticks (筷子 *kwai zi*)
Mustard (芥茉 *jie moh*)
Per portion (每份 *mei fen*)
Pepper (黑胡椒 *hei hu jiang*)
Salt (鹽 *yen*)
Soda (汽水 *chee sway*)
Sour (酸 *suan*)
Spoon (湯匙 *tang chih*)
Sweet (甜 *tian*)
Sugar (糖 *tang*)
Toothbrush (牙刷 *ya mao*)
Toothpaste (牙膏 *ya gao*)
Toothpick (牙籤 *ya chien*)
Water (水 *shui*)
Zoo (動物園 *dongwuyuen*)
Floss (牙線 *ya shien*)
Fork (叉子 *tsah zi*)
Lunch box, or boxed lunch (便當 *bien dang*)
Knife (刀子 *dao zi*)
Ketchup (番茄醬 *fan chieh jiang*)
Menu (菜單 *tsai dan*)

What Would You Like To Eat? (你想吃甚麼? *Ni Shang Chi Shenmuh*)

Food (食物 *shi wu*)	American-style (food) (美式 *Mei shi*)
Chinese-style (中式 *Zhong shi*)	European-style (歐式 *Ou shi*)
Japanese-style (日式 *Reh shi*)	Western-style (西式 *Shee shi*)
Thai-style (泰式 *Thai shi*)	Bread (麵包 *mian bao*)
Beef (牛肉 *niu roh*)	Beef steak (牛排 *niupai*)
Small beef steak (小牛排 *xiao niupai*)	Carrot (胡蘿蔔 *hu roh boh*)
Chicken (雞肉 *ji roh*)	Chicken leg steak (雞腿排 *ji tui pai*)
Duck (鴨肉 *ya roh*)	Ham (火腿 *huo tui*)
Lobster (龍蝦 *long xia*)	Pork (豬肉 *ju roh*)
Pork steak (豬排 *ju pie*)	Shrimp (蝦仁 *xia ren*)
Dessert (甜點 *tian dian*)	Egg (蛋 *dan*)

Fish (魚 *yu*)
White rice (白飯 *bai fan*)
Mushroom (香菇 *shang gu*)
Fried noodles (炒麵 *tsao mian*)
Fruit (水果 *shui guo*)
Salad (沙拉 *sa la*)
Sandwich (三明治 *san ming zhi*)

Goat (羊肉 *yang roh*)
Fried rice (炒飯 *tsao fan*)
Noodles (麵 *mian*)
Fried chicken (炸雞 *zha ji*)
Vegetables (蔬菜 *shu tsai*)
Hot dog (熱狗 *ruh goh*)
Toast (吐司 *tu si*)

What Would You Like To Drink? (你想喝甚麼? *Ni Shang Heh Shenmuh*)

Juice (果汁 *guo zhi*) Coffee (咖啡 *ka fei*) Mineral Water (礦泉水 *kuang chuen shui*)
Milk (牛奶 *niu nai*) Soybean Milk (黃豆牛奶 *huang dou niu nai*) Tea (茶 *cha*)
Black tea (紅茶 *hong cha*) Green tea (綠茶 *lu cha*) Oolong tea (烏龍茶 *wu long cha*)

Numbers (數目 *Shu Mu*)

One (一 *yi*)
Two (二 *er*)
Three (三 *san*)
Four (四 *si*)
Five (五 *wu*)
Six (六 *liu*)
Seven (七 *chee*)
Eight (八 *ba*)
Nine (九 *jiu*)
Ten (十 *shi*)

Eleven (十一 *shi yi*)
Twelve (十二 *shi er*)
Thirteen (十三 *shi san*)
Fourteen (十四 *shi sih*)
Fifteen (十五 *shi wu*)
Sixteen (十六 *shi liu*)
Seventeen (十七 *shi chee*)
Eighteen (十八 *shi ba*)
Ninteen (十九 *shi jiu*)
Twenty (二十 *er shi*)

Twenty-one (二十一 *er shi yi*)
Twenty-two (二十二 *er shi er*)
Twenty-three (二十三 *er shi san*)
Twenty-four (二十四 *er shi si*)
Twenty-five (二十五 *er shi wu*)
Thirty (三十 *san shi*)
Fourty (四十 *si shi*)
Fifty (五十 *wu shi*)
Sixty (六十 *liu shi*)
Seventy (七十 *chee shi*)

Eighty (八十 *ba shi*)
Ninety (九十 *jiu shi*)
One hundred (一百 *yi bai*)
One hundred twenty (一百二十 *yi bai er shi*)
One hundred fifty (一百五十 *yi bai wu shi*)
Two hundred (二百 *liang bai*)

Three hundred (三百 *san bai*)
Four hundred (四百 *si bai*)
Five hundred (五百 *wu bai*)
Seven hundred (七百 *chee bai*)
Nine hundred (九百 *jiu bai*)
One thousand (一千 *yi chian*)

Asking Directions (問方向 *Wen fangshang*)

Where is (are) the... (...在哪裡?...*zai nahli?*)
Where is the bathroom? (廁所在哪裡? *Tsuh swo zai nahli?*)
Bus Stop (車站 *che zhan*)
Hot spring (溫泉 *wen chuen*)
Hotel (飯店 *fan dian*)
MRT station (捷運站 *jieyun zhan*)
Mountain (山 *shan*)
Park (公園 *gongyuan*)
Restaurant (餐廳 *tsanting*)
Taxi (計程車 *jichengche*)
How much is the fare from X to Y? (從X到Y多少錢? *Tsong X dao Y, duoshao chian?*)
Right (右 *yo*)
Left (左 *zwo*)
Straight (一直走 *yi zhi zwo*)

Stop (停 *ting*)
Please turn right. (請右轉 *Ching yo zhuan.*)
Please turn left. (請左轉 *Ching zwo zhuan.*)
Please go straight. (請一直走 *Ching yi zhi zwo.*)
Please stop here. (請靠邊停 *Ching kao bien ting*)

VIDEO RENTALS
(影音租售連鎖店)

For video rental try **Blockbuster**® (百事達® *Baishida*). The one in Beitou is on Guangming Road, #212 (台北市北投區光明路212號) (02) 2897-2520, (02) 2897-2519 http://www.blockbuster.com.tw.

VISAS
(簽證)

Citizens of Australia, Belgium, Canada, France, Germany, Japan, Luxembourg, the Netherlands, New Zealand, Portugal, Spain, Sweden, and the U.S. are given two-week "landing visas" gratis upon arriving. For a longer stay, the "unofficial" (due to political reasons) Taiwan consulate in your country may offer a visitor visa that will permit you to reside for two months for up to six months. You must have a valid reason to remain on the island longer than two months, however, and sightseeing doesn't qualify. Studying Chinese does qualify, but you must present valid documentation (proof of enrollment) to local authorities. Employment on the island is not permitted with these kinds of visas.

If you overstay your visa you'll be required to pay a fine, which can range from NT $300 to NT $3,000, depending on the duration of overstay and how much sleep the police officer has had the previous evening. The police officer will proceed to stamp a series of nasty messages in your passport that say something to the effect of, "Hey peanut head, next time leave the island on time!" Upon returning home, you would probably have to purchase a new passport so the authorities in other countries don't glare and call you "peanut head" upon arrival. Don't overstay your visa.

Have the address and phone number of your country's consulate or trade representative office handy in case a conflict arises. However, it's best to settle disputes privately without contacting the authorities.

WEATHER
(天氣)

Formosa Television (FTV), Channel 6 or 53 (cable) boasts a nightly English news program 11 to 11:30 pm and rebroadcasts at 6:00 am the following morning.

Taiwan has a subtropical climate that may wrinkle your favorite shirt and pair of dress pants. Bring a small, portable umbrella, as it does rain often, particularly during the long, wet winters (compact umbrellas go for NT $100 and up at most convenience stores). Luckily, Taiwanese don't have to worry about light April showers bringing colorful May flowers, as the brief summer typhoons are sure to uproot the flowers soon after they've bloomed. For the most part, typhoons are nothing more than heavy summer rainstorms that miss the island by several hundred kilometers or pass quickly over the island. The "eye" of the typhoon tends to leave after a few hours, leaving little more than occasional bursts of wind, trees swaying and scattered twigs.

If there is a typhoon warning, turn on the news, you'll see meteorologists pointing at a small red dot with arrows circling around it. Kids like typhoons because most schools close after a public "typhoon warning" alert. While there is an occasional doozy, most typhoons bring downpours that end within a few hours and are less serious than the seasonal hurricanes that wreak havoc in Florida. Make sure you pick up a decent flashlight and new batteries, as typhoons may cause blackouts. Stay away from hiking trails as mudslides and falling rocks can turn a leisurely hiking trip into a veritable nightmare. Thankfully, typhoons are not especially prone to disrupt the vacations of travelers who have purchased **Taipei In A Day**.

Taipei winters are often cold and wet, with temperatures ranging from 45 to 55 degrees Fahrenheit, and summers are hot and humid, with temperatures averaging 85 to 90 in the north, with even hotter and stickier conditions down south. Summer mornings are usually pleasant, while clouds and occasional downpours wash away any thoughts you may have had of swimming during the afternoon. Although it may seem ironic, many Taiwanese appreciate the rain, as it tends to bring cooler, cleaner air.

If you visit during the winter, you'll find that Taiwan buildings are built with air conditioners but have no central heating. Dress in layers and bring an extra sweater. You may be surprised that Taiwanese turn on air conditioners even in winter to keep air in cars and residences cool and dry, not to turn expatriates into human ice cubes. Local drivers are also fond of trying out new designer air fresheners to hit the market.

Autumn and spring are good times to visit, as the weather tends to be neither too hot nor too cold. During the summer, the sun beats down on Taiwan the way my grandmother beats the dust out of her old sofa, meaning bring a good hat and sunscreen. Those new to the scooter scene find themselves sitting in the hot seat—literally! Be sure to bring a good bottle of suntan lotion, preferably one that offers a high level of Pf protection, but most important, bring a sunny disposition!

WINDOW ON CHINA (小人國)

Window On China, the world's second-largest miniature park, is in Taoyuan County, an hour southwest of Taipei. Discover miniature displays of famous Taiwan structures, such as National Taiwan Democracy Memorial Hall, Sun Yat-sen Freeway and Taiwan Taoyuan International Airport. You'll also see replicas of China's Great Wall, Forbidden City, Lungmen Caves, and Tienho Temple. View famous buildings and statues from around the world as well as ancient Egyptian civilizations. An electric train takes passengers around the park free of charge. Buses depart at the intersection of Hankou Street and Zhonghua Road in Taipei every thirty minutes. By train, go from Taipei Main Station to Jungli and catch a bus from Hsinchu Bus Company near the train station. Admission is NT $550/$360. Open 8:45 am to 5:30 pm, 8 am to 7 pm holidays. Gaoyuen Chuenhen Gangxia, #60-2 (桃園縣龍潭鄉高原村橫岡下60-2號) (03) 471-7211.

YUNLIN (雲林)
Population: 736,772

Located south of Changhua, west of Nantou and north of Chiayi, Yunlin is known for its agriculture and fishing industries, as well as for livestock farming. For international visitors heading north to Taichung or south to Tainan or Kaohsiung, Yunlin tends to be a scenic county to pass through rather than a tourist destination for adventurous travelers.

If you are intent on visiting every city on Taiwan, Yunlin holds a coffee festival from October to November since coffee is grown in the county's town of Gukeng. There are also several historic temples around town, and a Hakka cultural celebration takes place here in March. For more information visit http://www.OnTaiwan.com.

XY & Z (Useful Information)
(很有用的信息)

Air Raid Practice Drills
(萬安防空演習 *Wanan Fangkong Yanshi*)

If loud sirens blare and you're asked to remain indoors for a brief period, it's probably not because bombs are carpeting the city. However, the eerie silence and lack of cars, buses, people or mopeds zipping around town for half an hour is enough to make one appreciate not having a communist neighbor that lobs missiles within a few kilometers of where you reside. Even the most adventurous expatriates remark that these drills make them better appreciate freedom.

Chinese Calendar

The Chinese calendar, a lunar calendar that has been in existence for thousands of years, is tied to the fifteen-day cycles of the moon in which Chinese people knew the best time to fish, plant, harvest, and plan life events. Family rituals and festivals were also determined by the lunar calendar, and many of these traditions continue today.

Twelve animals were selected by Buddah to represent each of the twelve lunar years: the rat, ox, tiger, rabbit, dragon, snake, horse, sheep, monkey, rooster, dog and pig. According to the Chinese calendar, 2006 was the Year of the Dog, and many Chinese believed that showering their dogs with affection brought good luck. On Taiwan you can now spot dog designs on bags, bedding and clothing, as well as dogs wearing pooch clothing in restaurants enjoying local cuisine along with their owners. Since doggie style is now in vogue, the year of the pig also promises to be quite interesting.

Communication Corner: Important Cultural Do's & Don'ts

Let's start with the Do's…

DO bring a student ID for discounts.

DO go for a hair wash while in town, the experience is unlike that found in salons in the West. Here you're treated to a beverage (usually gratis) along with a soothing upper back, neck and scalp massage. For a wash sans haircut prices tend to range from NT $150 (US $4.50) to NT $200 (US $6.00).

DO ask for help if you need it. Taiwanese tend to be hospitable and are quick to offer assistance.

DO bargain. Bargaining is a traditional aspect of Chinese culture and you can bargain for just about anything, from clothing and food items to jade necklaces and beaded bracelets, as well as art and souvenirs. Bargaining is expected in day/night markets, and the price listed is the price you're expected to begin bargaining with. At the night market, if the price on an item says NT $290 (US $8.70), ask for NT $200 (US $6.00), the price will typically be lowered to NT $250 (US $7.50). Even if you visit a large retail outlet or department store, ask the salesperson if he or she could offer a slightly better price, a discount may be forthcoming.

DO compliment local residents on Taiwan's colorful traditional clothing, historic religious temples, delicious native foods, vast green mountains and breathtaking views. Talk about what you like about Taiwan, you'll be astonished at how overwhelmingly responsive Taiwanese people will be.

DO expect to see interesting expressions and misspellings on t-shirts and other paraphernalia. One expat colleague was particularly surprised to find an elderly Taiwanese woman sporting a t-shirt that read, "Deep Anal Penetration." Not only did she not understand the connotation, she looked as if she hadn't had any penetration aside from some intravenous medicine at the local hospital.

DO bring tissues or wet tissues to use in a restroom. Aside from Western restaurants, not all restaurants come equipped with toilet paper, nor a sit-down toilet, for that matter. Many local restaurants have "squats," bowls built onto a platform with a pull-down handle that hangs from a water basin for flushing. To use a squat toilet step onto the stall platform, carefully pull down your drawers, place one foot on each side of the bowl, and squat down as if you were crouching in the bushes. Squat toilets are not convenient for catching up on light reading. If you prefer to use a toilet with a seat, most department stores, Western restaurants and MRT stations have restrooms with sit-down toilets.

DO bring wet tissues to wipe your hands before meals.

DO be sensitive to Chinese holidays. Take into consideration which day the Chinese Lunar New Year falls on, for instance, and bear in mind that the festivities last for fifteen days. You may be surprised to find that parts of the city, which you had hoped would be brimming with excitement, become a virtual ghost town during this time.

DO give flowers. If you give someone flowers during Chinese New Year and they open on New Year's Day, the person receiving the flowers will be blessed with luck and good fortune in the year to come. However, make sure you don't give white flowers, as white flowers symbolize death in Chinese culture.

DO expect the waiter or waitress at most restaurants, even Western restaurants, to bring out one meal at a time for patrons, regardless of how many are dining. While this custom may appear strange to Westerners, serving one meal at a time, as opposed to bringing out a tray for all diners at one time, is the norm. If this troubles you, politely request to the waiter or waitress that meals be brought out and served to your party at the same time.

DO expect to see people using umbrellas to block the strong ultraviolet rays of the sun. Taiwan can become oven-like, and using an umbrella helps prevent getting baked. In crowds, elderly ladies may poke unsuspecting passerbys with their parasols. During a brief visit home two young ladies yelled, "It's not raining!" from a passing car. Stunned, I quickly remembered that carrying an umbrella during hot, sunny days, while practical, is not the norm in the West.

Now for the Don'ts...

DON'T drink the tap water, unless you enjoy diarrhea. Bottled water is inexpensive and in good supply at convenience and drug stores, department stores and bakeries. Some hotels and hot spring resorts also provide complimentary bottles of water to guests.

DON'T stick your chopsticks straight up in your bowl of rice, even after you have finished your meal, this is an extremely rude gesture that symbolizes death in Chinese culture. This is because Chinese people stick two incense straight up in a bowl of rice to pray for someone who has passed away.

DON'T be shocked when you see a sign on the bathroom stall requesting you not throw your used toilet paper into the toilet. This may seem unpleasant, but on Taiwan, it is considered socially improper to throw used toilet paper into the toilet. At department stores and hotels the sign in English may read, "Please flush the toilet and keep it clean," but the Chinese above it says don't put used paper into the toilet. Later, a cleaning person will use metal tongs (much like the ones used in the West for outdoor barbeques) to pick up the used tissue goodies left in wastebaskets and dispose of them in plastic bags. This is partly to keep antiquated city pipes, many of which were put in place during the Japanese occupation, from backing up and flooding.

DON'T leave a tip. Many Westerners are surprised to find that leaving a tip at a restaurant, which is not only common but also expected back home, is not the norm here. Some restaurants may include a 10% service charge in the bill, and that is considered the tip. As to taxi fares, the tip has already been included when the driver starts the meter. Not long ago, when the fare in Taipei was NT $50 per ride, passengers were expected to provide an extra NT $15 tip to the driver after each ride. Now the meter starts at NT $70. Unless you are patronizing a Western establishment, such as a coffee shop where you may find a "tip jar" at the counter, you are not expected to tip. Many international guests are also astounded (and a little embarrassed) to find that the service here is remarkable compared with the West. While it may seem odd, don't leave a tip. On Taiwan, a smile and simple "thank you" suffices.

DON'T point. Pointing is considered rude in Chinese culture. A subtle point to an object at a local shop or department store should not offend, but pointing directly at a person, even to say "I like that outfit!," is considered rude.

DON'T be surprised if some locals aren't comfortable with your taking pictures. While most understand that you're a visitor, police usually use cameras before issuing tickets.

DON'T give shoes to someone as a gift. Giving someone a pair of shoes symbolizes that you want him or her to walk away and leave you alone. If you give a Chinese person a pair of shoes you may receive at least NT $1 back so the shoes will not "technically" be a gift.

DON'T bargain at the local supermarket. There are only a few places on Taiwan where bargaining typically doesn't take place, and the supermarket is one of them. Bargaining is also typically not acceptable at restaurants and other eating establishments.

DON'T be astonished to see pets in restaurants, supermarkets and boutiques. While customers may cringe at your adorable poodle at shops in the West, it's not an uncommon sight here, and was particularly popular during the Year of the Dog.

DON'T purchase an item at a day/night market without a price on it. There are some opportunities in life that don't come along twice, so if you really want those Hello Kitty chopsticks, go for it. You should be aware, however, that when a price is listed, it's the price everyone is expected to begin bargaining with. If no price is listed, you will probably be hit with what I refer to as the "foreign face tax," a price higher than that offered to a local resident. Don't be taken for a fool. Avoid the foreign face tax and look at items that you can purchase for fair market value.

DON'T cringe at the sight of Taiwanese people eating stinky tofu (臭豆腐 *chou dofu*) or the black rectangular pig or chicken blood mixed with rice (豬血糕 *zhu shue gao*). Pig blood and stinky tofu are popular local snacks and are sold everywhere from amusement parks and ball games to high-class restaurants and cinemas. Try a bite of each during your visit. I mean, when else are you going to have the opportunity to try these interesting local delicacies, at the ballpark back home? I can just picture it now, "Stinky tofu here! Hot stinky tofu, get 'em while they're hot!"

DON'T be offended if residents ask your age or how much money you or your family earns. While it's taboo to discuss these topics in the West, Taiwanese people are naturally curious about visitors, and these kinds of personal questions are the norm in Chinese culture. You can avoid these kinds of questions with polite responses such as, "I'm old enough to be your friend," "I'm old enough to be my mother's/father's child" and "I earn enough to pay a visit to this beautiful island."

DON'T be shocked if no one says, "God bless you!" after you *dapenti*, or sneeze. This is a Western custom and is not well understood in the East. Westerners may also be discouraged to find that some Taiwanese don't cover their mouths as they cough or sneeze, choosing instead to share their mucus and germs with the sidewalk and the unfortunate pedestrians who happen to be passing by. Unless you want to give a ten-minute lecture on Western etiquette, keep quiet when locals sneeze. Instead, offer a tissue as a friendly, universal gesture of kindness.

DON'T be shocked if you hear some people burp in public. While there is some debate, the consensus seems to be that the burpee is satisfied with the meal. During college, as a student of Chinese language, history, art and literature in New York, some Taiwanese friends and I had taken a trip to the mountains of lovely, picturesque Vermont. While eating at a quaint, family-oriented restaurant, I unwittingly let out a tremendous belch. While my friends didn't blink an eye, the family sitting across from us were horrified. The mother's eyes must have widened greater than the Nile River and her jaw nearly hit the table. She sat aghast during the remainder of our time at the restaurant. East met West at a lovely, family-oriented restaurant in the mountains of Vermont, and needless to say, some Westerners weren't quite ready for the culture shock! After that incident, however, I tried to remember not to belch out loud in public while not in Chinatown.

DON'T be offended if someone makes a comment about the few extra pounds you gained during the holidays. In the West it's considered rude to discuss negative aspects of personal appearances, such as skin blemishes or weight gain. Here in the East, however, Chinese people will be the first to bring to your attention that nasty little zit on the tip of your nose or the few extra pounds around the abs you've been trying to lose. Even after a decade here I'm still somewhat taken aback when close Taiwanese friends remark, "My, you've put on weight!" Try not to take offense to these kinds of remarks, they indicate stark cultural differences and are not meant as personal insults. You can smile and quip back, "Why, thank you for noticing!" or "Fantastic, I've succeeded in getting out of shape!" You may wish to explain that back home we don't make these kinds of remarks.

DON'T give gifts in groups of four. The Chinese word for "four" sounds strikingly similar to the word for "death," thus giving gifts in four represents an ominous portent and is considered bad luck. This is especially important to remember during Chinese New Year, when Chinese people are especially superstitious.

DON'T give someone a clock! Chinese people are especially superstitious about death, and to a Chinese, receiving a clock signifies that his or her time will soon run out. Umbrellas are also taboo because they symbolizes that a family unit will split apart. Books also make unlucky presents. (This custom may be changing, however, as I recently received as a gift a copy of Sun Tzu's The Art of War.) Other holiday taboos include arguing, scolding children or crying, as bad feelings tend to bring bad luck. In addition, be especially careful not to break things. If something does break, you may hear someone remark, "*shway shway ping an*," or "may you be safer each year," a clever play on words because "*shway shway*" means "to break."

DON'T sign your name in red ink. While this may not be significant in the West, Chinese people feel it's not only impolite, it signifies misfortune or death. An expat English teacher at a local elementary school had to rewrite comments to parents in a hundred communication books because, to some Chinese, writing a child's name in red ink signifies that he or she will die. Sign your name with a blue or black pen.

DON'T be offended if some people stare at you. Chinese people tend to have very little body hair, so when they see Westerners it's natural for people to be curious.

DON'T be surprised if you're a male and encounter Taiwanese men who compliment your looks. In China, men as well as women compliment each other on appearance to help build "face" and good longstanding relationships. One fine Saturday I encountered a nice fellow while commuting on the MRT; unfortunately, speaking English with him was like trying to solve a Zen riddle. He approached me and said, "Handsome." I said, "Thank you very much." He said, "No, I Handsome." I said, "Okay, so you are. What's your name?" He said, "Handsome." I asked, "Is this a trick question?"

DON'T be surprised to see young women holding hands. It's common for young Taiwanese women who are close friends to hold hands as they walk or shop together.

DON'T expect to receive those nifty little fortune cookies after you finish your meal, fortune cookies are, oddly enough, a Western phenomenon. Invented in San Francisco at the turn of the 20th century, Westerners have come to expect these crunchy golden cookies at Chinese restaurants throughout the world. Don't expect to find them in Asia.

DON'T talk about politics or sex. While your next-door neighbor back home may boast of his sexual conquests on the local cable or radio talk show, sex isn't openly discussed here. This is slowly changing, however, with young Taiwanese keenly tuned into the latest TV programs from Japan and the West and eager to see the latest Hollywood hits, which are heavily promoted here. Taiwan is indeed chock-full-of irony. Conservative Buddhist commentators lecture on morality on late-night TV programs while channels in-between feature sexy tattooed strippers (that strip down to g-strings—not that I've ever noticed) swing around fire poles and hang upside-down from circus rings. Their talent for promoting insomnia on the island is uncanny. In addition, publications that depict explicit encounters between stars or politicians are now sold in most 24-hour convenience stores. The times, they may be a-changing, but in general, most Chinese people are uncomfortable discussing their private sexual thoughts and encounters in public.

DON'T have sex without a condom (as if you needed a **Taipei In A Day** public service announcement?) While it may not be difficult to find a fetching date, Taiwan is not without its share of sexually transmitted diseases. You wouldn't want to leave the island with anything more than a few interesting trinkets and fond memories. To put it bluntly, a half hour of hedonism isn't worth a lifetime of regret. If you engage in risky behavior and consider getting tested for HIV, you might want to wait until you return home. Those who test positive for HIV have three days to pack up their belongings and leave the island, regardless of how long they've been residing. Rest assured, the police will be happy to escort any individuals who test positive for HIV off the island.

Crime

Taipei is quite safe compared with most international cities. Every so often, however, a youth wearing a motorcycle helmet attempts to steal money from an ATM machine or rob a bank. Footage shot a few hours later shows the youth handcuffed and embarrassed at the local police station. Video cameras are conspicuously placed at many street corners and at MRT station platforms. If a bad person (壞人 huai ren) intends to create mischief, he or she is bound to be caught on film and arrested shortly thereafter. On Taiwan, unlike in the West, you are considered guilty until proven innocent, and the public feels little remorse towards criminals. Petty thefts do occur, however, so watch your wallet in crowded shopping areas and at night markets. And even though many females walk alone at night, just to be cautious, it's safer for females to be with a friend.

2-28 Incident (二二八 Er Er Ba)

While there are oral accounts of Japanese brutality during their occupation of Taiwan (1895 to 1945), Japan is credited with developing the infrastructure of Taiwan, instituting a national system of laws, and building modern schools. After Japan surrendered to the Allied Powers on September 2, 1945, Chiang Kai-shek and his troops occupied Taiwan. Locals originally rejoiced at the end of the Japanese colonial era, but Chiang appointed Chen Yi, a harsh Chinese general, to preside over the island. During the Japanese occupation there had been food surpluses. After Chiang's administration and Kuomintang (KMT) followers arrived, however, Taiwanese were faced with a corrupt regime that unjustly allocated land and food. Many feared starvation.

During the evening of February 27, 1947, a KMT State Monopoly Bureau police officer beat up a woman for peddling untaxed cigarettes on the street and accidentally killed a bystander in the process. When a crowd descended on the office of the Taipei State Monopoly Bureau the next day to protest, Governor Chen Yi ordered the police to use machine guns to open fire on the crowd, and a handful of people were killed. Rowdy public demonstrations ensued. Chiang Kai-shek, in China at

the time, sent poorly-trained and hostile Mainland Chinese troops to quash the unrest. On March 10, 1947, the KMT imposed martial law on the island, and a period known as "white terror" ensued, in which "dissonant" citizens were rounded up by police, severely injured or killed. Over thirty thousand Taiwanese were killed in what is now referred to as the 2-28 (二二八 Er Er Ba) incident. For years, the former ruling Nationalist KMT party struck the incident from history books and made public discussion or debate of the incident taboo. That finally began to change after Chiang Ching-kuo, son of Chiang Kai-shek and the second Republic of China (ROC) on Taiwan president, lifted martial law in 1987. Lee Teng-hui, Taiwan's first democratically elected president, later issued a formal apology for the 2-28 incident and introduced legislation that compensated victims' families. February 28 was declared a national holiday of remembrance in 1997.

Visitors can stroll through **2-28 Memorial Peace Park** (二二八和平公園), Shangyang Road, #2 (台北市襄陽路2號), near Taipei Main Station and the Presidential Office Building, as a reminder that painful wounds from the past must be acknowledged and given time to heal in order for society to progress. By MRT depart NTU Hospital Station.

Gay In Taipei

Taipei is progressive by modern standards, the city has been holding public gay pride parades and events for over half a decade that are growing in size and popularity. The first organized homosexual group on Taiwan is reported to have been lesbian group Between Us (我們之間). Soon thereafter, in 1993, a group of male students founded Gay Chat at National Taiwan University (國立台灣大學), or "Taida" (台大 Taida). Fembooks Publishing House & Bookstore (女書店 Nushudian), Taiwan's first lesbian and feminist bookstore, opened near the campus on Xinsheng South road, Section

3, Lane 56, #7, 2nd floor (台北市大安區新生南路3段56巷7號2樓) (02) 2363-8244. The bookstore remains an important source of moral and political support for the gay community on Taiwan.

In 1995, Lambda (浪達社 *Langdashi*), National Taiwan University's first lesbian group, co-sponsored Taiwan's first Gay Lesbian Awareness Day (GLAD). One year later GL (熱愛 *Ruh Ai*), the island's first gay magazine, was published. Coverage included a wedding between a Taiwanese author and his partner. In 1997, police began cracking down on gay social events taking place at 2-28 Memorial Peace Park (二二八和平公園), then known as New Park, and on Changde Street (常德街), considered a gay hangout of sorts. This outraged and mobilized members of the gay community who staged public demonstrations against blatant violations of their civil liberties. In the controversial 1998 Taipei mayorial race, DPP candidate Chen Shui-bien (Taiwan's current president) and Ma Ying-jeou (former Taipei mayor) both pledged to support the 1998 Election Gay Rights Alliance (1998 選舉同志人權聯盟). During the same year the Taiwan Tongzhi Hotline was established: (02) 2392-1970, 2392-1890, 2392-1969. After registering with the Ministry of the Interior two years later, the Taiwan Tongzhi Hotline Association (TTHA) (台灣同志諮詢熱線協會) became the first registered gay organization on Taiwan. According to the group's web site, "Taiwan Tongzhi Hotline Association (TTHA) is an organization that provides people with peer counseling, support networks, and a community resource center." Public services include a hotline, administrative support, events and lectures. To learn more visit the group's web site at http://www.hotline.org.tw.

In 1999, Gin Gin's (晶晶書庫 *Jin Jin Shuju*), Taiwan's first gay (male) bookstore, opened near National Taiwan University within walking distance from exit 1 of the Taipower Building Station (台電大樓站), Roosevelt Road, Section 3, Lane 210, Alley 8, #8 (北市羅斯福路3段210巷8弄8號1樓) (02) 2364-2006. Two years later the justices on Taiwan's high court administered the controversial "535 Interpretation," which stated that random searches (臨檢 *lin cheng*) must be based on probable cause. According to the law, gay individuals could no longer be rounded up and questioned at police stations unless they were under investigation, and police could no longer randomly show up at gay establishments to wreak financial havoc on owners. In spite of the 535 Interpretation, however, Gin Gin's has faced continued harassment, including a smashed storefront window and a questionable raid by Keelung police.

In addition to an annual gay pride parade held in June that winds through Taipei's Xinyi district, gay-sponsored events are sometimes held at **2-28 Memorial Peace Park** (二二八和平公園). Taipei pubs **Fresh** and **The Source**, both found under "Taipei Pub Guide (台北Pub 指南)," are also cool hangouts to meet both gay and gay-friendly people. Although some older Taiwanese may frown upon gay and alternative lifestyles, many younger Taiwanese are open to having gay friends and meeting gay people from abroad.

Lotto

Before Taiwan initiated the national lotto draw, residents would hold onto their receipts for a draw every third month. Now that "lotto fever" seems to have hit the island, however, many residents donate their receipts to charitable organizations, which place containers at fast food restaurants and supermarkets. Lotto stands appear in cities around the island. Who knows, maybe your six out of forty-two lucky lotto numbers will appear while you're visiting. The "small lotto" draw takes place every Monday, Wednesday and Friday while the "big lotto" is held every Tuesday and Thursday. Unlike in the West, lotto tickets aren't sold at 7-Eleven and other convenience stores (although seemingly just about everything else is). Lotto tickets cost NT $50 (US $1.50) per game.

A Funny Thing Happened...

I Love Condoms... Er, Popcorn

After living in Taipei for less than a month, a Taiwanese friend who had just returned from studying abroad brought me to her high school reunion. About twenty of her former classmates and I were sitting around a large table at a casual restaurant, snacking on appetizers. After nibbling on a few kernels of popcorn, I mustered the courage to try and impress everyone with my Chinese. "*Wo ai bao shien tao!*" I proudly stated. The room seemed to grow quiet and the reaction at the table was immediate: everyone turned to face me with a look of either shock or bewilderment. Embarrassed, my friend quickly turned to me and said, "You love what?" I caught my mistake too late—what I meant to say was "*Wo ai bao mi hua!*," or "I love popcorn!" What I had said was, "I love condoms!" A moment later, everyone in the room erupted with laughter, either from my Freudian slip or because my face had turned redder than a hot chili pepper. ^_*

The Toilet Requests Napkins

When I arrived on Taiwan I noticed that many bathrooms in traditional areas not only did not have traditional sit-down toilets, but they also did not have toilet paper. Most restaurants had squat toilets and, if lucky, some napkins placed behind the sink. I quickly learned how useful those little miniature tissue packets were! For this reason, tissues are often handed out to advertise new products, services or to promote politicians. Now THAT'S an appropriate time to think about the local candidates! At a local café I decided to muster up the courage to request some tissues prior to entering the restroom. I was surprised to find the young female servers behind the counter chuckling at my request in Mandarin of, "The toilet requests napkins." "It does? Did it tell you that?" I sheepishly accepted a packet of tissues and learned how to say, "The bathroom does not have toilet paper" (洗手間沒有衛生紙 *sheeshoujian meiyo wei sheng zhi*). ^_*

Not Foreign To Me

I was using my laptop in a small Guandu café when three young Taiwanese children started talking about me in the local dialect of Taiwanese (閩南語 *milanyu*). "A foreigner, look..." The youngest child said, "Where? I don't see any foreigner," replied the second. Then the older child exclaimed, "Right there! He's wearing glasses." I turned around and replied in Taiwanese, "What foreign guy? I don't see any foreign guy. I'm Taiwanese. Anyone can see I'm a Taiwanese." They were completely stunned, and as I walked away I heard the youngest child say, "See? I TOLD you he wasn't a foreigner!" ^_*

My Worst Sexual Nightmare

After I had moved into my new Taipei apartment, an elderly, somewhat senile woman continually called asking to speak to "Mr. Chou." This happened around nine o'clock in the evening, several times a week. After the eleventh time or so, I decided to have some fun. Much to her surprise, I would answer the phone in English, "Oh, my GOD, thank you for CALLING!!" in an excited, suggestive tone. You can imagine my shock and embarrassment when, one evening, I heard my mother's voice on the other end. I didn't answer the phone in that fashion after that. ^_*

Expiration Date: 2999

My international driver's license had expired. Since I wouldn't be returning home anytime soon and was unable to purchase a new one until my next visit (international licenses are not available on Taiwan), I simply wrote a "2" over the "1" in 1999. There. Now, instead of being valid for another year, my license was good for another millennium!

Unfortunately, the two police officers that stopped me at a red light in a quiet area in Tienmu, Taipei didn't find it so humorous. ^_*

All Out Of Love Songs

Taiwan is indeed one of the most interesting and exciting places to visit. Taiwanese work late into the night, and for this reason, night markets, convenience stores and supermarket chains remain open late or twenty-four hours. Taipei definitely gives New York a run for the money as being the city that never sleeps.

Taiwan is also a land of stark contradictions. While the majority of Taiwanese come from traditional households where religious traditions are strictly adhered to, it's not difficult to spot "spicy" girls (辣美 la mei) riding around on mopeds or sitting at road-side stands selling the legal but notorious betelnut (檳榔 bing lang), which contains the addictive arecoline drug.

You would never guess from the chaotic way Taiwanese people drive that their music of preference is predominantly dulcet love songs. Indeed, Taiwan is perhaps the only area in the world where Air Supply (of "All Out Of Love" fame) and REO Speedwagon ("Keep On Loving You") still top the charts, and billboards of Michael Jackson sometimes appear as if the self-proclaimed King of Pop had just released "Thriller." Also, for some bizarre reason, Chinese people seem to flip for the Eagles' classic "Hotel California." Chinese music stations play this song and it's one of the most requested English songs at KTVs and pubs that feature live music.

About Face!

Much has been written about the importance of face (面子 mian zi) in Asia. In one regard, face applies to status, and Chinese people, in particular, are extremely status-conscious. You may find it ironic that some people will nickel and dime over a bag of fruit, coffee or vegetables at the local day market, but won't think twice about purchasing expensive designer clothes, fancy cars and lavish jewelry to impress family, friends and neighbors.

On the other hand, there is a popular Chinese idiom, "Yi fen chian, yi fen huo," or "cost determines quality," and this holds particularly true on Taiwan. Imitation goods may be a dime a dozen (literally), but their quality tends to be lacking.

The concept of face also applies to the workplace and social situations. In general, "giving face" means more than being polite. It saves a professor from being embarrassed in front of his class or a superior from being embarrassed in front of her colleagues. Face leaves someone with a sense of dignity rather than humility in a social situation. For instance, a student realizes that the professor has made a mistake. However, instead of correcting the error in front of the class, the professor is approached afterwards in private. This avoids public humiliation. The same goes for the workplace. Get the picture?

When I had been on Taiwan for less than a week I quickly learned to appreciate the face aspect of Chinese culture. I had been exploring Taipei on my landlord's decrepit motorbike and continued to go straight on Zhongxiao East Road, Section 1, instead of making a right onto Zhongshan North Road, which leads north to Shilin and Tienmu. Unbeknownst to this naïve international traveler at the time, riding mopeds and motorcycles in front of Taipei Main Station is against the law, and I was duly pulled over. The officer, unable to communicate well in English, asked to see my driver's license. Fumbling around in my knapsack for my international driving permit, I nervously pulled out and handed the officer my New York State driver's license. The officer handed back the license, glanced nervously at the other five local Taiwanese mopedists he had pulled over and had been busily writing citations for, and whispered forcefully in my direction, "Five minutes! You go!" Had I ridden off immediately it would have given the officer the appearance of having no face, or power and authority, in the eyes of the other motorists. By waiting the five minutes, I allowed him to appear as if he were giving me the same fine. I quietly thanked the officer before riding away.

You may be surprised to find that some Taiwanese people act particularly rude given the emphasis on Confucian politeness and social correctness at the heart of Chinese society. By "rude" I mean throwing used cigarette butts onto the street, littering, or spitting blood-red betelnut juice onto the pavement, which leaves a rather nasty-looking purple stain. Signs hang in the area in English and Chinese, explicitly stating, "No Smoking" or "No Chewing Gums Of Any Sort." How could this be? While it is especially important for Chinese people to "give face" to friends, relatives and loved ones, it is not necessary to give face to strangers. For this reason, some Taiwanese people think nothing of pushing their way onto a crowded MRT train during rush hour while the poor souls who are attempting to leave the train are now forced to push their way out. This is a veritable nightmare, by the way, particularly once the MRT arrives at its final destination. This rudeness may stem from vast numbers of people being crowded into small spaces. Gradually, over time, some Taiwanese people must have lost patience with one another. It is also unfortunate that some young people feel no compunction sitting in Priority Seating (博愛座 bo ai zuo) and don't get up when elderly, handicapped, pregnant women or women with small children walk onto the MRT. As an aside, however, every good batch of ripened apples sometimes contains a few bad unripened ones.

If you stand too long trying to analyze the concept of face on a road on Taiwan, you're likely to lose your face—literally!

Think you've seen road rage? Actor Jack Nickelson pulling out his 9-Iron and smashing in the windshield of the Jaguar that cut in front of him on the exit ramp of a crowded L.A. expressway comes pretty close. Not to scare you, but even the most gentle of Taiwanese people seem to turn into untamed lions behind the wheel. It's uncanny. What happened to the search for spiritual enlightenment and kindness toward all living creatures?

By and large, however, Taiwanese are particularly hospitable towards international guests, and you shouldn't encounter any problems asking directions or finding your way around. Compared with people in other countries, Taiwanese are generally welcoming and helpful toward international travelers. Put on your best face and enjoy your stay!

All About Guanxi

Arriving in Asia to network and make business contacts has as much to do about building face (and showing your face) as it does to build relationships. To get things done on Taiwan and in China, you need to have a connected local contact to introduce you and your company to important people. This relationship building can be roughly translated as "guanxi," the grease that gets the squeaky wheel rolling. A good place to start would be the local chambers of commerce. Remember, establishing an Asian presence is all about guanxi.

"Barber Shops"

Now that prostitution has been officially outlawed on the island, prostitutes have found creative ways to drum up business. If you spot a "barber shop" with cloudy windows and a conspicuous white and red swirling lamp outside, chances are the attendants inside employ new methods of "blowing" and "styling." You should be able to distinguish between legitimate hair stylists and "barber shops." Be sure to avoid these kinds of facilities, the seedy looking characters hanging around outside don't appear welcoming, and you wouldn't want to return home with a "permanent" reminder of your visit.

On a similar note, some smaller motels offer three-hour "rest periods." Thanks in part to aggressive advertising on the Internet by companies selling spy devices and a public that feeds on scandal, it's not advisable to "rest" at these lodging establishments.

Dating On Taiwan

Taiwanese are undoubtedly some of the most beautiful people on the planet. Compared with the latest baggy styles in the West, you'll probably be amazed at how tight-fitting clothes are here. If you intend to stay for more than a week, be sure to bring your own wardrobe. Most clothing is tailored for the local population, who tend to be quite thin! Local residents wear spandex, short skirts and tight-fitting jeans that seem to hug every curve of their incredibly slender (according to Western standards) bodies.

It's not difficult to find a date on Taiwan, the personals on http://www.OnTaiwan. com are a good place to start. Taiwanese people are eager to befriend international guests, as they are naturally curious about visitors to the island. Much the way Asians appear "exotic" to Westerners back home, Taiwanese billboards, magazine ads and television commercials are rife with images of sexy Western models.

In spite of their alluring appearance, however, traditional Taiwanese tend not to express their sexuality the way Westerners might. For instance, if you're male and are spotted conspicuously checking out alluring women on Zhongxiao East Road, Section 4 (台北市忠孝東路4段), around Sogo Department Store, you may hear a local female refer to you as a "seh lang" or horny wolf, out to "pao nioh," or chase cows.

How To Find Love On Taiwan

So the fetching female at the Betelnut Pub rejected your snappy come-on of, "Empirically speaking I find you very attractive, would you care for a Taiwan Beer?" What could've possibly gone wrong? You rehearsed the line a hundred times before summoning the courage to approach her and thought for sure she would appreciate an ice-cold local favorite. Is there a better way to communicate with members of the opposite sex? You bet there is.

Listen, before you partake on your quest to find amoré it's important to recognize some of the cultural differences, many of which are subtle, between Taiwanese and people from the West. If you understand and respect Taiwanese culture it will be easier for you to communicate here, and good communication is the key to having good relationships.

For starters, dating on Taiwan is very different from dating in the West. Back home, dating typically begins in junior high school, and on weekends, movie theaters, pizza shops and shopping malls overflow with adolescents eager to get to know their latest beaus. On Taiwan, however, junior high and high school are mind-numbingly competitive, and teens study assiduously to keep their grades up as they prepare to take high school and college entrance exams.

Therefore, dating on Taiwan typically begins in college. Around this time young Taiwanese begin socializing together at Karaoke bars and KTV studios, small rooms where friends delight in eating and drinking while singing their favorite songs. Once upon a Taipei time young people also watched movies together at small MTV studios, but since most households now have at least one DVD player, MTV studios are likely to become a part of Taiwan's pop culture past. You can also spot young people sharing laughter, coffee, tea and sumptuous native and international foods at restaurants and night markets throughout the island.

In the West, it is not uncommon to date more than one person at a time to better understand which qualities one likes and dislikes. On Taiwan, however, it is more common for people to socialize in groups and remain friends for a considerable amount of time. If a man and woman are friends for a lengthy period of time and truly enjoy spending time with one another they agree to become a couple. While friends may hold hands in the West, a couple holding hands on Taiwan is taken as a more serious gesture.

Relationships on Taiwan also tend to be more exclusive. If you are a foreigner (外 國人 waiguoren), and a Taiwanese person wants to go out with you, he or she may assume that the two of you will be in a committed relationship from the outset. If you are uncomfortable getting too serious it's a good idea to remain friends and communicate your feelings so there are no misunderstandings. Taiwanese tend to be traditional when it comes to love and marriage. If you are being introduced to his or her parents, chances are you are considered a prospective spouse. Are those wedding bells I hear?

But let's not talk about marriage, you're still trying to figure out how to meet someone, right? On Taiwan (and in most places, for that matter), love comes along when you least expect it. Go dancing, bowling, or take a stroll through a local night market. You're not going to meet anyone by keeping your goldfish at home company. While the fish may appreciate the attention it'll do nothing to improve your social life.

While turning on the tube may be a waste of time in terms of "getting out there" in the West, some Taiwanese find a partner for life after he or she appears on a television show. This is because, on Taiwan, people call in to television stations to say they are interested in meeting someone (a common person like you or I, not pop stars like Madonna), and more often than not the person receives the messages. Popular dating shows include "The Dating Game" (男生女生配 Nanshen Nushen Pay), a bona fide hit with young people, and "About Man & Woman" (非常男女 Feichang Nannu), where many couples become sweethearts forever. The latter show has been on hiatus as of late, but expect to see more episodes and similar shows in the near future.

Nowadays, more young people are getting virtually active. A popular English site to find a dream lover on Taiwan is http://www.OnTaiwan.com. Taiwan also offers a plethora of pubs, restaurants and hotels (many with discos) to choose from. Heck, you could even go hospital-hopping, although the physicians may not appreciate that much. Having a good attitude means having a good time. Just be yourself. If people smile at you, smile back. Finding true love anywhere may not be easy, but if you're a nice person, making friends on Taiwan should be easier than making fishball soup. Happy hotel hopping!

Get With The Fad, Dad!

Taiwanese are quick to pick up on the latest fads from the West and Japan. This may be because, while Taiwanese companies produce goods that are exported around the world, many Taiwanese people believe that their homemade products don't compare in quality to those produced in the West or Japan. As large multinational corporations (MNCs) have discovered, the right combination of product, placement, promotion and timing can lead to quick, hefty profits. Japan, in particular, successfully capitalizes on its close proximity to the island by moving large quantities of a product into place just in time for a well-crafted marketing blitz.

Taiwanese people tend to trust advertisements they read in newspapers, hear on the radio and see on television. If a company is willing to shell out big bucks on an expensive television and radio marketing campaign, Taiwanese people figure the product must be of substantial quality and worth purchasing. Just take a stroll through any major department store or shopping district. Notice which products are selling well? Chances are, it's the name brands with flashy ad campaigns.

Although Japan had occupied the island for fifty years, many Taiwanese feel ambivalence rather than animosity, claiming they suffered harsher treatment and worse fates at the hands of Chiang Kai-shek and his administration. That may or may not be true, but what is true is that Japanese products tend to sell surprisingly well on Taiwan.

The Japanese have been keen to market their products by emphasizing high quality with sensitivity towards and an appreciation for the local culture. Just turn on the TV while you're in town and check out any of the ads for Suntory whisky, imported cars, or Japanese household products to understand what I'm referring to. Ads feature local families showing affection for one another and enjoying their daily lives while consuming Japanese goods. The ads for Suntory whisky are particularly clever. A Taiwanese father and his estranged daughter communicate better after a couple of shots of the whisky. Former local Taiwan classmates are better able to relate after the famous "clink ka clink!" sound of ice landing in the whisky glass. And here's my personal favorite, the imported Japanese whisky breaks writer's block for talented, well-known local musicians, and subsequently helps them to perform better in the recording studio. Imagine all the talented musicians who had no idea that a few shots of this dry Japanese whisky would forever enable them to crank out number one hits? Where was Suntory and its clever marketing campaign during the one-hit wonder eighties?

Japanese soap operas are also particularly popular with many young Taiwanese, who feel that more thought and creativity goes into the story and more work goes into the production and post-production compared with shows produced locally. Young people also tend to like Japanese pop, rock, and dance music, which basically sounds much like Taiwanese pop music, aside from the higher-pitched and slightly more whiny Japanese female crooners. In a nutshell, recycled melodies and formulaic lyrics are recorded by young singers, bubble-gum packaged and unloaded onto the ears of unsuspecting teeny-boppers or the unfortunate elderly souls getting their hair done at the local salon. "What is this noise?" they complain as indignant young hairdressers remove the final rollers from newly-permed silver quaffs. You may be surprised to hear that the latest hits bombarding the airwaves sound much like theme songs from children's television programs.

Take a stroll through Ximending in Taipei to see why young people are keen on the latest trends that arrive from the Land of the Rising Sun. From loud, colorful sticker machines, animated comic books and video arcade games to high-heeled platform shoes, all-too-cute dolls and colorful little trinkets for decorating cell phones and back packs, to wild hair-do's and funky clothing, it appears as if a Japanese tidal wave of music, fun and fashion has invaded Taiwan's youth culture. If you don't take it all too seriously, you may come to appreciate some of it yourself.

Macao Custard Tart, Anyone?

Expatriates are often amazed at the rate in which local businesses open and close. Clothing stores that had opened only a few months earlier may be out of business by the time you decide you like the new style enough to buy it, and many local restaurants last no more than a few years. This could be attributed to poor planning on the part of business owners, but it could also be due in part to the fad culture that persists. For instance, for some odd reason, egg custard tarts that are popular in Macao, the small island just south of Hong Kong, became the rage on Taiwan several years ago. Macao egg custard shops opened all over the city, and just about every bakery began selling their version of the golden brown yellow tart. Tarts were given as gifts and devoured by local residents as if they contained some sort of hidden panacea for aging, baldness and sexual dysfunction. A year later, however, you couldn't find a Macao custard tart even if you tried. What happened? More than likely, once the tart craze ended, everyone jumped off the Macao custard tart bandwagon, leaving little more than a few thousand empty tart boxes and stacks of promotional literature in warehouses and rubbish bins throughout the city. Macao custard tart, anyone?

Politics and Government

Taiwan has a Legislative Yuan, where representatives are elected for three-year terms, an Executive Yuan, which includes the president and vice-president, an Examination Yuan, made up of civil servants, a National Assembly, where members have no term limits, and a Control Yuan, where members are appointed by the president to six-year terms and are confirmed by the National Assembly. The president appoints fifteen justices to serve eight-year terms in the Judicial Yuan (lowered from nine years starting in 2008), and there is also a separate lower court, a court of appeals and a high court of appeals where justices are appointed to life terms. Taiwanese tend to be fervent about politics as shouting matches and all-out brawls are sometimes broadcast from the Legislative Yuan.

Taiwan has over ninety registered political parties but four remain the largest: The Kuomintang (KMT) (中國國民黨), the pro-indepence-leaning Democratic Progressive Party (DPP) (民主進步黨), the smaller pro-reunification New Party (NP) (新黨) and the newer People First Party (PFP) (親民黨). The Green Party (綠色本土清新黨) won a seat in the National Assembly in 1996 but doesn't wield much influence.

Since former president Chiang Ching-kuo (蔣經國) lifted martial law in 1987, Taiwan has rapidly become a full-fledged democracy with a vibrant free-market economy. Native-born Lee Teng-hui (李登輝) spent eight years in office before official democratic elections were held, and he easily won the first direct democratic presidential election in 1996. Lee was succeeded by Democratic Progressive Party (DPP) candidate Chen Shui-bian (陳水扁), who shocked the ruling KMT by defeating Lee's hand-picked successor Lien Chan (連戰). President Chen and Vice-President Annette Lu (呂秀蓮 *Lu Shiu Lian*) took office on May 20, 2000 and were subsequently re-elected in a controversial 2004 presidential race. During his second term, President Chen found himself mired in political controversy over scandal allegations involving his family.

More recently, the president caused a stir when he ordered that all statues of Chiang Kai-shek be removed from Taiwan's military bases and renamed Taiwan's international airport, removing Chiang's name. He subsequently created a brouhaha when he changed the name of "National Chiang Kai-shek Memorial Hall" to "National Taiwan Democracy Memorial Hall," over objections from the KMT and "pan-blue" camp, contending that the memorial hall has been the site of significant pro-democracy events. This is because the president and "pan-green" coalition view Chiang as an unrelenting dictator. But to better understand the root of President Chen's and his party's fervency, one would need to delve a bit into Taiwan's painful historical past.

On December 10, 1979, a large group of pro-democracy protesters were beaten and arrested in Kaohsiung in what has become known as the "Kaohsiung Incident." Many of the protesters had worked for Formosa Magazine, a publication used by the opposition to decry human rights abuses by the KMT. Vice-President Lu was one of the "Kaohsiung Eight" principle organizers tried in a military court and sentenced to twelve years in prison. President Chen, a young attorney and recent law graduate of National Taiwan University, Taiwan's top-ranking private university, had volunteered to defend the Kaohsiung Eight. The Kaohsiung Incident is said to have galvanized Taiwanese not only on Taiwan but also around the world, and eventually led to the lifting of martial law in the Republic of China.

Due in large part to economic concerns, the Kuomintang trounced President Chen and his party in the 2008 legislative elections, winning 86 of 113 seats. For the presidency former president Lee may endorse former Kaohsiung mayor and DPP premier Frank Hsieh (謝長廷 *Hsieh Zhang-ting*). James Soong (宋楚瑜 *Soong Zu Yu*), former premier under Lee Teng-hui and leader of the People First Party (PFP), the party he founded, is expected to throw his political weight into the presidential ring again; favored to win, however, is former Taipei mayor and current KMT heavyweight Ma Ying-jeou (馬英九). (In 2006, KMT veteran Hau Lung-bin won the Taipei mayoral race.)

Pop Goes The Culture

Taiwanese take pride in local artists, musicians and entertainers that make it big, particularly on the international stage. Perhaps one of the most famous Taiwanese singers to reach international acclaim, Teresa Teng (鄧麗君 *Teng Li Jun*) (January 29, 1953 to May 8, 1995), is remembered for her dulcet voice and captivating live performances. Her songs, including one of her most famous, "The Moon Represents My Heart" (月亮代表我的心), are still heard regularly at KTV studios and have been covered by some of Asia's biggest contemporary pop stars. After her sudden death from an asthma attack, she was buried on a remote Taipei County mountainside where her tomb continues to receive visits from loyal fans that pay their final respects.

Native-born, award-winning movie director **Ang Lee** (李安) draws large crowds whenever he returns from abroad to promote a film. Born in Pingtung (屏東) in 1954, Lee is known for tackling controversial topics such as interracial family life ("Pushing Hands") (推手), the rigors of traditional family life in modern society ("Eat Drink Man Woman") (飲食男女) and homosexuality ("Brokeback Mountain") (斷背山). Other Taiwanese directors who have received critical acclaim both at home and abroad include **Hou Hsiao-hsien** (侯孝賢) ("A Time to Live and a Time to Die") (童年往事), ("City of Sadness") (悲情城市) and **Tsai Ming-liang** (蔡明亮) ("Rebels of the Neon God") (青少年哪吒), ("Vive l'Amour") (愛情萬歲). Many upcoming Taiwanese actors and directors become famous at the annual **Golden Horse Film Festival** (台北金馬影展), the Asian equivalent of the Oscars, held on Taiwan during the fall or winter. Since arriving on Taiwan in 1997, the music and entertainment scene has changed drastically. While teens with adorable (好可愛 *hao ke ai*) images and bubble gum pop songs packaged for variety shows and the radio quickly come and go, proficient musicians and persistent Taiwanese bands now dominate the music scene.

May Day (五月天) are five seemingly irreverent Taiwanese men in their mid to late-twenties that perform catchy pop rock songs. Interestingly enough, their songs are performed mostly in Taiwanese, which has helped to make them a local sensation.

The melodic May Day blend of music is very Beatles meets pop punk, a la Blink 182 or Green Day, but their dulcet ballads could be performed by any international pop star (with English lyrics, of course). You can spot these five funny fellows on MRT billboards, bus advertisements and on TV commercials plugging everything from coffee and cell phones to national calling plans.

Compared with most of today's young artists, **Wu Bai** (伍佰) is an older, more established Taiwanese rock musician. With his tough persona, Wu Bai was a natural choice to do commercials for Taiwan Beer. Wu Bai is said to have received his entertainment moniker because his uncle gave him NT $500 (*wu bai*) every time he got an "A" in school. Wu Bai performs mostly in the Taiwanese dialect and is known for his unique native Taiwanese rock sound. Wu Bai's back-up band is called China Blue, and young people pack stadiums and large venues for Wu Bai & China Blue concerts.

Born May 2, 1974, Taiwanese rock musician **Zhang Zhen Yue** (張震嶽) and his band Free Night thrilled loyal fans with a recent tour across the U.S. His biggest Mandarin hits include "Love Me Don't Go" (愛我別走) and the punchy, anthemic "Freedom" (自由). Since obtaining pop stardom in the 1990s, Zhang has experimented with a heavier sound that blends punk rock and acid house with harsher lyrics. His public image also reveals a more sardonic side to his persona. On a recent overseas tour Zhang brought with him boisterous native rapper **MC Hot Dog** (熱狗), whose crass Mandarin and Taiwanese lyrics sometimes offend and often poke fun at Taiwan's bubble gum pop culture and starlets.One of MC Hot Dog's rap offerings is "I Love Tai Mei" (我愛台美). "Tai Mei" is short for Taiwan La Mei (台灣 辣美), or Taiwan's spicy girls. What's not to love?

Taiwanese pop diva **Zhang Hui-mei** (張惠妹), referred to as "Ah-mei" by her legion of loyal fans, is an aboriginal woman from Taitung (台東), southeastern Taiwan. Ah-mei burst onto the Taiwanese music scene in the early 1990's with her unrelenting smash hit "Jie Mei" (姊妹) and has gone on to sell millions of records worldwide. It's unfortunate that these records can no longer be purchased at two enormous Tower Records stores on Taiwan (or Tower Records anywhere, for that matter), as illegal music and movie downloading is taking a bite out of more than the artists' bottom line.

Religion On Taiwan

Religion plays an integral role on Taiwan, and most Taiwanese have alters for worship in their homes. Alters are usually found on the top floor, and in Taipei you can usually see these red alter lights aglow on the MRT from Yuanshan to Danshui. The first three stops after leaving Taipei Main Station, Zhongshan, Shuanglien and Minquan (Minchuan) West Road, are underground, and you won't see much aside from billboards and, if you're traveling on a weekend, lots of people.

While strolling around the city, these red alter lights may lead you to believe you've happened upon a red light district. Not so! Taiwanese people use red alter lights to help light red candles on top of their alters, and these electric red lights remain lit long after the red candles have gone out. The color red is considered lucky in Chinese culture, so red clothing, colors and lanterns are particularly apparent just before, during and after Chinese New Year, and during the Lantern Festival, a celebration that marks the culmination of the Chinese Lunar New Year. If you visit Taiwan during this time, expect to see streets illuminated with bright red lanterns.

Wooden prayer altars appear somewhat like old-fashioned hope chests or dressers used in the West for storing jewelry and clothes. There are cabinet drawers on either side for storing ghost money to offer to ancestors and gods. Ghost money to offer for ancestors to spend in heaven is yellow with a silver square in the middle. Money burned as an offering to the gods contains a shiny gold square in the middle. Ghost money has different designs, some have ancient Chinese writing scrolled across while others have pictures of clothes and other items ancestors could use in heaven (let's not give Nike or The Gap any ideas).

At home prayer alters and at city temples, Taiwanese people (拜拜 *bai bai*), or hold prayer ceremonies. Most temples have slightly different prayer rituals, which residents inquire about at a small information counter towards the entrance before praying. The basic rituals of prayer for each temple, however, remain generally the same. If at home, a Taiwanese person will first light red candles on the alter. Then, he or she will place food on the alter, which typically includes fruits, cakes and vegetables--but can also be as uncommon as a pizza! These food items are offered to ancestors and to various Buddhist gods. The person then lights incense and holds them at his or her chest, deep in prayer. After he or she has finished praying, the incense are waved to and fro, usually three times, and are placed inside a canister. Food consumed after being offered to ancestors and gods in prayer is considered lucky. Bon appetite!

At a temple, the worshipper enters the temple gates, usually guarded by statues of lions, tigers or other wild animals to protect the gods and those in the courtyard. Some of these temple courtyards, which may contain ponds, exotic trees or small waterfalls, are truly astounding. The worshipper enters the main prayer area of the temple and places food items to offer in prayer on a table, just inside the main prayer area. The worshipper then lights anywhere from three to twelve incense and bows his head while facing an image of a deity. After praying, he moves the incense up and down three times, hopeful that the deity will answer his prayers. Three incense are then placed into a large cauldron called a qian. If the worshipper chooses to pray to other deities within the temple, if there is more than one alter, he will bring his incense to the next statue, face the next image, bow his head and pray. After the *bai bai*, or prayer rituals, are complete, the food offered in prayer is consumed.

On special occasions, such as Chinese New Year, large red canisters are lit outside homes and offices, and ghost money is thrown inside the canister. This is to bring prosperity to the home or business. Unsuspecting travelers beware! Firecrackers are sometimes tossed haphazardly into the street, near the curb. Taiwanese people are not trying to scare you away, they're scaring away evil spirits from the business or neighborhood, thus ensuring luck will come.

Buddhism (佛教 *Fojiao*), which promotes morality, selflessness, and kindness toward all living creatures, prevails on the island. Siddartha Gautama (563 to 483 B.C.), an Indian prince, is credited with founding the religion. Guatama married at sixteen, had a son and lived lavishly for a decade until he began to question the rigid Brahman caste system of the day that led many to live in squalor. After observing a destitute monk content with his life, the Indian prince began a lifelong search for wisdom, value, and spiritual truth. He came to be called "Buddha" or "The Enlightened One" after his long journey led him to a banyan tree, called the "tree of wisdom." During this evening, which Buddhists refer to as "the sacred night," he arrived at "four noble truths." Guatama concluded that life is characterized by suffering, suffering originates in desire, suffering can only end by ending desire, and the steps that lead to the ending of suffering can be attained by following an eight-fold path: having the right views, intentions, speech, conduct, livelihood, effort, mindfulness, and concentration can end suffering, at which point nirvana, or eternal bliss and saintliness, can be attained.

There are many Buddhist gods (over eight thousand!), and Taiwanese people pray to different gods for different reasons. The principal Buddhist gods worshiped on Taiwan are **Guanyin** (觀音), the Goddess of Mercy, for whom the enormous mountain on Bali across from Danshui is dedicated, **Matzu** (馬祖), Goddess of the Sea, **Tu Di Gong** (土地公), the God of Land, and **Yuexia Laoren** (月下老人), "The Old Man Under The Moon," the God of Love. Chinese people believe that this elderly cupid determines who is meant to be together and ties a red line from one person's ankle to another. People both young and old pray to this elderly cupid for a good marriage. If he had gotten my parents together, however, he must have had one too many cocktails and applied his mystical power with reckless abandon! According to Buddhism, Yuexia Laoren pre-ordains all relationships throughout the world. **Guan Gong** (關公), the God of War, was a famous soldier who lived during the Three Kingdoms period in China. After he died he became immortalized in the eyes of the Chinese, who admired him for emerging victorious after every battle. Guan Gong temples with stupendous statues of the former war hero, found throughout the island, are particularly popular with businesspeople and law enforcement officials.

Taoism (道教 Daojiao) is a stark contrast to Buddhism or the teachings of Confucius. "**Tao**" or "**Dao**" (道) roughly translates to "the path" or "the way" to attain spiritual enlightenment. However, unlike Buddhism, which dictates its followers must follow an eight-fold path, Taoism draws upon nature and the unknown wonders of the universe. In Taoism, a balance, or harmony of opposites, exists in nature: yin (dark forces) and yang (light forces), black and white, male and female, light and dark, love and hate, Santa Claus and the Grinch, Luke

Skywalker and Darth Vader... you get the idea. The teachings of Taoism are found in the Tao Te Ching, an obscure collection of edicts written by Lao Tzu. Lao Tzu, (also spelled Laotzu, Laotzi, Lao Tse, or Lao Tzi) a philosopher who lived from 604 to 531 B.C., is believed to be the founder of Taoism. The debate continues as to whether he actually existed, however, or whether he worked alone, as some scholars contend that the Tao Te Ching may have been written by two or more individuals.

Taoists believe that the "Tao," a powerful, omnipotent force, flows through all things in the universe, and the goal of Taoism is to become one with the Tao. Therefore, pure Taoists don't believe in deities, as Buddhists do, nor do they believe in the scientific "big bang" theory in the creation of the universe nor in any secular explanation for creation. To Taoists, the Tao itself created the universe. (Most modern Taoists, however, belong to a combination of Taoist and Buddhist sects.) Taoists seek the answers to life's conundrums by searching within, through deep meditation, and by observing the world around them. On meditation and becoming one with the Tao, or this omnipotent force, Lao Tze had said, "Be still like a mountain and flow like a great river."

Taoists believe that for every action there is a reaction, if you act kindly towards another, that kindness, in turn, will be reciprocated. Taoists also believe strongly that everything in life happens for a reason, and advocate non-action (無為 wu wei) to allow nature to run its course. Taoists oppose interference in the natural flow of life events. For instance, Taoists would oppose the construction of a dam, regardless of its social or economic benefits, because it blocks the natural flow of water from the river to the sea. This attitude may not be prevalent in modern, capitalist societies, which emphasize development and economic growth; however, from a cultural standpoint, it may help to explain why Eastern people from a traditional Taoist society may come across as more passive than their Western counterparts.

Taoism, with its emphasis on balance, health and well-being, is at the heart of Eastern medicine. Chinese doctors, for instance, prescribe remedies that enable patients to nurture the life energy (氣 chi) that flows throughout the body. While many remedies may appear superstitious to Westerners, such as advising someone with a bad cold or flu not to consume cold foods and beverages and advising someone with an injured foot not to eat bananas, traditional Chinese medicine tends to emphasize natural remedies.

Taoism is also at the root of many forms of Chinese martial arts, particularly tai chi (太極拳 taijichuan). While practicing tai chi, Chinese people relax the body, focus the mind, and channel the intrinsic energy (氣 chi), irrespective of nearby noise. It's truly a sight to see! If you have an opportunity, visit a park or one of Taipei's memorial halls (National Taiwan Democracy or National Dr. Sun Yat-sen Memorial Hall) as the sun rises to catch a glimpse of Chinese people perform traditional techniques.

There are over eighty thousand Taoist temples on Taiwan, (most temples on the island are Taoist), stop by one during your stay. In Taipei, visit a historic temple, such as Longshan Temple or Xintian Temple, to admire the intricate colors and designs, ornate decorations and traditional Chinese architecture. You can distinguish between Taoist and Buddhist temples because in Buddhist temples, people offer only fruits and vegetables to the gods (no meat or animal-related products of any kind are offered, including foods prepared with animal fat). In Taoist temples, however, the gods enjoy just about any kind of food, from cakes, fruits, and vegetables, to seafood, burgers and sometimes even pizza.

Confucius

The teachings of **Confucius** (孔子 Kong Zi) (551 to 479 B.C.), a philosopher who lived during the Spring and Autumn Period, a time of tremendous political and social upheaval in China, have had a tremendous influence on Chinese society and the world. Just think about what those fortunes inside the cookies may read like had Confucius not lived. Confucius was born in the Lu district's village of Chou, in China's central Shandong province. Although born wealthy, Confucius' father died when he was only three, and his widowed mother raised him in poverty. Confucius was perspicacious, however, and realized at a young age that striving and personal aspiration could lead to success. ("Our greatest glory consists not never in failing, but in rising every time we fail.") At age fifteen, he began to study assiduously; as a consequence, he was chosen by a noble family to manage its farm, animals and land, and was later hired to teach the children of the manor Chinese classics and the importance of benevolence, ritual and virtue. He married at nineteen and had one son and two daughters.

Confucius briefly served as the Minister of Justice in his home district of Lu where he attended local government ceremonies and learned the rituals of the elite. He became deeply troubled by warring political factions in the region, attributing this increase in lawlessness to a lack of morality and virtue on the part of government officials. Confucius held great admiration for the Duke of Chou, a leader during his youth, and longed for a return to this "golden age" when art and culture flourished. When the Chou Empire began to implode, Confucius attempted, in vain, to convince local political leaders to adhere to tradition in order to remedy the chaotic political situation. After his mother died in 527 B.C., he wandered about the land, teaching to small crowds. He returned to his home district of Lu and died relatively poor and unknown at age 73. If not for his loyal students, who recorded many of his teachings and conversations in a book entitled, **The Analects**, the profound wisdom of Confucius may never have shaped the development of China.

The basic tenets of his teachings were having an appropriate state of being (仁 ren), moral doing (義 yi) and the ends (利 li), which can roughly be translated as profit. Confucius warned against the profit motive as it led to insidious behavior. Confucius also stressed filial piety (孝 xiao), virtue (德 de), good manners (禮 li) and loyalty (忠 zhong). Benevolence, or love for others, was a necessary requisite for good government, and subsequently, good society. Confucius taught that vying for personal profit or gain led to avarice and a breakdown of morals in society. Having the right conduct, duty and rituals, and fulfilling personal and societal obligations, were paramount. Perhaps because Confucius was raised without a father, he emphasized the importance of filial piety. To a group of students he once remarked, "It is not possible for one to teach others who cannot teach his own family."

There are many known Confucius quotes. On the subject of virtue, Confucius said, "Virtue is not left to stand alone. He who practices it will have," and, "To be able under all circumstances to practice five things constitutes perfect virtue; these five things are gravity, generosity of soul, sincerity, earnestness and kindness."

Many of Confucius' quotes have been taken to heart in the West, most notably, "A man should practice what he preaches, but a man should also preach what he practices," which has been interpreted as, "Practice what you preach." Many are also familiar with "The Golden Rule," namely, "Do unto others as you would have them do unto you." The Western "golden rule" is, in fact, a famous Confucius quote in its reverse, "Don't do unto others as you would not have them do unto you." And here's a personal Confucian favorite about the importance of enjoying what you do for a living: "If you enjoy what you do, you'll never work another day in your life."

After his death, Confucius was buried in the Shandong Province of China, within the vast green Kung Forest, which has been named in his honor. Today temples pay their respects to Confucius on his birthday, September 28th. Teacher's Day is a national holiday, on this day a Grand Ceremony Dedicated to Confucius (祭孔大典) is marked by loud music as well as dancers sporting colorful traditional costumes. Long live the eternal teacher!

Dr. Sun Yat-sen

Dr. Sun Yat-sen (孫中山 Sun Zhong Shan), often referred to in Chinese as "country father" (國父 guo fu), was born November 12, 1866 to a family of farmers in Guangdong, China. At age thirteen his family sent him to Hawaii to live with his elder brother. He studied there for three years before he relocated to Hong Kong, where he spent the next ten years studying medicine.

Although Dr. Sun obtained his doctorate and began to practice medicine, he was stirred by turbulent events during the turn of the century and decided to forgo his medical career for politics. From abroad, he organized several failed rebellions against the corrupt Ching dynasty regime. He continued to rally his followers around his "Three Principles of the People," a doctrine he wrote in 1905 which stated in no uncertain terms the inalienable rights of Chinese people to nationalism, livelihood, and civil rights.

After the Manchus fled China in 1911, due in part to the pressure Dr. Sun Yat-sen and his followers exerted, Dr. Sun was elected President of the new Republic of China in December, 1911. Sensing quite astutely that he did not have the political nor military clout to lead, he resigned the presidency two months later in favor of political veteran Yuan Shi-kai, focusing instead on reorganizing his national Kuomintang political party. Much to the chagrin of Dr. Sun and his supporters, however, Yuan Shi-kai declared himself the new "emperor" of China and abolished the legislature. After Dr. Sun led a failed revolt to oust Yuan Shi-kai, he enlisted the help of the Chinese communists and joined military forces with the USSR to reclaim Beijing. Dr. Sun died in Beijing on March 12, 1925.

Years after his death, Dr. Sun continues to be revered by both communists in China and democratic leaders on Taiwan. Communist leaders point to his cooperation with the Chinese communists and USSR and support for a strong central government to unite China. Taiwanese leaders hold dear his "Three Principles" doctrine and his goal for a full-fledged democratic nation. Both on Taiwan and in China you'll find roads named for the "Three Principles" doctrine, Nationalism (民族 *Mintsu*), Livelihood (民生 *Minsheng*) and Civil Rights (民權 *Minchuan*), and, of course, "Zhongshan," "Chong Shan" or "Chung Shan" (中山), in honor of Zhong Shan himself, Dr. Sun Yat-sen.

Women On Taiwan

While Taiwanese society is patriarchal at its core, women have made tremendous gains as of late, obtaining leading roles in business and politics. Taiwan's two-term vice-president is former governor of Taoyuan County Annette Lu. Women have obtained managerial positions at several international restaurant and retail chains as well as communications firms. In addition, many colleges and universities now offer courses that deal specifically with women's issues. In 2004, there were no differences in education levels (university-level and below) between men and women, and female participation in the labor force was nearly half (47.7%) and has been steadily increasing. In non-agricultural sectors, however, it was reported that women earned roughly 78% what male counterparts earned, and managerial and manual jobs

went mostly to males. A high percentage of teachers on Taiwan were female (98.4% kindergarten, 70% junior high school, 30% college and university), yet 75% of school administrators were male.

In 2004 the sex ratio was 104 males for every 100 females on the island; the sex ratio for newborn babies, however, was 111 males for every 100 females. While Taiwanese men and women married at 27.4 and 24 in 1983, a little over two decades later the median ages rose to 32.5 and 28.5, respectively. A recent Ministry of the Interior (MOI) report found that in Taipei, however, Taiwanese men marry on average at 34.4 and women at 30.4 years old. Over half (54.72%) of working Taiwanese females resigned from their jobs after marriage.

A slow but steady increase in violent crimes committed against women is becoming a major cause for concern. Males committed 94.6% of violent crimes, while 74.2% of women were reported as crime victims. Sexual assault was reported in 97.7% of all reported cases; 5,207 sexual offenses were reported, and of these cases, 4,130 of the victims, or 92.2%, were female. Just as alarming, almost half of the victims of sexual assault, or 48.3%, were females between the ages of 12 and 17.*

Although the Legislative Yuan passed the Domestic Violence Prevention Act in 1998, domestic violence is still a cause for concern on Taiwan. In 2004, 85.4% (38,881) of reported victims were female and men accounted for over 90% of the abusers (popular daytime soap operas often depict women slapped or beaten during domesetic disputes).

In some of the seedier areas on Taiwan, men have been caught videotaping women in hotels or spying in bathrooms. (It is said that cell phone manufacturers added the "click" sound after it was reported that men in Japan were photographing women on subways and crowded areas.) For this reason women on Taiwan (and women everywhere, in general) must be more cautious of their surroundings.

Using the Gender Empowerment Measure (GEM) of the United Nations Development Program, Taiwanese women were more politically and economically empowered compared with female counterparts in Japan and South Korea. Every year, Taiwanese government agencies pay public tribute to outstanding women on Women's Day, which is celebrated on March 8th. As women on Taiwan continue to shape politics and the private sector, Taiwan can continue to strive to become a more democratic, progressive and equitable society.

*data compiled from various government sources

Ylhas Formosa! A Brief History of Taiwan

You may be surprised to learn that Taiwan was once referred to as the "banana kingdom" for its prodigious banana exports. Japan received its first imported bananas from Taiwan, and early Japanese maps had Taiwan drawn in the shape of a banana.

Taiwan has a long history of invasion by foreign nations, beginning with the Portuguese, Spanish and Dutch, and ending with Japan. The first to arrive were the Portuguese in 1590, who, upon catching sight of its green mountains and pristine azure waters, exclaimed, "Ylhas Formosa!," which means "beautiful island." Thus, for centuries thereafter, this beautiful island came to be known as "Formosa." The next to occupy the island were the Dutch, who defeated the Portuguese and built Fort Zeelandia in the town of Anping, now the southern city of Tainan. The Dutch were interested in Taiwan not only for its natural resources and convenient location for trade, but also in converting inhabitants to Christianity. During the Dutch occupation, the Spanish landed on northern Taiwan in 1626. Two years later they built Fort San Domingo (紅毛城) in Danshui.

When the Manchus from Mongolia invaded China and ended the Ming dynasty (1368-1644), thousands of people, mainly from the southern Fujian and Guangdong provinces, fled to Taiwan. The Dutch welcomed these new settlers with land, cattle, and exorbitant taxes. As a consequence, the disgruntled farmers revolted in 1652, and Dutch rule on the island came to an end soonafter. This revolution was said to have lasted for eight months and was led by a Chinese warrior named Cheng Cheng-kung (鎮成功) (1624-1662), sometimes referred to as "Koxinga." Cheng established Chinese schools, laws and customs, and built the island's first Confucian temple. He had intended to build a substantial army to overthrow the Manchus in China but died before his dream could be actualized. Soon after Cheng's death, the Manchus sent a large fleet to Taiwan and defeated Cheng's small navy. In 1683, Cheng's family surrendered, and the island became a part of the Ch'ing dynasty (1644-1911), in the Fujian province of China. For the next two centuries, China considered the island and its inhabitants a nuisance, as revolts against the Ch'ing emperor occurred every few years.

At the end of the Sino-Japanese War, China signed the Treaty of Shimonoseki on April 17, 1895, ceding Taiwan and its surrounding territories to Japan in perpetuity. For the next fifty years, Japan occupied Taiwan. Many older Taiwanese speak fluent Japanese, as it was the required language of school instruction. On Taiwan, there are mixed accounts of the Japanese occupation. Some hold neither regard nor animosity toward the Japanese, claiming the Japanese treated them better than Chiang Kai-shek (蔣介石 Chiang Jie Shi) and his administration. Others claim that Japanese soldiers and police were harsh, sometimes even brutal.

After Japan's defeat in World War II, Japan was exiled from the island, and Chiang Kai-shek, then a powerful general in Mainland China, appointed general Chen Yi to preside over the island. After the violent February 28, 1947 (二二八 *er er ba*) incident in which over thirty thousand Taiwanese were slaughtered, Chiang found Chen Yi incapable of running the island, and subsequently ordered him decapitated.

After a brutal civil war with the communists, General Chiang and two million of his Kuomintang (KMT) supporters, mostly soldiers and their families, fled to Taiwan. Chiang imposed martial law on the island and, as the first self-elected president, intended to return to China to overthrow the communist government now in place. Like the mighty warrior Cheng Cheng-kung who had ruled centuries before him, however, Chiang's goal was never achieved. His son, Chiang Ching-kuo, succeeded him as president, followed by native-born Lee Teng-hui. Lee spent eight years in office before official democratic elections were held, and easily won the first direct democratic presidential election in 1996. Lee was succeeded by Democratic Progressive Party (DPP) candidate Chen Shui-bian, who shocked the ruling KMT by defeating Lee's hand-picked successor Lien Chan. President Chen and Vice-President Annette Lu took office on May 20, 2000, faced with a faltering economy and strained relations with Beijing. Chen and Lu were subsequently re-elected in a controversial 2004 race. Taiwan politics are lively, to say the least. For more information please see "Politics and Government" above.

The "Taiwan question" continues today, as a technologically advanced democracy struggles to gain respect in the eyes of the international community.

From Taipei to Danshui, All Aboard The MRT!

The MRT has changed much in recent years, with the addition of an underground shopping mall from Taipei Main Station to Zhongqing South Road. Another underground mall runs from Taipei Main Station towards Zhongshan, the second stop on the MRT heading towards Danshui. Expect road delays in Taipei's Xinyi district as construction is under way for a new Xinyi MRT line.

Coffee shops, pharmacies, and convenience stores are now located one floor below the main level of Taipei Main Station. The food court on the station's second floor boasts local, Western and Southeast Asian delights. During the weekends, many household helpers (外勞 *wai lao*) from Indonesia, Malaysia, Thailand and the Philippines, congregate here. On Sundays you may even see people dancing to Indonesian music on the first floor of the train station.

Select MRT stations have become wireless "hot spot" zones for commuting passengers with laptops. Locals and expatriates alike can register at Taipei City Hall or by faxing in a form from 7-Eleven. MRT attendants suggest that the service is free but information found online indicates that there is a monthly fee, which may not be practical for tourists. For more information visit http://wifly.com.tw.

You'll be pleased to know, especially if you are traveling on business, that you can use your cell phone on all MRT lines, even those that run underground. Even Ah Mah and Ah Gong (grandma and grandpa) stay connected! This is because four local telecom companies recently completed an underground cellular phone network. Taipei is indeed proving itself of being a 21st century cyber city.

Ticket vending machines are now computerized, and Easy Card magnetized tickets can be purchased at the ticket booth. Easy Cards are pressed against the side of the turn-style instead of inserting a card into the front and then removing it at top to enter the station. At every MRT station, commuters can determine the easiest route to arrive at their final destination from maps found on ticket machines. Thankfully, for those who can't read Chinese, station names also appear in English.

Video cameras are conspicuously placed at every station platform. On Taiwan, unlike the West, you are considered guilty until proven innocent, and the public feels little remorse towards criminals. Commuters can relax, Taiwan and its fine transit system are both safe and convenient.

Signs for "No Smoking," "No Littering," and "No Eating or Drinking" are also placed within eyesight on the station platform and on the MRT itself. Don't even think about chomping on that cheeseburger stashed in your purse, if an attendant catches you the fine is NT $1,500 (US $45.00), and fines are set to rise. While you may happen across an occasional scofflaw, police strictly enforce these laws and Taiwanese people keep the MRT clean.

The ongoing debate as to how to phonetically translate Chinese characters into English continues. Some expatriates comment that since international visitors are reading English signs, perhaps it would be wise for the government to ask them how they would phonetically translate Chinese characters. At MRT stations, Chungshan is now "Zhongshan," Min Chuan is "Minquan," Chientan is "Jiantan," Shih Lin is "Shilin," Chishan is "Zhishan," Chili An is "Qilian," and Chi Yen has been changed to a curious "Qiyan." Peitou now reads "Beitou," and Hsin Peitou? "Xinbeitou." Fushing Kang reads "Fuxinggang," Chungyi has been changed to "Zhongyi," Kuan Du is now "Guandu," Chu Wei is now "Zhuwei" and Hung Shulin now reads "Hongshulin" at that station.

Taipei Main Station (台北車站)

The clean, air-conditioned Mass Rapid Transit (MRT) (捷運 jieyun) railway pulls out of Taipei Main Station at exactly five-fifteen in the evening. The train is packed to near- seating capacity, and after an arduous day at the office, most people seem weary and deeply absorbed in life's subtle inconveniences. All aboard the MRT! We're off to the wonderful waterfront town of Danshui, famous on Taiwan for its breathtaking sunsets, sumptuous seafoods, and traditional teahouses. Danshui Historic Street, relics and a bustling night market on Yingzhuan Road are near the MRT station.

Zhongshan (中山)

Two minutes after leaving Taipei Main Station, the train pulls into Zhongshan, named in honor of Dr. Sun Yat-sen. *Hen kwai!* (很快), the ride is fast indeed. Inches from two incandescent ivory lines on the station platform, blinking scarlet lights warn swarms of mostly junior high and high school students of an approaching train. Students on Taiwan, like in Japan, are required to wear uniforms to school; unfortunately for the students, the uniforms here look surprisingly like my favorite pairs of green, blue and gray cotton pajamas.

Young and old alike scuttle to their feet, walk hurriedly to the small arrows indicating where the doors will open, and wait anxiously as the train slows to a halt. Once the train is in motion, it's apparent that education is paramount as exhausted students attempt to read textbooks and memorize English grammar while grasping the white straps dangling from bars attached to the ceiling.

You may be amazed to find that, in spite of intense pressure to excel in English grammar and conversation classes on Taiwan, students are typically embarrassed to speak with international guests in English. If you understand a little Mandarin and see a group of high school or college students together on the MRT, you'll often hear, "*Waiguoren! Ni gen ta jiang hua!*" ("A foreigner! Come on, speak with him/her!")

and perhaps the most common expression to encourage someone, "*Jia yo!*," which literally means "add gas," or "Go, go, go!"

If someone does muster the courage to speak with you, you will probably be asked the top-three questions to ask international guests to the island: "*Ni shi nai guo ren?*" or "You are what country person,"or "Where are you from?" This should be followed by "*Ni lai Taiwan duo juo?*" or "How long have you been on Taiwan?," followed by, "*Ni juede Taiwan zemeyang?*" or, "What do you think of Taiwan?" Taiwanese are curious to meet visitors to the island and are interested in hearing your thoughts. Unless you intend to have a long, deep, personal conversation with a curious stranger, however, it's best to keep your answers short and pleasant. You may mention the places you've been to or where you intend to visit, and ask for any suggestions he or she may be willing to offer. As always, thank the person for his or her insight before departing.

Shuanglien (雙連)

If you exit the MRT station here, there isn't much to see unless you walk for about twenty minutes to the historic district of Dadaocheng where you'll find a wharf and Dihua Street, famous for its variety of dried goods.

The train doors remain open for no more than five seconds before the station fills with a loud beeping noise. Is it a bird? Is it a child's toy laser gun? No, it's just an annoying loud beeping noise. This high-pitched noise is followed immediately by what sounds like an ambulance siren, possibly a warning to passengers that they will by laying in a real ambulance if they don't move away from the train doors, which close faster than a child's mouth at the sight of ching tsai, or vegetables. At the rear of the car, a newborn baby girl sleeps comfortably in the arms of her young mother.

Minquan West Road (民權西路)

The word "Minchuan" means "civil rights" and is one of Dr. Sun Yat-sen's famous "Three Principles of the People." Although the MRT runs mostly aboveground, the first four stops look much like the underground Bay Area Rapid Transit (BART) in Northern California and The Metro in Washington, D.C., both run on time and are clean railway systems. If you had time to explore other parts of the island, from here you could easily hop a cab in front of the MRT or go straight (一直走 *yi zhi zuo*) down Minchuan West Road and head to Songshan National Airport, a domestic airport in Taipei and a main airport on Taiwan. Dunhua North Road runs perpendicular from the airport and, crossing over Zhongxiao East Road, Dunhua South Road is a main road in Taipei that runs north to south across the city.

Yuanshan (圓山)

Only five minutes after leaving Taipei Main Station, the train emerges rapidly from the belly of the city and races onward toward the golden sun, setting slowly beyond tall buildings, towering trees, and gorgeous green mountains. As the train enters Yuanshan, the sight is urban indeed, as passengers bear witness to many of the factories that are keeping Taiwan's economy strong in spite of a recent economic downturn in Asia. The red and white corporate logo of Tatung, one of the world's largest manufacturing companies, is boldly printed on factory walls throughout Taiwan. The logo is visible on the right, after the train exits the tunnel. The logo is also visible to all on a local computer plant at the intersection of Dayeh Road and Dadu Road in Beitou.

The Grand Hotel (圓山大飯店 *Yuan Shan Da Fan Dian*), Zhongshan North Road, Section 4, #1 (台北市中山北路4段1號) 886 2 2596-5565, is one of the most renowned Chinese hotels in the world. The Grand Hotel operates a free shuttle bus that runs from here to the hotel year round and is visible from Yuanshan Station. Madame Chiang Kai-shek once owned this architectural masterpiece that appeared in the Ang Lee classic, "Eat Drink Man Woman." The hotel has a distinctly elegant Chinese persona, and tourists marvel at its outstanding façade. Its traditional Chinese structure, painted bright red with majestic gold frames and striking cardinal columns easily turns expatriate heads. During the evening the hotel lights up, and its immaculate walls take on a glossy silver appearance, akin to a costly cake purchased for privileged public servants. The Grand Hotel is a popular respite for dignitaries and prominent businesspeople from around the world and boasts a favored teatime and 60's disco.

Jiantan (劍潭)

After passing through Yuanshan, the environment begins to change. Scattered among the old, dilapidated buildings leading to Jiantan are new, modern-looking office structures and apartments. It almost looks as if the government began a building renovation project but stopped before the project was completed. A major Taipei towing lot (car impound) for traffic violators is located next to the Jiantan station. Had you parked illegally in the area, even for a few minutes while you ran into a fast food establishment to use the restroom, your car or moped would probably end up in this decrepit lot.

Traffic laws are erratically enforced, and the laws themselves are modified every few years, with new ones added, others revoked. For instance, yellow and red lines appear along many Taipei streets, indicating that parking is illegal, yet thousands of mopeds are parked either in front of these lines on the street or behind the lines, on the sidewalk. On a personal note, the author once paid NT $800 (US $24.00) to retrieve his moped from here. If you include the hassle of attempting to locate the lot in a taxi, combined with fear that the moped may have been stolen, it added up to one harrowing experience. When a car or moped is towed, an enforcement official is supposed to use chalk to write the license plate number on the ground to inform the owner his vehicle has been towed. No plate number was written. If you find yourself in this kind of unfortunate situation in Taipei, contact "Towed Vehicle Inquiry" at 886 2 2503-9589. In Kaohsiung the number is 886 7 225-7166.

Shilin (士林)

Unfortunately, **Shilin Night Market** (士林夜市), one of the greatest night markets on Taiwan, is barely visible from the rapidly passing MRT. Passengers can only catch a glimpse of some outside food venders and a crowded entrance area. The night market is within walking distance from either Jiantan or Shilin stations. Visit Shilin Night Market for a fantastic cultural, as well as eating and shopping, experience. Some truly delicious Taiwanese small foods (小吃 xiao chi) can be purchased at Shilin Night Market.

In Shilin there are several good eateries within walking distance of the MRT station. Small noodle stores, beverage and ice dessert shops, and pastry shops line either side of the road, and a new indoor swimming pool and physical fitness center called "My Island" is located here, in case you want to go for a quick dip to cool off during a hot afternoon or humid evening.

Zhishan (芝山)

On either side of the railway, hard-working Taiwanese entrepreneurs remain opened for business. Motorcycle repair shops, furniture stores, and small, family-run restaurants still welcome customers long after other businesses have closed. On the roofs of several tall apartment buildings are large satellite dishes and cable wires, indicating that residents may have access to the same crazy talk shows and television programs I had laughed at back home. After watching Jerry Springer it's no wonder some Taiwanese people think Americans are a tad bizarre. Damp clothes are hung to dry just inside apartment terraces, swaying gently in the spring breeze.

If you're interested in checking out a "hypermart," or an all-inclusive supermarket, depart here and walk one block north to arrive at Carrefour (家樂福 *Jialefu*), which means "house of happiness and luck" in Chinese. Taiwanese flock to Carrefour for everything from clothes to fresh fish and groceries, as well as bicycles, roller blades, CDs and VCDs, TVs, and household appliances.

Across the street from Zhishan Station, a bus shuttles passengers to Dayeh Takashimaya, a Tienmu department store, free of charge. The small bus only holds around twenty people, so during busy weekends and holidays expect a long line and a thirty-minute wait.

Mingde (明德)

Is it Tienmu, a town where locals go for coffee talk or to shop and observe the plethora of foreign residents in the area? No, but you may think it is from all the Tienmu store advertisements. Mingde is only a hop, skip, and ten-minute bus ride from Tienmu, and during weekends and holidays the roads become congested. To view hand-cut local flowers a large **flower mart** is ten minutes by foot from the MRT. Make a right onto Mingde Road, pass Taipei Municipal Mingde Junior High School (台北市明德國民中學), Mingde Road, #50, and cross the Wenlin North Road overpass. You should find yourself at Chiao Kung (巧工人造花有限公司), Wenlin North Road, #79-1 (台北市北投區文林北路 79 - 1 號) 886 2 2820-8942.

Shipai (石牌)

Around a hundred passengers depart the

train here. Hungry businesspeople head to the convenience store directly across the street to satisfy their craving for relatively inexpensive sandwiches and finger foods. A handful of foreigners (外國人 *waiguoren*) exit here. Some expats prefer to live in Shipai, which has a MRT stop and where the rent is cheaper than in Tienmu. Tienmu, which doesn't have a MRT station, borders Shipai. **Shipai Night Market** (石牌夜市) is only a few blocks from the MRT station and you'll find a traditional market located between the Mingde and Shipai MRT stations on Hsi-an Street, Lane 281 (台北市石牌區西安街281巷). Expect to see inexpensive clothing and consumer goods as well as the usual litany of fresh fruits and vegetables, fresh cut pig and chicken parts and other curious consumable goods.

Qilian (其哩岸)

Vegetable stands alongside the railway attract working adults eager to select the freshest fruits and vegetables for their families. Five customers sit outside a Mei Er Mei fast food breakfast chain munching on burgers and drinking colas. The food chain, easily spotted by its red and orange sign with white Chinese characters, offers reasonably priced chicken burgers. Try one and judge for yourself.

Beitou Incinerator (北投垃圾焚化廠) and its colorful tower stand out. Rather than protest, residents embrace this fixture since 1998. At the Beitou Refuse Incineration Plant (BTRIP) you'll find an outdoor heated swimming pool, a sports park, a children's playground, a car wash, and a multi-colored smoke stack that stands 150 meters above the ground. The observatory rotates 360 degrees, offering panoramic views of Shipai, Beitou, Yangmingshan and, off in the distance, Taipei. Observatory tickets cost NT $40, NT $20 for students. By MRT it's 1.55 kilometers from Qilian Station (其哩岸站). By bus the 217, 218, 266 and 302 stop at Ji Li Street, which is still about a kilometer hike from the plant. The quickest way to reach the plant would be to take the MRT to Qilian Station and take a taxi from there. The fare should cost between NT $120 (US $3.60) to NT $150 (US $4.50). Zhou Mei Street, #271, Beitou, Taipei (台北市政府環境保護局北投垃圾焚化廠, 台北市北投區洲美街271號) 886 2 2836-0500.

Qiyen (奇岩)

One stop from Beitou, to the left is the Morinaga & Co., Ltd. confectionary factory, where local caramels, gumdrops and Hi-Chew® chewy fruit candies are made. A young woman, preparing to exit the train, puts her wallet down on the seat next to her and hunts for her Easy Card. In many countries, her wallet would be long gone by the time she realized it was missing; fortunately for this young woman (小姐 shiao jie) this is Taiwan, and most citizens tend to be trustworthy. Her wallet remains on the seat untouched.

You may be surprised to find that on Taiwan, local residents leave their wallets and cell phones sticking out of their back pockets— even in crowded night markets, where bumping into others is not uncommon. Call it naiveté or trust in one's fellow man rarely found in big cities. Compared with other large international cities, crime is not a salient problem in Taipei. No man is an island, and no island is a utopia; however, on Taiwan thugs tend to mind their own illicit business dealings and not bother expats and international guests. If you don't go looking for trouble, chances are it won't find you.

Beitou (北投)

Twenty minutes after leaving Taipei Main Station the train pulls into Beitou (北投). A handful of passengers depart while a group of young passengers quickly board, eager to reach Danshui and meet up with friends. Beitou Station is where passengers transfer for Xinbeitou (New Beitou) (新北

投 Xinbeitou), Taipei city lines or Danshui. A separate MRT line runs to New Beitou (Xinbeitou) from Beitou Station.

While travelers once saw seas of trees instead of towering buildings around Beitou Station, exceedingly low interest rates has led to a real estate boom, and tall buildings are under construction in the immediate vicinity. Beitou is known for its fine schools and pristine parks, akin to a placid town in Long Island, New York. **New Beitou Park** (新北投公園 Xinbeitou Gongyuan), directly across from New Beitou Station, provides a literal breath of fresh air to the eyes and lungs of weary urban dwellers. Here you'll find a sparkling stream, full fountain and a rockin' roller blading rink. Elderly residents often dance here before dawn, start the day before the sun rises to learn a new move or two. This quaint park is just across the street from New Beitou Station and a Wellcome Supermarket, behind New Beitou Library.

Beitou has a fascinating volcanic topography, visit **Hell Valley** (地熱谷 Di Ruh Gu), a sulfuric pond that appears much like a large witch's cauldron and bathe in natural hot springs. A few choice options are **Hall Yard Resort** (花月生活館 Huayue Shenghuoguan), Xinming Road, Lane 1, #2.4 (北投區新民路1巷2.4號) 886 2 2893-9870, **Spa World** (水都 Shuidu), Guangming Road, #283 886 2 2897-9060 (台北市北投區光明路 283號), and **Spring City Resort** (春天酒店 Chuntien Jiudian), Youya Road, #18 (台北市北投區幽雅路18號) 886 2 2897-5555. Beitou is also famous for its close proximity to **Yangmingshan National Park** (陽明山國家公園). Discover fantastic flora and fauna, towering trees, magnificent mountain ranges, hiking trails, a manicured flower clock with the accurate local time, bright red pagodas, and immense, life-like monuments dedicated to significant figures in Chinese history.

Fuxinggang (復興崗)

This station is quite different from the previous ones. While the others are built with ordinary gray stones, the walls of Fuxinggang are lined with bright apricot ones, creating an almost Spanish-like appearance. Nearby vegetable fields hint that this once-placid area was far more rural. Small gray and red, three to four-story buildings stand near the railway, resembling garden apartments in the boroughs of New York City or in Boston. Here a warehouse area is where MRT trains are upgraded or repaired.

Zhongyi (忠義)

Near modern office buildings are older homes and low-level apartments, perhaps housing the employees of these new companies. You'll notice a lot of cars parked near the station, as many Zhongyi residents commute from here to Taipei.

Guandu (關渡)

It's difficult to see much of Guandu from the station because one's view is restricted as the train passes through a tunnel, and signals may drop on cellphones here. To the left of the train, sunlight sparkles on the scenic Danshui River, which winds through Taipei and flows to the waterfront town of Danshui. The grand red Guandu Bridge appears almost magestic when lit with purple lights at night, the bridge can be seen on the left as the train runs from Guandu to Zhuwei.

Guandu Temple (關渡宮), Zhi Hsing Road #360 (台北市北投區知行路360號) was constructed in 1661. The temple, one of the most elaborate, is said to be the oldest on Taiwan. Guandu may be forty minutes outside the city but it's still in Taipei. By foot, Guandu Temple is about a fifteen-minute walk from the MRT station. By bus the Red 35 (紅35) departs from Guandu Station and stops in front of the temple.

If you're in the mood to relax at a restful reserve, **Guandu Nature Park** (關渡自然公園 Guandu Ziran Gongyuan), Guandu Road, #55 (台北市關渡路55號) 886 2 2858-7417 is one long block south of Guandu Temple. The park is open 9 am to 6 pm weekdays, 9 am to 6:30 pm weekends. Admission is NT $50.

Bali (八里), once a remote town across from Danshui, is now easily accessible by crossing the scenic red Guandu Bridge (關渡橋) by motorcycle or car. You can also visit Bali by taking a quaint ferry from Danshui. On Bali, **Guan Yin Mountain** (觀音山 Guanyinshan) towers 616 meters, surrounded by 18 smaller peaks. The mountain is named after Guanyin, the Bodhisattva goddess of mercy, and is a northern Taiwan landmark. If you're in Danshui, take the boat across Danshui River to Bali, at NT $50 (US $1.50) for a round-trip ticket it's inexpensive and a fun, relaxing experience. On Bali take the Red 13 (紅13) bus to **Shihsanhang Museum of Archaeology** (十三行博物館), Bowuguan Road, #200 (台北縣八里鄉博物館路200號) 886 2 2 2619-1313, a Bali cultural attraction that boasts sui generis archeological findings.

Zhuwei (竹圍)

To the right of the train, cars enter the parking lot of Carrefour (家樂福), or, as the hypermart is known in Chinese, "house of happiness and luck." What an outstanding Chinese translation, the company couldn't have picked a better name to fit the location and culture. Just past the hypermart on the right are expensive car dealerships, seafood restaurants and Pfizer's corporate office. Interested in working overseas? Having an office with a view of Danshui River would make for quite a pleasant experience.

Hongshulin (紅樹林)

The town of Hongshulin got its name from the sprawling mangrove (樹林 hungshu) estuary alongside Danshui River; at one time vast reddened mangrove trees covered the entire area, hence the town name (紅 *hung* means "red"). Natural marshes and the dazzling Danshui River lie just beyond a barbed wire fence that runs from Fuxinggang to Danshui. Here you'll find the largest pure Kandelia candel (a type of mangrove) estuary in the world. You can learn more about the wetland food chain, mangroves of Taiwan and Danshui River Mangrove Nature Reserve at Mangrove Forest Exhibition Hall, just outside Exit 2, up a short flight of stairs at Hongshulin Station. Information is available in both English and Chinese. The Hall is open from 9 am to 4:30 pm daily except Mondays. Admission is free and all are welcome.

A scenic nature trail runs from behind this MRT station to Danshui where you'll often spot hikers and bikers trekking, especially during weekends. (Due to safety concerns, bikes are not allowed in Danshui Station.) To the right you'll notice contstruction in the area as residents invest in real estate due to extremely low interest rates.

Danshui (淡水)

Only forty-five minutes after leaving Taipei Main Station the train pulls slowly into Danshui. Children play in **Riverbank Park** (河濱公園 *Hobing Gongyuan*) just behind the MRT station as proud parents and grandparents look on. A flurry of shoppers crowd vendors selling food, toys, roller blades and other items along **Danshui River** (淡水河). Directly across the street, **Danshui Night Market** (淡水夜市) on Yingzhuan Road (英專路) teems with young people flocking to beverage shops, food stands and clothing stores.

Friends and families walk to **Danshui Historic Street** (淡水老街), the entrance of which is adjacent to the MRT park, where a magnificent market full of food, games, and toys awaits. Here you'll find traditional foods, toys, clothing, and eating establishments that serve food that is distinctly Danshui. Just behind Danshui Historic Street you can take the boat across to Bali.

From here you can also take a boat to Taipei's answer to San Francisco, **Fisherman's Wharf** (漁人碼頭). The wharf boasts a park with more kite-flyers than trees, talented artists, musicians, a sea wall, pier, various food and trinket shops and "Lover's Bridge" where you may fall in love with someone special. The Red 26 (紅26) bus runs to Fisherman's Wharf and stops at **Fort San Domingo** (紅毛城 *Hungmaocheng*), referred to by locals as "Fort of the Red Haired Barbarians" or "Red Hair Fort." This historic fort was built by the Portuguese and later run by the Dutch after they expelled the Portuguese from the island. Admission to Fort San Domingo costs NT $60 (U.S. $1.80) and an afternoon of exploration makes for quite an interesting experience.

The journey is over but the adventure has just begun. Have fun!

It is my hope that **Taipei In A Day** can help you to avoid some common cultural pitfalls and more thoroughly enjoy your visit. Once you arrive, you may choose to spend more time exploring temples, night markets or department stores, or add your own itinerary to the tour I present in this guide. You may also want to spend more of your vacation relaxing in the mountains or bathing in New Beitou's magnificent hot springs. It's your vacation, and how you choose to spend your time is ultimately your choice. For more detailed information the author recommends http://www.OnTaiwan.com.

Disclaimer:

The author tried to be as factually accurate as possible, and as such accepted no sweet gluttonous rice balls, Danshui fish balls, stinky beancurd or other delicious native foods, complimentary passes to hot springs or free stays at hotels. No gifts of any kind were accepted.

The author has tried to make the information in this tour guide as accurate as possible, but it is provided "as is" and as such the author accepts no responsibility for any loss, injury or inconvenience sustained by anyone as a result of using this information. You should verify critical information such as visas, health and safety, customs and transportation with the relevant authorities prior to travel. Although a moped ride through the mountains of Taipei is included in this book, the author does not recommend that visitors rent a moped. Riding a moped can be a dangerous activity and requires significant skill and experience. The author expressly disclaims all responsibility for any decision taken by a reader of **Taipei In A Day** to engage in such activity and thereby assume the attendant risks. By purchasing **Taipei In A Day** you are agreeing to use this tour guide at your own risk. The author expressly disclaims all responsibility for any decision taken by a reader of **Taipei In A Day**. For the reader's convenience, the author has provided links to content from external, third-party sites. By purchasing **Taipei In A Day**, you understand that the author neither endorses nor is responsible for any content on these external, third-party sites, as such responsibility lies exclusively with such sites' owners.

Some of the content provided in this tour guide may not be suitable for children. You understand that, by purchasing **Taipei In A Day**, you agree to indemnify, defend and hold harmless the author for material deemed offensive or inappropriate.

General Index

O-P

Q-S

T

Printed in the United States
212036BV00001B/189/P